SKETCHES OF THE HISTORY OF MAN

BOOK III

NATURAL LAW AND
ENLIGHTENMENT CLASSICS

Knud Haakonssen
General Editor

Henry Home, Lord Kames

NATURAL LAW AND
ENLIGHTENMENT CLASSICS

Sketches of the History of Man

Considerably Enlarged by
the Last Additions and
Corrections of the Author

BOOK III
Progress of Sciences

Henry Home, Lord Kames

Edited and with an Introduction by
James A. Harris

Major Works of Henry Home, Lord Kames

LIBERTY FUND
Indianapolis

Frontispiece and cover (detail): Portrait of Henry Home, Lord Kames, by David Martin.
Reproduced with permission of the National Galleries of Scotland.

Introduction, annotations © 2007 by Liberty Fund, Inc.

11 10 09 08 07 C 5 4 3 2 1
11 10 09 08 07 P 5 4 3 2 1

Library of Congress Cataloging-in-Publication Data
Kames, Henry Home, Lord, 1696–1782.
Sketches of the history of man/Henry Home, Lord Kames;
edited and with an introduction by James A. Harris.
v. cm.—(Natural law and enlightenment classics)
"Considerably enlarged by the last additions and corrections of the author."
Originally published in 4 v.: Edinburgh: A. Strahan and T. Cadell. 1788.
Includes bibliographical references and index.
Contents: bk. 1. Progress of men independent of society—
bk. 2. Progress of men in society—bk. 3. Progress of sciences.
ISBN 978-0-86597-500-2 (hardcover: set)   ISBN 978-0-86597-505-7 (pbk: set)
1. Civilization—History.   2. Human beings—History.
I. Harris, James A., 1968–   II. Title.
CB25.K3 2007
901—dc22   2006028369
ISBN 978-0-86597-503-3 (v. 3: hc)   ISBN 978-0-86597-508-8 (v. 3: sc)

LIBERTY FUND, INC.
8335 Allison Pointe Trail, Suite 300
Indianapolis, Indiana 46250-1684

CONTENTS

BOOK III

PROGRESS OF SCIENCES

CONTENTS[1]

1. The original page numbers from the 1788 edition are retained here.

APPENDIX.

Sketches concerning Scotland.

BOOK III
Progress of SCIENCES

Morality, Theology, and the Art of Reasoning, are three great branches of a learned education; and justly held to be so, being our only sure guides in passing through the intricate paths of life. They are indeed not essential to those termed men of the world: *the most profound philosopher makes but an insipid figure in fashionable company; would be somewhat ridiculous at a court-ball; and an absolute absurdity among the gamesters at Ar-<187>thur's, or jockeys at Newmarket. But, these cogent objections notwithstanding, I venture to pronounce such studies to be not altogether unsuitable to a gentleman. Man is a creature full of curiosity; and to gratify that appetite, many roam through the world, submitting to heat and cold, nay to hunger and thirst, without a sigh. Could indeed that troublesome guest be expelled, we might hug ourselves in ignorance; and, like true men of the world, undervalue knowledge that cannot procure money, nor a new sensual pleasure. But, alas! the expulsion is not in the power of every one; and those who must give vent to their curiosity, will naturally employ it upon studies that make them good members of society, and endear them to every person of virtue.*

And were we even men of the world in such perfection, as to regard nothing but our own interest; yet does not ignorance lay us open to the crafty and designing? and does not the art of reasoning guard many an honest man from being misled by subtile sophisms? With respect to right and wrong, not even passion is more dangerous than error. And as to religion, better it were to settle in a conviction that there is no God, than to be in <188> a state of wavering and fluctuation; sometimes indulging every loose desire, as if we were not ac-

581

countable beings; and sometimes yielding to superstitious fears, as if there were no god but the devil. To a well-disposed mind, the existence of a supreme benevolent Deity, appears highly probable: and if by the study of theology that probability be improved into a certainty, the conviction of a supreme Deity who rules with equity and mildness, will be a source of constant enjoyment, which I boldly set above the titillating pleasures of external sense. Possibly there may be less present amusement in abstract studies, than in newspapers, in party-pamphlets, or in Hoyl upon Whist: but let us for a moment anticipate futurity, and imagine that we are reviewing past transactions,—how pleasant the retrospect of those who have maintained the dignity of their nature, and employ'd their talents to the best purposes!

Contradictory opinions that have influence on practice, will be regretted by every person of a sound heart; and as erroneous opinions are commonly the result of imperfect education, I would gladly hope, that a remedy is not altogether out of reach. At the revival of arts and sciences, the learned languages <189> were our sole study, because in them were locked up all the treasures of useful knowledge. This study has long ago ceased to be the chief object of education; and yet the original plan is handed down to us with very little variation. Wishing to contribute to a more perfect system of education, I present to the public the following Sketches. The books that have been published on morality, theology, and the art of reasoning, are not eminent either for simplicity, or for perspicuity. To introduce these into the subjects mentioned, is my aim; with what success, is with deference submitted to the judgement of others. The historical part, hitherto much neglected, is necessary as a branch of my general plan; and I am hopeful, that, beside instruction, it will contribute to recreation, which, in abstract studies, is no less necessary than pleasant. <190>

Principles and Progress of Reason

SECTION I

Principles of Reason.

Affirmation is that sort of expression which the speaker uses, when he desires to be believed. What he affirms is termed a *proposition*.

Truth and error are qualities of propositions. A proposition that says a thing is what it is in reality, is termed a *true proposition*. A proposition that says a thing is what it is not in reality, is termed an *erroneous proposition*.

Truth is so essential in conducting affairs, that man would be a disjointed being were it not agreeable to him. Truth accordingly is agreeable to every human being, and falsehood or error disagreeable. <191> The pursuit of truth is no less pleasant than the pursuit of any other good.*[1]

Our knowledge of what is agreeable and disagreeable in objects is derived from the sense of beauty, handled in Elements of Criticism. Our knowledge of right and wrong in actions, is derived from the moral sense, to be handled in the sketch immediately following. Our knowledge of truth and error is derived from various sources.

Our external senses are one source of knowledge: they lay open to us external subjects, their qualities, their actions, with events produced by these actions. The internal senses are another source of knowledge: they lay open to us things passing in the mind; thinking, for example, deliber-

---

* It has been wisely observed, that truth is the same to the understanding that music is to the ear, or beauty to the eye.

1. This paragraph (with note) added in 2nd edition.

ating, inclining, resolving, willing, consenting, and other acts; and they also
lay open to us our emotions and passions. There is a sense by which we
perceive the truth of many propositions; such as, That every thing which
begins <192> to exist must have a cause; That every effect adapted to some
end or purpose, proceeds from a designing cause; and, That every effect
adapted to a good end or purpose, proceeds from a designing and benevolent cause. A multitude of axioms in every science, particularly in mathematics, are equally perceived to be true. By a peculiar sense, of which afterward, we know that there is a Deity. There is a sense by which we know,
that the external signs of passion are the same in all men; that animals of
the same external appearance, are of the same species, and that animals of
the same species, have the same properties (a). There is a sense that dives
into futurity: we know that the sun will rise to-morrow; that the earth will
perform its wonted course round the sun; that winter and summer will
follow each other in succession; that a stone dropt from the hand will fall
to the ground; and a thousand other such propositions.

There are many propositions, the truth of which is not so apparent: a
process of <193> reasoning is necessary, of which afterward.

Human testimony is another source of knowledge. So framed we are by
nature, as to rely on human testimony; by which we are informed of beings,
attributes, and events, that never came under any of our senses.

The knowledge that is derived from the sources mentioned, is of different kinds. In some cases, our knowledge includes absolute certainty, and
produces the highest degree of conviction: in other cases, probability comes
in place of certainty, and the conviction is inferior in degree. Knowledge
of the latter kind is distinguished into belief, which concerns facts; and
opinion, which concerns relations, and other things that fall not under the
denomination of facts. In contradistinction to opinion and belief, that sort
of knowledge which includes absolute certainty, and produces the highest
degree of conviction, retains its proper name. To explain what is here said,
I enter into particulars.

The sense of seeing, with very few exceptions, affords knowledge properly so <194> termed: it is not in our power to doubt of the existence of a

(a) Preliminary Discourse.

person we see, touch, and converse with. When such is our constitution, it is a vain attempt to call in question the authority of our sense of seeing, as some writers pretend to do. No one ever called in question the existence of internal actions and passions, laid open to us by internal sense; and there is as little ground for doubting of what we see. The sense of seeing, it is true, is not always correct: through different mediums the same object is seen differently: to a jaundic'd eye every thing appears yellow; and to one intoxicated with liquor, two candles sometimes appear four. But we are never left without a remedy in such a case: it is the province of the reasoning faculty to correct every error of that kind.

An object of sight recalled to mind by the power of memory, is termed an *idea* or secondary perception. An original perception, as said above, affords knowledge in its proper sense; but a secondary perception affords belief only. And Nature in this, as in all other instances, is faithful to truth; for it is evident, that we cannot be so certain of the existence <195> of an object in its absence, as when present.

With respect to many abstract propositions, of which instances are above given, we have an absolute certainty and conviction of their truth, derived to us from various senses. We can, for example, entertain as little doubt that every thing which begins to exist must have a cause, as that the sun is in the firmament; and as little doubt that he will rise to-morrow, as that he is now set. There are many other propositions, the truth of which is probable only, not absolutely certain; as, for example, that winter will be cold and summer warm. That natural operations are performed in the simplest manner, is an axiom of natural philosophy: it may be probable, but is far from being certain.* <196>

In every one of the instances given, conviction arises from a single act

---

* I have given this proposition a place, because it is assumed as an axiom by all writers on natural philosophy. And yet there appears some room for doubting, whether our conviction of it do not proceed from a bias in our nature, rather than from an original sense. Our taste for simplicity, which undoubtedly is natural, renders simple operations more agreeable than what are complex, and consequently makes them appear more natural. It deserves a most serious discussion, whether the operations of nature be always carried on with the greatest simplicity, or whether we be not misled by our taste for simplicity to be of that opinion.

of perception: for which reason, knowledge acquired by means of that perception, not only knowledge in its proper sense but also opinion and belief, are termed *intuitive knowledge.* But there are many things, the knowledge of which is not obtained with so much facility. Propositions for the most part require a process or operation in the mind, termed *reasoning;* leading, by certain intermediate steps, to the proposition that is to be demonstrated or made evident; which, in opposition to intuitive knowledge, is termed *discursive knowledge.* This process or operation must be explained, in order to understand the nature of reasoning. And as reasoning is mostly employ'd in discovering relations, I shall draw my examples from them. Every proposition concerning relations, is an affirmation of a certain relation between two subjects. If the relation affirmed appear not intuitively, we must search <197> for a third subject, intuitively connected with each of the others by the relation affirmed: and if such a subject be found, the proposition is demonstrated; for it is intuitively certain, that two subjects connected with a third by any particular relation, must be connected together by the same relation. The longest chain of reasoning may be linked together in this manner. Running over such a chain, every one of the subjects must appear intuitively to be connected with that immediately preceding, and with that immediately subsequent, by the relation affirmed in the proposition; and from the whole united, the proposition, as above mentioned, must appear intuitively certain. The last step of the process is termed *a conclusion,* being the last or concluding perception.

No other reasoning affords so clear a notion of the foregoing process, as that which is mathematical. Equality is the only mathematical relation; and comparison therefore is the only means by which mathematical propositions are ascertained. To that science belong a number of intuitive propositions, termed *axioms,* which are <198> all founded on equality. For example: Divide two equal lines, each of them, into a thousand equal parts, a single part of the one line must be equal to a single part of the other. Second: Take ten of these parts from the one line, and as many from the other, and the remaining parts must be equal; which is more shortly expressed thus: From two equal lines take equal parts, and the remainders will be equal; or add equal parts, and the sums will be equal. Third: If two things be, in the same respect, equal to a third, the one is equal to the other in the same respect. I proceed to show the use of these axioms. Two things may be equal without being intuitively so; which is the case of the equality between the three angles of a triangle and two right angles. To demonstrate that truth, it is necessary to search for some other angles that intuitively are equal to both. If this property cannot be discovered in any one set of angles, we must go more leisurely to work, and try to find angles that are equal to the three angles of a triangle. These being discovered, we next try to find other angles equal to the angles now disco-<199>vered; and so on in the comparison, till at last we discover a set of angles, equal not only to those thus introduced, but also to two right angles. We thus connect the two parts of the original proposition, by a number of intermediate equalities; and by that means perceive, that these two parts are equal among themselves; it being an intuitive proposition, as mentioned above, That two things are equal, each of which, in the same respect, is equal to a third.

I proceed to a different example, which concerns the relation between cause and effect. The proposition to be demonstrated is, "That there exists a good and intelligent Being, who is the cause of all the wise and benevolent effects that are produced in the government of this world." That there are such effects, is in the present example the fundamental proposition; which is taken for granted, because it is verified by experience. In order to discover the cause of these effects, I begin with an intuitive proposition mentioned above, "That every effect adapted to a good end or purpose, proceeds from a designing and benevolent cause." <200> The next step is, to examine whether man can be the cause: he is provided indeed with some share of wisdom and benevolence; but the effects mentioned are far above his power, and no less above his wisdom. Neither can this earth be the cause, nor the sun, the moon, the stars; for, far from being wise and benevolent, they are not even sensible. If these be excluded, we are unavoidably led to an invisible being, endowed with boundless power, goodness, and intelligence; and that invisible being is termed *God*.

Reasoning requires two mental powers, namely, the power of invention, and the power of perceiving relations. By the former are discovered intermediate propositions, equally related to the fundamental proposition and to the conclusion: by the latter we perceive, that the different links which compose the chain of reasoning, are all connected together by the same relation.

We can reason about matters of opinion and belief, as well as about matters of knowledge properly so termed. Hence reasoning is distinguished into two kinds; demonstrative, and probable. Demon-<201>strative reasoning is also of two kinds: in the first, the conclusion is drawn from the nature and inherent properties of the subject: in the other, the conclusion is drawn from some principle, of which we are certain by intuition. With respect to the first, we have no such knowledge of the nature or inherent properties of any being, material or immaterial, as to draw conclusions from it with certainty. I except not even figure considered as a quality of matter, tho' it is the object of mathematical reasoning. As we have no standard for determining with precision the figure of any portion of matter, we cannot with precision reason upon it: what appears to us a straight line may be a curve, and what appears a rectilinear angle may be curvilinear. How then comes mathematical reasoning to be demonstrative? This question may appear at first sight puzzling; and I know not that it has any where been distinctly explained. Perhaps what follows may be satisfactory.

The subjects of arithmetical reasoning are numbers. The subjects of mathematical reasoning are figures. But what figures? Not such as I see; but such as I <202> form an idea of, abstracting from every imperfection. I explain myself. There is a power in man to form images of things that never existed; a golden mountain, for example, or a river running upward. This power operates upon figures: there is perhaps no figure existing the sides of which are straight lines; but it is easy to form an idea of a line that has no waving or crookedness, and it is easy to form an idea of a figure bounded by such lines. Such ideal figures are the subjects of mathematical reasoning; and these being perfectly clear and distinct, are proper subjects for demonstrative reasoning of the first kind. Mathematical reasoning however is not merely a mental entertainment: it is of real use in life, by directing us to operate upon matter. There possibly may not be found any where a perfect globe, to answer the idea we form of that figure: but a globe may be made so near perfection, as to have nearly the properties of a perfect globe. In a word, tho' ideas are, properly speaking, the subject of mathematical evidence; yet the end and purpose of that evidence is, to direct us with respect to figures as they really exist; and <203> the nearer any real figure approaches to its ideal perfection, with the greater accuracy will the mathematical truth be applicable.

The component parts of figures, viz. lines and angles, are extremely simple, requiring no definition. Place before a child a crooked line, and one that has no appearance of being crooked: call the former a *crooked line,* the latter a *straight line;* and the child will use these terms familiarly, without hazard of a mistake. Draw a perpendicular upon paper: let the child advert, that the upward line leans neither to the right nor the left, and for that reason is termed *a perpendicular:* the child will apply that term familiarly to a tree, to the wall of a house, or to any other perpendicular. In the same manner, place before the child two lines diverging from each other, and two that have no appearance of diverging: call the latter *parallel lines,* and the child will have no difficulty of applying the same term to the sides of a door or of a window. Yet so accustomed are we to definitions, that even these simple ideas are not suffered to escape. A straight line, for example, is defined to be <204> the shortest that can be drawn between two given points. Is it so, that even a man, not to talk of a child, can have no idea of a straight line till he be told that the shortest line between two points is a straight line? How many talk familiarly of a straight line who never happened to think of that fact, which is an inference only, not a definition. If I had not beforehand an idea of a straight line, I should never be able to find out, that it is the shortest that can be drawn between two points. D'Alembert strains hard, but without success, for a definition of a straight line, and of the others mentioned. It is difficult to avoid smiling at his definition of parallel lines. Draw, says he, a straight line: erect upon it two perpendiculars of the same length: upon their two extremities draw another straight line; and that line is said to be parallel to the first mentioned; as if, to understand what is meant by the expression *two parallel lines,* we must first understand what is meant by a straight line, by a perpendicular, and by two lines equal in length. A very slight reflection upon the operations of his own mind, would have taught <205> this author, that he could form the idea of parallel lines without running through so many intermediate steps: sight alone is sufficient to explain the term to a boy, and even to a girl. At any rate, where is the necessity of introducing the line last mentioned? If the idea of parallels cannot be obtained from the two perpendiculars alone, the additional line drawn through their extremities will certainly not make it more clear.

Mathematical figures being in their nature complex, are capable of being defined; and from the foregoing simple ideas, it is easy to define every one of them. For example, a circle is a figure having a point within it, named the *centre,* through which all the straight lines that can be drawn, and extended to the circumference, are equal; a surface bounded by four equal straight lines, and having four right angles, is termed a *square;* and a cube is a solid, of which all the six surfaces are squares.

In the investigation of mathematical truths, we assist the imagination, by drawing figures upon paper that resemble our ideas. There is no necessity for a perfect <206> resemblance: a black spot, which in reality is a small round surface, serves to represent a mathematical point; and a black line, which in reality is a long narrow surface, serves to represent a mathematical line. When we reason about the figures composed of such lines, it is sufficient that these figures have some appearance of regularity: less or more is of no importance; because our reasoning is not founded upon them, but upon our ideas. Thus, to demonstrate that the three angles of a triangle are equal to two right angles, a triangle is drawn upon paper, in order to keep the mind steady to its object. After tracing the steps that lead to the conclusion, we are satisfied that the proposition is true; being conscious that the reasoning is built upon the ideal figure, not upon that which is drawn upon the paper. And being also conscious, that the enquiry is carried on independent of any particular length of the sides; we are satisfied of the universality of the proposition, and of its being applicable to all triangles whatever.

Numbers considered by themselves, abstractedly from things, make the subject <207> of arithmetic. And with respect both to mathematical and arithmetical reasonings, which frequently consist of many steps, the process is shortened by the invention of signs, which, by a single dash of the pen, express clearly what would require many words. By that means, a very long chain of reasoning is expressed by a few symbols; a method that contributes greatly to readiness of comprehension. If in such reasonings words were necessary, the mind, embarrassed with their multitude, would have great difficulty to follow any long chain of reasoning. A line drawn upon paper represents an ideal line, and a few simple characters represent the abstract ideas of number.

Arithmetical reasoning, like mathematical, depends entirely upon the relation of equality, which can be ascertained with the greatest certainty among many ideas. Hence, reasonings upon such ideas afford the highest degree of conviction. I do not say, however, that this is always the case; for a man who is conscious of his own fallibility, is seldom without some degree of diffidence, where the reasoning consists of many steps. And tho' on a re-<208>view no error be discovered, yet he is conscious that there may be errors, tho' they have escaped him.

As to the other kind of demonstrative reasoning, founded on propositions of which we are intuitively certain; I justly call it *demonstrative,* because it affords the same conviction that arises from mathematical reasoning. In both, the means of conviction are the same, viz. a clear perception of the relation between two ideas: and there are many relations of which we have ideas no less clear than of equality; witness substance and quality, the whole and its parts, cause and effect, and many others. From the intuitive proposition, for example, That nothing which begins to exist can exist without a cause, I can conclude, that some one being must have existed from all eternity, with no less certainty, than that the three angles of a triangle are equal to two right angles.

What falls next in order, is that inferior sort of knowledge which is termed *opinion;* and which, like knowledge properly so termed, is founded in some instances upon intuition, and in some upon reasoning. But it differs from knowledge <209> properly so termed in the following particular, that it produces different degrees of conviction, sometimes approaching to certainty, sometimes sinking toward the verge of improbability. The constancy and uniformity of natural operations, is a fit subject for illustrating that difference. The future successive changes of day and night, of winter and summer, and of other successions which have hitherto been constant and uniform, fall under intuitive knowledge, because of these we have the highest conviction. As the conviction is inferior of successions that hitherto have varied in any degree, these fall under intuitive opinion. We expect summer after winter with the utmost confidence; but we have not the same confidence in expecting a hot summer or a cold winter. And yet the probability approaches much nearer to certainty, than the intuitive opinion we have, that the operations of nature are extremely simple, a proposition that is little rely'd on.

As to opinion founded on reasoning, it is obvious, that the conviction produced by reasoning, can never rise above what is produced by the intuitive proposition <210> upon which the reasoning is founded. And that it may be weaker, will appear from considering, that even where the fundamental proposition is certain, it may lead to the conclusive opinion by intermediate propositions, that are probable only, not certain. In a word, it holds in general with respect to every sort of reasoning, that the conclusive proposition can never rise higher in point of conviction, than the very lowest of the intuitive propositions employ'd as steps in the reasoning.

The perception we have of the contingency of future events, opens a wide field to our reasoning about probabilities. That perception involves more or less doubt according to its subject. In some instances, the event is perceived to be extremely doubtful; in others, it is perceived to be less doubtful. It appears altogether doubtful, in throwing a dye, which of the six sides will turn up; and for that reason, we cannot justly conclude for one rather than for another. If one only of the six sides be marked with a figure, we conclude, that a blank will turn up; and five to one is an equal wager that such will be the effect. In judging of the future behaviour of a <211> man who has hitherto been governed by interest, we may conclude with a probability approaching to certainty, that interest will continue to prevail.

Belief comes last in order, which, as defined above, is knowledge of the truth of facts that falls below certainty, and involves in its nature some degree of doubt. It is also of two kinds; one founded upon intuition, and one upon reasoning. Thus, knowledge, opinion, belief, are all of them equally distinguishable into intuitive and discursive. Of intuitive belief, I discover three different sources or causes. First, A present object. Second, An object formerly present. Third, The testimony of others.

To have a clear conception of the first cause, it must be observed, that among the simple perceptions that compose the complex perception of a present object, a perception of real and present existence is one. This perception rises commonly to certainty; in which case it is a branch of knowledge properly so termed; and is handled as such above. But this perception falls below certainty in some instances; as where an object, seen at a <212> great distance or in a fog, is perceived to be a horse, but so indistinctly as to make it a probability only. The perception in such a case is termed *belief.*

Both perceptions are fundamentally of the same nature; being simple perceptions of real existence. They differ only in point of distinctness: the perception of reality that makes a branch of knowledge, is so clear and distinct as to exclude all doubt or hesitation: the perception of reality that occasions belief, being less clear and distinct, makes not the existence of the object certain to us, but only probable.

With respect to the second cause; the existence of an absent object, formerly seen, amounts not to a certainty; and therefore is the subject of belief only, not of knowledge. Things are in a continual flux from production to dissolution; and our senses are accommodated to that variable scene: a present object admits no doubt of its existence; but after it is removed, its existence becomes less certain, and in time sinks down to a slight degree of probability.

Human testimony, the third cause, produces belief, more or less strong, accor-<213>ding to circumstances. In general, nature leads us to rely upon the veracity of each other; and commonly the degree of reliance is proportioned to the degree of veracity. Sometimes belief approaches to certainty, as when it is founded on the evidence of persons above exception as to veracity. Sometimes it sinks to the lowest degree of probability, as when a fact is told by one who has no great reputation for truth. The nature of the fact, common or uncommon, has likewise an influence: an ordinary incident gains credit upon very slight evidence; but it requires the strongest evidence to overcome the improbability of an event that deviates from the ordinary course of nature. At the same time, it must be observed, that belief is not always founded upon rational principles. There are biasses and weaknesses in human nature that sometimes disturb the operation, and produce belief without sufficient or proper evidence: we are disposed to believe on very slight evidence, an interesting event, however rare or singular, that alarms and agitates the mind; because the mind in agitation is remarkably susceptible of impressions: for <214> which reason, stories of ghosts and apparitions pass current with the vulgar. Eloquence also has great power over the mind; and, by making deep impressions, enforces the belief of facts upon evidence that would not be regarded in a cool moment.

The dependence that our perception of real existence, and consequently belief, hath upon oral evidence, enlivens social intercourse, and promotes

society. But the perception of real existence has a still more extensive influence; for from that perception is derived a great part of the entertainment
we find in history, and in historical fables (*a*). At the same time, a perception
that may be raised by fiction as well as by truth, would often mislead were
we abandoned to its impulse: but the God of nature hath provided a remedy
for that evil, by erecting within the mind a tribunal, to which there lies an
appeal from the rash impressions of sense. When the delusion of eloquence
or of dread subsides, the perplexed mind is uncertain what to believe. A
regular process commences, counsel is heard, evidence pro-<215>duced,
and a final judgement pronounced, sometimes confirming, sometimes
varying, the belief impressed upon us by the lively perception of reality.
Thus, by a wise appointment of nature, intuitive belief is subjected to rational discussion: when confirmed by reason, it turns more vigorous and
authoritative: when contradicted by reason, it disappears among sensible
people. In some instances, it is too headstrong for reason; as in the case of
hobgoblins and apparitions, which pass current among the vulgar in spite
of reason.

We proceed to the other kind of belief, that which is founded on reasoning; to which, when intuition fails us, we must have recourse for ascertaining certain facts. Thus, from known effects, we infer the existence of
unknown causes. That an effect must have a cause, is an intuitive proposition; but to ascertain what particular thing is the cause, requires commonly a process of reasoning. This is one of the means by which the Deity,
the primary cause, is made known to us, as mentioned above. Reason, in
tracing causes from known effects, produces different degrees of conviction. It sometimes <216> produces certainty, as in proving the existence of
the Deity; which on that account is handled above, under the head of
knowledge. For the most part it produces belief only, which, according to
the strength of the reasoning, sometimes approaches to certainty, sometimes is so weak as barely to turn the scale on the side of probability. Take
the following examples of different degrees of belief founded on probable
reasoning. When Inigo Jones flourished, and was the only architect of note
in England; let it be supposed, that his model of the palace of Whitehall

(*a*) Elements of Criticism, ch. 2. part 1. § 7.

had been presented to a stranger, without mentioning the author. The stranger, in the first place, would be intuitively certain, that this was the work of some Being, intelligent and skilful. Secondly, He would have a conviction approaching to certainty, that the operator was a man. And, thirdly, He would have a conviction that the man was Inigo Jones; but less firm than the former. Let us next suppose another English architect little inferior in reputation to Jones: the stranger would still pronounce in favour of the latter; but his belief would be in the lowest degree. <217>

When we investigate the causes of certain effects, the reasoning is often founded upon the known nature of man. In the high country, for example, between Edinburgh and Glasgow, the people lay their coals at the end of their houses, without any fence to secure them from theft: whence it is rationally inferred, that coals are there in plenty. In the west of Scotland, the corn-stacks are covered with great care and nicety: whence it is inferred, that the climate is rainy. Placentia is the capital town of Biscay: the only town in Newfoundland bears the same name; from which circumstance it is conjectured, that the Biscayners were the first Europeans who made a settlement in that island.

Analogical reasoning, founded upon the uniformity of nature, is frequently employ'd in the investigation of facts; and we infer, that facts of which we are uncertain, must resemble those of the same kind that are known. The reasonings in natural philosophy are mostly of that kind. Take the following examples. We learn from experience, that proceeding from the humblest vegetable to man, there are num-<218>berless classes of beings rising one above another by differences scarce perceptible, and leaving no where a single gap or interval: and from conviction of the uniformity of nature we infer, that the line is not broken off here, but is carried on in other worlds, till it end in the Deity. I proceed to another example. Every man is conscious of a self-motive power in himself; and from the uniformity of nature, we infer the same power in every one of our own species. The argument here from analogy carries great weight, because we entertain no doubt of the uniformity of nature with respect to beings of our own kind. We apply the same argument to other animals; tho' their resemblance to man appears not so certain, as that of one man to another. But why not also apply the same argument to infer a self-motive power in matter? When we see matter in motion without an external mover, we naturally infer, that, like us, it moves itself. Another example is borrow'd from Maupertuis. "As there is no known space of the earth covered with water so large as the *Terra Australis incognita,* we may reasonably infer, that <219> so great a part of the earth is not altogether sea, but that there must be some proportion of land." The uniformity of nature with respect to the intermixture of sea and land, is an argument that affords but a very slender degree of conviction; and from late voyages it is discovered, that the argument holds not in fact. The following argument of the same kind, tho' it cannot be much rely'd on, seems however better founded. "The inhabitants of the northern hemisphere, have, in arts and sciences, excelled such of the southern as we have any knowledge of: and therefore among the latter we ought not to expect many arts, nor much cultivation."

After a fatiguing investigation of numberless particulars which divide and scatter the thought, it may not be unpleasant to bring all under one view by a succinct recapitulation.

We have two means for discovering truth and acquiring knowledge, viz. intuition and reasoning. By intuition we discover subjects and their attributes, passions, internal action, and in short every thing that is matter of fact. By intuition <220> we also discover several relations. There are some facts and many relations, that cannot be discovered by a single act of intuition, but require several such acts linked together in a chain of reasoning.

Knowledge acquired by intuition, includes for the most part certainty: in some instances it includes probability only. Knowledge acquired by reasoning, frequently includes certainty; but more frequently includes probability only.

Probable knowledge, whether founded on intuition or on reasoning, is termed *opinion* when it concerns relations; and is termed *belief* when it concerns facts. Where knowledge includes certainty, it retains its proper name.

Reasoning that produces certainty, is termed *demonstrative;* and is termed *probable,* when it only produces probability.

Demonstrative reasoning is of two kinds. The first is, where the conclusion is derived from the nature and inherent properties of the subject: mathematical reasoning is of that kind; and perhaps the only instance. The second is, where the conclusion is derived from some proposition, of which we are certain by intuition. <221>

Probable reasoning is endless in its varieties; and affords different degrees of conviction, depending on the nature of the subject upon which it is employ'd.

SECTION II

Progress of Reason.

A progress from infancy to maturity in the mind of man, similar to that in his body, has been often mentioned. The external senses, being early necessary for self-preservation, arrive quickly at maturity. The internal senses are of a slower growth, as well as every other mental power: their maturity would be of little or no use while the body is weak, and unfit for action. Reasoning, as observed in the first section, requires two mental powers, the power of invention, and that of perceiving relations. By the former are discovered intermediate propositions, having the same relation to the fundamental proposition and to the conclusion; <222> and that relation is verified by the latter. Both powers are necessary to the person who frames an argument, or a chain of reasoning: the latter only, to the person who judges of it. Savages are miserably deficient in both. With respect to the former, a savage may have from his nature a talent for invention; but it will stand him in little stead without a stock of ideas enabling him to select what may answer his purpose; and a savage has no opportunity to acquire such a stock. With respect to the latter, he knows little of relations. And how should he know, when both study and practice are necessary for distinguishing between relations? The understanding, at the same time, is among the illiterate obsequious to passion and prepossession; and among them the imagination acts without control, forming conclusions often no better than mere dreams. In short, considering the many causes that mislead from just reasoning, in days especially of ignorance, the erroneous and absurd opinions that have prevailed in the world, and that continue in some measure to prevail, are far from being surprising. Were reason our only <223> guide in the conduct of life, we should have cause to complain; but our Maker has provided us with the moral sense, a guide little subject to error in matters of importance. In the sciences, reason is essential; but in the conduct of life, which is our chief concern, reason may be an useful assistant; but to be our director is not its province.

The national progress of reason has been slower in Europe, than that of any other art: statuary, painting, architecture, and other fine arts, approach nearer perfection, as well as morality and natural history. Manners and every art that appears externally, may in part be acquired by imitation and example: in reasoning there is nothing external to be laid hold of. But there is beside a particular cause that regards Europe, which is the blind deference that for many ages was paid to Aristotle; who has kept the reasoning faculty in chains more than two thousand years. In his logic, the plain and simple mode of reasoning is rejected, that which Nature dictates; and in its stead is introduced an artificial mode, showy but unsubstantial, of no use for discovering truth; but con-<224>trived with great art for wrangling and disputation. Considering that reason for so many ages has been immured in the enchanted castle of syllogism, where phantoms pass for realities; the slow progress of reason toward maturity is far from being surprising. The taking of Constantinople by the Turks *ann.* 1453, unfolded a new scene, which in time relieved the world from the usurpation of Aristotle, and restored reason to her privileges. All the knowledge of Europe was centred in Constantinople; and the learned men of that city, abhorring the Turks and their government, took refuge in Italy. The Greek language was introduced among the western nations of Europe; and the study of Greek and Roman classics became fashionable. Men, having acquired new ideas, began to think for themselves: they exerted their native faculty of reason: the futility of Aristotle's logic became apparent to the penetrating; and is now apparent to all. Yet so late as the year 1621, several persons were banished from Paris for contradicting that philosopher, about matter and form, and about the number of the elements. And shortly after, the <225> parliament of Paris prohibited, under pain of death, any thing to be taught contrary to the doctrines of Aristotle. Julius II. and Leo X. Roman Pontiffs, contributed zealously to the reformation of letters; but they did not foresee that they were also contributing to the reformation of religion, and of every science that depends on reasoning. Though the fetters of syllogism have many years ago been shaken off; yet, like a limb long kept from motion, the reasoning faculty has scarcely to this day attained its free and natural exercise. Mathematics is the only science that never has been cramped by syllogism, and we find reasoning there in great perfection at an early period. The very slow progress of reasoning in other matters, will appear from the following induction.

To exemplify erroneous and absurd reasonings of every sort, would be endless. The reader, I presume, will be satisfied with a few instances; and I shall endeavour to select what are amusing. For the sake of order, I divide them into three heads. First, Instances showing the imbecillity of human reason during its nonage. Second, Erroneous reasoning occasioned by <226> natural biasses. Third, Erroneous reasoning occasioned by acquired biasses. With respect to the first, instances are endless of reasonings founded on erroneous premises. It was an Epicurean doctrine, That the gods have all of them a human figure; moved by the following argument, that no being of any other figure has the use of reason. Plato, taking for granted the following erroneous proposition, That every being which moves itself must have a soul, concludes that the world must have a soul, because it moves itself (a). Aristotle taking it for granted, without the least evidence and contrary to truth, that all heavy bodies tend to the centre of the universe, proves the earth to be the centre of the universe by the following argument. "Heavy bodies naturally tend to the centre of the universe: we know by experience that heavy bodies tend to the centre of the earth: therefore the centre of the earth is the centre of the universe." Appion ridicules the Jews for adhering literally to the precept of resting on their sabbath, so as to suffer Jerusalem to be taken that day by <227> Ptolomy son of Lagus. Mark the answer of Josephus: "Whoever passes a sober judgement on this matter, will find our practice agreeable to honour and virtue; for what can be more honourable and virtuous, than to postpone our country, and even life itself, to the service of God, and of his holy religion?" A strange idea of religion, to put it in direct opposition to every moral principle! A superstitious and absurd doctrine, That God will interpose by a miracle to declare what is right in every controversy, has occasioned much erroneous

(a) Cicero, De natura Deorum, lib. 2. § 12.

reasoning and absurd practice. The practice of determining controversies by single combat, commenced about the seventh century, when religion had degenerated into superstition, and courage was esteemed the only moral virtue. The parliament of Paris, in the reign of Charles VI. appointed a single combat between two gentlemen, in order to have the judgement of God whether the one had committed a rape on the other's wife. In 1454, John Picard being accused by his son-in-law for too great familiarity with his wife, a duel between them was appointed by the same <228> parliament. Voltaire justly observes, that the parliament decreed a parricide to be committed, in order to try an accusation of incest, which possibly was not committed. The trials by water and by fire, rest on the same erroneous foundation. In the former, if the person accused sunk to the bottom, it was a judgement pronounced by God, that he was innocent: if he kept above, it was a judgement that he was guilty. Fleury (*a*) remarks, that if ever the person accused was found guilty, it was his own fault. In Sicily, a woman accused of adultery, was compelled to swear to her innocence: the oath, taken down in writing, was laid on water; and if it did not sink, the woman was innocent. We find the same practice in Japan, and in Malabar. One of the articles insisted on by the reformers in Scotland, was, That public prayers be made and the sacraments administered in the vulgar tongue. The answer of a provincial council was in the following words: "That to conceive public prayers or administer the sacraments in any language but Latin, is contrary to the traditions and <229> practice of the Catholic church for many ages past; and that the demand cannot be granted, without impiety to God and disobedience to the church." Here it is taken for granted, that the practice of the church is always right; which is building an argument on a very rotten foundation. The Caribbeans abstain from swines flesh; taking it erroneously for granted, that such food would make them have small eyes, held by them a great deformity. They also abstain from eating turtle; which they think would infect them with the laziness and stupidity of that animal. Upon the same erroneous notion, the Brasilians abstain from the flesh of ducks, and of every creature that moves slowly. It is observed of northern nations, that they do not open the mouth sufficiently

(*a*) Histoire Ecclesiastique.

for distinct articulation; and the reason given is, that the coldness of the air makes them keep the mouth as close as possible. This reason is indolently copied by writers one from another: people enured to a cold climate feel little cold in the mouth; beside that a cause so weak could never operate equally among so many different nations. The real cause is, <230> that northern tongues abound with consonants, which admit but a small aperture of the mouth. (See Elements of Criticism, chap. Beauty of language.) A list of German names to be found in every catalogue of books, will make this evident, *Rutgersius,* for example, *Faesch.* To account for a fact that is certain, any reason commonly suffices.[2]

A talent for writing seems in Germany to be estimated by weight, as beauty is said to be in Holland. Cocceius for writing three weighty folio volumes on law, has obtained among his countrymen the epithet of *Great.* This author, handling the rules of succession in land-estates, has with most profound erudition founded all of them upon the following very simple proposition: In a competition, that descendent is entitled to be preferred who has the greatest quantity of the predecessor's blood in his veins. *Quaeritur,* has a man any of his predecessor's blood in his veins, otherwise than metaphorically? Simple indeed! to build an argument in law upon a pure metaphor.

Next of reasonings where the conclusion follows not from the premises, or funda-<231>mental proposition. Plato endeavours to prove, that the world is endowed with wisdom, by the following argument. "The world is greater than any of its parts: therefore it is endowed with wisdom; for otherwise a man who is endowed with wisdom would be greater than the world" (*a*). The conclusion here does not follow; for tho' man is endowed with wisdom, it follows not, that he is greater than the world in point of size. Zeno endeavours to prove, that the world has the use of reason, by an argument of the same kind. To convince the world of the truth of the four gospels, Ireneus (*b*) urges the following arguments, which he calls demonstration. "There are four quarters of the world and four cardinal winds,

(*a*) Cicero, De natura Deorum, lib. 2. § 12.
(*b*) Lib. 3. cap. 11.
2. "It is observed . . . reason commonly suffices": added in 2nd edition.

consequently there are four gospels in the church, as there are four pillars that support it, and four breaths of life that render it immortal." Again, "The four animals in Ezekiel's vision mark the four states of the Son of God. The lion is his royal dignity: <232> the calf, his priesthood: the beast with the face of man, his human nature: the eagle, his spirit which descends on the church. To these four animals correspond the four gospels, on which our Lord is seated. John, who teaches his celestial origin, is the lion, his gospel being full of confidence: Luke, who begins with the priesthood of Zachariah, is the calf: Matthew, who describes the genealogy of Christ according to the flesh, is the animal resembling a man: Mark, who begins with the prophetic spirit coming from above, is the eagle. This gospel is the shortest of all, because brevity is the character of prophecy." Take a third demonstration of the truth of the four gospels. "There have been four covenants; the first under Adam, the second under Noah, the third under Moses, the fourth under Jesus Christ." Whence Ireneus concludes, that they are vain, rash, and ignorant, who admit more or less than four gospels. St. Cyprian in his exhortation to martyrdom, after having applied the mysterious number seven, to the seven days of the creation, to the seven thousand years of the world's duration, to <233> the seven spirits that stand before God, to the seven lamps of the tabernacle, to the seven candlesticks of the Apocalypse, to the seven pillars of wisdom, to the seven children of the barren woman, to the seven women who took one man for their husband, to the seven brothers of the Maccabees; observes, that St. Paul mentions that number as a privileged number; which, says he, is the reason why he did not write but to seven churches.[3] Pope Gregory, writing in favour of the four councils, viz. Nice, Constantinople, Ephesus, and Calcedon, reasons thus: "That as there are four evangelists, there ought also to be four councils." What would he have said, if he had lived 100 years later, when there were many more than four? In administering the sacrament of the Lord's supper, it was ordered, that the host should be covered with a clean linen cloth; because, says the Canon law, the body of our Lord Jesus Christ was buried in a clean linen cloth. Josephus, in his answer to Appion, urges the following argument for the temple of Jerusalem: "As there is but one

---

3. "To convince the . . . to seven churches": added in 2nd edition.

God, and one world, it holds in analogy, that there should be but one <234> temple." At that rate, there should be but one worshipper. And why should that one temple be at Jerusalem rather than at Rome, or at Pekin? The Syrians and Greeks did not for a long time eat fish. Two reasons are assigned: one is, that fish is not sacrificed to the gods; the other, that being immersed in the sea, they look not up to heaven (a). The first would afford a more plausible argument for eating fish. And if the other have any weight, it would be an argument for sacrificing men, and neither fish nor cattle. In justification of the Salic law, which prohibits female succession, it was long held a conclusive argument, That in the scripture the lilies are said neither to work nor to spin. Vieira, termed by his countrymen *the Lusitanian Cicero,* published sermons, one of which begins thus, "Were the Supreme Being to show himself visibly, he would chuse the circle rather than the triangle, the square, the pentagon, the duodecagon, or any other figure." But why appear in any of these figures? And if he were obliged to appear in so mean a shape, a globe is un-<235>doubtedly more beautiful than a circle. Peter Hantz of Horn, who lived in the last century, imagined that Noah's ark is the true construction of a ship; "which," said he, "is the workmanship of God, and therefore perfect"; as if a vessel made merely for floating on the water, were the best also for sailing. Sixty or seventy years ago, the fashion prevailed, in imitation of birds, to swallow small stones for the sake of digestion; as if what is proper for birds, were equally proper for men. The Spaniards, who laid waste a great part of the West Indies, endeavoured to excuse their cruelties, by maintaining, that the natives were not men, but a species of the Ouran Outang; for no better reason, than that they were of a copper colour, spoke an unknown language, and had no beard. The Pope issued a bull, declaring, that it pleased him and the Holy Ghost to acknowledge the Americans to be of the human race. This bull was not received cordially; for in the council of Lima, *ann.* 1583, it was violently disputed, whether the Americans had so much understanding as to be admitted to the sacraments of the church. <236> In 1440, the Portuguese solicited the Pope's permission to double the Cape of Good Hope, and to reduce to perpetual servitude the negroes, because they had the colour of

(a) Sir John Marsham, p. 221.

the damned, and never went to church. In the Frederician Code, a proposition is laid down, That by the law of nature no man can make a testament. And in support of that proposition the following argument is urged, which is said to be a demonstration: "No deed can be a testament while a man is alive, because it is not necessarily his *ultima voluntas;* and no man can make a testament after his death." Both premises are true, but the negative conclusion does not follow: it is true a man's deed is not his *ultima voluntas,* while he is alive: but does it not become his *ultima voluntas,* when he dies without altering the deed?

Many reasonings have passed current in the world as good coin, where the premises are not true; nor, supposing them true, would they infer the conclusion. Plato in his Phaedon relies on the following argument for the immortality of the soul. "Is not death the opposite of life? <237> Certainly. And do they not give birth to each other? Certainly. What then is produced from life? Death. And what from death? Life. It is then from the dead that all things living proceed; and consequently souls exist after death." God, says Plato, made but five worlds, because according to his definition there are but five regular bodies in geometry. Is that a reason for confining the Almighty to five worlds, not one less or more.[4] Aristotle, who wrote a book upon mechanics, was much puzzled about the equilibrium of a balance, when unequal weights are hung upon it at different distances from the centre. Having observed, that the arms of the balance describe portions of a circle, he accounted for the equilibrium by a notable argument: "All the properties of the circle are wonderful: the equilibrium of the two weights that describe portions of a circle is wonderful. *Ergo,* the equilibrium must be one of the properties of the circle." What are we to think of Aristotle's Logic, when we find him capable of such childish reasoning? And yet that work has been the admiration of all the <238> world for centuries upon centuries. Nay, that foolish argument has been espoused and commented upon by his disciples, for the same length of time. To proceed to another instance: Marriage within the fourth degree of consanguinity, as well as of affinity, is prohibited by the Lateran council, and the reason given is, That the body being made up of the four elements, has four different humours

4. "Plato in his . . . less or more": added in 2nd edition.

in it.* The Roman Catholics began with beheading heretics, hanging them, or stoning them to death. But such punishments were discovered to be too slight, in matters of faith. It was demonstrated, that heretics ought to be burnt in a slow fire: it being taken for granted, that God punishes them in the other world with a slow fire; it was inferred, "That as every prince <239> and every magistrate is the image of God in this world, they ought to follow his example." Here is a double error in reasoning: first, the taking for granted the fundamental proposition, which is surely not self-evident; and next, the drawing a conclusion from it without any connection. The heat of the sun, by the reflection of its rays from the earth, is greatly increased in passing over the great country of Africa. Hence rich mines of gold, and the black complexion of the inhabitants. In passing over the Atlantic it is cooled: and by the time it reaches the continent of America, it has lost much of its vigour. Hence no gold on the east side of America. But being heated again in passing over a great space of land, it produces much gold in Peru. Is not this reasoning curious? What follows is no less so. Huetius Bishop of Auvranches, declaiming against the vanity of establishing a perpetual succession of descendents, observes, that other writers had exposed it upon moral principles, but that he would cut it down with a plain metaphysical argument. "Father and son are relative ideas; and the relation is at an end by <240> the death of either. My will therefore to leave my estate to my son, is absurd; because after my death, he is no longer my son." By the same sort of argument he demonstrates the vanity of fame. "The relation that subsists between a man and his character, is at an end by his death: and therefore, that the character given him by the world, belongs not to him nor to any person." Huetius is not the only writer who has urged metaphysical arguments contrary to common sense.[5]

It once was a general opinion among those who dwelt near the sea, that

---

* The original is curious: "Quaternarius enim numerus bene congruit prohibitioni conjugii corporalis; de quo dicit Apostolus, Quod vir non habet potestatem sui corporis, sed mulier; neque mulier habet potestatem sui corporis, sed vir; quia quatuor sunt humores in corpore, quod constat ex quatuor elementis." Were men who could be guilty of such nonsense, qualified to be our leaders in the most important of all concerns, that of eternal salvation?

5. "The heat of . . . to common sense": added in 2nd edition.

people never die but during the ebb of the tide. And there were not wanting plausible reasons. The sea, in flowing, carries with it vivifying particles that recruit the sick. The sea is salt, and salt preserves from rottenness. When the sea sinks in ebbing, every thing sinks with it: nature languishes: the sick are not vivified: they die.

What shall be said of a reasoning where the conclusion is a flat contradiction to the premises? If a man shooting at a wild pigeon happen unfortunately to kill his <241> neighbour, it is in the English law excusable homicide; because the shooting an animal that is no man's property, is a lawful act. If the aim be at a tame fowl for amusement, which is a trespass on the property of another, the death of the man is manslaughter. If the tame fowl be shot in order to be stolen, it is murder, by reason of the felonious intent. From this last the following consequence is drawn, that if a man, endeavouring to kill another, misses his blow and happeneth to kill himself, he is in judgement of law guilty *of wilful and deliberate self-murder* (*a*). Strange reasoning! to construe an act to be wilful and deliberate self-murder, contrary to the very thing that is supposed.

A plentiful source of inconclusive reasoning, which prevails greatly during the infancy of the rational faculty, is the making of no proper distinction between strong and weak relations. Minutius Felix, in his apology for the Christians, endeavours to prove the unity of the Deity from a most distant analogy or relation, "That there is but one king of the bees, <242> and that more than one chief magistrate would breed confusion." It is a prostitution of reason to offer such an argument for the unity of the Deity. But any argument passes current, in support of a proposition that we know beforehand to be true. Plutarch says, "that it seemed to have happened by the peculiar direction of the gods, that Numa was born on the 21st of April, the very day in which Rome was founded by Romulus"; a very childish inference from a mere accident. Supposing Italy to have been tolerably populous, as undoubtedly it was at that period, the 21st of April, or any day of April, might have given birth to thousands. In many countries, the surgeons and barbers are classed together, as members of the same trade, from a very slight relation, that both of them operate upon the human body. The Jews

(*a*) Hale, Pleas of the Crown, cap. 1. 413.

enjoy'd the reputation, for centuries, of being skilful physicians. Francis I. of France, having long laboured under a disease that eluded the art of his own physicians, apply'd to the Emperor Charles V. for a Jewish physician from Spain. Finding that the person sent had been convert-<243>ed to Christianity, the King refused to employ him; as if a Jew were to lose his skill upon being converted to Christianity. Why did not the King order one of his own physicians to be converted to Judaism? The following childish argument is built upon an extreme slight relation, that between our Saviour and the wooden cross he suffered on. "Believe me," says Julius Firmicus,

> that the devil omits nothing to destroy miserable mortals; converting him-
> self into every different form, and employing every sort of artifice. He
> appoints wood to be used in sacrificing to him, knowing that our Saviour,
> fixed to the cross, would bestow immortality upon all his followers. A pine-
> tree is cut down, and used in sacrificing to the mother of the gods. A
> wooden image of Osiris is buried in sacrificing to Isis. A wooden image
> of Proserpina is bemoaned for forty nights, and then thrown into the
> flames. Deluded mortals, these flames can do you no service. On the con-
> trary, the fire that is destined for your punishment rages without end.
> Learn from me to know that divine wood which will set <244> you free.
> A wooden ark saved the human race from the universal deluge. Abraham
> put wood upon the shoulders of his son Isaac. The wooden rod stretched
> out by Aaron brought the children of Israel out of the land of Egypt.
> Wood sweetened the bitter waters of Marah, and comforted the children
> of Israel after wandering three days without water. A wooden rod struck
> water out of the rock. The rod of God in the hand of Moses overcame
> Amalek. The patriarch dreamed, that he saw angels descending and as-
> cending upon a wooden ladder; and the law of God was inclosed in a
> wooden ark. These things were exhibited, that, as if it were by certain
> steps, we might ascend to the wood of the cross, which is our salvation.
> The wood of the cross sustains the heavenly machine, supports the foun-
> dations of the earth, and leads men to eternal life. The wood of the devil
> burns and perishes, and its ashes carries down sinners to the lowest pit of
> hell.

The very slightest relations make an impression on a weak understanding. It was a fancy of Anto-<245>ninus Geta, in ordering his table, to have services composed of dishes beginning with the same letter; such as lamb and lobster; broth, beef, blood-pudding; pork, plumb-cake, pigeons, potatoes. The name of John king of Scotland was changed into *Robert,* for no better reason than that the Johns of France and of England had been unfortunate.

In reasoning, instances are not rare, of mistaking the cause for the effect, and the effect for the cause. When a stone is thrown from the hand, the continuance of its motion in the air, was once universally accounted for as follows: "That the air follows the stone at the heels, and pushes it on." The effect here is mistaken for the cause: the air indeed follows the stone at the heels; but it only fills the vacuity made by the stone, and does not push it on. It has been slyly urged against the art of physic, that physicians are rare among temperate people, such as have no wants but those of nature; and that where physicians abound, diseases abound. This is mistaking the cause for the effect, and the effect for the cause: people in health have no occasion for a physician; <246> but indolence and luxury beget diseases, and diseases beget physicians.

During the nonage of reason, men are satisfied with words merely, instead of an argument. A sea-prospect is charming; but we soon tire of an unbounded prospect. It would not give satisfaction to say, that it is too extensive; for why should not a prospect be relished, however extensive? But employ a foreign term and say, that it is *trop vaste,* we enquire no farther: a term that is not familiar, makes an impression, and captivates weak reason. This observation accounts for a mode of writing formerly in common use, that of stuffing our language with Latin words and phrases. These are now laid aside as useless; because a proper emphasis in reading, makes an impression deeper than any foreign term can do.

There is one proof of the imbecillity of human reason in dark times, which would scarce be believed, were not the fact supported by incontestible evidence. Instead of explaining any natural appearance by searching for a cause, it has been common to account for it by inventing a fable, which gave satisfaction without enquiring <247> farther. For example, instead of giving the true cause of the succession of day and night, the sacred book of the Scandinavians, termed *Edda,* accounts for that succession by a tale: "The giant Nor had a daughter named *Night,* of a dark complexion. She was wedded to Daglingar, of the family of the gods. They had a male child,

which they named *Day*, beautiful and shining like all of his father's family.
The universal father took Night and Day, placed them in heaven, and gave
to each a horse and a car, that they might travel round the world, the one
after the other. Night goes first upon her horse named *Rimfaxe*, [Frosty
Mane], who moistens the earth with the foam that drops from his bit, which
is the dew. The horse belonging to Day is named *Skinfaxe*, [Shining Mane],
who by his radiant mane illuminates the air and the earth." It is observed
by the translator of the Edda, that this way of accounting for things is well
suited to the turn of the human mind, endowed with curiosity that is keen;
but easily satisfied, often with words instead of ideas. Zoroaster, by a similar
fable, accounts for the <248> growth of evil in this world. He invents a
good and an evil principle named *Oromazes* and *Arimanes,* who are in continual conflict for preference. At the last day, Oromazes will be reunited to
the supreme God, from whom he issued. Arimanes will be subdued, darkness destroyed; and the world, purified by an universal conflagration, will
become a luminous and shining abode, from which evil will be excluded.
I return to the Edda, which is stored with fables of this kind. The highest
notion savages can form of the gods, is that of men endowed with extraordinary power and knowledge. The only puzzling circumstance is, how they
differ so much from other men as to be immortal. The Edda accounts for
it by the following fable. "The gods prevented the effect of old age and
decay, by eating certain apples, trusted to the care of *Iduna. Loke,* the Mo-
mus of the Scandinavians, craftily convey'd away *Iduna,* and concealed her
in a wood, under the custody of a giant. The gods, beginning to wax old
and gray, detected the author of the theft; and, by terrible menaces, compelled him to employ his ut-<249>most cunning, for regaining Iduna and
her apples, in which he was successful." The origin of poetry is thus accounted for in the same work:

> The gods formed *Cuaser,* who traversed the earth, teaching wisdom to
> men. He was treacherously slain by two dwarfs, who mixed honey with
> his blood, and composed a liquor that renders all who drink of it poets.
> These dwarfs having incurred the resentment of a certain giant, were ex-
> posed by him upon a rock, surrounded on all sides with the sea. They gave
> for their ransom the said liquor, which the giant delivered to his daughter
> *Gunloda.* The precious potion was eagerly sought for by the gods; but how
> were they to come at it? *Odin,* in the shape of a worm, crept through a

crevice into the cavern where the liquor was concealed. Then resuming his natural shape, and obtaining Gunloda's consent to take three draughts, he sucked up the whole; and, transforming himself into an eagle, flew away to *Asgard.* The giant, who was a magician, flew with all speed after Odin, and came up with him near the gate of *Asgard.* The gods <250> issued out of their palaces to assist their master; and presented to him all the pitchers they could lay hands on, which he instantly filled with the precious liquor. But in the hurry of discharging his load, Odin poured only part of the liquor through his beak, the rest being emitted through a less pure vent. The former is bestow'd by the gods upon good poets, to inspire them with divine enthusiasm. The latter, which is in much greater plenty, is bestow'd liberally on all who apply for it; by which means the world is pestered with an endless quantity of wretched verses.

Ignorance is equally credulous in all ages. Albert, surnamed *the Great,* flourished in the thirteenth century, and was a man of real knowledge. During the course of his education he was remarkably dull; and some years before he died became a sort of changeling. That singularity produced the following story. The holy Virgin, appearing to him, demanded, whether he would excel in philosophy or in theology: upon his chusing the former, she promised, that he should become an incomparable philosopher; but added, that to punish <251> him for not preferring theology, he should become stupid again as at first.

Upon a slight view, it may appear unaccountable, that even the grossest savages should take a childish tale for a solid reason. But nature aids the deception: where things are related in a lively manner, and every circumstance appears as passing in our sight, we take all for granted as true (*a*). Can an ignorant rustic doubt of inspiration, when he sees as it were the poet sipping the pure celestial liquor? And how can that poet fail to produce bad verses, who feeds on the excrements that drop from the fundament even of a deity?

In accounting for natural appearances, even good writers have betray'd a weakness in reasoning, little inferior to that above mentioned. They do not indeed put off their disciples with a tale; but they put them off with a

---

(*a*) Elements of Criticism, vol. 1. p. 100. edit. 5.

mere supposition, not more real than the tale. Descartes ascribes the motion of the planets to a vortex of ether whirling round and round. He thought not of enquiring whether there really be such a vortex, nor what makes it <252> move. M. Buffon forms the earth out of a splinter of the sun, struck off by a comet. May not one be permitted humbly to enquire at that eminent philosopher, what formed the comet? This passes for solid reasoning; and yet we laugh at the poor Indian, who supports the earth from falling by an elephant, and the elephant by a tortoise.

It is still more ridiculous to reason upon what is acknowledged to be a fiction, as if it were real. Such are the fictions admitted in the Roman law. A Roman taken captive in war, lost his privilege of being a Roman citizen; for freedom was held essential to that privilege. But what if he made his escape after perhaps an hour's detention? The hardship in that case ought to have suggested an alteration of the law, so far as to suspend the privilege no longer than the captivity subsisted. But the ancient Romans were not so ingenious. They remedied the hardship by a fiction, that the man never had been a captive. The Frederician code banishes from the law of Prussia an endless number of fictions found in the Roman law (a). Yet <253> afterward, treating of personal rights, it is laid down as a rule, That a child in the womb is feigned or supposed to be born when the fiction is for its advantage (b). To a weak reasoner, a fiction is a happy contrivance for resolving intricate questions. Such is the constitution of England, that the English law-courts are merely territorial; and that no fact happening abroad comes under their cognisance. An Englishman, after murdering his fellow-traveller in France, returns to his native country. What is to be done, for guilt ought not to pass unpunished? The crime is feigned to have been committed in England.

Ancient histories are full of incredible facts that passed current during the infancy of reason, which at present would be rejected with contempt. Every one who is conversant in the history of ancient nations, can recall instances without end. Does any person believe at present, tho' gravely reported by historians, that in old Rome there was a law, for cutting into

(a) Preface, § 28.
(b) Part 1. book 1. title 4. § 4.

pieces the body of a bankrupt, and distri-<254>buting the parts among his creditors? The story of Porsenna and Scevola is highly romantic; and the story of Vampires in Hungary, shamefully absurd. There is no reason to believe, there ever was such a state as that of the Amazons; and the story of Thalestris and Alexander the Great is certainly a fiction. Scotch historians describe gravely and circumstantially the battle of Luncarty, as if they had been eye-witnesses. A peasant and his two sons, it is said, were ploughing in an adjacent field, during the heat of the action. Enraged at their countrymen for turning their backs, they broke the plough in pieces; and each laying hold of a part, rushed into the midst of the battle, and obtained a complete victory over the Danes. This story has every mark of fiction: A man following out unconcernedly his ordinary occupation of ploughing, in sight of a battle, on which depended his wife and children, his goods, and perhaps his own life: three men, without rank or figure, with only a stick in the hand of each, stemming the tide of victory, and turning the fate of battle. I mention not that a plough was unknown <255> in Scotland for a century or two after that battle; for that circumstance could not create a doubt in the historian, if he was ignorant of it.

Reason, with respect to its progress, is singular. Morals, manners, and every thing that appears externally, may in part be acquired by imitation and example; which have not the slightest influence upon the reasoning faculty. The only means for advancing that faculty to maturity, are indefatigable study and practice; and even these will not carry a man one step beyond the subjects he is conversant about: examples are not rare of men extremely expert in one science, and grossly deficient in others. Many able mathematicians are novices in politics, and even in the common arts of life: study and practice have ripened them in every relation of equality, while they remain ignorant, like the vulgar, about other relations. A man, in like manner, who has bestowed much time and thought in political matters, may be a child as to other branches of knowledge.* <256>

* Pascal, the celebrated author of *Lettres Provinciales,* in order to explain the infinity and indivisibility of the Deity, has the following words. "I will show you a thing both infinite and indivisible. It is a point moving with infinite celerity: that point is in all places at once, and entire in every place." What an absurdity, says Voltaire, to ascribe

I proceed to the second article, containing erroneous reasoning occasioned by natural biasses. The first bias I shall mention has an extensive
influence. What is seen, makes a deeper impression than what is reported,
or discovered by reflection. Hence it is, that in judging of right and wrong,
the ignorant and illiterate are struck with the external act only, without
penetrating into will or intention which lie out of sight. Thus with respect
to covenants, laws, vows, and other acts that are completed by words, the
whole weight in days of ignorance is laid upon the external expression, with
no regard to the meaning of the speaker or writer. The blessing bestow'd
by Isaac upon his son <257> Jacob, mistaking him for Esau, is an illustrious
instance. Not only was the blessing intended for Esau, but Jacob, by de-
ceiving his father, had rendered himself unworthy of it (*a*); yet Isaac had
pronounced the sounds, and it was not in his power to unsay them: *Nescit
vox emissa reverti.*[6] Joshua, grossly imposed on by the Gibeonites denying
that they were Canaanites, made a covenant with them; and yet, tho' he
found them to be Canaanites, he held himself to be bound. Led by the
same bias, people think it sufficient to fulfil the words of a vow, however
short of intention. The Duke of Lancaster, vexed at the obstinate resistance
of Rennes, a town in Britany, vowed in wrath not to raise the siege till he
had planted the English colours upon one of the gates. He found it necessary to raise the siege; but his vow stood in the way. The governor relieved
him from his <258> scruple, permitting him to plant his colours upon one
of the gates; and he was satisfied that his vow was fulfilled. The following
is an example of an absurd conclusion deduced from a precept taken literally, against common sense. We are ordered by the Apostle, to pray always;
from which Jerom, one of the fathers, argues thus: "Conjugal enjoyment
is inconsistent with praying; *ergo,* conjugal enjoyment is a sin." By the same

---

motion to a mathematical point, that has no existence but in the mind of the geometer!
that it can be every where at the same instant, and that it can move with infinite celerity!
as if infinite celerity could actually exist. Every word, adds he, is big with absurdity; and
yet he was a great man who uttered that stuff.

* Many more are killed by a fall from a horse or by a fever, than by thunder. Yet we
are much more afraid of the latter. It is the sound that terrifies; tho' every man knows
that the danger is over when he hears the sound.

(*a*) Genesis, chap. 27.

6. "The word once sent forth can never come back": Horace, *Ars poetica,* l. 390.

argument it may be proved, that eating and drinking are sins; and that sleeping is a great sin, being a great interruption to praying. With respect to another text, "That a bishop must be blameless, the husband of one wife" taken literally, a very different conclusion is drawn in Abyssinia, That no man can be ordained a presbyter till he be married. Prohibitions have been interpreted in the same shallow manner. Lord Clarendon gives two instances, both of them relative to the great fire of London. The mayor proposing to pull down a house in order to stop the progress of the fire, was opposed by the lawyers, who declared the act to be unlawful; and the house was burnt without being <259> pulled down. About the same time it was proposed to break open some houses in the temple for saving the furniture, the possessors being in the country; but it was declared burglary to force open a door without consent of the possessor. Such literal interpretation, contrary to common sense, has been extended even to inflict punishment. Isadas was bathing when the alarm was given in Lacedemon, that Epaminondas was at hand with a numerous army. Naked as he was, he rushed against the enemy with a spear in one hand and a sword in the other, bearing down all before him. The Ephori fined him for going to battle unarmed; but honoured him with a garland for his gallant behaviour. How absurd to think that the law was intended for such a case! and how much more absurd to think, that the same act ought to be both punished and rewarded! The King of Castile being carried off his horse by a hunted hart, was saved by a person at hand, who cut his belt. The judges thought a pardon absolutely requisite, to relieve from capital punishment a man who had lifted a sword <260> against his sovereign.* It is a salutary regulation, that a man who is absent cannot be tried for his life. Pope Formosus died suddenly without suffering any punishment for his crimes. He was raised from his grave, dressed in his pontifical habit; and in that shape a criminal process went on against him. Could it seriously be thought, that a rotten carcase brought into court was sufficient to fulfil the law? The same absurd farce was play'd in Scotland, upon the body of Logan of Restalrig, several years after his

* A person unacquainted with the history of law, will imagine that Swift has carried beyond all bounds his satire against lawyers, in saying, that Gulliver had incurred a capital punishment, for saving the Emperor's palace by pissing out the fire; it being capital in any person of what quality soever, to make water within the precincts of the palace.

interment. The body of Tancred King of Sicily was raised from the grave, and the head cut off for supposed rebellion. Henry IV. of Castile was deposed in absence; but, for a colour of justice, the following ridiculous scene was acted. A wooden statue dressed in a royal habit, was placed on a theatre; and the sentence of deposition was solemnly <261> read to it, as if it had been the King himself. The Archbishop of Toledo seized the crown, another the sceptre, a third the sword; and the ceremony was concluded with proclaiming another king. How humbling are such scenes to man, who values himself upon the faculty of reason as his prime attribute! An expedient of that kind would now be rejected with disdain, as fit only to amuse children; and yet it grieves me to observe that law-proceedings are not yet totally purged of such absurdities. By a law in Holland, the criminal's confession is essential to a capital punishment, no other evidence being held sufficient: and yet if he insist on his innocence, he is tortured till he pronounce the words of confession; as if sounds merely were sufficient, without will or intention. The practice of England in a similar case, is no less absurd. Confession is not there required; but it is required, that the person accused shall plead, and say whether he be innocent or guilty. But what if he stand mute? He is pressed down by weights till he plead; and if he continue mute, he is pressed till he give up the ghost, a tor-<262>ture known by the name of *Peine forte et dure.** Further, law copying religion, has exalted ceremonies above the substantial part. In England, so strictly has form been adhered to, as to make the most trivial defect in words fatal, however certain the meaning be. *Murdredavit* for *murdravit, feloniter* for *felonice,* have been adjudged to vitiate an indictment. *Burgariter* for *burglariter* hath been a fatal objection; but *burgulariter* hath been holden good. Webster being indicted for murder, and the stroke being laid "sinistro *bracio*" instead of *"brachio,"* he was dismissed. *A. B. alias dictus A. C. Butcher,* was found to vitiate the indictment; because it ought to have been *A. B. Butcher, alias dictus A. C. Butcher.* So *gladium in dextra sua,* without *manu.*

No bias in human nature is more prevalent than a desire to anticipate

* Since the above was written, the parliament has enacted, That persons arraigned for felony or piracy, who stand mute, or refuse to answer directly to the indictment, shall be held as confessing, and judgement shall pass against them, as if they had been convicted by verdict or confession.

futurity, by being made acquainted beforehand <263> with what will happen. It was indulged without reserve in dark times; and hence omens, auguries, dreams, judicial astrology, oracles, and prophecies, without end. It shows strange weakness not to see, that such foreknowledge would be a gift more pernicious to man than Pandora's box: it would deprive him of every motive to action; and leave no place for sagacity, nor for contriving means to bring about a desired event. Life is an enchanted castle, opening to interesting views that inflame the imagination and excite industry. Remove the vail that hides futurity.—To an active, bustling, animating scene, succeeds a dead stupor, men converted into statues; passive like inert matter, because there remains not a single motive to action. Anxiety about futurity rouses our sagacity to prepare for what may happen; but an appetite to know what sagacity cannot discover, is a weakness in nature inconsistent with every rational principle.* <264>

Propensity to things rare and wonderful, is a natural bias no less universal than the former. Any strange or unaccountable event rouses the attention, and enflames the mind: we suck it in greedily, wish it to be true, and believe it to be true upon the slightest evidence (*a*). A hart taken in the forest of Senlis by Charles VI. of France, bore a collar upon which was inscribed, *Caesar hoc me donavit.*† Every one believed that a Roman Emperor was meant, and that the beast must have lived at least a thousand years; overlooking that the Emperor of Germany is also styled *Caesar,* and that it was not necessary to go back fifty years. This propensity displays itself even in childhood: stories of ghosts and apparitions are anxiously listened to; and firmly believed, by the terror they occasion: the vulgar accordingly have been captivated with such stories, upon evidence that would not be sufficient to ascertain the simplest fact. The absurd and childish prodigies that are every where scattered through the history of Titus Li-<265>vius, not to mention other ancient historians, would be unaccountable in a writer of sense and gravity, were it not for the propensity mentioned. But human

---

* Foreknowledge of future events, differs widely from a conviction, that all events are fixed and immutable: the latter leaves us free to activity; the former annihilates all activity.

† "Caesar gave me this."

(*a*) See Elements of Criticism, vol. I. p. 163. ed. 5.

belief is not left at the mercy of every irregular bias: our maker has subjected belief to the correction of the rational faculty; and accordingly, in proportion as reason advances towards maturity, wonders, prodigies, apparitions, incantations, witchcraft, and such stuff, lose their influence. That reformation however has been exceedingly slow, because the propensity is exceedingly strong. Such absurdities found credit among wise men, even as late as the last age. I am ready to verify the charge, by introducing two men of the first rank for understanding: were a greater number necessary, there would be no difficulty of making a very long catalogue. The celebrated Grotius shall lead the van. Procopius in his Vandal history relates, that some orthodox Christians, whose tongues were cut out by the Arians, continued miraculously to speak as formerly. And to vouch the fact, he appeals to some of those miraculous persons, alive in Constantinople at the time of his writing. In <266> the dark ages of Christianity, when different sects were violently enflamed against each other, it is not surprising that gross absurdities were swallowed as real miracles: but is it not surprising, and also mortifying, to find Grotius, the greatest genius of the age he lived in, adopting such absurdities? For the truth of the foregoing miracle, he appeals not only to Procopius, but to several other writers (a); as if the hearsay of a few writers were sufficient to make us believe an impossibility. Could it seriously be his opinion, that the great God who governs by general laws, permitting the sun to shine alike upon men of whatever religion, would miraculously suspend the laws of nature, in order to testify his displeasure at an honest sect of Christians, led innocently into error? Did he also believe what Procopius adds, that two of these orthodox Christians were again deprived of speech, as a punishment inflicted by the Almighty for cohabiting with prostitutes?

I proceed to our famous historian, the Earl of Clarendon, the other person I had in view. A man long in public business, <267> a consummate politician and well stored with knowledge from books as well as from experience, might be fortified against foolish miracles, if any man can be fortified: and yet behold his superstitious credulity in childish stories; no less weak in that particular, than was his cotemporary Grotius. He gravely re-

(a) Prolegomena to his History of the Goths.

lates an incident concerning the assassination of the Duke of Buckingham, the sum of which follows.

There were many stories scattered abroad at that time, of prophecies and predictions of the Duke's untimely and violent death; one of which was upon a better foundation of credit, than usually such discourses are founded upon. There was an officer in the King's wardrobe in Windsor castle, of reputation for honesty and discretion, and at that time about the age of fifty. About six months before the miserable end of the Duke, this man being in bed and in good health, there appeared to him at midnight a man of a venerable aspect, who drawing the curtains and fixing his eye upon him, said, Do you know me, Sir. The poor man, half dead with fear, answered, That he <268> thought him to be Sir George Villiers, father to the Duke. Upon which he was ordered by the apparition, to go to the Duke and tell him, that if he did not somewhat to ingratiate himself with the people, he would be suffered to live but a short time. The same person appeared to him a second and a third time, reproaching him bitterly for not performing his promise. The poor man pluck'd up as much courage as to excuse himself, that it was difficult to find access to the Duke, and that he would be thought a madman. The apparition imparted to him some secrets, which he said would be his credentials to the Duke. The officer, introduced to the Duke by Sir Ralph Freeman, was received courteously. They walked together near an hour; and the Duke sometimes spoke with great commotion, tho' his servants with Sir Ralph were at such a distance that they could not hear a word. The officer, returning from the Duke, told Sir Ralph, that when he mentioned the particulars that were to gain him credit, the Duke's colour changed; and he swore the officer could <269> come to that knowledge only by the devil; for that these particulars were known only to himself, and to one person more, of whose fidelity he was secure. The Duke, who went to accompany the King at hunting, was observed to ride all the morning in deep thought; and before the morning was spent, left the field and alighted at his mother's house, with whom he was shut up for two or three hours. When the Duke left her, his countenance appeared full of trouble, with a mixture of anger, which never appeared before in conversing with her: and she was found overwhelmed with tears, and in great agony. Whatever there was of all this, it is a notorious truth, that when she heard of the Duke's murder, she seemed not in the least surprised, nor did express much sorrow.

The name of Lord Clarendon calls for more attention to the foregoing relation than otherwise it would deserve. It is no article of the Christian faith, that the dead preserve their connection with the living, or are ever suffered to return to this world: we have no solid evidence for such a fact; <270> and rarely hear of it, except in tales for amusing or terrifying children. Secondly, The story is inconsistent with the system of Providence; which, for the best purposes, has drawn an impenetrable veil between us and futurity. Thirdly, This apparition, tho' supposed to be endowed with a miraculous knowledge of future events, is however deficient in the sagacity that belongs to a person of ordinary understanding. It appears twice to the officer, without thinking of giving him proper credentials; nor does it think of them till suggested by the officer. Fourthly, Why did not the apparition go directly to the Duke himself; what necessity for employing a third person? The Duke must have been much more affected with an apparition to himself, than with the hearing it at second hand. The officer was afraid of being taken for a madman; and the Duke had some reason to think him such. Lastly, The apparition happened above three months before the Duke's death; and yet we hear not of a single step taken by him, in pursuance of the advice he got. The authority of the historian and the regard we owe him, have drawn from <271> me the foregoing reflections, which with respect to the story itself are very little necessary; for the evidence is really not such as to verify any ordinary occurrence. His Lordship acknowledges, that he had no evidence but common report, saying, that it was one of the many stories scattered abroad at that time. He does not say, that the story was related to him by the officer, whose name he does not even mention, or by Sir Ralph Freeman, or by the Duke, or by the Duke's mother. If any thing happened like what is related, it may with good reason be supposed that the officer was crazy or enthusiastically mad: nor have we any evidence beyond common report, that he communicated any secret to the Duke. Here are two remarkable instances of an observation made above, that a man may be high in one science and very low in another. Had Grotius, or had Clarendon, studied the fundamentals of reason and religion coolly and impartially, as they did other sciences, they would never have given faith to reports so ill vouched, and so contradictory to every sound principle of theology.

Another source of erroneous reasoning, <272> is a singular tendency in the mind of man to mysteries and hidden meanings. Where an object makes a deep impression, the busy mind is seldom satisfied with the simple and obvious intendment: invention is roused to allegorize, and to pierce into hidden views and purposes. I have a notable example at hand, with respect to forms and ceremonies in religious worship, Josephus (*a*), talking of the tabernacle, has the following passage.

> Let any man consider the structure of the tabernacle, the sacerdotal vestments, the vessels dedicated to the service of the altar; and he must of necessity be convinced, that our lawgiver was a pious man, and that all the clamours against us and our profession, are mere calumny. For what are all of these but the image of the whole world? This will appear to any man who soberly and impartially examines the matter. The tabernacle of thirty cubits is divided into three parts; two for the priests in general, and as free to them as the earth and the sea; the third, where no mortal must be admitted, is as the heaven, <273> reserved for God himself. The twelve loaves of shew-bread signify the twelve months of the year. The candlestick, composed of seven branches, refers to the twelve signs of the zodiac, through which the seven planets shape their course; and the seven lamps on the top of the seven branches bear an analogy to the planets themselves. The curtains of four colours represent the four elements. The fine linen signifies the earth, as flax is raised there. By the purple is understood the sea, from the blood of the murex, which dies that colour. The violet colour is a symbol of the air; and the scarlet of the fire. By the linen garment of the high-priest, is designed the whole body of the earth: by the violet colour the heavens. The pomegranates signify lightning: the bells tolling signify thunder. The four-coloured ephod bears a resemblance to the very nature of the universe, and the interweaving it with gold has a regard to the rays of light. The girdle about the body of the priest is as the sea about the globe of the earth. The two sardonyx stones are a kind of <274> figure of the sun and moon; and the twelve other stones may be understood, either of the twelve months, or of the twelve signs in the zodiac. The violet-coloured tiara is a resemblance of heaven; and it would be irreverent to have written the sacred name of God upon any other colour. The triple

(*a*) Jewish Antiquities, book 3.

crown and plate of gold give us to understand the glory and majesty of Almighty God. This is a plain illustration of these matters; and I would not lose any opportunity of doing justice to the honour and wisdom of our incomparable lawgiver.

How wire-drawn and how remote from any appearance of truth, are the foregoing allusions and imagined resemblances! But religious forms and ceremonies, however arbitrary, are never held to be so. If an useful purpose do not appear, it is taken for granted that there must be a hidden meaning; and any meaning, however childish, will serve when a better cannot be found. Such propensity there is in dark ages for allegorizing, that even our Saviour's miracles have not escaped. Where-ever any seeming difficulty occurs in the plain sense, <275> the fathers of the church, Origen, Augustine, and Hilary, are never at a loss for a mystic meaning. "Sacrifice to the celestial gods with an odd number, and to the terrestrial gods with an even number," is a precept of Pythagoras. Another is, "Turn round in adoring the gods, and sit down when thou hast worshipped." The learned make a strange pother about the hidden meaning of these precepts. But, after all, have they any hidden meaning? Forms and ceremonies are useful in external worship, for occupying the vulgar; and it is of no importance what they be, provided they prevent the mind from wandering. Why such partiality to ancient ceremonies, when no hidden meaning is supposed in those of Christians, such as bowing to the east, or the priest performing the liturgy, partly in a black upper garment, partly in a white? No ideas are more simple than of numbers, nor less susceptible of any hidden meaning; and yet the profound Pythagoras has imagined many such meanings. The number *one,* says he, having no parts, represents the Deity: it represents also order, peace, and tranquillity, which result from unity of <276> sentiment. The number *two* represents disorder, confusion, and change. He discovered in the number *three* the most sublime mysteries: all things are composed, says he, of three substances. The number *four* is holy in its nature, and constitutes the divine essence, which consists in unity, power, benevolence, and wisdom. Would one believe, that the great philosopher, who demonstrated the 47th proposition of the first book of Euclid, was the inventor of such childish conceits? Perhaps Pythagoras meant only to divert himself with them. Whether so or not, it seems difficult to be explained, how such trifles were preserved in memory, and handed down to us through so many generations. All that can be said is, that during the infancy of knowledge, every novelty makes a figure, and that it requires a long course of time to separate the corn from the chaff.* A certain writer, smit-<277>ten with the conceit of hidden meanings, has applied his talent to the constellations of the zodiac. The *lion* typifies the force or heat of the sun in the month of July, when he enters that constellation. The constellation where the sun is in the month of August is termed the *virgin,* signifying the time of harvest. He enters the *balance* in September, denoting the equality of day and night. The *scorpion,* where he is found in October, is an emblem of the diseases that are frequent during that month, &c. The *balance,* I acknowledge, is well hit off; but I see not clearly the resemblance of the force of a lion to the heat of the sun; and still less that of harvest to a virgin: the spring would be more happily represented by a virgin, and the harvest by a woman in the act of delivery.

Our tendency to mystery and allegory, <278> displays itself with great vigour in thinking of our forefathers and of the ancients in general, by means of the veneration that is paid them. Before writing was known, ancient history is made up of traditional fables. A Trojan Brutus peopled England; and the Scots are descended from Scota, daughter to an Egyptian king. Have we not equally reason to think, that the histories of the heathen gods are involved in fable? We pretend not to draw any hidden meaning from the former: why should we suspect any such meaning in the latter? Allegory is a species of writing too refined for a savage or barbarian: it is the fruit of a cultivated imagination; and was a late invention even in Greece. The allegories of Esop are of the simplest kind: yet they were composed after learning began to flourish; and Cebes, whose allegory about the life of man is justly celebrated, was a disciple of Socrates. Prepossession

---

* The following precepts of the same philosopher, tho' now only fit for the *Child's Guide,* were originally cherished, and preserved in memory, as emanations of superior wisdom. "Do not enter a temple for worship, but with a decent air. Render not life painful by undertaking too many affairs. Be always ready for what may happen. Never bind yourself by a vow, nor by an oath. Irritate not a man who is angry." The seven wise men of Greece made a figure in their time; but it would be unreasonable to expect, that what they taught during the infancy of knowledge, should make a figure in its maturity.

however in favour of the ancients makes us conclude, that there must be some hidden meaning or allegory in their historical fables; for no better reason than that they are destitute of common sense. In the Greek mythology, there <279> are numberless fables related as historical facts merely; witness the fable of gods mixing with women, and procreating giants, like what we find in the fabulous histories of many other nations. These giants attempt to dethrone Jupiter: Apollo keeps the sheep of Admetus: Minerva springs from the head of Jove:* Bacchus is cut out of his thigh: Orpheus goes to hell for his wife: Mars and Venus are caught by Vulcan in a net; and a thousand other such childish stories. But the Greeks, many centuries after the invention of such foolish fables, became illustrious for arts and sciences; and nothing would satisfy writers in later times, but to dub them profound philosophers, even when mere savages. Hence endless attempts to <280> detect mysteries and hidden meanings in their fables. Let other interpreters of that kind pass: they give me no concern. But I cannot, without the deepest concern, behold our illustrious philosopher Bacon employing his talents so absurdly. What imbecillity must there be in human nature, when so great a genius is capable of such puerilities! As a subject so humbling is far from being agreeable, I confine myself to a few instances.[7] In an ancient fable, Prometheus formed man out of clay; and kindling a bundle of birch rods at the chariot of the sun, brought down fire to the earth for the use of his creature man. And tho' ungrateful man complained to Jupiter of that theft, yet the god, pleased with the ingenuity of Prometheus, not only confirmed to man the use of fire, but conferred on him a gift much more considerable: the gift was perpetual youth, which was laid upon an ass to be carried to the earth. The ass, wanting to drink at a brook, was opposed by a serpent, who insisted to have the burden, without which, no drink for the poor ass.

---

* However easy it may be to draw an allegorical meaning out of that fable, I cannot admit any such meaning to have been intended. An allegory is a fable contrived to illustrate some acknowledged truth, by making a deeper impression than the truth would make in plain words; of which we have several beautiful instances in the Spectator (Elements of Criticism, chap. 20. § 6.). But the fable here was understood to be a matter of fact, Minerva being worshipped by the Greeks as a real goddess, the daughter of Jupiter without a mother.

7. Kames draws from Bacon's *De Sapientia Veterum* in what follows.

And thus, for a draught of plain water, was perpetual youth transferred from man <281> to the serpent. This fable has a striking resemblance to many in the Edda; and, in the manner of the Edda, accounts for the invention of fire, and for the mortality of man. Nor is there in all the Edda one more childish, or more distant from any appearance of a rational meaning. It is handled however by our philosopher with much solemn gravity, as if every source of wisdom were locked up in it. The explanation he gives, being too long to be copied here, shall be reduced to a few particulars. After an elogium upon fire, his Lordship proceeds thus. "The manner wherein Prometheus stole his fire, is properly described from the nature of the thing; he being said to have done it by applying a rod of birch to the chariot of the sun: for birch is used in striking and beating; which clearly denotes fire to proceed from violent percussions and collisions of bodies, whereby the matters struck are subtilized, rarefied, put into motion, and so prepared to receive the heat of the celestial bodies. And accordingly they, in a clandestine and secret manner, snatch fire, as it were by stealth, from the <282> chariot of the sun." He goes on as follows. "The next is a remarkable part of the fable; which represents, that men, instead of gratitude, accused both Prometheus and his fire to Jupiter: and yet the accusation proved so pleasant to Jupiter, that he not only indulged mankind the use of fire, but conferred upon them perpetual youth. Here it may seem strange, that the sin of ingratitude should meet with approbation or reward. But the allegory has another view; and denotes, that the accusation both of human nature and human art, proceeds from a noble and laudable temper of mind, viz. modesty; and also tends to a very good purpose, viz. to stir up fresh industry and new discoveries." Can any thing be more wire-drawn?

Vulcan, attempting the chastity of Minerva, had recourse to force. In the struggle, his *semen,* falling upon the ground, produced Erictonius; whose body from the middle upward was comely and well proportioned, his thighs and legs small and deformed like an eel. Conscious of that defect, he was the inventor of chariots; which showed the graceful part of <283> his body, and concealed what was deformed. Listen to the explanation of this ridiculous fable. "Art, by the various uses it makes of fire, is here represented by Vulcan: and Nature is represented by Minerva, because of the industry employ'd in her works. Art, when it offers violence to Nature in order to bend her to its purpose, seldom attains the end proposed. Yet, upon great struggle and application, there proceed certain imperfect births, or lame abortive works; which however, with great pomp and deceitful appearances, are triumphantly carried about, and shown by impostors." I admit the ingenuity of that forc'd meaning; but had the inventor of that fable any latent meaning? If he had, why did he conceal it? The ingenious meaning would have merited praise; the fable itself none at all.

I shall add but one other instance, for they grow tiresome. Sphinx was a monster, having the face and voice of a virgin, the wings of a bird, and the talons of a gryphin. She resided on the summit of a mountain, near the city Thebes. Her manner was, to lie in ambush for travel-<284>lers, to propose dark riddles which she received from the Muses, and to tear those to pieces who could not solve them. The Thebans having offered their kingdom to the man who should interpret these riddles, Oedipus presented himself before the monster, and he was required to explain the following riddle: What creature is that, which being born four-footed, becomes afterwards two-footed, then three-footed, and lastly four-footed again. Oedipus answered, It was man, who in his infancy crawls upon his hands and feet, then walks upright upon his two feet, walks in old age with a stick, and at last lies four-footed in bed. Oedipus having thus obtained the victory, slew the monster; and laying the carcase upon an ass, carried it off in triumph. Now for the explanation. "This is an elegant and instructive fable, invented to represent science: for Science may be called a monster, being strangely gazed at and admired by the ignorant. Her figure and form is various, by reason of the vast variety of subjects that science considers. Her voice and countenance are represented female, by reason of her gay appear-<285>ance, and volubility of speech. Wings are added, because the sciences and their inventions fly about in a moment; for knowledge, like light communicated from torch to torch, is presently catched, and copiously diffused. Sharp and hooked talons are elegantly attributed to her; because the axioms and arguments of science fix down the mind, and keep it from moving or slipping away." Again: "All science seems placed on high, as it were on the tops of mountains that are hard to climb: for science is justly imagined a sublime and lofty thing, looking down upon ignorance, and at the same time taking an extensive view on all sides, as is usual on the tops of mountains. Sphinx is said to propose difficult questions and riddles, which she received from the Muses. These questions, while they remain with the Muses, may be pleasant, as contemplation and enquiry are when knowledge is their only aim: but after they are delivered to Sphinx, that is, to practice, which impels to action, choice, and determination; then it is that they become severe and torturing; and un-<286>less solved, strangely perplex the human mind, and tear it to pieces. It is with the utmost elegance added in the fable, that the carcase of Sphinx was laid upon an ass; for there is nothing so subtile and abstruse, but after being made plain, may be conceived by the slowest capacity." According to such latitude of interpretation, there is nothing more easy than to make *quidlibet ex quolibet*.

> *Who would not laugh if such a man there be?*
> *Who would not weep if Atticus were he?*[8]

I will detain the reader but a moment longer, to hear what our author says in justification of such mysterious meaning. Out of many reasons, I select the two following. "It may pass for a farther indication of a concealed and secret meaning, that some of these fables are so absurd and idle in their narration, as to proclaim an allegory even afar off. A fable that carries probability with it, may be supposed invented for pleasure, or in imitation of history; but what could never be conceived or related in this way, must surely have a different use. For example, what a monstrous fiction <287> is this, That Jupiter should take *Metis* to wife; and as soon as he found her pregnant eat her up; whereby he also conceived, and out of his head brought forth *Pallas* armed! Certainly no mortal could, but for the sake of the moral it couches, invent such an absurd dream as this, so much out of the road of thought." At that rate, the more ridiculous or absurd a fable is, the more instructive it must be. This opinion resembles that of the ancient Germans with respect to mad women, who were held to be so wise, as that every thing they uttered was prophetic. Did it never occur to our author, that in the infancy of the reasoning faculty, the imagination is suffered to roam without controul, as in a dream; and that the vulgar in all

---

8. Pope, "Epistle to Dr. Arbuthnot, Being a Prologue to the Satires," ll. 213–14.

ages are delighted with wonderful stories; the more out of nature, the more to their taste?

We proceed to the other reason. "The argument of most weight with me is, That many of these fables appear not to have been invented by the persons who relate and divulge them, whether Homer, Hesiod, or others; for if I were assured they first flowed from those later <288> times and authors, I should never expect any thing singularly great or noble from such an origin. But whoever attentively considers the thing, will find, that these fables are delivered down by those writers, not as matters then first invented, but as received and embraced in earlier ages. And this principally raises my esteem of those fables; which I receive, not as the product of the age, or invention of the poets, but as sacred relics, gentle whispers, and the breath of better times, that from the traditions of more ancient nations, came at length into the flutes and trumpets of the Greeks." Was it our author's sincere opinion, that the farther back we trace the history of man, the more of science and knowledge is found; and consequently that savages are the most learned of all men?

The following fable of the savage Canadians ought to be mysterious, if either of the reasons urged above be conclusive. "There were in the beginning but six men in the world, (from whence sprung is not said): one of these ascended to <289> heaven in quest of a woman named *Atahentsic,* and had carnal knowledge of her. She being thrown headlong from the height of the empyrean, was received on the back of a tortoise, and delivered of two children, one of whom slew the other." This fable is so absurd, that it must have a latent meaning; and one needs but copy our author to pump a deep mystery out of it, however little intended by the inventer. And if either absurdity or antiquity entitle fables to be held sacred relics, gentle whispers, and the breath of better times, the following Japanese fables are well intitled to these distinguishing epithets. "Bunsio, in wedlock, having had no children for many years, addressed her prayers to the gods, was heard, and was delivered of 500 eggs. Fearing that the eggs might produce monsters, she packed them up in a box, and threw them into the river. An old fisherman finding the box, hatched the eggs in an oven, every one of which produced a child. The children were fed with boiled rice and mugwort-leaves; and being at last left to shift for themselves, they fell arobbing on the highway. Hear-<290>ing of a man famous for great wealth, they told their story at his gate, and begged some food. This happening to be the house of their mother, she own'd them for her children, and gave a great entertainment to her friends and neighbours. She was afterward in-listed among the goddesses by the name of *Bensaiten:* her 500 sons were appointed to be her attendants; and to this day she is worshipped in Japan as the goddess of riches." Take another fable of the same stamp. The Japanese have a table of lucky and unlucky days, which they believe to have been composed by Abino Seimei, a famous astrologer, and a sort of demi-god. They have the following tradition of him. "A young fox, pursued by hunters, fled into a temple, and took shelter in the bosom of Abino Jassima, son and heir to the king of the country. Refusing to yield the poor creature to the unmerciful hunters, he defended himself with great bravery, and set the fox at liberty. The hunters, through resentment against the young prince, murdered his royal father; but Jassima revenged his father's death, killing the traitors with his own hand. Up-<291>on this signal victory, a lady of incomparable beauty appeared to him, and made such an impression on his heart, that he took her to wife. Abino Seimei, procreated of that marriage, was endowed with divine wisdom, and with the precious gift of prophecy. Jassima was ignorant that his wife was the very fox whose life he had saved, till she resumed by degrees her former shape." If there be any hidden mystery in this tale, I shall not despair of finding a mystery in every fairy-tale invented by Madam Gomez.

It is lamentable to observe the slow progress of human understanding and the faculty of reason. If this reflection be verified in our celebrated philosopher Bacon, how much more in others? It is comfortable, however, that human understanding is in a progress toward maturity, however slow. The fancy of allegorizing ancient fables, is now out of fashion: enlightened reason has unmasked these fables, and left them in their nakedness, as the invention of illiterate ages when wonder was the prevailing passion.

Having discussed the first two heads, I proceed to the third, viz. Erroneous rea-<292>soning occasioned by acquired biasses. And one of these that has the greatest influence in perverting the rational faculty, is blind religious zeal. There is not in nature a system more simple or perspicuous than that of pure religion; and yet what a complication do we find in it of metaphysical subtilties and unintelligible jargon! That subject being too well known to need illustration, I shall confine myself to a few instances of the influence that religious superstition has on other subjects.

A history-painter and a player require the same sort of genius. The one by colours, the other by looks and gestures, express various modifications of passion, even what are beyond the reach of words; and to accomplish these ends, great sensibility is requisite as well as judgement. Why then is not a player equally respected with a history-painter? It was thought by zealots, that a play is an entertainment too splendid for a mortified Christian; upon which account players fell under church-censure, and were even held unworthy of Christian burial. A history-painter, on the contrary, being frequently employ'd < 293 > in painting for the church, was always in high esteem. It is only among Protestants that players are beginning to be restored to their privileges as free citizens; and there perhaps never existed a history-painter more justly esteemed, than Garrick, a player, is in Great Britain. Aristarchus, having taught that the earth moves round the sun, was accused by the Heathen priests, for troubling the repose of their household-gods. Copernicus, for the same doctrine, was accused by Christian priests, as contradicting the scriptures, which talk of the sun's moving. And Galileo, for adhering to Copernicus, was condemned to prison and penance: he found it necessary to recant upon his knees. A bias acquired from Aristotle, kept reason in chains for centuries. Scholastic divinity in particular, founded on the philosophy of that author, was more hurtful to the reasoning faculty than the Goths and Huns. Tycho Braché suffered great persecution for maintaining, that the heavens were so far empty of matter as to give free course to the comets; contrary to Aristotle, who taught, that the heavens are harder than a diamond: it < 294 > was extremely ill taken, that a simple mortal should pretend to give Aristotle the lie. During the infancy of reason, authority is the prevailing argument.*

---

* Aristotle, it would appear, was less regarded by his cotemporaries than by the moderns. Some persons having travelled from Macedon all the way to Persia, with complaints against Antipater; Alexander observed, that they would not have made so long a journey had they received no injury. And Cassander, son of Antipater, replying, that their long journey was an argument against them, trusting that witnesses would not be brought

Reason is easily warped by habit. In the disputes among the Athenians about adjusting the form of their government, those who lived in the high country were for democracy; the inhabitants of the plains were for oligarchy; and the seamen for monarchy. Shepherds are all equal: in a corn-country, there are a few masters and many servants: on shipboard, there is one commander, and all the rest subjects. Habit was their adviser: none of them thought of consulting reason, in order to judge what was the best form <295> upon the whole. Habit of a different kind has an influence no less powerful. Persons who are in the habit of reasoning, require demonstration for every thing: even a self-evident proposition is not suffered to escape. Such demonstrations occur more than once in the Elements of Euclid, nor has Aristotle, with all his skill in logic, entirely avoided them. Can any thing be more self-evident, than the difference between pleasure and motion? Yet Aristotle attempts to demonstrate, that they are different. "No motion," says he, "except circular motion, is perfect in any one point of time; there is always something wanting during its course, and it is not perfected till it arrive at its end. But pleasure is perfect in every point of time; being the same from the beginning to the end." The difference is clear from perception: but instead of being clear from this demonstration, it should rather follow from it, that pleasure is the same with motion in a circle. Plato also attempts to demonstrate a self-evident proposition, that a quality is not a body. "Every body," says he, "is a subject: <296> quality is not a subject, but an accident; *ergo,* quality is not a body. Again, A body cannot be in a subject: every quality is in a subject; *ergo,* quality is not a body." But Descartes affords the most illustrious instance of the kind. He was the greatest geometer of the age he lived in, and one of the greatest of any age; which insensibly led him to overlook intuitive knowledge, and to admit no proposition but what is demonstrated or proved in the regular form of syllogism. He took a fancy to doubt even of his own existence, till he was convinced of it by the following argument. *Cogito, ergo sum: I think, therefore I exist.* And what sort of a demonstration is this after all? In the very fundamental proposition he acknowledges his existence by the term

from such a distance to give evidence of their calumny; Alexander, smiling, said, "Your argument is one of Aristotle's sophisms, which will serve either side equally."

I; and how absurd is it, to imagine a proof necessary of what is admitted in the fundamental proposition? In the next place, How does our author know that he thinks? If nothing is to be taken for granted, an argument is no less necessary to prove that he thinks, than to prove that he exists. It is true, that he has intuitive knowledge of his thinking; but has he <297> not the same of his existing? Would not a man deserve to be laughed at, who, after warming himself at a fire, should imagine the following argument necessary to prove its existence, "The fire burns, *ergo* it exists"? Listen to an author of high reputation attempting to demonstrate a self-evident proposition. "The *labour* of B cannot be the labour of C; because it is the application of the organs and powers of B, not of C, to the effecting of something; and therefore the labour is as much B's, as the *limbs* and *faculties* made use of are his. Again, the *effect* or *produce* of the labour of B, is not the effect of the labour of C: and therefore this effect or produce is B's, not C's; as much B's, as the *labour* was B's, and not C's: Because, what the labour of B causes or produces, B produces by his labour; or it is the product of B by his labour: that is, it is B's product, not C's or any other's. And if C should pretend to any *property* in that which B can truly call *his,* he would act contrary to truth" (*a*).

In every subject of reasoning, to define <298> terms is necessary in order to avoid mistakes: and the only possible way of defining a term, is to express its meaning in more simple terms. Terms expressing ideas that are simple without parts, admit not of being defined, because there are no terms more simple to express their meaning. To say that every term is capable of a definition, is in effect to say, that terms resemble matter; that as the latter is divisible without end, so the former is reducible into simpler terms without end. The habit however of defining is so inveterate in some men, that they will attempt to define words signifying simple ideas. Is there any necessity to define motion: do not children understand the meaning of the word? And how is it possible to define it, when there are not words more simple to define it by? Yet Worster (*b*) attempts that bold task. "A continual change

---

(*a*) [[William Wollaston,]] Religion of Nature delineated, sect. 6. parag. 2.
(*b*) Natural Philosophy, p. 31.

of place," says he, "or leaving one place for another, without remaining for any space of time in the same place, is called *motion.*" That every body in motion is continually changing place, is true: but change of place is not <299> motion; it is the effect of motion. Gravesend (*a*) defines motion thus, "Motus est translatio de loco in locum, sive continua loci mutatio";* which is the same with the former. Yet this very author admits *locus* or *place* to signify a simple idea, incapable of a definition. Is it more simple or more intelligible than motion? But, of all, the most remarkable definition of motion is that of Aristotle, famous for its impenetrability, or rather absurdity, "Actus entis in potentia, quatenus in potentia."† His definition of time is *numerus motus secundum prius ac posterius.*[9] This definition as well as that of motion, may more properly be considered as riddles propounded for exercising invention. Not a few writers on algebra define negative quantities to be quantities less than nothing.

Extension enters into the conception of every particle of matter; because every <300> particle of matter has length, breadth, and thickness. Figure in the same manner enters into the conception of every particle of matter; because every particle of matter is bounded. By the power of abstraction, figure may be conceived independent of the body that is figured; and extension may be conceived independent of the body that is extended. These particulars are abundantly plain and obvious; and yet observe what a heap of jargon is employ'd by the followers of Leibnitz, in their fruitless endeavours to define extension. They begin with *simple existences,* which they say are unextended, and without parts. According to that definition, simple existences cannot belong to matter, because the smallest particle of matter has both parts and extension. But to let that pass, they endeavour to show as follows, how the idea of extension arises from these simple existences. "We may look upon simple existences, as having mutual relations with respect to their internal state: relations that form a certain order in their manner of existence. And this order or arrangement of things, coexisting and

---

* "Motion is, the removing from one place to another, or a continual change of place."
† "The action of a being in power, so far as it is in power."
(*a*) Elements of Physics, p. 23.
9. Literally, "the number of motion in respect of the before and after."

linked toge-<301>ther but so as we do not distinctly understand how, causes in us a confused idea, from whence arises the appearance of extension." A Peripatetic philosopher being asked, What sort of things the sensible species of Aristotle are, answered, That they are neither entities nor nonentities, but something intermediate between the two. The famous astronomer Ismael Bulialdus lays down the following proposition, and attempts a mathematical demonstration of it, "That light is a mean-proportional between corporeal substance and incorporeal."

I close with a curious sort of reasoning, so singular indeed as not to come under any of the foregoing heads. The first editions of the latest version of the Bible into English, have the following preface.

> Another thing we think good to admonish thee of, gentle reader, that we have not tied ourselves to an uniformity of phrasing, or to an identity of words, as some peradventure would wish that we had done, because they observe, that some learned men somewhere have been as exact as they could be that way. Truly, that we might not vary from the <302> sense of that which we have translated before, if the word signified the same in both places, (for there be some words that be not of the same sense every where), we were especially careful, and made a conscience according to our duty. But that we should express the same notion in the same particular word; as, for example, if we translate the Hebrew or Greek word once by *purpose,* never to call it *intent;* if one where *journeying,* never *travelling;* if one where *think,* never *suppose;* if one where *pain,* never *ache;* if one where *joy,* never *gladness,* &c.; thus to mince the matter, we thought to favour more of curiosity than wisdom, and that rather it would breed scorn in the Atheist, than bring profit to the godly reader. For is the kingdom of God become words or syllables? Why should we be in bondage to them, if we may be free; use one precisely, when we may use another, no less fit, as commodiously? We might also be charged by scoffers, with some unequal dealing toward a great number of good English words. For as it is written by a certain great philosopher, that he <303> should say, that those logs were happy that were made images to be worshipped; for their fellows, as good as they, lay for blocks behind the fire: so if we should say, as it were, unto certain words, Stand up higher, have a place in the Bible always; and to others of like quality, Get ye hence, be banished for

ever, we might be taxed peradventure with St. James his words, namely, to be partial in ourselves, and judges of evil thoughts.

Quaeritur, Can this translation be safely rely'd on as the rule of faith, when such are the translators? <304>

APPENDIX

In reviewing the foregoing sketch, it occurred, that a fair analysis of Aristotle's logic, would be a valuable addition to the historical branch. A distinct and candid account of a system that for many ages governed the reasoning part of mankind, cannot but be acceptable to the public. Curiosity will be gratified, in seeing a phantom delineated that so long fascinated the learned world; a phantom, which shows infinite genius, but like the pyramids of Egypt or hanging gardens of Babylon, is absolutely useless unless for raising wonder. Dr. Reid, professor of moral philosophy in the college of Glasgow, relished the thought; and his friendship to me prevailed on him, after much solicitation, to undertake the laborious task. No man is better acquainted with Aristotle's writings; and, without any enthusiastic attachment, he holds that philosopher to be a first-rate genius. <305>

The logic of Aristotle has been on the decline more than a century; and is at present relegated to schools and colleges. It has occasionally been criticised by different writers; but this is the first attempt to draw it out of its obscurity into day-light. From what follows, one will be enabled to pass a true judgement on that work, and to determine whether it ought to make a branch of education. The Doctor's essay, as a capital article in the progress and history of the sciences, will be made welcome, even with the fatigue of squeezing through many thorny paths, before a distinct view can be got of that ancient and stupendous fabric.

It will at the same time show the hurt that Aristotle has done to the reasoning faculty, by drawing it out of its natural course into devious paths. His artificial mode of reasoning, is no less superficial than intricate: I say, superficial; for in none of his logical works, is a single truth attempted to be proved by syllogism that requires a proof: the propositions he undertakes to prove by syllogism, are all of them self-evident. Take for instance the following proposition, That man has a <306> power of self-motion. To prove this, he assumes the following axiom, upon which indeed every one of his syllogisms are founded, That whatever is true of a number of particulars joined together, holds true of every one separately; which is thus expressed in logical terms, Whatever is true of the genus, holds true of every species. Founding upon that axiom, he reasons thus: "All animals have a power of self-motion: man is an animal: *ergo,* man has a power of self-motion." Now if all animals have a power of self-motion, it requires no argument to prove, that man, an animal, has that power: and therefore, what he gives as a conclusion or consequence, is not really so; it is not *inferred* from the fundamental proposition, but is *included* in it. At the same time, the self-motive power of man, is a fact that cannot be known but from experience; and it is more clearly known from experience than that of any other animal. Now, in attempting to prove man to be a self-motive animal, is it not absurd, to found the argument on a proposition less clear than that undertaken to be demonstrated? What is here observed, will be found ap-<307>plicable to the greater part, if not the whole, of his syllogisms.

Unless for the reason now given, it would appear singular, that Aristotle never attempts to apply his syllogistic mode of reasoning to any subject handled by himself: on ethics, on rhetoric, and on poetry, he argues like a rational being, without once putting in practice any of his own rules. It is not supposable that a man of his capacity could be ignorant, how insufficient a syllogism is for discovering any latent truth. He certainly intended his system of logic, chiefly if not solely, for disputation: and if such was his purpose, he has been wonderfully successful; for nothing can be better contrived for wrangling and disputing without end. He indeed in a manner professes this to be his aim, in his books *De Sophisticis elenchis.* [10]

Some ages hence, when the goodly fabric of the Romish spiritual power shall be laid low in the dust, and scarce a vestige remain; it will among antiquaries be a curious enquiry, What was the nature and extent of a tyranny, more oppressive to the minds of men, than the tyranny of ancient Rome was to their persons. During every <308> step of the enquiry, posterity will rejoice over mental liberty, no less precious than personal liberty. The despotism of Aristotle with respect to the faculty of reason, was no

---

10. *On Sophistical Refutations.*

less complete, than that of the Bishop of Rome with respect to religion; and it is now a proper subject of curiosity, to enquire into the nature and extent of that despotism. One cannot peruse the following sheets, without sympathetic pain for the weakness of man with respect to his noblest faculty; but that pain will redouble his satisfaction, in now being left free to the dictates of reason and common sense.

In my reveries, I have more than once compared Aristotle's logic to a bubble made of soap-water for amusing children; a beautiful figure with splendid colours; fair on the outside, empty within. It has for more than two thousand years been the hard fate of Aristotle's followers, Ixion like, to embrace a cloud for a goddess.—But this is more than sufficient for a preface: and I had almost forgot, that I am detaining my readers from better entertainment, in listening to Dr. Reid.[11] <309>

A Brief Account of ARISTOTLE'S LOGIC.
With REMARKS.

CHAPTER I.

Of the First Three Treatises.

SECTION I

Of the Author.

Aristotle had very uncommon advantages: born in an age when the philosophical spirit in Greece had long flourished, and was in its greatest vigour; brought up in the court of Macedon, where his father was the King's phy-

---

11. Reid's account of Aristotle's logic was published separately in 1806. It was added to later editions of Reid's *Essays on the Powers of the Human Mind* and was included by Sir William Hamilton in his 1846 edition of Reid's works. For a fully annotated modern edition, with introductory material, see *Thomas Reid on Logic, Rhetoric and the Fine Arts,* ed. Alexander Broadie (Edinburgh: Edinburgh University Press and Pennsylvania State University Press, 2004).

sician; twenty years a favourite scholar of Plato, and tutor to Alexander the Great; who both honoured him with his friendship, and supplied him with every thing necessary for the prosecution of his enquiries.

These advantages he improved by indefatigable study, and immense reading. He was the first, we know, says Strabo, <310> who composed a library. And in this the Egyptian and Pergamenian kings, copied his example. As to his genius, it would be disrespectful to mankind, not to allow an uncommon share to a man who governed the opinions of the most enlightened part of the species near two thousand years.

If his talents had been laid out solely for the discovery of truth and the good of mankind, his laurels would have remained for ever fresh: but he seems to have had a greater passion for fame than for truth, and to have wanted rather to be admired as the prince of philosophers than to be useful: so that it is dubious, whether there be in his character, most of the philosopher or of the sophist. The opinion of Lord Bacon is not without probability, That his ambition was as boundless as that of his royal pupil; the one aspiring at universal monarchy over the bodies and fortunes of men, the other over their opinions. If this was the case, it cannot be said, that the philosopher pursued his aim with less industry, less ability, or less success than the hero.

His writings carry too evident marks <311> of that philosophical pride, vanity, and envy, which have often sullied the character of the learned. He determines boldly things above all human knowledge; and enters upon the most difficult questions, as his pupil entered on a battle, with full assurance of success. He delivers his decisions oracularly, and without any fear of mistake. Rather than confess his ignorance, he hides it under hard words and ambiguous expressions, of which his interpreters can make what they please. There is even reason to suspect, that he wrote often with affected obscurity, either that the air of mystery might procure greater veneration, or that his books might be understood only by the adepts who had been initiated in his philosophy.

His conduct towards the writers that went before him has been much censured. After the manner of the Ottoman princes, says Lord Verulam, he thought his throne could not be secure unless he killed all his brethren. Ludovicus Vives charges him with detracting from all philosophers, that he might derive that glory to himself, of which he robbed them. He rarely quotes an author but with a view to censure, and <312> is not very fair in representing the opinions which he censures.

The faults we have mentioned are such as might be expected in a man, who had the daring ambition to be transmitted to all future ages, as the prince of philosophers, as one who had carried every branch of human knowledge to its utmost limit; and who was not very scrupulous about the means he took to obtain his end.

We ought, however, to do him the justice to observe, that although the pride and vanity of the sophist appear too much in his writings in abstract philosophy; yet in natural history the fidelity of his narrations seems to be equal to his industry; and he always distinguishes between what he knew and what he had by report. And even in abstract philosophy, it would be unfair to impute to Aristotle all the faults, all the obscurities, and all the contradictions, that are to be found in his writings. The greatest part, and perhaps the best part, of his writings is lost. There is reason to doubt whether some of those we ascribe to him be really his; and whether what are his be not much vitiated and <313> interpolated. These suspicions are justified by the fate of Aristotle's writings, which is judiciously related, from the best authorities, in Bayle's dictionary, under the article *Tyrannion,* to which I refer.

His books in logic which remain, are, 1. One book of the Categories. 2. One of Interpretation. 3. First Analytics, two books. 4. Last Analytics, two books. 5. Topics, eight books. 6. Of Sophisms, one book. Diogenes Laertius mentions many others that are lost. Those I have mentioned have commonly been published together, under the name of *Aristotle's Organon,* or *his Logic;* and for many ages, Porphyry's Introduction to the Categories has been prefixed to them.

SECTION 2

Of Porphyry's Introduction.

In this Introduction, which is addressed to Chrysoarius, the author observes, That in order to understand Aristotle's doctrine concerning the categories, it is necessary to know what a *genus* is, what a *species,* what a *specific difference,* what a *property,* and what an *accident;* that the knowledge of these is also very useful in definition, <314> in division, and even in demonstration: therefore he proposes, in this little tract, to deliver shortly and simply the doctrine of the ancients, and chiefly of the Peripatetics, concerning these five *predicables;* avoiding the more intricate questions concerning them; such as, Whether *genera* and *species* do really exist in nature? or, Whether they are only conceptions of the human mind? If they exist in nature, Whether they are corporeal or incorporeal? and, Whether they are inherent in the objects of sense, or disjoined from them? These, he says, are very difficult questions, and require accurate discussion; but that he is not to meddle with them.

After this preface, he explains very minutely each of the five words above mentioned, divides and subdivides each of them, and then pursues all the agreements and differences between one and another through sixteen chapters.

SECTION 3

Of the Categories.

The book begins with an explication of what is meant by univocal words, what <315> by equivocal, and what by denominative. Then it is observed, that what we say is either simple, without composition or structure, as *man, horse;* or, it has composition and structure, as, *a man fights, the horse runs.* Next comes a distinction between a subject of predication; that is, a subject of which any thing is affirmed or denied, and a subject of inhesion. These things are said to be inherent in a subject, which although they are not a part of the subject, cannot possibly exist without it, as figure in the thing figured. Of things that are, says Aristotle, some may be predicated of a subject, but are in no subject; as *man* may be predicated of James or John, but is not in any subject. Some again are in a subject, but can be predicated of no subject. Thus, my knowledge in grammar is in me as its subject, but it can be predicated of no subject; because it is an individual thing. Some are both in a subject, and may be predicated of a subject, as science; which is in the mind as its subject, and may be predicated of geometry. Lastly, Some things can neither be in a subject, nor be predicated of any subject. Such are all individual sub-<316>stances, which cannot be predicated, because they are individuals; and cannot be in a subject, because they are substances. After some other subtilties about predicates and subjects, we come to the categories themselves; the things above mentioned being called by the schoolmen the *antepraedicamenta.* It may be observed, however, that notwithstanding the distinction now explained, the *being in a subject,* and the *being predicated truly of a subject,* are in the Analytics used as synonymous phrases; and this variation of style has led some persons to think that the Categories were not written by Aristotle.

Things that may be expressed without composition or structure, are, says the author, reducible to the following heads. They are either *substance,* or *quantity,* or *quality,* or *relatives,* or *place,* or *time,* or *having,* or *doing,* or *suffering.* These are the predicaments or categories. The first four are largely treated of in four chapters; the others are slightly passed over, as sufficiently clear of themselves. As a specimen, I shall give a summary of what he says on the category of substance.

Substances are either primary, to wit <317> individual substances, or secondary, to wit, the genera and species of substances. Primary substances neither are in a subject, nor can be predicated of a subject; but all other things that exist, either are in primary substances, or may be predicated of them. For whatever can be predicated of that which is in a subject, may also be predicated of the subject itself. Primary substances are more substances than the secondary; and of the secondary, the species is more a substance than the genus. If there were no primary, there could be no secondary substances.

The properties of substance are these: 1. No substance is capable of intension or remission. 2. No substance can be in any other thing as its subject of inhesion. 3. No substance has a contrary; for one substance cannot be contrary to another; nor can there be contrariety between a substance and that which is no substance. 4. The most remarkable property of substance, is, that one and the same substance may, by some change in itself, become the subject of things that are contrary. Thus, the same body may be at one time hot, at another cold. <318>

Let this serve as a specimen of Aristotle's manner of treating the categories. After them, we have some chapters, which the schoolmen call *post-praedicamenta;* wherein first, the four kinds of opposition of terms are explained; to wit, *relative, privative,* of *contrariety,* and of *contradiction.* This is repeated in all systems of logic. Last of all we have distinctions of the four Greek words which answer to the Latin ones, *prius, simul, motus,* and *habere.* [12]

SECTION 4

Of the book concerning Interpretation.

We are to consider, says Aristotle, what a noun is, what a verb, what affirmation, what negation, what speech. Words are the signs of what passeth in the mind; writing is the sign of words. The signs both of writing and of words are different in different nations, but the operations of mind signified by them are the same. There are some operations of thought which are neither true nor false. These are expressed by nouns or verbs singly, and without composition. <319>

A noun is a sound which by compact signifies something without respect to time, and of which no part has signification by itself. The cries of beasts may have a natural signification, but they are not nouns: we give that name only to sounds which have their signification by compact. The cases of a noun, as the genitive, dative, are not nouns. *Non homo* is not a noun, but, for distinction's sake, may be called a *nomen infinitum.* [13]

A verb signifies something by compact with relation to time. Thus *valet* is a verb; but *valetudo* is a noun, because its signification has no relation to time.[14] It is only the present tense of the indicative that is properly called a verb; the other tenses and moods are variations of the verb. *Non valet* may be called a *verbum infinitum.*

Speech is sound significant by compact, of which some part is also significant. And it is either enunciative, or not enunciative. Enunciative speech

12. "Earlier," "at the same time," "movement" (or "change"), "having."
13. *Non homo* means "not a man"; *nomen infinitum* means "indefinite name."
14. *Valet* means "(he) is well"; *valetudo* means "good health."

is that which affirms or denies. As to speech which is not enunciative, such as a prayer or wish, the consideration of it belongs to oratory, or poetry. Every enunciative speech must have <320> a verb, or some variation of a verb. Affirmation is the enunciation of one thing concerning another. Negation is the enunciation of one thing from another. Contradiction is an affirmation and negation that are opposite. This is a summary of the first six chapters.

The seventh and eighth treat of the various kinds of enunciations or propositions, universal, particular, indefinite, and singular; and of the various kinds of opposition in propositions, and the axioms concerning them. These things are repeated in every system of logic. In the ninth chapter he endeavours to prove by a long metaphysical reasoning, that propositions respecting future contingencies are not, determinately, either true or false; and that if they were, it would follow, that all things happen necessarily, and could not have been otherwise than as they are. The remaining chapters contain many minute observations concerning the equipollency of propositions both pure and modal. <321>

CHAPTER II.

Remarks.

SECTION I

On the Five Predicables.

The writers on logic have borrowed their materials almost entirely from Aristotle's Organon, and Porphyry's Introduction. The Organon however was not written by Aristotle as one work. It comprehends various tracts, written without the view of making them parts of one whole, and afterwards thrown together by his editors under one name on account of their affinity. Many of his books that are lost, would have made a part of the Organon if they had been saved.

The three treatises of which we have given a brief account, are unconnected with each other, and with those that follow. And although the first was undoubtedly compiled by Porphyry and the two last probably by Aristotle, yet I consider <322> them as the venerable remains of a philosophy more ancient than Aristotle. Archytas of Tarentum, an eminent mathematician and philosopher of the Pythagorean school, is said to have wrote upon the ten categories; and the five predicables probably had their origin in the same school. Aristotle, though abundantly careful to do justice to himself, does not claim the invention of either. And Porphyry, without ascribing the latter to Aristotle, professes only to deliver the doctrine of the ancients and chiefly of the Peripatetics, concerning them.

The writers on logic have divided that science into three parts; the first treating of simple apprehension and of terms; the second, of judgement and of propositions; and the third, of reasoning and of syllogisms. The materials of the first part are taken from Porphyry's Introduction and the Categories; and those of the second from the book of Interpretation.

A predicable, according to the grammatical form of the word, might seem to signify, whatever may be predicated, that is, affirmed or denied, of a subject: and in that sense every predicate would be a <323> predicable. But logicians give a different meaning to the word. They divide propositions into certain classes, according to the relation which the predicate of the proposition bears to the subject. The first class is that wherein the predicate is the *genus* of the subject; as when we say, *This is a triangle, Jupiter is a planet.* In the second class, the predicate is a *species* of the subject; as when we say, *This triangle is right-angled.* A third class is when the predicate is the specific difference of the subject; as when we say, *Every triangle has three sides and three angles.* A fourth when the predicate is a property of the subject; as when we say, *The angles of every triangle are equal to two right angles.* And a fifth class is when the predicate is something accidental to the subject; as when we say, *This triangle is neatly drawn.*

Each of these classes comprehends a great variety of propositions, having different subjects, and different predicates; but in each class the relation between the predicate and the subject is the same. Now it is to this relation that logicians have given the name of *a predicable.* Hence it is, that <324> although the number of predicates be infinite, yet the number of predicables can be no greater than that of the different relations which may be in prop-

ositions between the predicate and the subject. And if all propositions belong
to one or other of the five classes above mentioned, there can be but five
predicables, to wit, *genus, species, differentia, proprium,* and *accidens.* These
might, with more propriety perhaps, have been called *the five classes of predicates;* but use has determined them to be called *the five predicables.*

It may also be observed, that as some objects of thought are individuals,
such as, *Julius Caesar, the city Rome;* so others are common to many individuals, as *good, great, virtuous, vicious.* Of this last kind are all the things
that are expressed by adjectives. Things common to many individuals, were
by the ancients called *universals.* All predicates are universals, for they have
the nature of adjectives; and, on the other hand, all universals may be predicates. On this account, universals may be divided into the same classes as
predicates; and as the five classes of predicates <325> above mentioned have
been called the five predicables, so by the same kind of phraseology they
have been called *the five universals;* altho' they may more properly be called
the *five classes of universals.*

The doctrine of the five universals or predicables makes an essential part
of every system of logic, and has been handed down without any change
to this day. The very name of *predicables* shews, that the author of this
division, whoever he was, intended it as a complete enumeration of all the
kinds of things that can be affirmed of any subject; and so it has always
been understood. It is accordingly implied in this division, that all that can
be affirmed of any thing whatever, is either the *genus* of the thing, or its
species, or its *specific difference,* or some *property* or *accident* belonging to it.

Burgersdick, a very acute writer in logic, seems to have been aware, that
strong objections might be made to the five predicables, considered as a
complete enumeration: but, unwilling to allow any imperfection in this
ancient division, he endeavours to restrain the meaning of the word *predicable,* so as to obviate objec-<326>tions. Those things only, says he, are to
be accounted predicables, which may be affirmed of *many individuals, truly,
properly,* and *immediately.* The consequence of putting such limitations
upon the word *predicable* is, that in many propositions, perhaps in most,
the predicate is not a predicable. But admitting all his limitations, the enumeration will still be very incomplete: for of many things we may affirm
truly, properly, and immediately, their existence, their end, their cause, their

effect, and various relations which they bear to other things. These, and perhaps many more, are predicables in the strict sense of the word, no less than the five which have been so long famous.

Altho' Porphyry and all subsequent writers, make the predicables to be, in number, five; yet Aristotle himself, in the beginning of the Topics, reduces them to four; and demonstrates, that there can be no more. We shall give his demonstration when we come to the Topics; and shall only here observe, that as Burgersdick justifies the fivefold division, by restraining the meaning of the word *predicable;* so Aristotle justifies the fourfold di-<327>vision, by enlarging the meaning of the words *property* and *accident.*

After all, I apprehend, that this ancient division of predicables with all its imperfections, will bear a comparison with those which have been substituted in its stead by the most celebrated modern philosophers.

Locke, in his Essay on the Human Understanding, having laid it down as a principle, That all our knowledge consists in perceiving certain agreements and disagreements between our ideas, reduces these agreements and disagreements to four heads: to wit, 1. Identity and diversity; 2. Relation; 3. Coexistence; 4. Real Existence (*a*). Here are four predicables given as a complete enumeration, and yet not one of the ancient predicables is included in the number.

The author of the Treatise of Human Nature,[15] proceeding upon the same principle that all our knowledge is only a perception of the relations of our ideas, observes, "That it may perhaps be esteemed an endless task, to enumerate all those <328> qualities which admit of comparison, and by which the ideas of philosophical relation are produced: but if we diligently consider them, we shall find, that without difficulty they may be comprised under seven general heads: 1. Resemblance; 2. Identity; 3. Relations of Space and Time; 4. Relations of Quantity and Number; 5. Degrees of Quality; 6. Contrariety; 7. Causation" (*b*). Here again are seven predicables given as a complete enumeration, wherein all the predicables of the ancients, as well as two of Locke's are left out.

(*a*) Book 4. chap. 1.
(*b*) Vol. 1. p. 33. and 125.
15. Hume.

The ancients in their division attended only to categorical propositions which have one subject and one predicate; and of these to such only as have a general term for their subject. The moderns, by their definition of knowledge, have been led to attend only to relative propositions, which express a relation between two subjects, and these subjects they suppose to be always ideas. <329>

SECTION 2

On the Ten Categories, and on Divisions in general.

The intention of the categories or predicaments is, to muster every object of human apprehension under ten heads: for the categories are given as a complete enumeration of every thing which can be expressed without *composition* and *structure;* that is, of every thing that can be either the subject or the predicate of a proposition. So that as every soldier belongs to some company, and every company to some regiment; in like manner every thing that can be the object of human thought, has its place in one or other of the ten categories; and by dividing and subdividing properly the several categories, all the notions that enter into the human mind may be mustered in rank and file, like an army in the day of battle.

The perfection of the division of categories into ten heads, has been strenuously defended by the followers of Aristotle, as well as that of the five predicables. They are indeed of kin to each other: <330> they breathe the same spirit, and probably had the same origin. By the one we are taught to marshal every term that can enter into a proposition, either as subject or predicate; and by the other, we are taught all the possible relations which the subject can have to the predicate. Thus, the whole furniture of the human mind is presented to us at one view, and contracted, as it were, into a nut-shell. To attempt, in so early a period, a methodical delineation of the vast region of human knowledge, actual and possible, and to point out the limits of every district, was indeed magnanimous in a high degree, and deserves our admiration, while we lament that the human powers are unequal to so bold a flight.

A regular distribution of things under proper classes or heads, is, without doubt, a great help both to memory and judgement. As the philosopher's province includes all things human and divine that can be objects of enquiry, he is naturally led to attempt some general division, like that of the categories. And the invention of a division of this kind, which the speculative part of mankind acquiesced in <331> for two thousand years, marks a superiority of genius in the inventer, whoever he was. Nor does it appear, that the general divisions which, since the decline of the Peripatetic philosophy, have been substituted in place of the ten categories, are more perfect.

Locke has reduced all things to three categories; to wit, substances, modes, and relations. In this division, time, space, and number, three great objects of human thought, are omitted.

The author of the Treatise of Human Nature has reduced all things to two categories; to wit, ideas, and impressions: a division which is very well adapted to his system; and which puts me in mind of another made by an excellent mathematician in a printed thesis I have seen.[16] In it the author, after a severe censure of the ten categories of the Peripatetics, maintains, that there neither are nor can be more than two categories of things; to wit, *data* and *quaesita*.[17]

There are two ends that may be proposed by such divisions. The first is, to methodize or digest in order what a man actually knows. This is neither unim-<332>portant nor impracticable; and in proportion to the solidity and accuracy of a man's judgement, his divisions of the things he knows, will be elegant and useful. The same subject may admit, and even require, various divisions, according to the different points of view from which we contemplate it: nor does it follow, that because one division is good, therefore another is naught. To be acquainted with the divisions of the logicians and metaphysicians, without a superstitious attachment to them, may be of use in dividing the same subjects, or even those of a different nature. Thus, Quintilian borrows from the ten categories his division of the topics of rhetorical argumentation. Of all methods of arrangement, the most an-

16. Reid means James Gregory, professor of natural philosophy at St. Andrews in the late seventeenth century.
17. "Things that are granted" and "things that are sought after."

tiphilosophical seems to be the invention of this age; I mean, the arranging the arts and sciences by the letters of the alphabet, in dictionaries and encyclopedies. With these authors the categories are, A, B, C, &c.

Another end commonly proposed by such divisions, but very rarely attained, is to exhaust the subject divided; so that nothing that belongs to it shall be omit-<333>ted. It is one of the general rules of division in all systems of logic, That the division should be adequate to the subject divided: a good rule, without doubt; but very often beyond the reach of human power. To make a perfect division, a man must have a perfect comprehension of the whole subject at one view. When our knowledge of the subject is imperfect, any division we can make, must be like the first sketch of a painter, to be extended, contracted, or mended, as the subject shall be found to require. Yet nothing is more common, not only among the ancient, but even among modern philosophers, than to draw, from their incomplete divisions, conclusions which suppose them to be perfect.

A division is a repository which the philosopher frames for holding his ware in convenient order. The philosopher maintains, that such or such a thing is not good ware, because there is no place in his ware-room that fits it. We are apt to yield to this argument in philosophy, but it would appear ridiculous in any other traffic.

Peter Ramus, who had the spirit of a re-<334>former in philosophy, and who had force of genius sufficient to shake the Aristotelian fabric in many parts, but insufficient to erect any thing more solid in its place, tried to remedy the imperfection of philosophical divisions, by introducing a new manner of dividing. His divisions always consisted of two members, one of which was contradictory of the other; as if one should divide England into Middlesex and what is not Middlesex. It is evident that these two members comprehend all England: for the logicians observe, that a term along with its contradictory, comprehend all things. In the same manner, we may divide what is not Middlesex into Kent and what is not Kent. Thus one may go on by divisions and subdivisions that are absolutely complete. This example may serve to give an idea of the spirit of Ramean divisions, which were in no small reputation about two hundred years ago.

Aristotle was not ignorant of this kind of division. But he used it only as a touchstone to prove by induction the perfection of some other division, which indeed is the best use that can be made of it. When <335> applied to the common purpose of division, it is both inelegant, and burdensome to the memory; and, after it has put one out of breath by endless subdivisions, there is still a negative term left behind, which shows that you are no nearer the end of your journey than when you began.

Until some more effectual remedy be found for the imperfection of divisions, I beg leave to propose one more simple than that of Ramus. It is this: When you meet with a division of any subject imperfectly comprehended, add to the last member an *et caetera*. That this *et caetera* makes the division complete, is undeniable; and therefore it ought to hold its place as a member, and to be always understood, whether expressed or not, until clear and positive proof be brought that the division is complete without it. And this same *et caetera* is to be the repository of all members that shall in any future time shew a good and valid right to a place in the subject.

SECTION 3

On Distinctions.

Having said so much of logical divi-<336>sions, we shall next make some remarks upon distinctions.

Since the philosophy of Aristotle fell into disrepute, it has been a common topic of wit and raillery, to enveigh against metaphysical distinctions. Indeed the abuse of them in the scholastic ages, seems to justify a general prejudice against them: and shallow thinkers and writers have good reason to be jealous of distinctions, because they make sad work when applied to their flimsy compositions. But every man of true judgement, while he condemns distinctions that have no foundation in the nature of things, must perceive, that indiscriminately to decry distinctions, is to renounce all pretensions to just reasoning: for as false reasoning commonly proceeds from confounding things that are different; so without distinguishing such things, it is impossible to avoid error, or detect sophistry. The authority of Aquinas, or Suarez, or even of Aristotle, can neither stamp a real value upon distinctions of base metal, nor hinder the currency of those of true metal.

Some distinctions are verbal, others are real. The first kind distinguish the va-<337>rious meanings of a word; whether proper, or metaphorical. Distinctions of this kind make a part of the grammar of a language, and are often absurd when translated into another language. Real distinctions are equally good in all languages, and suffer no hurt by translation. They distinguish the different species contained under some general notion, or the different parts contained in one whole.

Many of Aristotle's distinctions are verbal merely; and therefore, more proper materials for a dictionary of the Greek language, than for a philosophical treatise. At least, they ought never to have been translated into other languages, when the idiom of the language will not justify them: for this is to adulterate the language, to introduce foreign idioms into it without necessity or use, and to make it ambiguous where it was not. The distinctions in the end of the Categories of the four words, *prius, simul, motus,* and *habere,* are all verbal.

The modes or species of *prius,* according to Aristotle, are five. One thing may be prior to another; first, in point of time; secondly, in point of dignity; thirdly, in <338> point of order; and so forth. The modes of *simul* are only three. It seems this word was not used in the Greek with so great latitude as the other, although they are relative terms.

The modes or species of *motion* he makes to be six, to wit, generation, corruption, increase, decrease, alteration, and change of place.

The modes or species of *having* are eight. 1. Having a quality or habit, as having wisdom. 2. Having quantity or magnitude. 3. Having things adjacent, as having a sword. 4. Having things as parts, as having hands or feet. 5. Having in a part or on a part, as having a ring on one's finger. 6. Containing, as a cask is said to have wine. 7. Possessing, as having lands or houses. 8. Having a wife.

Another distinction of this kind is Aristotle's distinction of causes; of which he makes four kinds, efficient, material, formal, and final. These distinctions may deserve a place in a dictionary of the Greek language; but in English or Latin they adulterate the language. Yet so fond were the schoolmen of distinctions of this kind, that they added to Aristotle's enumeration, <339> an impulsive cause, an exemplary cause, and I don't know how many more. We seem to have adopted into English a final cause; but it is merely a term of art, borrowed from the Peripatetic philosophy, without necessity or use: for the English word *end* is as good as *final cause,* though not so long nor so learned.

SECTION 4

On Definitions.

It remains that we make some remarks on Aristotle's definitions, which have exposed him to much censure and ridicule. Yet I think it must be allowed, that in things which need definition and admit of it, his definitions are commonly judicious and accurate; and had he attempted to define such things only, his enemies had wanted great matter of triumph. I believe it may likewise be said in his favour, that until Locke's essay was wrote, there was nothing of importance delivered by philosophers with regard to definition, beyond what Aristotle has said upon that subject. <340>

He considers a definition as a speech declaring what a thing is. Every thing essential to the thing defined, and nothing more, must be contained in the definition. Now the essence of a thing consists of these two parts: First, What is common to it with other things of the same kind; and, secondly, What distinguishes it from other things of the same kind. The first is called the *genus* of the thing, the second its *specific difference.* The definition therefore consists of these two parts. And for finding them, we must have recourse to the ten categories; in one or other of which every thing in nature is to be found. Each category is a *genus,* and is divided into so many species, which are distinguished by their specific differences. Each of these species is again subdivided into so many species, with regard to which it is a genus. This division and subdivision continues until we come to the lowest species, which can only be divided into individuals, distinguished from one another, not by any specific difference, but by accidental differences of time, place, and other circumstances.

The category itself being the highest genus, is in no respect a species, and the <341> lowest *species* is in no respect a *genus;* but every intermediate order is a genus compared with those that are below it, and a species compared with those above it. To find the definition of any thing, therefore, you must take the genus which is immediately above its place in the category, and the specific *difference,* by which it is distinguished from other species of the same *genus.* These two make a perfect definition. This I take to be the substance of Aristotle's system; and probably the system of the Pythagorean school before Aristotle, concerning definition.

But notwithstanding the specious appearance of this system, it has its defects. Not to repeat what was before said of the imperfection of the division of things into ten categories, the subdivisions of each category are no less imperfect. Aristotle has given some subdivisions of a few of them; and as far as he goes, his followers pretty unanimously take the same road. But when they attempt to go farther, they take very different roads. It is evident, that if the series of each category could be completed, and the division of things into categories could be made perfect, still the <342> highest genus in each category could not be defined, because it is not a species; nor could individuals be defined, because they have no specific difference. There are also many species of things, whose specific difference cannot be expressed in language, even when it is evident to sense, or to the understanding. Thus green, red, and blue, are very distinct species of colour; but who can express in words wherein green differs from red or blue?

Without borrowing light from the ancient system, we may perceive, that every definition must consist of words that need no definition; and that to define the common words of a language that have no ambiguity, is trifling, if it could be done; the only use of a definition being to give a clear and adequate conception of the meaning of a word.

The logicians indeed distinguish between the definition of a word, and the definition of a thing; considering the former as the mean office of a lexicographer, but the last as the grand work of a philosopher. But what they have said about the definition of a thing, if it have a meaning, is beyond my comprehension. All <343> the rules of definition agree to the definition of a word: and if they mean by the definition of a thing, the giving an adequate conception of the nature and essence of any thing that exists; this is impossible, and is the vain boast of men unconscious of the weakness of human understanding.

The works of God are but imperfectly known by us. We see their outside; or perhaps we discover some of their qualities and relations, by observation and experiment assisted by reasoning: but even of the simplest of them we can give no definition that comprehends its real essence. It is justly observed by Locke, that nominal essences only, which are the creatures of our own minds, are perfectly comprehended by us, or can be properly defined; and even of these there are many too simple in their nature to admit of definition. When we cannot give precision to our notions by a definition, we must endeavour to do it by attentive reflection upon them, by observing minutely their agreements and differences, and especially by a right understanding of the powers of our own minds by which such notions are formed. <344>

The principles laid down by Locke with regard to definition and with regard to the abuse of words, carry conviction along with them. I take them to be one of the most important improvements made in logic since the days of Aristotle: not so much because they enlarge our knowledge, as because they make us sensible of our ignorance; and shew that a great part of what speculative men have admired as profound philosophy, is only a darkening of knowledge by words without understanding.

If Aristotle had understood these principles, many of his definitions, which furnish matter of triumph to his enemies, had never seen the light: let us impute them to the times rather than to the man. The sublime Plato, it is said, thought it necessary to have the definition of a man, and could find none better than *Animal implume bipes;*[18] upon which Diogenes sent to his school a cock with his feathers plucked off, desiring to know whether it was a man or not. <345>

SECTION 5

On the Structure of Speech.

The few hints contained in the beginning of the book concerning Interpretation relating to the structure of speech, have been left out in treatises of logic, as belonging rather to grammar; yet I apprehend this is a rich field of philosophical speculation. Language being the express image of human thought, the analysis of the one must correspond to that of the other. Nouns adjective and substantive, verbs active and passive, with their various

18. "Two-footed animal without feathers."

moods, tenses, and persons, must be expressive of a like variety in the modes of thought. Things that are distinguished in all languages, such as substance and quality, action and passion, cause and effect, must be distinguished by the natural powers of the human mind. The philosophy of grammar, and that of the human understanding, are more nearly allied than is commonly imagined.

The structure of language was pursued to a considerable extent, by the ancient commentators upon this book of Aristotle. Their speculations upon this subject, which <346> are neither the least ingenious nor the least useful part of the Peripatetic philosophy, were neglected for many ages, and lay buried in ancient manuscripts, or in books little known, till they were lately brought to light by the learned Mr. Harris in his Hermes.

The definitions given by Aristotle, of a noun, of a verb, and of speech, will hardly bear examination. It is easy in practice to distinguish the various parts of speech; but very difficult, if at all possible, to give accurate definitions of them.

He observes justly, that besides that kind of speech called a *proposition,* which is always either true or false, there are other kinds which are neither true nor false; such as, a prayer, or wish; to which we may add, a question, a command, a promise, a contract, and many others. These Aristotle pronounces to have nothing to do with his subject, and remits them to oratory, or poetry; and so they have remained banished from the regions of philosophy to this day: yet I apprehend, that an analysis of such speeches, and of the operations of mind which they express, would be of real use, and perhaps would <347> discover how imperfect an enumeration the logicians have given of the powers of human understanding, when they reduce them to simple apprehension, judgement, and reasoning.

SECTION 6

On Propositions.

Mathematicians use the word *proposition* in a larger sense than logicians. A problem is called a *proposition* in mathematics, but in logic it is not a proposition: it is one of those speeches which are not enunciative, and which Aristotle remits to oratory or poetry.

A proposition, according to Aristotle, is a speech wherein one thing is affirmed or denied of another. Hence it is easy to distinguish the thing affirmed or denied, which is called *the predicate,* from the thing of which it is affirmed or denied, which is called *the subject;* and these two are called *the terms of the proposition.* Hence likewise it appears, that propositions are either affirmative or negative; and this is called *their quality.* All affirmative propositions have the same quality, so likewise have all <348> negative; but an affirmative and a negative are contrary in their quality.

When the subject of a proposition is a general term, the predicate is affirmed or denied, either of the whole, or of a part. Hence propositions are distinguished into universal and particular. *All men are mortal,* is an universal proposition; *Some men are learned,* is a particular; and this is called *the quantity of the proposition.* All universal propositions agree in quantity, as also all particular: but an universal and a particular are said to differ in quantity. A proposition is called *indefinite,* when there is no mark either of universality or particularity annexed to the subject: thus, *Man is of few days,* is an indefinite proposition; but it must be understood either as universal or as particular, and therefore is not a third species, but by interpretation is brought under one of the other two.

There are also singular propositions, which have not a general term but an individual for their subject; as, *Alexander was a great conqueror.* These are considered by logicians as universal, because, the subject being indivisible, the predicate <349> is affirmed or denied of the whole, and not of a part only. Thus all propositions, with regard to quality, are either affirmative or negative; and with regard to quantity, are universal or particular; and taking in both quantity and quality, they are universal affirmatives, or universal negatives, or particular affirmatives, or particular negatives. These four kinds, after the days of Aristotle, came to be named by the names of the four first vowels, A, E, I, O, according to the following distich:

> *Asserit A, negat E, sed universaliter ambae;*
> *Asserit I, negat O, sed particulariter ambo.* [19]

---

19. "A asserts, E denies, but both do so universally; I asserts, O denies, but both do so particularly."

When the young logician is thus far instructed in the nature of propositions, he is apt to think there is no difficulty in analysing any proposition, and shewing its subject and predicate, its quantity and quality; and indeed, unless he can do this, he will be unable to apply the rules of logic to use. Yet he will find, there are some difficulties in this analysis, which are overlooked by Aristotle altogether; and although they are sometimes touched, they are not removed by his followers. For, 1. There are propositions in which it is difficult to find a subject and a predicate; <350> as in these, *It rains, It snows.* 2. In some propositions either term may be made the subject or the predicate as you like best; as in this, *Virtue is the road to happiness.* 3. The same example may serve to shew, that it is sometimes difficult to say, whether a proposition be universal or particular. 4. The quality of some propositions is so dubious, that logicians have never been able to agree whether they be affirmative or negative; as in this proposition, *Whatever is insentient is not an animal.* 5. As there is one class of propositions which have only two terms, to wit, one subject and one predicate, which are called *categorical propositions;* so there are many classes that have more than two terms. What Aristotle delivers in this book is applicable only to categorical propositions; and to them only the rules concerning the conversion of propositions, and concerning the figures and modes of syllogisms, are accommodated. The subsequent writers of logic have taken notice of some of the many classes of complex propositions, and have given rules adapted to them; but finding this work endless, they have left us to manage the rest by the rules of common sense. <351>

CHAPTER III.

Account of the First Analytics.[20]

SECTION I

Of the Conversion of Propositions.

In attempting to give some account of the Analytics and of the Topics of Aristotle, ingenuity requires me to confess, that though I have often purposed to read the whole with care, and to understand what is intelligible, yet my courage and patience always failed before I had done. Why should I throw away so much time and painful attention upon a thing of so little real use? If I had lived in those ages when the knowledge of Aristotle's Organon intitled a man to the highest rank in philosophy, ambition might have induced me to employ upon it some years of painful study; and less, I conceive, would not be sufficient. Such reflections as these, always got the better of my resolution, <352> when the first ardor began to cool. All I can say is, that I have read some parts of the different books with care, some slightly, and some perhaps not at all. I have glanced over the whole often, and when any thing attracted my attention, have dipped into it till my appetite was satisfied. Of all reading it is the most dry and the most painful, employing an infinite labour of demonstration, about things of the most abstract nature, delivered in a laconic style, and often, I think, with affected obscurity; and all to prove general propositions, which when applied to particular instances appear self-evident.

There is probably but little in the Categories or in the book of Interpretation, that Aristotle could claim as his own invention: but the whole theory of syllogisms he claims as his own, and as the fruit of much time and labour. And indeed it is a stately fabric, a monument of a great genius, which we could wish to have been more usefully employed. There must be something however adapted to please the human understanding, or to flat-

---

20. Now generally known as the *Prior Analytics.*

ter human pride, in a work which occupied men of speculation for more than a thousand <353> years. These books are called *Analytics,* because the intention of them is to resolve all reasoning into its simple ingredients.

The first book of the First Analytics, consisting of forty-six chapters, may be divided into four parts; the first treating of the conversion of propositions; the second, of the structure of syllogisms in all the different figures and modes; the third, of the invention of a middle term; and the last, of the resolution of syllogisms. We shall give a brief account of each.

To convert a proposition, is to infer from it another proposition, whose subject is the predicate of the first, and whose predicate is the subject of the first. This is reduced by Aristotle to three rules. 1. An universal negative may be converted into an universal negative: thus, *No man is a quadruped;* therefore, *No quadruped is a man.* 2. An universal affirmative can be converted only into a particular affirmative: thus, *All men are mortal;* therefore, *Some mortal beings are men.* 3. A particular affirmative may be converted into a particular affirmative: as, *Some men are just;* therefore, *Some just persons are men.* When a proposition may be con-<354>verted without changing its quantity, this is called *simple conversion;* but when the quantity is diminished, as in the universal affirmative, it is called conversion *per accidens.*

There is another kind of conversion, omitted in this place by Aristotle, but supplied by his followers, called *conversion by contraposition,* in which the term that is contradictory to the predicate is put for the subject, and the quality of the proposition is changed; as, *All animals are sentient;* therefore, *What is insentient is not an animal.* A fourth rule of conversion therefore is, That an universal affirmative, and a particular negative, may be converted by contraposition.

SECTION 2

Of the Figures and Modes of pure Syllogisms.

A syllogism is an argument, or reasoning, consisting of three propositions, the last of which, called *the conclusion,* is inferred from the two preceding, which are called *the premises.* The conclusion having two terms, a subject and a predicate, its <355> predicate is called the *major* term, and its subject the *minor* term. In order to prove the conclusion, each of its terms is, in the premises, compared with a third term, called the *middle* term. By this means one of the premises will have for its two terms the major term and the middle term; and this premise is called the *major* premise, or the *major* proposition of the syllogism. The other premise must have for its two terms the minor term and the middle term, and it is called the *minor* proposition. Thus the syllogism consists of three propositions, distinguished by the names of the *major,* the *minor,* and the *conclusion:* and altho' each of these has two terms, a subject and a predicate, yet there are only three different terms in all. The major term is always the predicate of the conclusion, and is also either the subject or predicate of the major proposition. The minor term is always the subject of the conclusion, and is also either the subject or predicate of the minor proposition. The middle term never enters into the conclusion, but stands in both premises, either in the position of subject or of predicate. <356>

According to the various positions which the middle term may have in the premises, syllogisms are said to be of various figures. Now all the possible positions of the middle term are only four: for, first, it may be the subject of the major proposition, and the predicate of the minor, and then the syllogism is of the first figure; or it may be the predicate of both premises, and then the syllogism is of the second figure; or it may be the subject of both, which makes a syllogism of the third figure; or it may be the predicate of the major proposition, and the subject of the minor, which makes the fourth figure. Aristotle takes no notice of the fourth figure. It was added by the famous Galen, and is often called *the Galenical figure.*

There is another division of syllogisms according to their modes. The mode of a syllogism is determined by the quality and quantity of the propositions of which it consists. Each of the three propositions must be either an universal affirmative, or an universal negative, or a particular affirmative, or a particular negative. These four kinds of propositions, as was before observed, have been named by the four vowels, <357> A, E, I, O; by which means the mode of a syllogism is marked by any three of those four vowels. Thus A, A, A, denotes that mode in which the major, minor, and conclusion, are all universal affirmatives; E, A, E, denotes that mode in which the major and conclusion are universal negatives, and the minor is an universal affirmative.

To know all the possible modes of syllogism, we must find how many different combinations may be made of three out of the four vowels, and from the art of combination the number is found to be sixty-four. So many possible modes there are in every figure, consequently in the three figures of Aristotle there are one hundred and ninety-two, and in all the four figures two hundred and fifty-six.

Now the theory of syllogism requires, that we shew what are the particular modes in each figure, which do, or do not, form a just and conclusive syllogism, that so the legitimate may be adopted, and the spurious rejected. This Aristotle has shewn in the first three figures, examining all the modes one by one, and passing sentence upon each; and from this examination he <358> collects some rules which may aid the memory in distinguishing the false from the true, and point out the properties of each figure.

The first figure has only four legitimate modes. The major proposition in this figure must be universal, and the minor affirmative; and it has this property, that it yields conclusions of all kinds, affirmative and negative, universal and particular.

The second figure has also four legitimate modes. Its major proposition must be universal, and one of the premises must be negative. It yields conclusions both universal and particular, but all negative.

The third figure has six legitimate modes. Its minor must always be affirmative; and it yields conclusions both affirmative and negative, but all particular.

Besides the rules that are proper to each figure, Aristotle has given some that are common to all, by which the legitimacy of syllogisms may be tried. These may, I think, be reduced to five. 1. There must be only three terms in a syllogism. As each term occurs in two of the propositions, it must be precisely the same in both: if it be not, the syllogism is said to <359> have four terms, which makes a vitious syllogism. 2. The middle term must be taken universally in one of the premises. 3. Both premises must not be particular propositions, nor both negative. 4. The conclusion must be particular, if either of the premises be particular; and negative, if either of the premises be negative. 5. No term can be taken universally in the conclusion, if it be not taken universally in the premises.

For understanding the second and fifth of these rules, it is necessary to observe, that a term is said to be taken universally, not only when it is the subject of an universal proposition, but when it is the predicate of a negative proposition; on the other hand, a term is said to be taken particularly, when it is either the subject of a particular, or the predicate of an affirmative proposition.

SECTION 3

Of the Invention of a Middle Term.

The third part of this book contains rules general and special for the invention of a middle term; and this the author <360> conceives to be of great utility. The general rules amount to this, That you are to consider well both terms of the proposition to be proved; their definition, their properties, the things which may be affirmed or denied of them, and those of which they may be affirmed or denied: these things collected together, are the materials from which your middle term is to be taken.

The special rules require you to consider the quantity and quality of the proposition to be proved, that you may discover in what mode and figure of syllogism the proof is to proceed. Then from the materials before collected, you must seek a middle term which has that relation to the subject and predicate of the proposition to be proved, which the nature of the syllogism requires. Thus, suppose the proposition I would prove is an universal affirmative, I know by the rules of syllogisms, that there is only one legitimate mode in which an universal affirmative proposition can be proved; and that is the first mode of the first figure. I know likewise, that in this mode both the premises must be universal affirmatives; and that the middle <361> term must be the subject of the major, and the predicate of the minor. Therefore of the terms collected according to the general rule, I seek out one or more which have these two properties; first, That the predicate of the proposition to be proved can be universally affirmed of it;

and secondly, That it can be universally affirmed of the subject of the proposition to be proved. Every term you can find which has those two properties, will serve you as a middle term, but no other. In this way, the author gives special rules for all the various kinds of propositions to be proved; points out the various modes in which they may be proved, and the properties which the middle term must have to make it fit for answering that end. And the rules are illustrated, or rather, in my opinion, purposely darkened, by putting letters of the alphabet for the several terms.

SECTION 4

Of the remaining part of the First Book.

The resolution of syllogisms requires no other principles but these before laid down <362> for constructing them. However it is treated of largely, and rules laid down for reducing reasoning to syllogisms, by supplying one of the premises when it is understood, by rectifying inversions, and putting the propositions in the proper order.

Here he speaks also of hypothetical syllogisms; which he acknowledges cannot be resolved into any of the figures, although there be many kinds of them that ought diligently to be observed; and which he promises to handle afterwards. But this promise is not fulfilled, as far as I know, in any of his works that are extant.

SECTION 5

Of the Second Book of the First Analytics.

The second book treats of the powers of syllogisms, and shows, in twenty-seven chapters, how we may perform many feats by them, and what figures and modes are adapted to each. Thus, in some syllogisms several distinct conclusions may be drawn from the same premises: in some, <363> true conclusions may be drawn from false premises: in some, by assuming the conclusion and one premise, you may prove the other; you may turn a direct syllogism into one leading to an absurdity.

We have likewise precepts given in this book, both to the assailant in a syllogistical dispute, how to carry on his attack with art, so as to obtain the victory; and to the defendant, how to keep the enemy at such a distance as that he shall never be obliged to yield. From which we learn, that Aristotle introduced in his own school, the practice of syllogistical disputation, instead of the rhetorical disputations which the sophists were wont to use in more ancient times.

CHAPTER IV.

Remarks.

SECTION I

Of the Conversion of Propositions.

We have given a summary view of the theory of pure syllogisms as delivered by Aristotle, a theory of which he <364> claims the sole invention. And I believe it will be difficult, in any science, to find so large a system of truths of so very abstract and so general a nature, all fortified by demonstration, and all invented and perfected by one man. It shows a force of genius and labour of investigation, equal to the most arduous attempts. I shall now make some remarks upon it.

As to the conversion of propositions, the writers on logic commonly satisfy themselves with illustrating each of the rules by an example, conceiving them to be self-evident when applied to particular cases. But Aristotle has given demonstrations of the rules he mentions. As a specimen, I shall give his demonstration of the first rule. "Let A B be an universal negative proposition; I say, that if A is in no B, it will follow that B is in no A. If you deny this consequence, let B be in some A, for example, in C; then the first supposition will not be true; for C is of the B's." In this demonstration, if I understand it, the third rule of conversion is assumed, that if B is in some A, then A must be in some B, which indeed is contrary to the first supposition. If <365> the third rule be assumed for proof of the first, the proof of all the three goes round in a circle; for the second and third rules are proved by the first. This is a fault in reasoning which Aristotle condemns, and which I would be very unwilling to charge him with, if I could find any better meaning in his demonstration. But it is indeed a fault very difficult to be avoided, when men attempt to prove things that are self-evident.

The rules of conversion cannot be applied to all propositions, but only to those that are categorical; and we are left to the direction of common sense in the conversion of other propositions. To give an example: Alexander was the son of Philip; therefore Philip was the father of Alexander: A is greater than B; therefore B is less than A. These are conversions which, as far as I know, do not fall within any rule in logic; nor do we find any loss for want of a rule in such cases.

Even in the conversion of categorical propositions, it is not enough to transpose the subject and predicate. Both must undergo some change, in order to fit them for their new station: for in every pro-<366>position the subject must be a substantive, or have the force of a substantive; and the predicate must be an adjective, or have the force of an adjective. Hence it follows, that when the subject is an individual, the proposition admits not of conversion. How, for instance, shall we convert this proposition, God is omniscient?

These observations show, that the doctrine of the conversion of propositions is not so complete as it appears. The rules are laid down without any limitation; yet they are fitted only to one class of propositions, to wit, the categorical; and of these only to such as have a general term for their subject.

SECTION 2

On Additions made to Aristotle's Theory.

Although the logicians have enlarged the first and second parts of logic, by explaining some technical words and distinctions which Aristotle has omitted, and by giving names to some kinds of propositions which he overlooks; yet in what concerns the theory of categorical syllo-<367>gisms, he is more full, more minute and particular, than any of them: so that they seem to have thought this capital part of the Organon rather redundant than deficient.

It is true, that Galen added a fourth figure to the three mentioned by Aristotle. But there is reason to think that Aristotle omitted the fourth figure, not through ignorance or inattention, but of design, as containing only some indirect modes, which, when properly expressed, fall into the first figure.

It is true also, that Peter Ramus, a professed enemy of Aristotle, introduced some new modes that are adapted to singular propositions; and that Aristotle takes no notice of singular propositions, either in his rules of conversion, or in the modes of syllogism. But the friends of Aristotle have shewn, that this improvement of Ramus is more specious than useful. Singular propositions have the force of universal propositions, and are subject to the same rules. The definition given by Aristotle of an universal proposition applies to them; and therefore he might think, that there was no occasion to mul-<368>tiply the modes of syllogism upon their account.

These attempts, therefore, show rather inclination than power, to discover any material defect in Aristotle's theory.

The most valuable addition made to the theory of categorical syllogisms, seems to be the invention of those technical names given to the legitimate modes, by which they may be easily remembered, and which have been comprised in these barbarous verses.

> *Barbara, Celarent, Darii, Ferio,* dato primae;
> *Cesare, Camestris, Festino, Baroco,* secundae;
> Tertia grande sonans recitat *Darapti, Felapton;*
> Adjungens *Disamis, Datisi, Bocardo, Ferison.*

In these verses, every legitimate mode belonging to the three figures has a name given to it, by which it may be distinguished and remembered. And this name is so contrived as to denote its nature: for the name has three vowels, which denote the kind of each of its propositions.

Thus, a syllogism in *Bocardo* must be made up of the propositions denoted by the three vowels, O, A, O; that is, its major and conclusion must be particular negative propositions, and its minor an <369> universal affirmative; and being in the third figure, the middle term must be the subject of both premises.

This is the mystery contained in the vowels of those barbarous words. But there are other mysteries contained in their consonants: for, by their means, a child may be taught to reduce any syllogism of the second or third figure to one of the first. So that the four modes of the first figure being directly proved to be conclusive, all the modes of the other two are proved at the same time, by means of this operation of reduction. For the rules and manner of this reduction, and the different species of it, called *ostensive* and *per impossible,* I refer to the logicians, that I may not disclose all their mysteries.

The invention contained in these verses is so ingenious, and so great an adminicle to the dextrous management of syllogisms, that I think it very probable that Aristotle had some contrivance of this kind, which was kept as one of the secret doctrines of his school, and handed down by tradition, until some person brought it to light. This is offered only as a conjecture, leaving it to those who are better <370> acquainted with the most ancient commentators on the Analytics, either to refute or to confirm it.

SECTION 3

On Examples used to illustrate this Theory.

We may observe, that Aristotle hardly ever gives examples of real syllogisms to illustrate his rules. In demonstrating the legitimate modes, he takes A, B, C, for the terms of the syllogism. Thus, the first mode of the first figure is demonstrated by him in this manner. "For," says he, "if A is attributed to every B, and B to every C, it follows necessarily, that A may be attributed to every C." For disproving the illegitimate modes, he uses the same manner; with this difference, that he commonly for an example gives three real terms, such as, *bonum, habitus, prudentia;* of which three terms you are to make up a syllogism of the figure and mode in question, which will appear to be inconclusive.

The commentators and systematical writers in logic, have supplied this defect; <371> and given us real examples of every legitimate mode in all the figures. We acknowledge this to be charitably done, in order to assist the conception in matters so very abstract; but whether it was prudently done for the honour of the art, may be doubted. I am afraid this was to uncover the nakedness of the theory: it has undoubtedly contributed to bring it into contempt; for when one considers the silly and uninstructive reasonings that have been brought forth by this grand organ of science, he can hardly forbear crying out, *Parturiunt montes, et nascitur ridiculus mus.* [21] Many of the writers of logic are acute and ingenious, and much practised in the syllogistical art; and there must be some reason why the examples they have given of syllogisms are so lean.

We shall speak of the reason afterwards; and shall now give a syllogism in each figure as an example.

> No work of God is bad;
> The natural passions and appetites of men are the work of God;
> Therefore none of them is bad.

In this syllogism, the middle term, *work of God,* is the subject of the major and <372> the predicate of the minor; so that the syllogism is of the first figure. The mode is that called *Celarent;* the major and conclusion being both universal negatives, and the minor an universal affirmative. It agrees to the rules of the figure, as the major is universal, and the minor affirmative; it is also agreeable to all the general rules; so that it maintains its character in every trial. And to show of what ductile materials syllogisms are made, we may, by converting simply the major proposition, reduce it to a good syllogism of the second figure, and of the mode *Cesare,* thus:

> Whatever is bad is not the work of God;
> All the natural passions and appetites of men are the work of God;
> Therefore they are not bad.

Another example:

> Every thing virtuous is praise-worthy;
> Some pleasures are not praise-worthy;
> Therefore some pleasures are not virtuous.

---

21. "Mountains will labour, to birth will come a laughter-rousing mouse": Horace, *Ars poetica,* l. 139 (trans. Rushton Fairclough).

Here the middle term *praise-worthy* being the predicate of both premises, the syllogism is of the second figure; and seeing it is made up of the
propositions, A, <373> O, O, the mode is *Baroco.* It will be found to agree
both with the general and special rules: and it may be reduced into a good
syllogism of the first figure upon converting the major by contraposition,
thus:

> What is not praise-worthy is not virtuous;
> Some pleasures are not praise-worthy;
> Therefore some pleasures are not virtuous.

That this syllogism is conclusive, common sense pronounces, and all
logicians must allow; but it is somewhat unpliable to rules, and requires a
little straining to make it tally with them.

That it is of the first figure is beyond dispute; but to what mode of that
figure shall we refer it? This is a question of some difficulty. For, in the first
place, the premises seem to be both negative, which contradicts the third
general rule; and moreover, it is contrary to a special rule of the first figure,
That the minor should be negative. These are the difficulties to be removed.

Some logicians think, that the two negative particles in the major are
equivalent <374> to an affirmative; and that therefore the major proposition, *What is not praise-worthy, is not virtuous,* is to be accounted an affirmative proposition. This, if granted, solves one difficulty; but the other
remains. The most ingenious solution, therefore, is this: Let the middle
term be *not praise-worthy.* Thus, making the negative particle a part of the
middle term, the syllogism stands thus:

> Whatever is *not praise-worthy* is not virtuous;
> Some pleasures are *not praise-worthy;*
> Therefore some pleasures are not virtuous.

By this analysis, the major becomes an universal negative, the minor a particular affirmative, and the conclusion a particular negative, and so we have
a just syllogism in *Ferio.*

We see, by this example, that the quality of propositions is not so invariable, but that, when occasion requires, an affirmative may be degraded
into a negative, or a negative exalted to an affirmative. Another example:

All Africans are black;
All Africans are men; <375>
Therefore some men are black.

This is of the third figure, and of the mode *Darapti;* and it may be reduced to *Darii* in the first figure, by converting the minor.

All Africans are black;
Some men are Africans;
Therefore some men are black.

By this time I apprehend the reader has got as many examples of syllogisms as will stay his appetite for that kind of entertainment.

SECTION 4

On the Demonstration of the Theory.

Aristotle and all his followers have thought it necessary, in order to bring this theory of categorical syllogisms to a science, to demonstrate, both that the fourteen authorised modes conclude justly, and that none of the rest do. Let us now see how this has been executed.

As to the legitimate modes, Aristotle and those who follow him the most closely, demonstrate the four modes of the first figure directly from an axiom called the <376> *Dictum de omni et nullo.* The amount of the axiom is, That what is affirmed of a whole *genus,* may be affirmed of all the species and individuals belonging to that *genus;* and that what is denied of the whole genus, may be denied of its species and individuals. The four modes of the first figure are evidently included in this axiom. And as to the legitimate modes of the other figures, they are proved by reducing them to some mode of the first. Nor is there any other principle assumed in these reductions but the axioms concerning the conversion of propositions, and in some cases the axioms concerning the opposition of propositions.

As to the illegitimate modes, Aristotle has taken the labour to try and condemn them one by one in all the three figures: but this is done in such a manner that it is very painful to follow him. To give a specimen. In order to prove, that those modes of the first figure in which the major is particular, do not conclude, he proceeds thus: "If A is or is not in some B, and B in every C, no conclusion follows. Take for the terms in the affirmative case, *good, habit, prudence,* in the nega-<377>tive, *good, habit, ignorance."* This laconic style, the use of symbols not familiar, and, in place of giving an example, his leaving us to form one from three assigned terms, give such embarrassment to a reader, that he is like one reading a book of riddles.

Having thus ascertained the true and false modes of a figure, he subjoins the particular rules of that figure, which seem to be deduced from the particular cases before determined. The general rules come last of all, as a general corollary from what goes before.

I know not whether it is from a diffidence of Aristotle's demonstrations, or from an apprehension of their obscurity, or from a desire of improving upon his method, that almost all the writers in logic I have met with, have inverted his order, beginning where he ends, and ending where he begins. They first demonstrate the general rules, which belong to all the figures, from three axioms; then from the general rules and the nature of each figure, they demonstrate the special rules of each figure. When this is done, nothing remains but to apply these general and <378> special rules, and to reject every mode which contradicts them.

This method has a very scientific appearance: and when we consider, that by a few rules once demonstrated, an hundred and seventy-eight false modes are destroyed at one blow, which Aristotle had the trouble to put to death one by one, it seems to be a great improvement. I have only one objection to the three axioms.

The three axioms are these: 1. Things which agree with the same third, agree with one another. 2. When one agrees with the third, and the other does not, they do not agree with one another. 3. When neither agrees with the third, you cannot thence conclude, either that they do, or do not agree with one another. If these axioms are applied to mathematical quantities, to which they seem to relate when taken literally, they have all the evidence that an axiom ought to have: but the logicians apply them in an analogical sense to things of another nature. In order, therefore, to judge whether they are truly axioms, we ought to strip them of their figurative dress, and to set them down in plain English, as the logicians <379> understand them. They amount therefore to this. 1. If two things be affirmed of a third, or the third be affirmed of them; or if one be affirmed of the third, and the third affirmed of the other; then they may be affirmed one of the other. 2. If one is affirmed of the third, or the third of it, and the other denied of the third, or the third of it, they may be denied one of the other. 3. If both are denied of the third, or the third of them; or if one is denied of the third, and the third denied of the other; nothing can be inferred.

When the three axioms are thus put in plain English, they seem not to have that degree of evidence which axioms ought to have; and if there is any defect of evidence in the axioms, this defect will be communicated to the whole edifice raised upon them.

It may even be suspected, that an attempt by any method to demonstrate that a syllogism is conclusive, is an impropriety somewhat like that of attempting to demonstrate an axiom. In a just syllogism, the connection between the premises and the conclusion is not only real, but <380> immediate; so that no proposition can come between them to make their connection more apparent. The very intention of a syllogism is, to leave nothing to be supplied that is necessary to a complete demonstration. Therefore a man of common understanding who has a perfect comprehension of the premises, finds himself under a necessity of admitting the conclusion, supposing the premises to be true; and the conclusion is connected with the premises with all the force of intuitive evidence. In a word, an immediate conclusion is seen in the premises, by the light of common sense; and where that is wanting, no kind of reasoning will supply its place.

SECTION 5

On this Theory, considered as an Engine of Science.

The slow progress of useful knowledge, during the many ages in which the syllogistic art was most highly cultivated as the only guide to science, and its quick progress since that art was disused, suggest a presumption against it; and this presump-<381>tion is strengthened by the puerility of the examples which have always been brought to illustrate its rules.

The ancients seem to have had too high notions, both of the force of the reasoning power in man, and of the art of syllogism as its guide. Mere reasoning can carry us but a very little way in most subjects. By observation, and experiments properly conducted, the stock of human knowledge may be enlarged without end; but the power of reasoning alone, applied with vigour through a long life, would only carry a man round, like a horse in a mill who labours hard but makes no progress. There is indeed an exception to this observation in the mathematical sciences. The relations of quantity are so various and so susceptible of exact mensuration, that long trains of accurate reasoning on that subject may be formed, and conclusions drawn very remote from the first principles. It is in this science and those which depend upon it, that the power of reasoning triumphs; in other matters its trophies are inconsiderable. If any man doubt this, let him produce, in any subject unconnected with mathematics, a train <382> of reasoning of some length, leading to a conclusion, which without this train of reasoning would never have been brought within human sight. Every man acquainted with mathematics can produce thousands of such trains of reasoning. I do not say, that none such can be produced in other sciences; but I believe they are few, and not easily found; and that if they are found, it will not be in subjects that can be expressed by categorical propositions, to which alone the theory of figure and mode extends.

In matters to which that theory extends, a man of good sense, who can distinguish things that differ, can avoid the snares of ambiguous words, and is moderately practised in such matters, sees at once all that can be inferred from the premises; or finds, that there is but a very short step to the conclusion.

When the power of reasoning is so feeble by nature, especially in subjects to which this theory can be applied, it would be unreasonable to expect great effects from it. And hence we see the reason why the examples brought to illustrate it <383> by the most ingenious logicians, have rather tended to bring it into contempt.

If it should be thought, that the syllogistic art may be an useful engine in mathematics, in which pure reasoning has ample scope: First, It may be observed, That facts are unfavourable to this opinion: for it does not appear, that Euclid, or Apollonius, or Archimedes, or Hugens, or Newton, ever made the least use of this art; and I am even of opinion, that no use can be made of it in mathematics. I would not wish to advance this rashly, since

Aristotle has said, that mathematicians reason for the most part in the first figure. What led him to think so was, that the first figure only yields conclusions that are universal and affirmative, and the conclusions of mathematics are commonly of that kind. But it is to be observed, that the propositions of mathematics are not categorical propositions, consisting of one subject and one predicate. They express some relation which one quantity bears to another, and on that account must have three terms. The quantities compared make two, and the relation between them is a third. Now to such pro-<384>positions we can neither apply the rules concerning the conversion of propositions, nor can they enter into a syllogism of any of the figures or modes. We observed before, that this conversion, *A is greater than B,* therefore *B is less than A,* does not fall within the rules of conversion given by Aristotle or the logicians; and we now add, that this simple reasoning, *A is equal to B, and B to C;* therefore *A is equal to C,* cannot be brought into any syllogism in figure and mode. There are indeed syllogisms into which mathematical propositions may enter, and of such we shall afterwards speak: but they have nothing to do with the system of figure and mode.

When we go without the circle of the mathematical sciences, I know nothing in which there seems to be so much demonstration as in that part of logic which treats of the figures and modes of syllogism; but the few remarks we have made, shew, that it has some weak places: and besides, this system cannot be used as an engine to rear itself.

The compass of the syllogistic system as an engine of science, may be discerned by <385> a compendious and general view of the conclusion drawn, and the argument used to prove it, in each of the three figures.

In the first figure, the conclusion affirms or denies something of a certain species or individual; and the argument to prove this conclusion is, That the same thing may be affirmed or denied of the whole genus to which that species or individual belongs.

In the second figure, the conclusion is, That some species or individual does not belong to such a genus; and the argument is, That some attribute common to the whole genus does not belong to that species or individual.

In the third figure, the conclusion is, That such an attribute belongs to part of a genus; and the argument is, That the attribute in question belongs to a species or individual which is part of that genus.

I apprehend, that in this short view, every conclusion that falls within the compass of the three figures, as well as the mean of proof, is comprehended. The rules of all the figures might be easily deduced from it; and it appears, that there <386> is only one principle of reasoning in all the three; so that it is not strange, that a syllogism of one figure should be reduced to one of another figure.

The general principle in which the whole terminates, and of which every categorical syllogism is only a particular application, is this, That what is affirmed or denied of the whole genus, may be affirmed or denied of every species and individual belonging to it. This is a principle of undoubted certainty indeed, but of no great depth. Aristotle and all the logicians assume it as an axiom or first principle, from which the syllogistic system, as it were, takes its departure: and after a tedious voyage, and great expence of demonstration, it lands at last in this principle as its ultimate conclusion. *O curas hominum! O quantum est in rebus inane!*[22]

SECTION 6

On Modal Syllogisms.

Categorical propositions, besides their quantity and quality, have another affection, by which they are divided into pure and modal. In a pure proposition, the <387> predicate is barely affirmed or denied of the subject; but in a modal proposition, the affirmation or negation is modified, by being declared to be necessary, or contingent, or possible, or impossible. These are the four modes observed by Aristotle, from which he denominates a proposition modal. His genuine disciples maintain, that these are all the modes that can affect an affirmation or negation, and that the enumeration is complete. Others maintain, that this enumeration is incomplete; and that when an affirmation or negation is said to be certain or uncertain, probable or improbable, this makes a modal proposition, no less than the four modes of Aristotle. We shall not enter into this dispute; but proceed to observe, that the epithets of *pure* and *modal* are applied to syllogisms as well as to

22. "O the vanity of mankind! How vast the void in human affairs!": Persius Flaccus, *Satires,* I, l. 1 (trans. Ramsay).

propositions. A pure syllogism is that in which both premises are pure propositions. A modal syllogism is that in which either of the premises is a modal proposition.

The syllogisms of which we have already said so much, are those only which are pure as well as categorical. But when we consider, that through all the figures <388> and modes, a syllogism may have one premise modal of any of the four modes, while the other is pure, or it may have both premises modal, and that they may be either of the same mode or of different modes; what prodigious variety arises from all these combinations? Now it is the business of a logician, to shew how the conclusion is affected in all this variety of cases. Aristotle has done this in his First Analytics, with immense labour; and it will not be thought strange, that when he had employed only four chapters in discussing one hundred and ninety-two modes, true and false, of pure syllogisms, he should employ fifteen upon modal syllogisms.

I am very willing to excuse myself from entering upon this great branch of logic, by the judgement and example of those who cannot be charged either with want of respect to Aristotle, or with a low esteem of the syllogistic art.

Keckerman, a famous Dantzican professor, who spent his life in teaching and writing logic, in his huge folio system of that science, published *ann.* 1600, calls the doctrine of the modals the *crux logi-*<389>*corum.* With regard to the scholastic doctors, among whom this was a proverb, *De modalibus non gustabit asinus,* [23] he thinks it very dubious, whether they tortured most the modal syllogisms, or were most tortured by them. But those crabbed geniuses, says he, made this doctrine so very thorny, that it is fitter to tear a man's wits in pieces than to give them solidity. He desires it to be observed, that the doctrine of the modals is adapted to the Greek language. The modal terms were frequently used by the Greeks in their disputations; and, on that account, are so fully handled by Aristotle: but in the Latin tongue you shall hardly ever meet with them. Nor do I remember, in all my experience, says he, to have observed any man in danger of being foiled in a dispute, through his ignorance of the modals.

23. "Even a donkey will not eat the modes [of syllogisms]."

This author, however, out of respect to Aristotle, treats pretty fully of modal propositions, shewing how to distinguish their subject and predicate, their quantity and quality. But the modal syllogisms he passes over altogether.

Ludovicus Vives, whom I mention, not as a devotee of Aristotle, but on ac-<390>count of his own judgement and learning, thinks that the doctrine of modals ought to be banished out of logic, and remitted to grammar; and that if the grammar of the Greek tongue had been brought to a system in the time of Aristotle, that most acute philosopher would have saved the great labour he has bestowed on this subject.

Burgersdick, after enumerating five classes of modal syllogisms, observes, that they require many rules and cautions, which Aristotle hath handled diligently; but that as the use of them is not great and their rules difficult, he thinks it not worth while to enter into the discussion of them; recommending to those who would understand them, the most learned paraphrase of Joannes Monlorius upon the first book of the First Analytics.

All the writers of logic for two hundred years back that have fallen into my hands, have passed over the rules of modal syllogisms with as little ceremony. So that this great branch of the doctrine of syllogism, so diligently handled by Aristotle, fell into neglect, if not contempt, even while the doctrine of pure syllogisms con-<391>tinued in the highest esteem. Moved by these authorities, I shall let this doctrine rest in peace, without giving the least disturbance to its ashes.

SECTION 7

On Syllogisms that do not belong to Figure and Mode.

Aristotle gives some observations upon imperfect syllogisms: such as, the Enthimema, in which one of the premises is not expressed but understood: Induction, wherein we collect an universal from a full enumeration of particulars: and Examples, which are an imperfect induction. The logicians have copied Aristotle upon these kinds of reasoning, without any considerable improvement. But to compensate the modal syllogisms, which they have laid aside, they have given rules for several kinds of syllogism, of which Aristotle takes no notice. These may be reduced to two classes.

The first class comprehends the syllogisms into which any exclusive, re-
strictive, exceptive, or reduplicative proposition enters. Such propositions
are by some called <392> *exponible,* by others *imperfectly modal.* The rules
given with regard to these are obvious, from a just interpretation of the
propositions.

The second class is that of hypothetical syllogisms, which take that denomination from having a hypothetical proposition for one or both premises. Most logicians give the name of *hypothetical* to all complex propositions which have more terms than one subject and one predicate. I use the
word in this large sense; and mean by hypothetical syllogisms, all those in
which either of the premises consists of more terms than two. How many
various kinds there may be of such syllogisms, has never been ascertained.
The logicians have given names to some; such as, the copulative, the con-
ditional by some called hypothetical, and the disjunctive.

Such syllogisms cannot be tried by the rules of figure and mode. Every
kind would require rules peculiar to itself. Logicians have given rules for
some kinds; but there are many that have not so much as a name.

The Dilemma is considered by most logicians as a species of the disjunctive syl-<393>logism. A remarkable property of this kind is, that it may
sometimes be happily retorted: it is, it seems, like a hand-grenade, which
by dextrous management may be thrown back, so as to spend its force upon
the assailant. We shall conclude this tedious account of syllogisms, with a
dilemma mentioned by *A. Gellius,* and from him by many logicians, as
insoluble in any other way.

> Euathlus, a rich young man, desirous of learning the art of pleading, ap-
> plied to Protagoras, a celebrated sophist, to instruct him, promising a great
> sum of money as his reward; one half of which was paid down; the other
> half he bound himself to pay as soon as he should plead a cause before
> the judges, and gain it. Protagoras found him a very apt scholar; but, after
> he had made good progress, he was in no haste to plead causes. The master,
> conceiving that he intended by this means to shift off his second payment,
> took, as he thought, a sure method to get the better of his delay. He sued
> Euathlus before the judges; and, having opened his cause at the bar, he
> pleaded to this <394> purpose. O most foolish young man, do you not
> see, that, in any event, I must gain my point? for if the judges give sentence

for me, you must pay by their sentence; if against me, the condition of our bargain is fulfilled, and you have no plea left for your delay, after having pleaded and gained a cause. To which Euathlus answered. O most wise master, I might have avoided the force of your argument, by not pleading my own cause. But, giving up this advantage, do you not see, that whatever sentence the judges pass, I am safe? If they give sentence for me, I am acquitted by their sentence; if against me, the condition of our bargain is not fulfilled, by my pleading a cause, and losing it. The judges, thinking the arguments unanswerable on both sides, put off the cause to a long day. <395>

CHAPTER V.

Account of the remaining books of the Organon.

SECTION I

Of the Last Analytics.[24]

In the First Analytics, syllogisms are considered in respect of their form; they are now to be considered in respect of their matter. The form lies in the necessary connection between the premises and the conclusion; and where such a connection is wanting, they are said to be informal, or vicious in point of form.

But where there is no fault in the form, there may be in the matter; that is, in the propositions of which they are composed, which may be true or false, probable or improbable.

When the premises are certain, and the conclusion drawn from them in due form, this is demonstration, and produces science. Such syllogisms are called *apodic-*<396>*tical;* and are handled in the two books of the Last Analytics. When the premises are not certain, but probable only, such syllo-

---

24. Now generally known as the *Posterior Analytics.*

gisins are called *dialectical;* and of them he treats in the eight books of the
Topics. But there are some syllogisms which seem to be perfect both in
matter and form, when they are not really so: as, a face may seem beautiful
which is but painted. These being apt to deceive, and produce a false opinion, are called *sophistical;* and they are the subject of the book concerning
Sophisms.

To return to the Last Analytics, which treat of demonstration and of
science: We shall not pretend to abridge these books; for Aristotle's writings
do not admit of abridgement: no man in fewer words can say what he says;
and he is not often guilty of repetition. We shall only give some of his
capital conclusions, omitting his long reasonings and nice distinctions, of
which his genius was wonderfully productive.

All demonstration must be built upon principles already known; and
these upon others of the same kind; until we come at last to first principles,
which neither <397> can be demonstrated, nor need to be, being evident
of themselves.

We cannot demonstrate things in a circle, supporting the conclusion by
the premises, and the premises by the conclusion. Nor can there be an infinite
number of middle terms between the first principle and the conclusion.

In all demonstration, the first principles, the conclusion, and all the intermediate propositions, must be necessary, general, and eternal truths: for
of things fortuitous, contingent, or mutable, or of individual things, there
is no demonstration.

Some demonstrations prove only, that the thing is thus affected; others
prove, why it is thus affected. The former may be drawn from a remote
cause, or from an effect: but the latter must be drawn from an immediate
cause; and are the most perfect.

The first figure is best adapted to demonstration, because it affords conclusions universally affirmative; and this figure is commonly used by the
mathematicians.

The demonstration of an affirmative proposition is preferable to that of
a nega-<398>tive; the demonstration of an universal to that of a particular;
and direct demonstration to that *ad absurdum.*

The principles are more certain than the conclusion.

There cannot be opinion and science of the same thing at the same time.

In the second book we are taught, that the questions that may be put with regard to any thing, are four: 1. Whether the thing be thus affected. 2. Why it is thus affected. 3. Whether it exists. 4. What it is.

The last of these questions Aristotle, in good Greek, calls the *What is it* of a thing. The schoolmen, in very barbarous Latin, called this, the *quiddity* of a thing. This quiddity, he proves by many arguments, cannot be demonstrated, but must be fixed by a definition. This gives occasion to treat of definition, and how a right definition should be formed. As an example, he gives a definition of the number *three,* and defines it to be the first odd number.

In this book he treats also of the four kinds of causes; efficient, material, formal, and final.

Another thing treated of in this book is, <399> the manner in which we acquire first principles, which are the foundation of all demonstration. These are not innate, because we may be for a great part of life ignorant of them: nor can they be deduced demonstratively from any antecedent knowledge, otherwise they would not be first principles. Therefore he concludes, that first principles are got by induction, from the informations of sense. The senses give us informations of individual things, and from these by induction we draw general conclusions: for it is a maxim with Aristotle, That there is nothing in the understanding which was not before in some sense.

The knowledge of first principles, as it is not acquired by demonstration, ought not to be called science; and therefore he calls it *intelligence.*

SECTION 2

Of the Topics.

The professed design of the Topics is, to shew a method by which a man may be able to reason with probability and con-<400>sistency upon every question that can occur.

Every question is either about the genus of the subject, or its specific difference, or some thing proper to it, or something accidental.

To prove that this division is complete, Aristotle reasons thus: Whatever

is attributed to a subject, it must either be, that the subject can be recip-
rocally attributed to it, or that it cannot. If the subject and attribute can
be reciprocated, the attribute either declares what the subject is, and then
it is a definition; or it does not declare what the subject is, and then it is a
property. If the attribute cannot be reciprocated, it must be something contained in the definition, or not. If it be contained in the definition of the
subject, it must be the genus of the subject, or its specific difference; for
the definition consists of these two. If it be not contained in the definition
of the subject, it must be an accident.

The furniture proper to fit a man for arguing dialectically may be reduced
to these four heads: 1. Probable propositions of all sorts, which may on
occasion be assumed <401> in an argument. 2. Distinctions of words which
are nearly of the same signification. 3. Distinctions of things which are not
so far asunder but that they may be taken for one and the same. 4. Simil-
itudes.

The second and the five following books are taken up in enumerating the
topics or heads of argument that may be used in questions about the genus,
the definition, the properties, and the accidents of a thing; and occasionally
he introduces the topics for proving things to be the same, or different; and
the topics for proving one thing to be better or worse than another.

In this enumeration of topics, Aristotle has shewn more the fertility of
his genius, than the accuracy of method. The writers of logic seem to be
of this opinion: for I know none of them that has followed him closely
upon this subject. They have considered the topics of argumentation as
reducible to certain axioms. For instance, when the question is about the
genus of a thing, it must be determined by some axiom about genus and
species; when it is about a definition, it must be determined by some axiom
relating to definition, and things defined: and so of other questions. <402>
They have therefore reduced the doctrine of the topics to certain axioms
or canons, and disposed these axioms in order under certain heads.

This method seems to be more commodious and elegant than that of
Aristotle. Yet it must be acknowledged, that Aristotle has furnished the materials from which all the logicians have borrowed their doctrine of topics:
and even Cicero, Quintilian, and other rhetorical writers, have been much
indebted to the topics of Aristotle.

He was the first, as far as I know, who made an attempt of this kind: and in this he acted up to the magnanimity of his own genius, and that of ancient philosophy. Every subject of human thought had been reduced to ten categories; every thing that can be attributed to any subject, to five predicables: he attempted to reduce all the forms of reasoning to fixed rules of figure and mode, and to reduce all the topics of argumentation under certain heads; and by that means to collect as it were into one store all that can be said on one side or the other of every question, and to provide a grand arsenal, from <403> which all future combatants might be furnished with arms offensive and defensive in every cause, so as to leave no room to future generations to invent any thing new.

The last book of the Topics is a code of the laws according to which a syllogistical disputation ought to be managed, both on the part of the assailant and defendant. From which it is evident, that this philosopher trained his disciples to contend, not for truth merely, but for victory.

SECTION 3

Of the book concerning Sophisms.

A syllogism which leads to a false conclusion, must be vicious, either in matter or form: for from true principles nothing but truth can be justly deduced. If the matter be faulty, that is, if either of the premises be false, that premise must be denied by the defendant. If the form be faulty, some rule of syllogism is transgressed; and it is the part of the defendant to shew, what general or special rule it is that is transgressed. So that, if he be an able logician, he will be impregnable in the <404> defence of truth, and may resist all the attacks of the sophist. But as there are syllogisms which may seem to be perfect both in matter and form, when they are not really so, as a piece of money may seem to be good coin when it is adulterate; such fallacious syllogisms are considered in this treatise, in order to make a defendant more expert in the use of his defensive weapons.

And here the author, with his usual magnanimity, attempts to bring all the fallacies that can enter into a syllogism under thirteen heads; of which six lie in the diction or language, and seven not in the diction.

The fallacies in diction are, 1. When an ambiguous word is taken at one time in one sense, and at another time in another. 2. When an ambiguous phrase is taken in the same manner. 3. and 4. are ambiguities in syntax; when words are conjoined in syntax that ought to be disjoined; or disjoined when they ought to be conjoined. 5. is an ambiguity in prosody, accent, or pronunciation. 6. An ambiguity arising from some figure of speech. <405>

When a sophism of any of these kinds is translated into another language, or even rendered into unambiguous expressions in the same language, the fallacy is evident, and the syllogism appears to have four terms.

The seven fallacies which are said not to be in the diction, but in the thing, have their proper names in Greek and in Latin, by which they are distinguished. Without minding their names, we shall give a brief account of their nature.

1. The first is, Taking an accidental conjunction of things for a natural or necessary connection: as, when from an accident we infer a property; when from an example we infer a rule; when from a single act we infer a habit.

2. Taking that absolutely which ought to be taken comparatively, or with a certain limitation. The construction of language often leads into this fallacy: for in all languages, it is common to use absolute terms to signify things that carry in them some secret comparison; or to use unlimited terms, to signify what from its nature must be limited.

3. Taking that for the cause of a thing <406> which is only an occasion, or concomitant.

4. Begging the question. This is done, when the thing to be proved, or some thing equivalent, is assumed in the premises.

5. Mistaking the question. When the conclusion of the syllogism is not the thing that ought to be proved, but something else that is mistaken for it.

6. When that which is not a consequence is mistaken for a consequence; as if, because all Africans are black, it were taken for granted that all blacks are Africans.

7. The last fallacy lies in propositions that are complex, and imply two affirmations, whereof one may be true, and the other false; so that whether you grant the proposition, or deny it, you are intangled: as when it is affirmed, that such a man has left off playing the fool. If it be granted, it

implies, that he did play the fool formerly. If it be denied, it implies, or seems to imply, that he plays the fool still.

In this enumeration, we ought, in justice to Aristotle, to expect only the fallacies incident to categorical syllogisms. <407> And I do not find, that the logicians have made any additions to it when taken in this view; although they have given some other fallacies that are incident to syllogisms of the hypothetical kind, particularly the fallacy of an incomplete enumeration in disjunctive syllogisms and dilemmas.

The different species of sophisms above mentioned are not so precisely defined by Aristotle, or by subsequent logicians, but that they allow of great latitude in the application; and it is often dubious under what particular species a sophistical syllogism ought to be classed. We even find the same example brought under one species by one author, and under another species by another. Nay, what is more strange, Aristotle himself employs a long chapter in proving by a particular induction, that all the seven may be brought under that which we have called *mistaking the question,* and which is commonly called *ignoratio elenchi.* And indeed the proof of this is easy, without that laborious detail which Aristotle uses for the purpose: for if you lop off from the conclusion of a sophistical syllogism all that is not sup-<408>ported by the premises, the conclusion, in that case, will always be found different from that which ought to have been proved; and so it falls under the *ignoratio elenchi.*

It was probably Aristotle's aim, to reduce all the possible variety of sophisms, as he had attempted to do of just syllogisms, to certain definite species: but he seems to be sensible that he had fallen short in this last attempt. When a genus is properly divided into its species, the species should not only, when taken together, exhaust the whole genus; but every species should have its own precinct so accurately defined, that one shall not encroach upon another. And when an individual can be said to belong to two or three different species, the division is imperfect; yet this is the case of Aristotle's division of the sophisms, by his own acknowledgement. It ought not therefore to be taken for a division strictly logical. It may rather be compared to the several species or forms of action invented in law for the redress of wrongs. For every wrong there is a remedy in law by one action or another: but sometimes a man <409> may take his choice among several different actions. So every sophistical syllogism may, by a little art, be brought under one or other of the species mentioned by Aristotle, and very often you may take your choice of two or three.

Besides the enumeration of the various kinds of sophisms, there are many other things in this treatise concerning the art of managing a syllogistical dispute with an antagonist. And indeed, if the passion for this kind of litigation, which reigned for so many ages, should ever again lift up its head, we may predict, that the Organon of Aristotle will then become a fashionable study: for it contains such admirable materials and documents for this art, that it may be said to have brought it to a science.

The conclusion of this treatise ought not to be overlooked: it manifestly relates, not to the present treatise only, but also to the whole analytics and topics of the author. I shall therefore give the substance of it.

> Of those who may be called inventers, some have made important additions to things long before begun, and carried < 410 > on through a course of ages; others have given a small beginning to things which, in succeeding times, will be brought to greater perfection. The beginning of a thing, though small, is the chief part of it, and requires the greatest degree of invention; for it is easy to make additions to inventions once begun. Now with regard to the dialectical art, there was not something done, and something remaining to be done. There was absolutely nothing done: for those who professed the art of disputation, had only a set of orations composed, and of arguments, and of captious questions, which might suit many occasions. These their scholars soon learned, and fitted to the occasion. This was not to teach you the art, but to furnish you with the materials produced by the art: as if a man professing to teach you the art of making shoes, should bring you a parcel of shoes of various sizes and shapes, from which you may provide those who want. This may have its use; but it is not to teach the art of making shoes. And indeed, with regard to rhetorical decla-<411>mation, there are many precepts handed down from ancient times; but with regard to the construction of syllogisms, not one.
>
> We have therefore employed much time and labour upon this subject; and if our system appear to you not to be in the number of those things, which, being before carried a certain length, were left to be perfected; we hope for your favourable acceptance of what is done, and your indulgence in what is left imperfect.

CHAPTER VI.

Reflections on the Utility of Logic, and the Means of its improvement.

SECTION I

Of the Utility of Logic.

Men rarely leave one extreme without running into the contrary. It is no wonder, therefore, that the excessive admiration of Aristotle, which continued for <412> so many ages, should end in an undue contempt; and that the high esteem of logic as the grand engine of science, should at last make way for too unfavourable an opinion, which seems now prevalent, of its being unworthy of a place in a liberal education. Those who think according to the fashion, as the greatest part of men do, will be as prone to go into this extreme, as their grandfathers were to go into the contrary.

Laying aside prejudice, whether fashionable or unfashionable, let us consider whether logic is, or may be made, subservient to any good purpose. Its professed end is, to teach men to think, to judge, and to reason, with precision and accuracy. No man will say that this is a matter of no importance; the only thing therefore that admits of doubt, is, whether it can be taught.

To resolve this doubt, it may be observed, that our rational faculty is the gift of God, given to men in very different measure. Some have a large portion, some a less; and where there is a remarkable defect of the natural power, it cannot be supplied by any culture. But this natural <413> power, even where it is the strongest, may lie dead for want of the means of improvement: a savage may have been born with as good faculties as a Bacon or a Newton: but his talent was buried, being never put to use; while theirs was cultivated to the best advantage.

It may likewise be observed, that the chief mean of improving our rational power, is the vigorous exercise of it, in various ways and in different subjects, by which the habit is acquired of exercising it properly. Without such exercise, and good sense over and above, a man who has studied logic all his life, may after all be only a petulant wrangler, without true judgement or skill of reasoning in any science.

I take this to be Locke's meaning, when in his Thoughts on Education he says, "If you would have your son to reason well, let him read Chillingworth." The state of things is much altered since Locke wrote. Logic has been much improved, chiefly by his writings; and yet much less stress is laid upon it, and less time consumed in it. His counsel, therefore, was judicious and seasonable; to wit, <414> That the improvement of our reasoning power is to be expected much more from an intimate acquaintance with the authors who reason the best, than from studying voluminous systems of logic. But if he had meant, that the study of logic was of no use nor deserved any attention, he surely would not have taken the pains to have made so considerable an addition to it, by his *Essay on the Human Understanding,* and by his *Thoughts on the Conduct of the Understanding.* Nor would he have remitted his pupil to Chillingworth, the acutest logician as well as the best reasoner of his age; and one who, in innumerable places of his excellent book, without pedantry even in that pedantic age, makes the happiest application of the rules of logic, for unravelling the sophistical reasoning of his antagonist.

Our reasoning power makes no appearance in infancy; but as we grow up, it unfolds itself by degrees, like the bud of a tree. When a child first draws an inference, or perceives the force of an inference drawn by another, we may call this *the birth of his reason:* but it is yet like a new-born babe, weak and tender; it must <415> be cherished, carried in arms, and have food of easy digestion, till it gather strength.

I believe no man remembers the birth of his reason: but it is probable that his decisions are at first weak and wavering; and, compared with that steady conviction which he acquires in ripe years, are like the dawn of the morning compared with noon-day. We see that the reason of children yields to authority, as a reed to the wind; nay, that it clings to it, and leans upon it, as if conscious of its own weakness.

When reason acquires such strength as to stand on its own bottom, without the aid of authority or even in opposition to authority, this may be called its *manly age.* But in most men, it hardly ever arrives at this period.

Many, by their situation in life, have not the opportunity of cultivating their rational powers. Many, from the habit they have acquired of submitting their opinions to the authority of others, or from some other principle which operates more powerfully than the love of truth, suffer their judgement to be carried along to the end of their days, either by <416> the authority of a leader, or of a party, or of the multitude, or by their own passions. Such persons, however learned, however acute, may be said to be all their days children in understanding. They reason, they dispute, and perhaps write: but it is not that they may find the truth; but that they may defend opinions which have descended to them by inheritance, or into which they have fallen by accident, or been led by affection.

I agree with Mr. Locke, that there is no study better fitted to exercise and strengthen the reasoning powers, than that of the mathematical sciences; for two reasons; first, Because there is no other branch of science which gives such scope to long and accurate trains of reasoning; and, secondly, Because in mathematics there is no room for authority, nor for prejudice of any kind, which may give a false bias to the judgement.

When a youth of moderate parts begins to study Euclid, every thing at first is new to him. His apprehension is unsteady: his judgement is feeble; and rests partly upon the evidence of the thing, and partly upon the authority of his teacher. But <417> every time he goes over the definitions, the axioms, the elementary propositions, more light breaks in upon him: the language becomes familiar, and conveys clear and steady conceptions: the judgement is confirmed: he begins to see what demonstration is; and it is impossible to see it without being charmed with it. He perceives it to be a kind of evidence that has no need of authority to strengthen it. He finds himself emancipated from that bondage; and exults so much in this new state of independence, that he spurns at authority, and would have demonstration for every thing; until experience teaches him, that this is a kind of evidence that cannot be had in most things; and that in his most important concerns, he must rest contented with probability.

As he goes on in mathematics, the road of demonstration becomes smooth and easy: he can walk in it firmly, and take wider steps: and at last he acquires the habit, not only of understanding a demonstration, but of discovering and demonstrating mathematical truths.

Thus, a man, without rules of logic, may acquire a habit of reasoning justly in <418> mathematics; and, I believe, he may, by like means, acquire a habit of reasoning justly in mechanics, in jurisprudence, in politics, or in any other science. Good sense, good examples, and assiduous exercise, may bring a man to reason justly and acutely in his own profession, without rules.

But if any man think, that from this concession he may infer the inutility of logic, he betrays a great want of that art by this inference: for it is no better reasoning than this, That because a man may go from Edinburgh to London by the way of Paris, therefore any other road is useless.

There is perhaps no practical art which may not be acquired, in a very considerable degree, by example and practice, without reducing it to rules. But practice, joined with rules, may carry a man on in his art farther and more quickly, than practice without rules. Every ingenious artist knows the utility of having his art reduced to rules, and by that means made a science. He is thereby enlightened in his practice, and works with more assurance. By rules, he sometimes corrects <419> his own errors, and often detects the errors of others: he finds them of great use to confirm his judgement, to justify what is right, and to condemn what is wrong.

Is it of no use in reasoning, to be well acquainted with the various powers of the human understanding, by which we reason? Is it of no use, to resolve the various kinds of reasoning into their simple elements; and to discover, as far as we are able, the rules by which these elements are combined in judging and in reasoning? Is it of no use, to mark the various fallacies in reasoning, by which even the most ingenious men have been led into error? It must surely betray great want of understanding, to think these things useless or unimportant. These are the things which logicians have attempted; and which they have executed; not indeed so completely as to leave no room for improvement, but in such a manner as to give very considerable aid to our reasoning powers. That the principles laid down with regard to definition and division, with regard to the conversion and opposition of propositions and the general rules of reasoning, are not without use, is suffi-<420>ciently apparent from the blunders committed by those who disdain any acquaintance with them.

Although the art of categorical syllogism is better fitted for scholastic litigation, than for real improvement in knowledge, it is a venerable piece of antiquity, and a great effort of human genius. We admire the pyramids of Egypt, and the wall of China, though useless burdens upon the earth. We can bear the most minute description of them, and travel hundreds of leagues to see them. If any person should with sacrilegious hands destroy or deface them, his memory would be had in abhorrence. The predicaments and predicables, the rules of syllogism, and the topics, have a like title to our veneration as antiquities: they are uncommon efforts, not of human power, but of human genius; and they make a remarkable period in the progress of human reason.

The prejudice against logic has probably been strengthened by its being taught too early in life. Boys are often taught logic as they are taught their creed, when it is an exercise of memory only, without understanding. One may as well expect <421> to understand grammar before he can speak, as to understand logic before he can reason. It must even be acknowledged, that commonly we are capable of reasoning in mathematics more early than in logic. The objects presented to the mind in this science, are of a very abstract nature, and can be distinctly conceived only when we are capable of attentive reflection upon the operations of our own understanding, and after we have been accustomed to reason. There may be an elementary logic, level to the capacity of those who have been but little exercised in reasoning; but the most important parts of this science require a ripe understanding, capable of reflecting upon its own operations. Therefore to make logic the first branch of science that is to be taught, is an old error that ought to be corrected.

SECTION 2

Of the Improvement of Logic.

In compositions of human thought expressed by speech or by writing, whatever is excellent and whatever is faulty, fall within the province, either of grammar, <422> or of rhetoric, or of logic. Propriety of expression is the province of grammar; grace, elegance, and force, in thought and in expression, are the province of rhetoric; justness and accuracy of thought are the province of logic.

The faults in composition, therefore, which fall under the censure of logic, are obscure and indistinct conceptions, false judgement, inconclusive reasoning, and all improprieties in distinctions, definitions, division, or method. To aid our rational powers, in avoiding these faults and in attaining the opposite excellencies, is the end of logic; and whatever there is in it that has no tendency to promote this end, ought to be thrown out.

The rules of logic being of a very abstract nature, ought to be illustrated by a variety of real and striking examples taken from the writings of good authors. It is both instructive and entertaining, to observe the virtues of accurate composition in writers of fame. We cannot see them, without being drawn to the imitation of them, in a more powerful manner than we can be by dry rules. Nor are the faults of such writers, less instructive or <423> less powerful monitors. A wreck, left upon a shoal or upon a rock, is not more useful to the sailor, than the faults of good writers, when set up to view, are to those who come after them. It was a happy thought in a late ingenious writer of English grammar, to collect under the several rules, examples of bad English found in the most approved authors. It were to be wished that the rules of logic were illustrated in the same manner. By these means, a system of logic would become a repository; wherein whatever is most acute in judging and in reasoning, whatever is most accurate in dividing, distinguishing, and defining, should be laid up and disposed in order for our imitation; and wherein the false steps of eminent authors should be recorded for our admonition.

After men had laboured in the search of truth near two thousand years by the help of syllogisms, Lord Bacon proposed the method of induction, as a more effectual engine for that purpose. His *Novum Organum* gave a new turn to the thoughts and labours of the inquisitive, more remarkable and more useful than that which <424> the *Organum* of Aristotle had given before; and may be considered as a second grand aera in the progress of human reason.

The art of syllogism produced numberless disputes; and numberless sects who fought against each other with much animosity, without gaining or losing ground, but did nothing considerable for the benefit of human life. The art of induction, first delineated by Lord Bacon, produced numberless laboratories and observatories; in which Nature has been put to the question by thousands of experiments, and forced to confess many of her secrets, that before were hid from mortals. And by these, arts have been improved, and human knowledge wonderfully increased.

In reasoning by syllogism, from general principles we descend to a conclusion virtually contained in them. The process of induction is more arduous; being an ascent from particular premises to a general conclusion. The evidence of such general conclusions is probable only, not demonstrative: but when the induction is sufficiently copious, and carried on according <425> to the rules of art, it forces conviction no less than demonstration itself does.

The greatest part of human knowledge rests upon evidence of this kind. Indeed we can have no other for general truths which are contingent in their nature, and depend upon the will and ordination of the Maker of the world. He governs the world he has made, by general laws. The effects of these laws in particular phenomena, are open to our observation; and by observing a train of uniform effects with due caution, we may at last decypher the law of nature by which they are regulated.

Lord Bacon has displayed no less force of genius in reducing to rules this method of reasoning, than Aristotle did in the method of syllogism. His *Novum Organum* ought therefore to be held as a most important addition to the ancient logic. Those who understand it, and enter into its spirit, will be able to distinguish the chaff from the wheat in philosophical disquisitions into the works of God. They will learn to hold in due contempt all hypotheses and theories, the creatures of human imagination; and to respect nothing <426> but facts sufficiently vouched, or conclusions drawn from them by a fair and chaste interpretation of nature.

Most arts have been reduced to rules, after they had been brought to a considerable degree of perfection by the natural sagacity of artists; and the rules have been drawn from the best examples of the art, that had been before exhibited: but the art of philosophical induction was delineated by Lord Bacon in a very ample manner, before the world had seen any tolerable example of it. This, altho' it adds greatly to the merit of the author, must have produced some obscurity in the work, and a defect of proper examples for illustration. This defect may now be easily supplied, from those authors who, in their philosophical disquisitions, have the most strictly pursued the

path pointed out in the *Novum Organum*. Among these Sir Isaac Newton
appears to hold the first rank; having, in the third book of his *Principia*
and in his Optics, had the rules of the *Novum Organum* constantly in his
eye.

I think Lord Bacon was also the first who endeavoured to reduce to a
system the prejudices or biasses of the mind, <427> which are the causes
of false judgement, and which he calls *the idols of the human understanding.*
Some late writers of logic have very properly introduced this into their
system; but it deserves to be more copiously handled, and to be illustrated
by real examples.

It is of great consequence to accurate reasoning, to distinguish first principles which are to be taken for granted, from propositions which require
proof. All the real knowledge of mankind may be divided into two parts:
the first consisting of self-evident propositions; the second, of those which
are deduced by just reasoning from self-evident propositions. The line that
divides these two parts ought to be marked as distinctly as possible; and the
principles that are self-evident reduced, as far as can be done, to general
axioms. This has been done in mathematics from the beginning, and has
tended greatly to the advancement of that science. It has lately been done
in natural philosophy: and by this means that science has advanced more
in an hundred and fifty years, than it had done before in two thousand.
Every science is in an unformed state until <428> its first principles are
ascertained: after which, it advances regularly, and secures the ground it has
gained.

Although first principles do not admit of direct proof, yet there must be
certain marks and characters, by which those that are truly such may be
distinguished from counterfeits. These marks ought to be described, and
applied, to distinguish the genuine from the spurious.

In the ancient philosophy, there is a redundance, rather than a defect,
of first principles. Many things were assumed under that character without
a just title: That nature abhors a *vacuum;* That bodies do not gravitate in
their proper place; That the heavenly bodies undergo no change; That they
move in perfect circles, and with an equable motion. Such principles as
these were assumed in the Peripatetic philosophy, without proof, as if they
were self-evident.

Des Cartes, sensible of this weakness in the ancient philosophy, and de-
sirous to guard against it in his own system, resolved to admit nothing until
his assent was forced by irresistible evidence. The first thing that he found
to be certain and e-<429>vident was, that he thought, and reasoned, and
doubted. He found himself under a necessity of believing the existence of
those mental operations of which he was conscious: and having thus found
sure footing in this one principle of consciousness, he rested satisfied with
it, hoping to be able to build the whole fabric of his knowledge upon it;
like Archimedes, who wanted but one fixed point to move the whole earth.
But the foundation was too narrow; and in his progress he unawares assumes many things less evident than those which he attempts to prove.
Altho' he was not able to suspect the testimony of consciousness; yet he
thought the testimony of sense, of memory, and of every other faculty,
might be suspected, and ought not to be received until proof was brought
that they are not fallacious. Therefore he applies these faculties, whose character is yet in question, to prove, That there is an infinitely perfect Being,
who made him, and who made his senses, his memory, his reason, and all
his faculties; That this Being is no deceiver, and therefore could not give
him faculties that are <430> fallacious; and that on this account they deserve credit.

It is strange, that this philosopher, who found himself under a necessity
of yielding to the testimony of consciousness, did not find the same necessity of yielding to the testimony of his senses, his memory, and his understanding: and that while he was certain that he doubted, and reasoned,
he was uncertain whether two and three made five, and whether he was
dreaming or awake. It is more strange, that so acute a reasoner should not
perceive, that his whole train of reasoning to prove that his faculties were
not fallacious, was mere sophistry; for if his faculties were fallacious, they
might deceive him in this train of reasoning; and so the conclusion, That
they were not fallacious, was only the testimony of his faculties in their own
favour, and might be a fallacy.

It is difficult to give any reason for distrusting our other faculties, that
will not reach consciousness itself. And he who distrusts the faculties of
judging and reasoning which God hath given him, must even rest in his
scepticism, till he <431> come to a sound mind, or until God give him new

faculties to sit in judgement upon the old. If it be not a first principle, That our faculties are not fallacious, we must be absolute sceptics: for this principle is incapable of proof; and if it is not certain, nothing else can be certain.

Since the time of Des Cartes, it has been fashionable with those who dealt in abstract philosophy, to employ their invention in finding philosophical arguments, either to prove those truths which ought to be received as first principles, or to overturn them: and it is not easy to say, whether the authority of first principles is more hurt by the first of these attempts, or by the last: for such principles can stand secure only upon their own bottom; and to place them upon any other foundation than that of their intrinsic evidence, is in effect to overturn them.

I have lately met with a very sensible and judicious treatise, wrote by Father Buffier about fifty years ago, concerning first principles and the source of human judgements, which, with great propriety, he prefixed to his treatise of logic. And <432> indeed I apprehend it is a subject of such consequence, that if inquisitive men can be brought to the same unanimity in the first principles of the other sciences, as in those of mathematics and natural philosophy, (and why should we despair of a general agreement in things that are self-evident?), this might be considered as a third grand aera in the progress of human reason.

END of the Third Volume.

SKETCHES

OF THE

HISTORY OF MAN.

CONSIDERABLY ENLARGED
BY THE LAST ADDITIONS
AND CORRECTIONS
OF THE AUTHOR.

IN FOUR VOLUMES.

VOLUME IV.

EDINBURGH:

PRINTED FOR A. STRAHAN AND T. CADELL, LONDON;
AND FOR WILLIAM CREECH, EDINBURGH.

M,DCC,LXXXVIII.

CONTENTS[1]

1. The original page numbers from the 1788 edition are retained here.

APPENDIX.

Sketches concerning Scotland.

BOOK III

Progress of SCIENCES

Principles and Progress of Morality

The principles of morality are little understood among savages: and if they arrive at maturity among enlightened nations, it is by slow degrees. This progress points out the historical part, as first in order: but as that history would give little satisfaction, without a rule for comparing the morals of different ages, and of different nations, <2> I begin with the principles of morality, such as ought to govern at all times, and in all nations. The present sketch accordingly is divided into two parts. In the first, the principles are unfolded; and the second is altogether historical.

PART I

Principles of Morality

SECTION I

Human Actions analysed.

The hand of God is no where more visible, than in the nice adjustment of our internal frame to our situation in this world. An animal is endued with a power of self-motion; and in performing animal functions, requires no external aid. This in particular is the case of man, the noblest of terrestrial beings. His heart beats, his blood circulates, his stomach digests, &c. &c. By what means? Not <3> surely by the laws of mechanism, which are far from being adequate to such operations. They are effects of an internal power, bestow'd on man for preserving life. The power is exerted uniformly, and without interruption, independent of will, and without consciousness.

Man is a being susceptible of pleasure and pain: these generate desire to attain what is agreeable, and to shun what is disagreeable; and he is possessed of other powers which enable him to gratify his desires. One power, termed *instinct,* is exerted indeed with consciousness; but without will, and consequently without desiring or intending to produce any effect. Brute animals act for the most part by instinct: hunger prompts them to eat, and cold to take shelter; knowingly indeed, but without exerting any act of will, and without foresight of what will happen. Infants of the human species are, like brutes, governed by instinct: they apply to the nipple, without knowing that sucking will satisfy their hunger; and they weep when pained, without any view of relief.[1] But men commonly are governed by desire and intention. In the progress from infancy <4> to maturity, the mind opens to objects without end, agreeable and disagreeable, which raise in us a desire to attain the former and avoid the latter. The will is influenced by desire; and the actions thus performed are termed *voluntary.*

But to have an accurate conception of human nature, it is necessary to be more particular. To incline, to intend, to consent, to resolve, to will, are acts of the mind preparatory to external action. These several acts are well understood, tho' they cannot be defined, being perfectly simple. As every act implies a power to act, the acts mentioned must be the effects of mental

---

1. In the 1st edition the following note is added here: "Akin to these, are certain habitual acts done without thought, such as snuffing or grinning. Custom enables one to move the fingers on an instrument of music, without being directed by will: the motion is often too quick for an act of will. Some arrive at great perfection in the art of balancing: the slightest deviation from the just balance is instantly redressed: were a preceding act of will necessary, it would be too late. An unexpected hollow in walking, occasions a violent shock: is not this evidence, that external motion is governed by the mind, frequently without consciousness; and that in walking, the body is adjusted beforehand to what is expected?" [2:243].

powers. The mind cannot determine without having a power to determine, nor will without having a power to will.

Instinctive actions are exerted without any previous desire or motive, and without any previous act of will. Actions influenced by desire or motives are very different. In such actions, will is essential to connect the desire or motive with the external act. A man who desires or is moved to perform an external act in view, must have a power to determine himself: that power is termed *will;* and the deter-<5>mination is an act of will. With respect to external acts influenced by desire, we cannot even move a finger, without a previous act of will directing that motion. We are very sensible of this determination or act of will, when we deliberate upon motives that tend to different ends. The mind for some time is suspended, deliberates, and at last determines according to the strongest motive. But there must also be a determination where there is but a single motive, though not so perceptible. Being called to dinner when hungry, I instantly obey the call. I cannot go to dinner without first determining to rise from my seat. And it is this determination that intitles it to be called a voluntary act, as much as where the determination is the result of the most anxious deliberation.[2]

Some effects require a train of actions; walking, reading, singing. Where these actions are uniform, as in walking, or nearly so, as in playing on a musical instrument, an act of will is only necessary at the commencement: the train proceeds by habit without any new act of will. The body is antecedently adjusted to the uniform progress; and is disturbed if any <6> thing unexpected happen: in walking, for example, a man feels a shock if he happen to tread on ground higher or lower than his body was prepared for. The power thus acquired by habit of acting without will, is an illustrious branch of our nature; for upon it depend all the arts, both the fine and the useful. To play on the violin, requires wonderful swiftness of fingers, every motion of which in a learner is preceded by an act of will: and yet by habit solely, an artist moves his fingers with no less accuracy than celerity. Let the most handy person try for the first time to knit a stocking: every motion of the needle demands the strictest attention; and yet a girl of nine or ten will move the needle so swiftly as almost to escape the eye,

2. This paragraph and the preceding one on p. 702 were added in the 3rd edition.

without once looking on her work. If every motion in the arts required a new act of will, they would remain in infancy for ever; and what would man be in that case? In the foregoing instances, we are conscious of the external operation without being conscious of a cause. But there are various internal operations of which we have no consciousness; and yet that they have existed is made known by their <7> effects. Often have I gone to bed with a confused notion of what I was studying; and have awaked in the morning completely master of the subject. I have heard a new tune of which I carried away but an imperfect conception. A week or perhaps a fortnight after, the tune has occurred to me in perfection; recollecting with difficulty where I heard it. Such things have happened to me frequently, and probably also to others. My mind must have been active in these instances, though I knew nothing of it.[3]

There still remains another species of actions, termed *involuntary.* Strictly speaking, every action influenced by a motive is *voluntary,* because no such action can be done but by an antecedent act of will. But in a less strict sense, actions done contrary to desire are termed *involuntary;* and they have more or less of that character according to the strength of the motive. A man to free himself from torture, reveals the secrets of his party: his confession is in a degree involuntary, being extorted from him with great reluctance. But let us suppose, that after the firmest resolution to reveal nothing, his mind is unhinged by <8> exquisite torture: the discovery he makes is in the highest degree *involuntary.*

Man is by his nature an accountable being, answerable for his conduct to God and man. In doing any action that wears a double face, he is prompted by his nature to explain the same to his relations, his friends, his acquaintance; and above all, to those who have authority over him. He hopes for praise for every right action, and dreads blame for every one that is wrong. But for what sort of actions does he hold himself accountable? Not surely for an instinctive action, which is done blindly, without intention and without will: neither for an involuntary action, because it is extorted from him reluctantly, and contrary to his desire; and least of all, for actions done without consciousness. What only remain are voluntary ac-

3. Paragraph added in 2nd edition.

tions proceeding from desire, which are done as we say wittingly and willingly: for these we must account, if at all accountable; and for these every man in conscience holds himself bound to account.

Further upon voluntary actions. To intend and to will, though commonly held synonymous, signify different acts of the <9> mind. Intention respects the effect: Will respects the action that is exerted for producing the effect. It is my Intention, for example, to relieve my friend from distress: upon seeing him, it is my Will to give him a sum for his relief: the external act of giving follows; and my friend is relieved, which is the effect intended. But these internal acts are always united: I cannot will the means, without intending the effect; and I cannot intend the effect, without willing the means.[4]

Some effects of voluntary action follow necessarily: A wound is an effect that necessarily follows the stabbing a person with a dagger: death is a necessary effect of throwing one down from the battlements of a high tower. Some effects are probable only: I labour in order to provide for my family; fight for my country to rescue it from oppressors; take physic for my health. In such cases, the event intended does not necessarily nor always follow.

A man, when he wills to act, must intend the necessary effect: a person who stabs, certainly intends to wound. But where the effect is probable only, one may <10> act without intending the effect that follows: a stone thrown by me at random into the market-place, may happen to wound a man without my intending it. One acts by instinct, without either will or intention: voluntary actions that necessarily produce their effect, imply intention: voluntary actions, when the effect is probable only, are sometimes intended, sometimes not.

Human actions are distinguished from each other by certain *qualities,* termed *right* and *wrong.* But as these make the corner-stone of morality, they are reserved to the following section.

4. In the 1st and 2nd editions the following note is added here: "To incline, to resolve, to intend, to will, are acts of the mind relative to external action. These several acts are well understood; tho' they cannot be defined, being perfectly simple" [2:245].

SECTION II

Division of Human Actions into Right, Wrong, and Indifferent.

The qualities of right and wrong in voluntary actions, are universally acknowledged as the foundation of morality; and yet philosophers have been strangely perplexed about them. The hi-<11>story of their various opinions, would signify little but to darken the subject: the reader will have more satisfaction in seeing these qualities explained, without entering at all into controversy.

No person is ignorant of primary and secondary qualities, a distinction much insisted on by philosophers. Primary qualities, such as figure, cohesion, weight, are permanent qualities, that exist in a subject whether perceived or not. Secondary qualities, such as colour, taste, smell, depend on the percipient as much as on the subject, being nothing when not perceived. Beauty and ugliness are qualities of the latter sort: they have no existence but when perceived; and, like all other secondary qualities, they are perceived intuitively; having no dependence on reason nor on judgement, more than colour has, or smell, or taste (*a*).

The qualities of right and wrong in voluntary actions, are secondary, like beauty and ugliness and the other secondary qualities mentioned. Like them, they are objects of intuitive perception, and depend not in any degree on reason. No argu-<12>ment is requisite to prove, that to rescue an innocent babe from the jaws of a wolf, to feed the hungry, to clothe the naked, are right actions: they are perceived to be so intuitively. As little is an argument requisite to prove, that murder, deceit, perjury, are wrong actions: they are perceived to be so intuitively. The Deity has bestow'd on man, different faculties for different purposes. Truth and falsehood are investigated by the reasoning faculty. Beauty and ugliness are objects of a sense, known by the name of *taste*. Right and wrong are objects of a sense termed the *moral sense* or *conscience*. And supposing these qualities to be hid from our perception, in vain would we try to discover them by any argument or

(*a*) Elements of Criticism, vol. 1. p. 207. edit. 5.

process of reasoning: the attempt would be absurd; no less so than an attempt to discover by reasoning colour, or taste, or smell.* <13>

Right and wrong, as mentioned above, are qualities of voluntary actions, and of no other kind. An instinctive action may be agreeable, may be disagreeable; but it cannot properly be denominated either right or wrong. An involuntary act is hurtful to the agent, and disagreeable to the spectator; but it is neither right nor wrong. These qualities also depend in no degree on the event. Thus, if to save my friend from drowning I plunge into a river, the action is right, tho' I happen to come too late. And if I aim a stroke at a man behind his back, the action is wrong, tho' I happen not to touch him.

The qualities of right and of agreeable, are inseparable; and so are the qualities of wrong and of disagreeable. A right action is agreeable, not only in the direct perception, but equally so in every subse-<14>quent recollection. And in both circumstances equally, a wrong action is disagreeable.

Right actions are distinguished by the moral sense into two kinds, what *ought* to be done, and what *may* be done, or left undone. Wrong actions admit not that distinction: they are all prohibited to be done. To say that an action ought to be done, means that we are tied or obliged to perform; and to say that an action ought not to be done, means that we are restrained from doing it. Tho' the necessity implied in the being tied or obliged, is not physical, but only what is commonly termed *moral;* yet we conceive ourselves deprived of liberty or freedom, and necessarily bound to act or to forbear acting, in opposition to every other motive. The necessity here described is termed *duty.* The moral necessity we are under to forbear harming the innocent, is a proper example: the moral sense declares the restraint to be our duty, which no motive whatever will excuse us for transgressing.

---

* Every perception must proceed from some faculty or power of perception, termed *sense.* The moral sense, by which we perceive the qualities of right and wrong, may be considered either as a branch of the sense of seeing, by which we perceive the actions to which these qualities belong, or as a sense distinct from all others. The senses by which objects are perceived, are not separated from each other by distinct boundaries: the sorting or classing them, seems to depend more on taste and fancy, than on nature. I have followed the plan laid down by former writers; which is, to consider the moral sense as a sense distinct from others, because it is the easiest and clearest manner of conceiving it.

The duty of performing or forbearing any action, implies a *right* in some person to exact performance of that duty; and <15> accordingly, a duty or obligation necessarily infers a corresponding right. My promise to pay L. 100 to John, confers a right on him to demand performance. The man who commits an injury, violates the *right* of the person injured; which entitles that person to demand reparation of the wrong.

Duty is twofold; duty to others, and duty to ourselves. With respect to the former, the doing what we ought to do, is termed *just:* the doing what we ought not to do, and the omitting what we ought to do, are termed *unjust.* With respect to ourselves, the doing what we ought to do, is termed *proper:* the doing what we ought not to do, and the omitting what we ought to do, are termed *improper.* Thus, *right,* signifying a quality of certain actions, is a genus; of which *just* and *proper* are species: *wrong,* signifying a quality of other actions, is a genus; of which *unjust* and *improper* are species.

Right actions left to our free will, to be done or left undone, come next in order. They are, like the former, right when done; but they differ, in not being wrong when left undone. To remit a just debt <16> for the sake of a growing family, to yield a subject in controversy rather than go to law with a neighbour, generously to return good for ill, are examples of this species. They are universally approved as right actions: but as no person has a right or title to oblige us to perform such actions, the leaving them undone is not a wrong: no person is injured by the forbearance. Actions that come under this class, shall be termed *arbitrary* or *discretionary,* for want of a more proper designation.

So much for right actions, and their divisions. Wrong actions are of two kinds, *criminal* and *culpable.* What are done intentionally to produce mischief, are *criminal:* rash or unguarded actions that produce mischief without intention, are *culpable.* The former are restrained by punishment, to be handled in the 5th section; the latter by reparation, to be handled in the 6th.

The divisions of voluntary actions are not yet exhausted. Some there are that, properly speaking, cannot be denominated either right or wrong. Actions done merely for amusement or pastime, without in-<17>tention to produce good or ill, are of that kind; leaping, for example, running, jumping over a stick, throwing a stone to make circles in the water. Such actions are neither approved nor disapproved: they may be termed *indifferent*.

There is no cause for doubting the existence of the moral sense, more than for doubting the existence of the sense of beauty, of seeing, or of hearing. In fact, the perception of right and wrong as qualities of actions, is no less distinct and clear, than that of beauty, of colour, or of any other quality; and as every perception is an act of sense, the sense of beauty is not with greater certainty evinced from the perception of beauty, than the moral sense is from the perception of right and wrong. We find this sense distributed among individuals in different degrees of perfection: but there perhaps never existed any one above the condition of an idiot, who possessed it not in some degree; and were any man entirely destitute of it, the terms *right* and *wrong* would be to him no less unintelligible, than the term colour is to one born blind. <18>

That every individual is endued with a sense of right and wrong, more or less distinct, will probably be granted; but whether there be among men what may be termed a *common sense* of right and wrong, producing uniformity of opinion as to right and wrong, is not so evident. There is no absurdity in supposing the opinions of men about right and wrong, to be as various as about beauty and deformity. And that the supposition is not destitute of foundation, we are led to suspect, upon discovering that in different countries, and even in the same country at different times, the opinions publicly espoused with regard to right and wrong, are extremely various; that among some nations it was held lawful for a man to sell his children for slaves, and in their infancy to abandon them to wild beasts; that it was held equally lawful to punish children, even capitally, for the crime of their parent; that the murdering an enemy in cold blood, was once a common practice; that human sacrifices, impious no less than immoral according to our notions, were of old universal; that even in later times, it has been held meritorious, <19> to inflict cruel torments for the slightest deviations from the religious creed of the plurality; and that among the most enlightened nations, there are at this day considerable differences with respect to the rules of morality.

These facts tend not to disprove the reality of a common sense in morals: they only prove, that the moral sense has not been equally perfect at all times, nor in all countries. This branch of the history of morality, is reserved for the second part. To give some interim satisfaction, I shall shortly observe, that the savage state is the infancy of man; during which, the more delicate senses lie dormant, leaving nations to the authority of custom, of imitation, and of passion, without any just taste of morals more than of the fine arts. But a nation, like an individual, ripens gradually, and acquires a refined taste in morals as well as in the fine arts: after which we find great uniformity of opinion about the rules of right and wrong; with few exceptions, but what may proceed from imbecillity, or corrupted education. There may be found, it is true, even in the most enlightened ages, men <20> who have singular notions in morality, and in many other subjects; which no more affords an argument against a common sense or standard of right and wrong, than a monster doth against the standard that regulates our external form, or than an exception doth against the truth of a general proposition.

That there is in mankind an uniformity of opinion with respect to right and wrong, is a matter of fact of which the only infallible evidence is observation and experience: and to that evidence I appeal; entering only a caveat, that, for the reason above given, the inquiry be confined to enlightened nations. In the mean time, I take liberty to suggest an argument from analogy, That if there be great uniformity among the different tribes of men in seeing and hearing, in pleasure and pain, in judging of truth and error, the same uniformity ought to be expected with respect to right and wrong. Whatever minute differences there may be to distinguish one person from another, yet in the general principles that constitute our nature, internal and external, there is wonderful uniformity. <21>

This uniformity of sentiment, which may be termed *the common sense of mankind with respect to right and wrong,* is essential to social beings. Did the moral sentiments of men differ as much as their faces, they would be unfit for society: discord and controversy would be endless, and *major vis* would be the only rule of right and wrong.

But such uniformity of sentiment, tho' general, is not altogether universal: men there are, as above mentioned, who differ from the common sense of mankind with respect to various points of morality. What ought to be the conduct of such men? ought they to regulate their conduct by

that standard, or by their private conviction? There will be occasion afterward to observe, that we judge of others as we believe they judge of themselves; and that private conviction is the standard for rewards and punishments (*a*). But with respect to every controversy about property and
pecuniary interest, and, in general, about every civil right and obligation,
the common sense of mankind is to every individual the standard, and not
private con-<22>viction or conscience; for proof of which take what
follows.

We have an innate sense of a common nature, not only in our own species, but in every species of animals. And that our perception holds true in
fact, is verified by experience; for there appears a remarkable uniformity in
creatures of the same kind, and a difformity, no less remarkable, in creatures
of different kinds. It is accordingly a subject of wonder, to find an individual deviating from the common nature of the species, whether in its
internal or external structure: a child born with aversion to its mother's
milk, is a wonder, no less than if born without a mouth, or with more than
one.

Secondly, This sense dictates, that the common nature of man in particular, is invariable as well as universal; that it will be the same hereafter as
it is at present, and as it was in time past; the same among all nations, and
in all corners of the earth: nor are we deceived; because, allowing for slight
differences occasioned by culture and other accidental circumstances, the
fact corresponds to our perception.

Thirdly, We perceive that this common <23> nature is *right* and *perfect*,
and that it *ought* to be a model or standard for every human being. Any
remarkable deviation from it in the structure of an individual, appears imperfect or irregular; and raises a painful emotion: a monstrous birth, excit-
ing curiosity in a philosopher, fails not at the same time to excite aversion
in every spectator.

This sense of perfection in the common nature of man, comprehends
every branch of his nature, and particularly the common sense of right and
wrong; which accordingly is perceived by all to be perfect, having authority
over every individual as the ultimate and unerring standard of morals, even

(*a*) Sect. 5.

in contradiction to private conviction. Thus, a law in our nature binds us to regulate our conduct by that standard: and its authority is universally acknowledged; as nothing is more ordinary in every dispute about *meum et tuum,* than an appeal to common sense as the ultimate and unerring standard.

At the same time, as that standard, through infirmity or prejudice, is not conspicuous to every individual; many are misled into erroneous opinions, by mis-<24>taking a false standard for that of nature. And hence a distinction between a right and a wrong sense in morals; a distinction which every one understands, but which, unless for the conviction of a moral standard, would have no meaning.

The final cause of this branch of our Nature is conspicuous. Were there no standard of right and wrong for determining endless controversies about matters of interest, the strong would have recourse to force, the weak to cunning, and society would dissolve. Courts of law could afford no remedy; for without a standard of morals, their decisions would be arbitrary, and of no authority. Happy it is for men to be provided with such a standard: it is necessary in society that our actions be uniform with respect to right and wrong; and in order to uniformity of action, it is necessary that our perceptions of right and wrong be also uniform: to produce such uniformity, a standard of morals is indispensable. Nature has provided us with that standard, which is daily apply'd by courts of law with success (*a*). <25>

In reviewing what is said, it must afford great satisfaction, to find morality established upon the solid foundations of intuitive perception; which is a single mental act complete in itself, having no dependence on any antecedent proposition. The most accurate reasoning affords not equal conviction; for every sort of reasoning, as explained in the sketch immediately foregoing, requires not only self-evident truths or axioms to found upon, but employs over and above various propositions to bring out its conclusions. By intuitive perception solely, without reasoning, we acquire knowledge of right and wrong; of what we may do, of what we ought to do, and of what we ought to abstain from: and considering that we have thus greater certainty of moral laws than of any proposition discoverable by reasoning,

---

(*a*) See Elements of Criticism, vol. 2. p. 490. edit. 5. [[Note added in 2nd edition.]]

man may well be deemed a favourite of Heaven, when he is so admirably qualified for doing his duty. The moral sense or conscience is the voice of God within us; constantly admonishing us of our duty, and requiring from us no exercise of our faculties but attention merely. The celebrated Locke ventured <26> what he thought a bold conjecture, That moral duties are susceptible of demonstration: how agreeable to him would have been the discovery, that they are founded upon intuitive perception, still more convincing and authoritative!

By one branch of the moral sense, we are taught what we ought to do, and what we ought not to do; and by another branch, what we may do, or leave undone. But society would be imperfect, if the moral sense stopped here. There is a third branch that makes us accountable for our conduct to our fellow-creatures; and it will be made evident afterward in the third sketch, that we are accountable to our Maker, as well as to our fellow-creatures.

It follows from the standard of right and wrong, that an action is right or wrong, independent of what the agent may think. Thus, when a man, excited by friendship or pity, rescues a heretic from the flames, the action is right, even tho' he think it wrong, from a conviction that heretics ought to be burnt. But we apply a different standard to the agent: a man is approved and held to be inno-<27>cent in doing what he himself thinks right: he is disapproved and held to be guilty in doing what he himself thinks wrong. Thus, to assassinate an atheist for the sake of religion, is a wrong action; and yet the enthusiast who commits that wrong, may be innocent: and one is guilty, who against conscience eats meat in Lent, tho' the action is not wrong. In short, an action is perceived to be right or wrong, independent of the actor's own opinion: but he is approved or disapproved, held to be innocent or guilty, according to his own opinion.

SECTION III

Laws of Nature respecting our
Moral Conduct in Society.

A standard being thus established for regulating our moral conduct in society, we proceed to investigate the laws that result from it. But first we take under consideration, what other principles <28> concur with the moral sense to qualify men for society.

When we reflect on the different branches of human knowledge, it might seem, that of all subjects human nature should be the best understood; because every man has daily opportunities to study it, in his own passions and in his own actions. But human nature, an interesting subject, is seldom left to the investigation of philosophy. Writers of a sweet disposition and warm imagination, hold, that man is a benevolent being, and that every man ought to direct his conduct for the good of all, without regarding himself but as one of the number (a). Those of a cold temperament and contracted mind, hold him to be an animal entirely selfish; to evince which, examples are accumulated without end (b). Neither of these systems is that of nature. The selfish system is contradicted by the experience of all ages, affording the clearest evidence, that men frequently act for the sake of others, without regarding themselves, and sometimes in direct opposition to their own <29> interest.* And however much selfishness may prevail in action; man cannot be an animal entirely selfish, when all men conspire to put a high estimation upon generosity, benevolence, and other social virtues: even the most selfish are disgusted with selfishness in others, and endeavour to hide it in themselves. The most zealous patron of the selfish principle, will not venture to maintain, that it renders us altogether indifferent about our fellow-creatures. Laying aside self-interest with every connection of love and hatred, good fortune happening to any one gives pleasure to all, and bad fortune happening to any one is painful to all. On the other hand, the system of universal benevolence, is no less contradictory to experience; <30> from which we learn, that men commonly are disposed to prefer their own interest before that of others, es-

---

* Whatever wiredrawn arguments may be urged for the selfish system, as if benevolence were but refined selfishness, the emptiness of such arguments will clearly appear when applied to children, who know no refinement. In them, the rudiments of the social principle are no less visible than of the selfish principle. Nothing is more common, than mutual good-will and fondness between children: which must be the work of nature; for to reflect upon what is one's interest, is far above the capacity of children. [[Note added in 2nd edition.]]

(a) Lord Shaftesbury.

(b) Helvetius.

pecially where there is no strict connection: nor do we find that such bias is condemned by the moral sense. Man in fact is a complex being, composed of principles, some benevolent, some selfish: and these principles are so justly blended in his nature, as to fit him for acting a proper part in society. It would indeed be losing time to prove, that without some affection for his fellow-creatures he would be ill qualified for society. And it will be made evident afterward (*a*), that universal benevolence would be more hurtful to society, than even absolute selfishness.* <31>

We are now prepared for investigating the laws that result from the foregoing principles. The several duties we owe to others shall be first discussed, taking them in order according to the extent of their influence. And for the sake of perspicuity, I shall first present them in a general view, and then proceed to particulars. Of our duties to others, one there is so extensive, as to have for its object all the innocent part of mankind. It is the duty that prohibits us to hurt others: than which no law is more clearly dictated by the moral sense; nor is the transgression of any other law more deeply stamped with the character of wrong. A man may be hurt externally in his goods, in his person, in his relations, and in his reputation. Hence the laws, Do not steal; Defraud not others; Do not kill nor wound; Be not guilty of defamation. A man may be hurt internally, by an action that occasions to him distress of mind, or by be-<32>ing impressed with false notions of men and things. Therefore conscience dictates, that we ought not to treat men disrespectfully; that we ought not causelessly to alienate their affections from others; and, in general, that we ought to forbear whatever may tend to break their peace of mind, or tend to unqualify them for being good men and good citizens.

---

* "Many moralists enter so deeply into one passion or bias of human nature, that, to use the painter's phrase, they quite overcharge it. Thus I have seen a whole system of morals founded upon a single pillar of the inward frame; and the entire conduct of life and all the characters in it accounted for, sometimes from superstition, sometimes from pride, and most commonly from interest. They forget how various a creature it is they are painting; how many springs and weights, nicely adjusted and balanced, enter into the movement, and require allowance to be made for their several clogs and impulses, ere you can define its operation and effects." [[Thomas Blackwell,]] *Enquiry into the life and writings of Homer.*

(*a*) Sect. 4.

The duties mentioned are duties of restraint. Our active duties regard particular persons; such as our relations, our friends, our benefactors, our masters, our servants. It is our duty to honour and obey our parents; and to establish our children in the world, with all advantages internal and external: we ought to be faithful to our friends, grateful to our benefactors, submissive to our masters, kind to our servants; and to aid and comfort every one of these persons when in distress. To be obliged to do good to others beyond these bounds, must depend on positive engagement; for, as will appear afterward, universal benevolence is not a duty.

This general sketch will prepare us for particulars. The duty of restraint comes first in view, that which bars us from <33> harming the innocent; and to it corresponds a right in the innocent to be safe from harm. This is the great law preparatory to society; because without it, society could never have existed. Here the moral sense is inflexible: it dictates, that we ought to submit to any distress, even death itself, rather than procure our own safety by laying violent hands upon an innocent person. And we are under the same restraint with respect to the property of another; for robbery and theft are never upon any pretext indulged. It is indeed true, that in extreme hunger I may lawfully take food where it can be found; and may freely lay hold of my neighbour's horse, to carry me from an enemy who threatens death. But it is his duty as a fellow-creature to assist me in distress; and when there is no time for delay, I may lawfully use what he ought to offer were he present, and what I may presume he would offer. For the same reason, if in a storm my ship be driven among the anchor-ropes of another ship, I may lawfully cut the ropes in order to get free. But in every case of this kind, it would be a wrong in me to use my neighbour's <34> property, without resolving to pay the value. If my neighbour be bound to aid me in distress, conscience binds me to make up his loss.* <35>

---

* This doctrine is obviously founded on justice; and yet, in the Roman law, there are two passages which deny any recompence in such cases. "Item Labeo scribit, si cum vi ventorum navis impulsa esset in funes anchorarum alterius, et nautae funes praecidissent; si nullo alio modo, nisi praecisis funibus, explicare se potuit, nullam actionem dandam"; *l.* 29. § 3. *ad leg. Aquil.* "Quod dicitur *damnum injuria datum Aquilia persequi,* sic erit accipiendum, ut videatur damnum injuria datum quod cum damno injuriam attulerit; nisi magna vi cogente, fuerit factum. Ut Celsus scribit circa eum, qui incendii arcendi

The prohibition of hurting others internally, is perhaps not essential to the formation of societies, because the transgression of that law doth not much alarm plain people: but where manners and refined sentiments prevail, the mind is susceptible of more grievous wounds than the body; and therefore, without that law, a polished society could have no long endurance.

By adultery, mischief is done both external and internal. Each sex is so constituted, as to require strict fidelity and attachment in a mate. The breach of these duties is the greatest external harm <36> that can befal them: it harms them also internally, by breaking their peace of mind. It has indeed been urged, that no harm will ensue, if the adultery be kept secret; and consequently, that there can be no crime where the fact is kept secret. But such as reason thus do not advert, that to declare secret adultery to be lawful, is in effect to overturn every foundation of mutual trust and fidelity in the matrimonial state. It is clear beyond all doubt, says a reputable writer, that no man is permitted to violate his faith; and that the man is unjust and barbarous who deprives his wife of the only reward she has for adhering to the austere duties of her sex. But an unfaithful wife is still more criminal,

---

gratia vicinas aedes intercidit: et sive pervenit ignis, sive antea extinctus est, existimat legis Aquiliae actionem cessare." *l.* 49. § 1. *eod.* [[The *Lex Aquila,* framed in the early third century B.C., introduced into Roman law civil liability for willful negligence in the damage of another's property.]]—[*In English thus:* "In the opinion of Labeo, if a ship is driven by the violence of a tempest among the anchor-ropes of another ship, and the sailors cut the ropes, having no other means of getting free, there is no action competent.—The Aquilian law must be understood to apply only to such damage as carries the idea of an injury along with it, unless such injury has not been wilfully done, but from necessity. Thus Celsus puts the case of a person who, to stop the progress of a fire, pulls down his neighbour's house; and whether the fire had reached that house which is pulled down, or was extinguished before it got to it, in neither case, he thinks, will an action be competent from the Aquilian law."]—These opinions are undoubtedly erroneous. And it is not difficult to say what has occasioned the error: the cases mentioned are treated as belonging to the *lex Aquilia;* which being confined to the reparation of wrongs, lays it justly down for a rule, That no action for reparation can lie, where there is no *culpa.* But had Labeo and Celsus adverted, that these cases belong to a different head, viz. the duty of recompence, where one suffers loss by benefiting another, they themselves would have had no difficulty of sustaining a claim for making up that loss.

by dissolving the whole ties of nature: in giving to her husband children that are not his, she betrays both, and joins perfidy to infidelity (*a*).

Veracity is commonly ranked among the active duties; but erroneously: for if a man be not bound to speak, he cannot be bound to speak truth. It is therefore only a restraining duty, prohibiting us to deceive others, <37> by affirming what is not true. Among the many corresponding principles in the human mind that in conjunction tend to make society comfortable, a principle of veracity,* and a principle that leads us to rely on human testimony, are two: without the latter, the former would be an useless principle; and without the former, the latter would lay us open to fraud and treachery. The moral sense accordingly dictates, that we ought to adhere strictly to truth, without regard to consequences.

It must not be inferred, that we are bound to explain our thoughts, when truth is demanded from us by unlawful means. Words uttered voluntarily, are na-<38>turally relied on, as expressing the speaker's mind; and if his mind differ from his words, he tells a lie, and is guilty of deceit. But words drawn from a man by torture, are no indication of his mind; and he is not guilty of deceit in uttering whatever words may be agreeable, however alien from his thoughts: if the author of the unlawful violence suffer himself to be deceived, he ought to blame himself, not the speaker.

It need scarce be mentioned, that the duty of veracity excludes not fable, nor any liberty of speech intended for amusement only.

Active duties, as hinted above, are all of them directed to particular persons. And the first I shall mention, is that between parent and child. The relation of parent and child, the strongest that can exist between individuals, binds these persons to exert their utmost powers in mutual good of-

---

* Truth is always uppermost, being the natural issue of the mind: it requires no art nor training, no inducement nor temptation, but only that we yield to natural impulse. Lying, on the contrary, is doing violence to our nature; and is never practised, even by the worst of men, without some temptation. Speaking truth is like using our natural food, which we would do from appetite although it answered no end: lying is like taking physic, which is nauseous to the taste, and which no man takes but for some end which he cannot otherwise attain. *Dr. Reid's Enquiry into the human mind.*

(*a*) [[Rousseau,]] Emile, liv. 5.

fices. Benevolence among other blood-relations, is also a duty; but not so indispensable, being proportioned to the inferior degree of relation.

Gratitude is a duty directed to our benefactors. But tho' gratitude is strictly a <39> duty, the measure of performance, and the kind, are left mostly to our own choice. It is scarce necessary to add, that the active duties now mentioned, are acknowledged by all to be absolutely inflexible, perhaps more so than the restraining duties: many find excuses for doing harm; but no one hears with patience an excuse for deviating from truth, friendship, or gratitude.

Distress, tho' it has a tendency to convert benevolence into a duty, is not sufficient without other concurring circumstances; for to relieve every person in distress, is beyond the power of any human being. Our relations in distress claim that duty from us, and even our neighbours: but distant distress, without a particular connection, scarce rouses our sympathy, and never is an object of duty. Many other connections, too numerous for this short essay, extend the duty of relieving others from distress; and these make a large branch of equity. Tho' in various instances benevolence is converted into a duty by distress, it follows not, that the duty is always proportioned to the degree of distress. Nature has more wisely pro-<40>vided for the support of virtue: a virtuous person in distress commands our pity: a vicious person in distress has much less influence; and if by vice he have brought on the distress, indignation is raised, not pity (*a*).

One great advantage of society, is the co-operation of many to accomplish some useful work, where a single hand would be insufficient. Arts, manufactures, and commerce, require many hands: but as hands cannot be secured without a previous engagement, the performance of promises and covenants is, upon that account, a capital duty in society. In their original occupations of hunting and fishing, men living scattered and dispersed, have seldom opportunity to aid and benefit each other; and in that situation, covenants, being of little use, are little regarded: but husbandry, requiring the co-operation of many hands, draws men together for mutual assistance; and then covenants make a figure: arts and commerce make

(*a*) See Elements of Criticism, vol. 1. p. 187. edit. 5.

them more and more necessary; and in a polished society great regard is paid to them. <41>

But contracts and promises are not confined to commercial dealings: they serve also to make benevolence a duty; and are even extended to connect the living with the dead: a man would die with regret, if he thought his friends were not bound by their promises to fulfil his will after his death: and to quiet the minds of men with respect to futurity, the moral sense makes the performing such promises our duty. Thus, if I promise to my friend to erect a monument for him after his death, conscience binds me, even tho' no person alive be entitled to demand performance: every one perceives this to be my duty; and I must expect to suffer reproach and blame, if I neglect my engagement.

To fulfil a rational promise or covenant, deliberately made, is a duty no less inflexible than those duties are which arise independent of consent. But as man is fallible, often misled by ignorance, and liable to be deceived, his condition would be deplorable, did the moral sense compel him to fulfil every engagement, however imprudent or irrational. Here the moral sense gives way to human infirmity: it relieves from deceit, from imposition, <42> from ignorance, from error; and binds a man by no engagement but what answers the end fairly intended. There is still less doubt that it will relieve us from an engagement extorted by external violence, or by overbearing passion. The dread of torture will force most men to submit to any terms; and a man in imminent hazard of drowning, will voluntarily promise all he has in the world to save him. The moral sense would be ill suited to the imbecillity of our nature, did it bind men in conscience to fulfil engagements made in such circumstances.[5]

The other branch of duties, those we owe to ourselves, shall be discussed in a few words. *Propriety,* a branch of the moral sense, regulates our conduct with respect to ourselves; as *Justice,* another branch of the moral sense, regulates our conduct with respect to others. Propriety dictates, that we ought to act up to the dignity of our nature, and to the station allotted us by Providence: it dictates in particular, that temperance, prudence, modesty, and uniformity of conduct, are self-duties. These duties contribute to

5. "There is still . . . in such circumstances": added in 2nd edition.

private happiness, by preserving health, <43> peace of mind, and self-esteem; which are inestimable blessings: they contribute no less to happiness in society, by gaining the love and esteem of others, and aid and support in time of need.

Upon reviewing the foregoing duties respecting others, we find them more or less extensive; but none so extensive as to have for their end the good of mankind in general. The most extensive duty is that of restraint, prohibiting us to harm others: but even that duty has a limited end; for its purpose is only to protect others from mischief, not to do them any positive good. The active duties of doing positive good are circumscribed within still narrower bounds, requiring some relation that connects us with others; such as those of parent, child, friend, benefactor. The slighter relations, unless in peculiar circumstances, are not the foundation of any active duty: neighbourhood, for example, does not alone make benevolence a duty: but supposing a neighbour to be in distress, relief becomes our duty, if it can be done without distress to ourselves. The duty of relieving from distress, seldom goes farther; for tho' we always sympa-<44>thise with our relations, and with those under our eye, the distresses of the remote and unknown affect us very little. Pactions and agreements become necessary, if we would extend the duty of benevolence beyond the limits mentioned. Men, it is true, are capable of doing more good than is required of them as a duty; but every such good must be a free-will offering.

And this leads to arbitrary or discretionary actions, such as may be done or left undone; which make the second general head of moral actions. With respect to these, the moral sense leaves us at freedom: a benevolent act is approved, but the omission is not condemned. This holds strictly in single acts; but in viewing the whole of a man's conduct, the moral sense appears to vary a little. As the nature of man is complex, partly social, partly selfish, we have an intuitive perception, that our conduct ought to be conformable to our nature; and that in advancing our own interest, we ought not altogether to neglect that of others. The man accordingly who confines his whole time and thoughts within his own little <45> sphere, is condemned by all the world as guilty of wrong conduct; and the man himself, if his moral perceptions be not blunted by selfishness, must be sensible that he deserves to be condemned. On the other hand, it is possible that free benevolence may be extended beyond proper bounds: where it prevails, it commonly leads to excess, by prompting a man to sacrifice a great interest of his own to a small interest of others; and the moral sense dictates, that such conduct is wrong. The just temperament, is a subordination of benevolence to self-love.

Thus, moral actions are divided into two classes: the first regards our duty, containing actions that ought to be done, and actions that ought not to be done; the other regards arbitrary or discretionary actions, containing actions that are right when done, but not wrong when left undone. Society is indeed promoted by the latter; but it can scarce subsist, unless the former be made our duty. Hence it is, that actions only of the first class are made indispensable; those of the other class being left to our free-will. And hence also it is, that the various propensities that dis-<46>pose us to actions of the first class, are distinguished by the name of *primary virtues;* leaving the name of *secondary virtues* to those propensities which dispose us to actions of the other class.*

The deduction above given makes it evident, that the general tendency of right actions is to promote the good of society, and of wrong actions, to obstruct that good. Universal benevolence is indeed not required of man; because to put it in practice, is beyond his utmost abilities. But for promoting the general good, every thing is required of him that he can accomplish; which will appear from reviewing the foregoing duties. The prohibition of harming others is an easy task; and upon that account is made universal. Our active duties are very different: man is circumscribed both in capacity and power: he cannot do good but in a slow succession; and therefore it is wisely ordered, that his obligation to do good should be confined to his relations, his <47> friends, his benefactors. Even distress makes not benevolence a general duty: all a man can readily do, is to relieve those at hand; and accordingly we hear of distant misfortunes with little or no concern.

But let not the moral system be misapprehended, as if it were our duty,

---

* Virtue signifies that disposition of mind which gives the ascendant to moral principles. Vice signifies that disposition of mind which gives little or no ascendant to moral principles.

or even lawful, to prosecute what upon the whole we reckon the most beneficial to society, balancing ill with good. The moral sense permits not a violation of any person's right, however trivial, whatever benefit may thereby accrue to another. A man for example in low circumstances, by denying a debt he owes to a rich miser, saves himself and a hopeful family from ruin. In that case, the good effect far outweighs the ill, or rather has no counterbalance: but the moral sense permits not the debtor to balance ill with good; nor gives countenance to an unjust act, whatever benefit it may produce. And hence a maxim in which all moralists agree, That we must not do ill to bring about good; the final cause of which shall be given below (a). <48>

SECTION IV

Principles of Duty and of Benevolence.

Having thus shortly delineated the moral laws of our nature, we proceed to an article of great importance, which is, to enquire into the means provided by our Maker for compelling obedience to these laws. The moral sense is an unerring guide; but the most expert guide will not profit those who are not disposed to be led. This consideration makes it evident, that to complete the moral system, man ought to be endued with some principle or propensity, some impulsive power, to enforce obedience to the laws dictated by the moral sense.

The author of our nature leaves none of his works imperfect. In order to render us obsequious to the moral sense as our guide, he hath implanted in our nature the principles of duty, of benevolence, of rewards and punishments, and of repara-<49>tion. It may possibly be thought, that rewards and punishments, of which afterward, are sufficient of themselves to enforce the laws of nature, without necessity of any other principle. Human laws, it is true, are enforc'd by these means; because no higher sanction is under command of a terrestrial legislator. But the celestial legislator, with power that knows no control, and benevolence that knows no bounds, hath

(a) Sect. 7.

enforc'd his laws by means no less remarkable for mildness than for efficacy: he employs no external compulsion; but, in order to engage our will on the right side, hath in the breast of individuals established the principles of duty and of benevolence, which efficaciously excite them to obey the dictates of the moral sense.

The restraining and active duties being both of them essential to society, our Maker has wisely ordered, that the principle which enforces these duties, should be the most cogent of all that belong to our nature. Other principles may solicit, allure, or terrify; but the principle of duty assumes authority, commands, and insists <50> to be obey'd, without giving ear to any opposing motive.

As one great purpose of society, is to furnish opportunities of mutual aid and support; nature seconding that purpose, hath provided the principle of benevolence, which excites us to be kindly, beneficent, and generous. Nor ought it to escape observation, that the author of nature, attentive to our wants and to our well-being, hath endued us with a liberal portion of that principle. It excites us to be kind, not only to those we are connected with, but to our neighbours, and even to those we are barely acquainted with. Providence is peculiarly attentive to objects in distress, who require immediate aid and relief. To the principle of benevolence, it hath superadded the passion of pity, which in every feeling heart is irresistible. To make benevolence more extensive, would be fruitless; because here are objects in plenty to fill the most capacious mind. It would not be fruitless only, but hurtful to society: I say hurtful; because frequent disappointments in attempting to gratify our benevolence, would render it a troublesome guest, and <51> make us cling rather to selfishness, which we can always gratify. At the same time, tho' there is not room for a more extensive list of particular objects, yet the faculty we have of uniting numberless individuals into one complex object, enlarges greatly the sphere of benevolence. By that faculty our country, our government, our religion, become objects of public spirit, and of a lively affection. The individuals that compose the group, considered apart, may be too minute, or too distant, for our benevolence: but when united into one whole, accumulation makes them great, greatness makes them conspicuous; and affection, preserved entire and undivided, is bestow'd upon an abstract object, as upon one that is single and visible; but with energy proportioned to its greater dignity and importance. Thus the principle of benevolence is not too sparingly scattered among men. It is indeed made subordinate to self-interest, which is wisely ordered, as will afterward be made evident (*a*): but its power and extent are nicely proportioned to the limited capacity of man, and to his situation in this world; < 52 > so as better to fulfil its destination, than if it were an overmatch for self-interest, and for every other principle.

SECTION V

Laws respecting Rewards and Punishments.

Reflecting on the moral branch of our nature qualifying us for society in a manner suited to our capacity, we cannot overlook the hand of our Maker; for means so finely adjusted to an important end, never happen by chance. It must however be acknowledged, that in many individuals, the principle of duty has not vigour nor authority sufficient to stem every tide of unruly passion: by the vigilance of some passions, we are taken unguarded; deluded by the sly insinuations of others; or overwhelmed with the stormy impetuosity of a third sort. Moral evil is thus introduced, and much wrong is done. This new scene suggests to us, that there must be some article still want-<53>ing to complete the moral system; some means for redressing such wrongs, and for preventing the reiteration of them. To accomplish these important ends, there are added to the moral system, laws relative to rewards and punishments, and to reparation; of which in their order.

Many animals are qualified for society by instinct merely; such as beavers, sheep, monkeys, bees, rooks. But men are seldom led by instinct: their actions are commonly prompted by passions; of which there is an endless variety, social and selfish, benevolent and malevolent. And were every passion equally entitled to gratification, man would be utterly unqualified for society: he would be a ship without a rudder, obedient to every wind, and moving at random without any ultimate destination. The faculty of reason would make no opposition; for were there no sense of wrong, it

(*a*) Sect. 7.

would be reasonable to gratify every desire that harms not ourselves: and to talk of punishment would be absurd; for punishment, in its very idea, implies some wrong that ought to be redressed. Hence the necessity of the moral sense, to qualify us for society: by in-<54>structing us in our duty, it renders us accountable for our conduct, and makes us susceptible of rewards and punishments. The moral sense fulfils another valuable purpose: it erects in man an unerring standard for the application and measure of rewards and punishments.

To complete the system of rewards and punishments, it is necessary that a provision be made, both of power and of willingness to reward and punish. The author of our nature hath provided amply for the former, by entitling every man to reward and punish as his native privilege. And he has provided for the latter, by a noted principle in our nature, prompting us to exercise the power. Impelled by that principle, we reward the virtuous with approbation and esteem, and punish the vicious with disapprobation and contempt. And there is an additional motive for exercising that principle, which is, that we have great satisfaction in rewarding, and no less in punishing.

As to punishment in particular, an action done intentionally to produce mischief, is criminal, and merits punishment. Such an action, being disagree-<55>able, raises my resentment, even where I have no connection with the person injured; and the principle mentioned impells me to chastise the delinquent with indignation and hatred. An injury done to myself raises my resentment to a higher tone: I am not satisfied with so slight a punishment as indignation and hatred: the author must by my hand suffer mischief, as great as he has made me suffer.

Even the most secret crime escapes not punishment. The delinquent is tortured with remorse: he even desires to be punished, sometimes so ardently as to punish himself.* There cannot be imagined <56> a contrivance

---

* Mr. John Kello, minister of Spot in East Lothian, had an extraordinary talent for preaching, and was universally held a man of singular piety. His wife was handsome, chearful, tender-hearted, and in a word possessed all the qualities that can endear a woman to her husband. A pious and rich widow in the neighbourhood tempted his avarice. She clung to him as a spiritual guide; and but for his little wife, he had no doubt of obtaining her in marriage. He turned gradually peevish and discontented. His change

more effectual to deter one from vice, than remorse, which itself is a grievous punishment. Self-punishment goes still farther: every criminal, sensible that he ought to be punished, dreads punishment from others; and this dread, <57> however smothered during prosperity, breaks out in adversity, or in depression of mind: his crime stares him in the face, and every accidental misfortune is in his disturbed imagination interpreted to be a punishment: "And they said one to another, We are verily guilty concerning our brother, in that we saw the anguish of his soul, when he besought us; and we would not hear: therefore is this distress come upon us. And Reuben answered them, saying, Spake I not unto you, saying, Do not sin against the child; and ye would not hear? therefore behold also his blood is required" (a).* <58>

---

of behaviour made a deep impression on his wife, for she loved him dearly; and yet she was anxious to conceal her treatment from the world. Her meekness, her submission, her patience, tended but to increase his sullenness. Upon a Sunday morning when on her knees she was offering up her devotions, he came softly behind her, put a rope about her neck, and hung her up to the ceiling. He bolted his gate, creeped out at a window, walked demurely to church, and charmed his hearers with a most pathetic sermon. After divine service, he invited two or three of his neighbours to pass the evening, at his house, telling them that his wife was indisposed, and of late inclined to melancholy; but that she would be glad to see them. It surprised them to find the gate bolted and none to answer: much more when, upon its being forc'd open, they found her in the posture mentioned. The husband seemed to be struck dumb; and counterfeited sorrow so much to the life, that his guests, forgetting the deceased, were wholly interested about the living. His feign'd tears however became real: his soul was oppressed with the weight of his guilt. Finding no relief from agonizing remorse, and from the image of his murdered wife constantly haunting him, he about six weeks after the horrid deed went to Edinburgh and delivered himself up to justice. He was condemned upon his own confession, and executed 4th October 1570. [[Note added in 2nd edition.]]

(a) Genesis xlii. 21.

* John Duke of Britany, commonly termed *the Good Duke,* illustrious for generosity, clemency, and piety, reigned forty-three years, wholly employ'd about the good of his subjects. He was succeeded by his eldest son Francis, a prince weak and suspicious, and consequently liable to be misled by favourites. Arthur of Montauban, in love with the wife of Gilles, brother to the Duke, persuaded the Duke that his brother was laying plots to dethrone him. Gilles being imprisoned, the Duke's best friends conjured him to pity his unhappy brother, who might be imprudent, but assuredly was innocent;—all in vain. Gilles being prosecuted before the three estates of the province for high treason, was unanimously absolved; which irritated the Duke more and more. Arthur of Montauban artfully suggested to his master to try poison; which having miscarried, they next resolved

The usurper Oliver Cromwell found to his dire experience, that the grandeur <59> which he had attained with so much cunning and courage, did not contribute to his happiness; for with happiness guilt is inconsistent. Conscious that he deserved punishment for his crimes, and dreading its being inflicted upon him, all around appeared to him treacherous friends or bitter enemies. Death, which with intrepidity he had braved in the field, was now timorously apprehended from assassins. With a piercing and anxious eye he surveyed every new face. He wore armour under his cloaths, and never moved a step without his guards. Seldom he slept three nights together in the same chamber; nor in any but what had a back-door, at which centinels were placed. Society terrified him by reflecting on his unknown enemies, numerous and implacable. Solitude astonished him by leaving him without protection. Can all the glory and power that this earth can afford be a counterbalance for such misery?[6]

No transgression of self-duty escapes punishment, more than transgression of duty to others. The punishments, tho' not the same, differ in degree more than in kind. Injustice is punished with re-<60>morse: impropriety with shame, which is remorse in a lower degree. Injustice raises indignation in the beholder, and so doth every flagrant impropriety: slighter improprieties receive a milder punishment, being rebuked with some degree of contempt, and commonly with derision (*a*).

---

to starve the prisoner to death. The unfortunate prince, through the bars of a window, cried aloud for bread; but the passengers durst not supply him. One poor woman only had courage more than once to slip some bread within the window. He charged a priest, who had received his confession, to declare to the Duke, "That seeing justice was refused him in this world, he appealed to Heaven; and called upon the Duke to appear before the judgement-seat of God in forty days." The Duke and his favourite, amazed that the prince lived so long without nourishment, employed assassins to smother him with his bed-cloaths. The priest, in obedience to the orders he had received, presented himself before the Duke, and with a loud voice cited him in name of the deceased Lord Gilles to appear before God in forty days. Shame and remorse verified the prediction. The Duke was seized with a sudden terror; and the image of his brother, expiring by his orders, haunted him day and night. He decay'd daily without any marks of a regular disease, and died within the forty days in frightful agony.

See this subject further illustrated in the Sketch *Principles and Progress of Theology,* chap. 1.

(*a*) See Elements of Criticism, chap. 10.

6. Paragraph added in 3rd edition.

So far we have been led in a beaten track; but in attempting to proceed, we are entangled in mazes and intricacies. An action well intended may happen to produce no good; and an action ill intended may happen to produce no mischief: a man overawed by fear, may be led to do mischief against his will; and a person, mistaking the standard of right and wrong, may be innocently led to do acts of injustice. By what rule, in such cases, are rewards and punishments to be apply'd? Ought a man to be rewarded when he does no good, or punished when he does no mischief: ought he to be punished for doing mischief against his will, or for doing mischief when he thinks he is acting innocently? These questions suggest a doubt, whether the standard of <61> right and wrong be applicable to rewards and punishments.

We have seen that there is an invariable standard of right and wrong, which depends not in any degree on private opinion or conviction. By that standard, all pecuniary claims are judged, all claims of property, and, in a word, every demand founded on interest, not excepting reparation, as will afterward appear. But with respect to the moral characters of men, and with respect to rewards and punishments, a different standard is erected in the common sense of mankind, neither rigid nor inflexible; which is, the opinion that men have of their own actions. It is mentioned above, that a man is esteemed innocent in doing what he himself thinks right, and guilty in doing what he himself thinks wrong. In applying this standard to rewards and punishments, we reward those who in doing wrong are however convinced that they are innocent; and punish those who in doing right are however convinced that they are guilty.* Some, it is true, are so pervert-<62>ed by improper education or by superstition, as to espouse numberless absurd tenets, contradictory to the standard of right and wrong; and yet such men are no exception from the general rule: if they act according to conscience, they are innocent, and safe against punishment however wrong the action may be; and if they act against conscience, they are guilty and punishable however right the action may be: it is abhorrent to every moral

---

* Virtuous and vicious, innocent and guilty, signify qualities both of men and of their actions. Approbation and disapprobation, praise and blame, signify certain emotions or sentiments of those who see or contemplate men and their actions.

perception, that a guilty person be rewarded, or an innocent person punished. Further, if mischief be done contrary to Will, as where a man is compelled by fear or by torture, to reveal the secrets of his party; he may be grieved for yielding to the weakness of his nature, contrary to his firmest resolves; but he has no check of conscience, and upon that account is not liable to punishment. And lastly, in order that personal merit and demerit may not in any measure depend on chance, we are so constituted as to place innocence and guilt, not on the event, but on the in-<63>tention of doing right or wrong; and accordingly, whatever be the event, a man is praised for an action well intended, and condemned for an action ill intended.

But what if a man intending a certain wrong happen by accident to do a wrong he did not intend; as, for example, intending to rob a warren by shooting the rabbits, he accidentally wounds a child unseen behind a bush? The delinquent ought to be punished for intending to rob; and he is also subjected to repair the hurt done to the child: but he cannot be punished for the accidental wound; because our nature regulates punishment by the intention, and not by the event.* <64>

---

* During the infancy of nations, pecuniary compositions for crimes were universal; and during that long period, very little weight was laid upon intention. This proceeded from the cloudiness and obscurity of moral perceptions among barbarians, making no distinction between reparation and pecuniary punishment. Where a man does mischief intentionally, or is *versans in illicito,* as expressed in the Roman law, he is justly bound to repair all the harm that ensues, however accidentally; and from the resemblance of pecuniary punishment to reparation, the rule was childishly extended to punishment. But this rule, so little consistent with moral principles, could not long subsist after pecuniary compositions gave place to corporal punishment; and accordingly, among civilized nations, the law of nature is restored, which prohibits punishment for any mischief that is not intentional. The English must be excepted, who, remarkably tenacious of their original laws and customs, preserve in force, even as to capital punishment, the above-mentioned rule that obtained among barbarians, when pecuniary compositions were in vigour. The following passage is from Hales (Pleas of the Crown, chap. 39). "Regularly he that voluntarily and knowingly intends hurt to the person of a man, as for example to beat him, tho' he intend not death, yet if death ensues, it excuseth not from the guilt of murder, or manslaughter at least, as the circumstances of the case happen." And Foster, in his Crown law, teaches the same doctrine, never once suspecting in it the least deviation from moral principles. "A shooteth at the poultry of B, and by accident killeth a man: if his intention was to steal the poultry, which must be collected

A crime against any primary virtue is attended with severe and never-failing punishment, more efficacious than any that have been invented to enforce municipal laws: on the other hand, the preserving <65> primary virtues inviolate, is attended with little merit. The secondary virtues are directly opposite: the neglecting them is not attended with any punishment; but the practice of them is attended with illustrious rewards. Offices of undeserved kindness, returns of good for ill, generous toils and sufferings for our friends or for our country, are attended with consciousness of self-merit, and with universal praise and admiration; the highest rewards a generous mind is susceptible of.

From what is said, the following observation will occur: The pain of transgressing justice, fidelity, or any duty, is much greater than the pleasure of performing; but the pain of neglecting a generous action, or any secondary virtue, is as nothing compared with the pleasure of performing. Among the vices opposite to the primary virtues, the most striking moral deformity is found; among the secondary virtues, the most striking moral beauty. <66>

SECTION VI

Laws respecting Reparation.

The principle of reparation is made a branch of the moral system for accomplishing two ends: which are, to repress wrongs that are not criminal, and to make up the loss sustained by wrongs of whatever kind. With respect to the former, reparation is a species of punishment: with respect to the latter, it is an act of justice. These ends will be better understood, after ascertaining the nature and foundation of reparation; to which the following division of actions is necessary. First, actions that we are bound to perform. Second, actions that we perform in prosecution of a right or privilege. Third, indifferent actions, described above. Actions of the first kind subject

---

from circumstances, it will be murder by reason of that felonious intent; but if it was done wantonly, and without that intention, it will be barely manslaughter." (p. 259.)

not a man to reparation, whatever damage ensues; because it is his duty to perform them, and it would be inconsist-<67>ent with morality that a man should be subjected to reparation for doing his duty. The laws of reparation that concern actions of the second kind, are more complex. The social state, highly beneficial by affording opportunity for mutual good offices, is attended with some inconveniencies; as where a person happens to be in a situation of necessarily harming others by exercising a right or privilege. If the foresight of harming another restrain me not from exercising my right, the interest of that other is made subservient to mine: on the other hand, if such foresight restrain me from exercising my right, my interest is made subservient to his. What doth the moral sense provide in that case? To preserve as far as possible an equality among persons born free and by nature equal in rank, the moral sense dictates a rule, no less beautiful than salutary; which is, That the exercising a right will not justify me for doing direct mischief; but will justify me, tho' I foresee that mischief may possibly happen. The first branch of the rule resolves into a proposition established above, That no interest of mine, not even life itself, will authorise <68> me to hurt an innocent person. The other branch is supported by expediency: for if the bare possibility of hurting others were sufficient to restrain a man from prosecuting his rights and privileges; men would be too much cramped in action, or rather would be reduced to a state of absolute inactivity. With respect to the first branch, I am criminal, and liable even to punishment: with respect to the other, I am not even culpable, nor bound to repair the mischief that happens to ensue. But this proposition admits a temperament, which is, that if any danger be foreseen, I am in some degree culpable, if I be not at due pains to prevent it. For example, where in pulling down an old house I happen to wound one passing accidentally, without calling aloud to beware.[7]

With respect to indifferent actions, the moral sense dictates, that we ought carefully to avoid doing mischief, either direct or consequential. As we suffer no loss by forbearing actions that are done for pastime merely, such an action is *culpable* or *faulty*, if the consequent mischief was foreseen or might have been foreseen; and the actor of course is subjected to re-

---

7. "But this proposition . . . aloud to beware": added in 2nd edition.

<69>paration. As this is a cardinal point in the doctrine of reparation, I shall endeavour to explain it more fully. Without intending any harm, a man may foresee, that what he is about to do will probably or possibly produce mischief; and sometimes mischief follows that was neither intended nor foreseen. The action in the former case is not criminal; because ill intention is essential to a crime: but it is culpable or faulty; and if mischief ensue, the actor blames himself, and is blamed by others, for having done what he ought not to have done. Thus, a man who throws a large stone among a crowd of people, is highly culpable; because he must foresee that mischief will probably ensue, tho' he has no intention to hurt any person. As to the latter case, tho' mischief was neither intended nor foreseen, yet if it might have been foreseen, the action is rash or uncautious, and consequently culpable or faulty in some degree. Thus, if a man, shooting at a mark for recreation near a high road, happen to wound one passing accidentally, without calling aloud to keep out of the way, the action is in some degree culpable, <70> because the mischief might have been foreseen. But tho' mischief ensue, an action is not culpable or faulty if all reasonable precaution have been adhibited: the moral sense declares the author to be innocent* and blameless: the mischief is accidental; and the action may be termed *unlucky,* but comes not under the denomination of either right or wrong. In general, when we act merely for amusement, our nature makes us answerable for the harm that ensues, if it was either foreseen or might with due attention have been foreseen. But our rights and privileges would profit us little, if their exercise were put under the same restraint: it is more wisely ordered, that the probability of mischief, even foreseen, should not restrain a man from prosecuting his concerns, which may often be of consequence to him; provided that he act with due precaution. He proceeds accordingly with a safe conscience, and is not afraid of being blamed either by God or man. <71>

With respect to rash or uncautious actions, where the mischief might have been foreseen tho' not actually foreseen; it is not sufficient to escape

---

* *Innocent* here is opposed to *culpable:* in a broader sense it is opposed to *criminal.* With respect to punishment, an action tho' culpable is innocent, if it be not criminal: with respect to reparation, it is not innocent if it be culpable.

blame, that a man, naturally rash or inattentive, acts according to his character: a degree of precaution is required, both by himself and by others, such as is natural to the generality of men: he perceives that he might and *ought* to have acted more cautiously; and his conscience reproaches him for his inattention, no less than if he were naturally more sedate and attentive. Thus the circumspection natural to mankind in general, is applied as a standard to every individual; and if a man fall short of that standard he is culpable and blameable, however unforeseen by him the mischief may have been.

What is said upon culpable actions, is equally applicable to culpable omissions; for by these also mischief may be occasioned, entitling the sufferer to reparation. If we forbear to do our duty with an intention to occasion mischief, the forbearance is criminal. The only question is, how far forbearance without such intention is culpable: supposing the probabi- <72>lity of mischief to have been foreseen, tho' not intended, the omission is highly culpable; and tho' neither intended nor foreseen, yet the omission is culpable in a lower degree, if there have been less care and attention than are proper in performing the duty required. But supposing all due care, the omission of extreme care and diligence is not culpable.*

By ascertaining what acts and omissions are culpable or faulty, the doctrine of reparation is rendered extremely simple; for it may be laid down as a rule without a single exception, That every culpable act, and every culpable omission, binds us in conscience to repair the mischief occasioned by it. The moral sense binds us no <73> farther; for it loads not with reparation the man who is blameless and innocent: the harm is accidental; and we are so constituted as not to be responsible in conscience for what happens by accident. But here it is requisite, that the man be in every respect

---

* *Culpa lata aequiparatur dolo* [[gross negligence is equivalent to fraud]], says the Roman law. They are equal with respect to reparation and to every civil consequence; but they are certainly not equal in a criminal view. The essence of a crime consists in the intention to do mischief; upon which account no fault or *culpa* however gross amounts to a crime. But may not gross negligence be a subject of punishment? A jailor sees a state-prisoner taking steps to make his escape; and yet will not give himself the trouble to prevent it; and so the prisoner escapes. Damages cannot be qualified, because no person is hurt; and if the jailor cannot be punished, he escapes free. [[Note added in 2nd edition.]]

innocent: for if he intend harm, tho' not what he has done, he will find himself bound in conscience to repair the accidental harm he has done; as, for example, when aiming a blow unjustly at one in the dark, he happens to wound another whom he did not suspect to be there. And hence it is a rule in all municipal laws, That one *versans in illicito*[8] is liable to repair every consequent damage. That these particulars are wisely ordered by the Author of our nature for the good of society, will appear afterward (*a*). In general, the rules above mentioned are dictated by the moral sense; and we are compelled to obey them by the principle of reparation.

We are now prepared for a more particular inspection of the two ends of reparation above mentioned, The repressing wrongs that are not criminal, and the ma-<74>king up what loss is sustained by wrongs of whatever kind. With respect to the first, it is clear, that punishment in its proper sense cannot be inflicted for a wrong that is culpable only; and if nature did not provide some means for repressing such wrongs, society would scarce be a comfortable state. Laying conscience aside, pecuniary reparation is the only remedy that can be provided against culpable omissions: and with respect to culpable commissions, the necessity of reparation is still more apparent; for conscience alone, without the sanction of reparation, would seldom have authority sufficient to restrain us from acting rashly or uncautiously, even where the possibility of mischief is foreseen, and far less where it is not foreseen.

With respect to the second end of reparation, my conscience dictates to me, that if a man suffer by my fault, whether the mischief was foreseen or not foreseen, it is my duty to make up his loss; and I perceive intuitively, that the loss ought to rest ultimately upon me, and not upon the sufferer, who has not been culpable in any degree. <75>

In every case where the mischief done can be estimated by a pecuniary compensation, the two ends of reparation coincide. The sum is taken from the one as a sort of punishment for his fault, and is bestow'd on the other to make up the loss he has sustained. But in numberless cases where mischief done cannot be compensated with money, reparation is in its nature

(*a*) Sect. 7.
8. I.e., a trespasser.

a sort of punishment. Defamation, contemptuous treatment, personal restraint, the breaking one's peace of mind, are injuries that cannot be repaired with money; and the pecuniary reparation decreed against the
wrong-doer, can only be considered as a punishment inflicted in order to
deter him from reiterating such injuries: the sum, it is true, is awarded to
the person injured; but not as sufficient to make up his loss, which money
cannot do, but only as a *solatium* for what he has suffered.

Hitherto it is supposed, that the man who intends a wrong action, is at
the same time conscious of its being so. But a man may intend a wrong
action, thinking erroneously that it is right; or a right action, thinking erroneously that it is <76> wrong; and the question is, What shall be the
consequence of such errors with respect to reparation. The latter case is
clear: the person who occasionally suffers loss by a right action, has not a
claim for reparation, because he has no just cause of complaint. On the
other hand, if the action be wrong, the innocence of the author, for which
he is indebted to an error in judgement, will not relieve him from reparation. When he is made sensible of his error, he feels himself bound in conscience to repair the harm he has done by a wrong action: and others, sensible of his error from the beginning, have the same feeling: nor will his
obstinacy in resisting conviction, nor his dullness in not apprehending his
error, mend the matter: it is well that these defects relieve him from punishment, without wronging others by denying a claim for reparation. A
man's errors ought to affect himself only, and not those who have not erred.
Hence in general, reparation always follows wrong; and is not affected by
any erroneous opinion of a wrong action being right, more than of a right
action being wrong. <77>

But this doctrine suffers an exception with respect to one who, having
undertaken a trust, is bound in duty to act. A judge is in that state: it is his
duty to pronounce sentence in every case that comes before him; and if he
judge according to his knowledge, he is not liable for consequences. A judge
cannot be subjected to reparation, unless the judgement he gave was intentionally wrong. An officer of the revenue is in the same predicament.
Led by a doubtful clause in a statute, he makes a seizure of goods as forfeited
to the crown, which afterward, in the proper court, are found not to be
seizable: he ought not to be subjected to reparation, if he have acted to the

best of his judgement. This rule however must be taken with a limitation: a public officer who is grossly ignorant, will not be excused; for he ought to know better.

Reparation is due, tho' the immediate act be involuntary, provided it be connected with a preceding voluntary act. Example: "If A ride an unruly horse in Lincolns-inn fields, to tame him, and the horse breaking from A, run over B and grievously hurt him; B shall have <78> an action against A: for tho' the mischief was done against the will of A, yet since it was his fault to bring a wild horse into a frequented place where mischief might ensue, he must answer for the consequences." Gaius seems to carry this rule still farther, holding in general, that if a horse, by the weakness or unskilfulness of the rider, break away and do mischief, the rider is liable (*a*). But Gaius probably had in his eye a frequented place, where the mischief might have been foreseen. Thus in general, a man is made liable for the mischief occasioned by his voluntary deed, tho' the immediate act that occasioned the mischief be involuntary.

SECTION VII

Final Causes of the foregoing Laws of Nature.

Several final causes have been already mentioned, which could not conveni- <79>ently be reserved for the present section, being necessary for explaining the subjects to which they relate; the final cause for instance of erecting a standard of morals upon the common sense of mankind. I proceed now to what have not been mentioned, or but slightly mentioned.

The final cause that presents itself first to view, respects man considered as an accountable being. The sense of being accountable, is one of our most vigilant guards against the silent attacks of vice. When a temptation moves me it immediately occurs, What will the world say? I imagine my friends expostulating, my enemies reviling—it would be in vain to dissemble—my spirits sink—the temptation vanishes. 2dly, Praise and blame, especially

---

(*a*) 1. 8. §. 1. ad leg. Aquil.

from those we regard, are strong incentives to virtue: but if we were not accountable for our conduct, praise and blame would seldom be well directed; for how shall a man's intentions be known, without calling him to account? And praise or blame, frequently ill-directed, would lose their influence. 3dly, This branch of our nature, is the corner-stone <80> of the criminal law. Did not a man think himself accountable to all the world, and to his judge in a peculiar manner, it would be natural for him to think, that the justest sentence pronounced against him, is oppression, not justice. 4thly, It promotes society. If we were not accountable beings, those connected by blood, or by country, would be no less shy and reserved, than if they were utter strangers to each other.

The final cause that next occurs, being simple and obvious, is mentioned only that it may not seem to have been overlooked. All right actions are agreeable, all wrong actions, disagreeable. This is a wise appointment of Providence. We meet with so many temptations against duty, that it is not always easy to persevere in the right path: would we persevere, were duty disagreeable? And were acts of pure benevolence disagreeable, they would be rare, however worthy of praise.

Another final cause respects duty, in contradistinction to pure benevolence. All the moral laws are founded on intuitive perception; and are so simple and plain, as to be perfectly apprehended by the most <81> ignorant. Were they in any degree complex or obscure, they would be perverted by selfishness and prejudice. No conviction inferior to what is afforded by intuitive perception, could produce in mankind a common sense in moral duties. Reason would afford no general conviction; because that faculty is distributed in portions so unequal, as to bar all hopes from it of uniformity either in practice or in opinion. We are taught beside by woful experience, that reason even the most convincing, has no commanding influence over the greater part of men. Reason, it is true, aided by experience, supports morality; by convincing us, that we cannot be happy if we abandon duty for any other interest. But conviction seldom weighs much against imperious passion; to control which the vigorous and commanding principle of duty is requisite, directed by the shining light of intuition.

A proposition laid down above, appears a sort of mystery in the moral system, That tho' evidently all moral duties are contrived for promoting the general good, yet that a choice is not permitted among different goods, or between good and ill; <82> but that we are strictly tied down to perform or forbear certain particular acts, without regard to consequences; or, in other words, that we must not do wrong, whatever good it may produce. The final cause I am about to unfold, will clear this mystery, and set the beauty of the moral system in a conspicuous light. I begin with observing, that as the general good of mankind, or even of the society we live in, results from many and various circumstances intricately combined; it is far above the capacity of man, to judge in every instance what particular action will tend the most to that end. The authorising therefore a man to trace out his duty by weighing endless circumstances good and ill, would open a wide door to partiality and passion, and often lead him unwittingly to prefer the preponderating ill, under a false appearance of being the greater good. At that rate, the opinions of men about right and wrong, would be as various as their faces; which, as observed above, would totally unhinge society. It is better ordered by Providence even for the general good, that, avoiding complex and obscure objects, we are di-<83>rected by the moral sense to perform certain plain and simple acts, which admit no ambiguity.

In the next place, To permit ill in order to produce greater good, may suit a being of universal benevolence; but is repugnant to the nature of man, composed of selfish and benevolent principles. We have seen above, that the true moral balance depends on a subordination of self-love to duty, and of discretionary benevolence to self-love; and accordingly every man is sensible of injustice when he is hurt in order to benefit another. Were it a rule in society, That a greater good to any other would make it an act of justice to deprive me of my life, of my reputation, or of my property, I should renounce the society of men, and associate with more harmless animals.

Thirdly, The true moral system, that which is display'd above, is not only better suited to the nature of man and to his limited capacity, but contributes more to the general good, which I now proceed to demonstrate. It would be losing time to prove, that one entirely selfish is ill fitted <84> for society; and we have seen (a), that universal benevolence, were it a duty,

(a) Sect. 4.

would contribute to the general good perhaps less than absolute selfishness. Man is too limited in capacity and in power for universal benevolence. Even the greatest monarch has not power to exercise his benevolence, but within a very narrow sphere; and if so, how unfit would such a duty be for private persons, who have very little power? Serving only to distress them by inability of performance, they would endeavour to smother it altogether, and give full scope to selfishness. Man is much better qualified for doing good, by a constitution in which benevolence is duly blended with self-love. Benevolence as a duty, takes place of self-love; a regulation essential to society: benevolence as a virtue, not a duty, gives place to self-love; because as every man has more power, knowledge, and opportunity, to promote his own good than that of others, a greater quantity of good is produced, than if benevolence were our only principle of action. This holds, even supposing no harm done to any per-<85>son: much more would it hold, were we permitted to hurt some, in order to produce more good to others.

The foregoing final causes respect morality in general. We now proceed to particulars; and the first and most important is the law of restraint. Man is evidently framed for society: and as there can be no society among creatures who prey upon each other, it was necessary to provide against mutual injuries; which is effectually done by this law. Its necessity with respect to personal security is self-evident; and with respect to property, its necessity will appear from what follows. In the nature of every man there is a propensity to hoard or store up things useful to himself and family. But this natural propensity would be rendered ineffectual, were he not secured in the possession of what he thus stores up; for no man will toil to accumulate what he cannot securely possess. This security is afforded by the moral sense, which dictates, that the first occupant of goods provided by nature for the subsistence of man, ought to be protected in the possession, and that such goods ought to be inviolably his pro-<86>perty. Thus, by the great law of restraint, men have a protection for their goods, as well as for their persons; and are no less secure in society, than if they were separated from each other by impregnable walls.

Several other duties are little less essential than that of restraint, to the existence of society. Mutual trust and confidence, without which society would be an uncomfortable state, enter into the character of the human species; to which the duties of veracity and fidelity correspond. The final cause of these corresponding duties is obvious: the latter would be of no use in society without the former; and the former, without the latter, would be hurtful by laying men open to fraud and deceit.

With respect to veracity in particular, man is so constituted, that he must be indebted to information for the knowledge of most things that benefit or hurt him; and if he could not depend upon information, society would be very little beneficial. Further, it is wisely ordered, that we should be bound by the moral sense to speak truth, even where we perceive no <87> harm in transgressing that duty; because it is sufficient that harm may ensue, tho' not foreseen. At the same time, falsehood always does mischief: it may happen not to injure us externally in our reputation, or in our goods; but it never fails to injure us internally: the sweetest and most refined pleasure of society, is a candid intercourse of sentiments, of opinions, of desires, and wishes; and it would be poisonous to indulge any falsehood in such intercourse.

Because man is the weakest of all animals in a state of separation, and the very strongest in society by mutual aid and support; covenants and promises, which greatly contribute to these, are made binding by the moral sense.

The final cause of the law of propriety, which enforces the duty we owe to ourselves, comes next in order. In discoursing upon those laws of nature which concern society, there is no occasion to mention any self-duty but what relates to society; of which kind are prudence, temperance, industry, firmness of mind. And that such qualities should be made our duty, is wisely ordered in a double <88> respect; first, as qualifying us to act a proper part in society; and next, as intitling us to good-will from others. It is the interest, no doubt, of every man, to suit his behaviour to the dignity of his nature, and to the station allotted him by Providence; for such rational conduct contributes to happiness, by preserving health, procuring plenty, gaining the esteem of others, and, which of all is the greatest blessing, by gaining a justly-founded self-esteem. But here interest solely is not relied on: the powerful authority of duty is added, that in a matter of the utmost importance to ourselves, and of some importance to the society we live in, our conduct may be regular and steady. These duties tend not only to render a man happy in himself; but also, by procuring the good-will and esteem of others, to command their aid and assistance in time of need.

I proceed to the final causes of natural rewards and punishments. It is laid down above, that controversies about property and about other matters of interest, must be adjusted by the standard of right and wrong. But to bring rewards and punishments under the same standard, with-<89>out regard to private conscience, would be a plan unworthy of our Maker. It is clear, that to reward one who is not conscious of merit, or to punish one who is not conscious of demerit, cannot answer any good end; and in particular, cannot tend either to improvement or to reformation of manners. How much more like the Deity is the plan of nature, which rewards no man who is not conscious that he merits reward, and punishes no man who is not conscious that he merits punishment! By that plan, and by that only, rewards and punishments accomplish every good end, a final cause most illustrious!

The rewards and punishments that attend the primary and secondary virtues, are finely contrived for supporting the distinction between them set forth above. Punishment must be confined to the transgression of primary virtues, it being the intention of nature that secondary virtues be entirely free. On the other hand, secondary virtues are more highly rewarded than primary: generosity, for example, makes a greater figure than justice; and magnanimity, heroism, undaunted cou-<90>rage, a still greater figure. One would imagine at first view, that the primary virtues, being more essential, should be intitled to the first place in our esteem, and be more amply rewarded than the secondary; and yet in elevating the latter above the former, peculiar wisdom and foresight are conspicuous. Punishment is appropriated to enforce primary virtues; and if these virtues were also attended with the highest rewards, secondary virtues, degraded to a lower rank, would be deprived of that enthusiastic admiration which is their chief support: self-interest would universally prevail over benevolence; and would banish those numberless favours we receive from each other in society, which are beneficial in point of interest, and still more so by generating affection and friendship.

In our progress through final causes, we come at last to reparation, one of the principles destined by Providence for redressing wrongs committed, and for preventing reiteration. The final cause of this principle where the mischief arises from intention, is clear: for to protect individuals in society, it is not sufficient that the <91> delinquent be punished; it is necessary over and above, that the mischief be repaired.

Secondly, Where the act is wrong or unjust, tho' not understood by the author to be so, it is wisely ordered that reparation should follow; which will thus appear. Considering the fallibility of man, it would be too severe never to give any allowance for error. On the other hand, to make it a law in our nature, never to take advantage of error, would be giving too much indulgence to indolence and remission of mind, tending to make us neglect the improvement of our rational faculties. Our nature is so happily framed, as to avoid these extremes by distinguishing between gain and loss. No man is conscious of wrong, when he takes advantage of an error committed by another to save himself from loss: if there must be a loss, common sense dictates, that it ought to rest upon the person who has erred, however innocently, rather than upon the person who has not erred. Thus, in a competition among creditors about the estate of their bankrupt debtor, every one is at liberty to avail himself of an er-<92>ror committed by his competitor, in order to recover payment. But *in lucro captando,* the moral sense teacheth a different lesson; which is, that no man ought to lay hold of another's error to make gain by it. Thus, an heir finding a rough diamond in the repositories of his ancestor, gives it away, mistaking it for a common pebble: the purchaser is in conscience and equity bound to restore, or to pay a just price.

Thirdly, The following considerations respecting the precaution that is necessary in acting, unfold a final cause, no less beautiful than that last mentioned. Society could not subsist in any tolerable manner, were full scope given to rashness and negligence, and to every action that strictly speaking is not criminal; whence it is a maxim founded no less upon utility than upon justice, That men in society ought to be extremely circumspect, as to every action that may possibly do harm. On the other hand, it is also a maxim, That as the prosperity and happiness of man depend on action, activity ought to be encouraged, instead of being discouraged by dread of consequences. These <93> maxims, seemingly in opposition, have natural limits that prevent their encroaching one upon the other. There is a certain degree of attention and circumspection that men generally bestow upon affairs, proportioned to their importance: if that degree were not sufficient to defend against a claim of reparation, individuals would be too much cramped in action; which would be a great discouragement to activity: if a less degree were sufficient, there would be too great scope for rash or remiss conduct; which would prove the bane of society. These limits, which evidently tend to the good of society, are adjusted by the moral sense; which dictates, as laid down in the section of Reparation, that the man who acts with foresight of the probability of mischief, or acts rashly and uncautiously without such foresight, ought to be liable for consequences; but that the man who acts cautiously, without foreseeing or suspecting any mischief, ought not to be liable for consequences.

In the same section it is laid down, that the moral sense requires from every man, not his own degree of vigilance and at-<94>tention, which may be very small, but that which belongs to the common nature of the species. The final cause of that regulation will appear upon considering, that were reparation to depend upon personal circumstances, there would be a necessity of enquiring into the character of individuals, their education, their manner of living, and the extent of their understanding; which would render judges arbitrary, and such law-suits inextricable. But by assuming the common nature of the species as a standard, by which every man in conscience judges of his own actions, law-suits about reparation are rendered easy and expeditious.

SECTION VIII

Liberty and Necessity considered with respect to Morality.

Having in the foregoing sections ascertained the reality of a moral sense, with its sentiments of approbation and dis-<95>approbation, praise and blame; the purpose of the present section is, to shew, that these sentiments are consistent with the laws that govern the actions of man as a rational being. In order to which, it is first necessary to explain these laws; for there has been much controversy about them, especially among divines of the Arminian and Calvinist sects.

Human actions, as laid down in the first section, are of three kinds: one, where we act by instinct, without any view to consequences; one, where we act by will in order to produce some effect; and one, where we act against will. With respect to the first, the agent acts blindly, without deliberation or choice; and the external act follows necessarily from the instinctive impulse.* <96> Voluntary actions done with a view to an end, are in a very different condition: into these, desire and will, enter: desire to accomplish the end goes first; the will to act in order to accomplish the end is next; and the external act follows of course. Desire considered as what influences the will, is termed a *motive.* Thus, hearing that my friend is in the hands of robbers, I burn with desire to free him: desire influences my will to arm my servants, and to fly to his relief. Actions done against will come in afterward.

But what is it that raises desire? The answer is ready: it is the prospect of attaining some agreeable end, or of avoiding one that is disagreeable. And if it be enquired, What makes an object agreeable or disagreeable; the answer is equally ready, that our nature makes it so. <97> Certain visible objects are agreeable, certain sounds, and certain smells: other objects of these senses are disagreeable. But there we must stop; for we are far from being so intimately acquainted with our own nature as to assign the causes. These hints are sufficient for my present purpose: if one be curious to know more, the theory of desire, and of agreeableness and disagreeableness, will be found in Elements of Criticism (*a*).

With respect to instinctive actions, no person, I presume, thinks that there is any freedom: an infant applies to the nipple, and a bird builds a nest, no less necessarily than a stone falls to the ground. With respect to voluntary actions, done in order to produce some effect, the necessity is the

---

* A stonechatter makes its nest on the ground or near it; and the young, as soon as they can shift for themselves, leave the nest instinctively. An egg of that bird was laid in a swallow's nest, fixed to the roof of a church. The swallow fed all the young equally, without distinction. The young stonechatter left the nest at the usual time before it could fly; and falling to the ground, it was taken up dead. Here is instinct in purity, exerting itself blindly without regard to variation of circumstances. The same is observable in our dunghill-fowl. They feed on worms, corn, and other seeds dropt on the ground. In order to discover their food, nature has provided them with an instinct to scrape with the foot; and the instinct is so regularly exercised, that they scrape even when they are set upon a heap of corn.

(*a*) Chap. 2.

same, tho' less apparent at first view. The external action is determined by
the will: the will is determined by desire: and desire by what is agreeable or
disagreeable. Here is a chain of causes and effects, not one link of which
is arbitrary, or under command of the agent: he cannot will but according
to his desire: he cannot desire <98> but according to what is agreeable or
disagreeable in the objects perceived: nor do these qualities depend on his
inclination or fancy; he has no power to make a beautiful woman appear
ugly, nor to make a rotten carcase smell sweetly.

Many good men apprehending danger to morality from holding our
actions to be necessary, endeavour to break the chain of causes and effects
above mentioned, maintaining, "That whatever influence desire or motives
may have, it is the agent himself who is the cause of every action; that desire
may advise, but cannot command; and therefore that a man is still free to
act in contradiction to desire and to the strongest motives." That a being
may exist, which in every case acts blindly and arbitrarily, without having
any end in view, I can make a shift to conceive: but it is difficult for me
even to imagine a thinking and rational being, that has affections and passions, that has a desirable end in view, that can easily accomplish this end;
and yet, after all, can fly off, or remain at rest, without any cause, reason,
or motive, to sway it. If such a whimsical being can possibly ex-<99>ist, I
am certain that man is not the being. There is perhaps not a person above
the condition of a changeling, but can say why he did so and so, what
moved him, what he intended. Nor is a single fact stated to make us believe,
that ever a man acted against his own desire, who was not compelled by
external force. On the contrary, constant and universal experience proves,
that human actions are governed by certain inflexible laws; and that a man
cannot exert his self-motive power, but in pursuance of some desire or
motive.

Had a motive always the same influence, actions proceeding from it
would appear no less necessary than the actions of matter. The various degrees of influence that motives have on different men at the same time, and
on the same man at different times, occasion a doubt by suggesting a notion
of chance. Some motives however have such influence, as to leave no doubt:
a timid female has a physical power to throw herself into the mouth of a
lion, roaring for food; but she is withheld by terror no less effectually than

by cords: if she should rush upon the lion, <100> would not every one conclude that she was frantic? A man, tho' in a deep sleep, retains a physical power to act, but he cannot exert it. A man, tho' desperately in love, retains a physical power to refuse the hand of his mistress; but he cannot exert that power in contradiction to his own ardent desire, more than if he were fast asleep. Now if a strong motive have a necessary influence, there is no reason for doubting, but that a weak motive must also have its influence, the same in kind, tho' not in degree. Some actions indeed are strangely irregular: but let the wildest action be scrutiniz'd, there will always be discovered some motive or desire, which, however whimsical or capricious, was what influenced the person to act. Of two contending motives, is it not natural to expect that the stronger will prevail, however little its excess may be? If there by any doubt, it must arise from a supposition that a weak motive can be resisted arbitrarily. Where then are we to fix the boundary between a weak and a strong motive? If a weak motive can be resisted, why not one a little stronger, and why not the strongest? In Elements of <101> Criticism (a) the reader will find many examples of contrary motives weighing against each other. Let him ponder these with the strictest attention: his conclusion will be, that between two motives, however nearly balanced, a man has not an arbitrary choice, but must yield to the stronger. The mind indeed fluctuates for some time, and feels itself in a measure loose: at last, however, it is determined by the more powerful motive, as a balance is by the greater weight after many vibrations.

Such then are the laws that govern our voluntary actions. A man is absolutely free to act according to his own will; greater freedom than which is not conceivable. At the same time, as man is made accountable for his conduct, to his Maker, to his fellow-creatures, and to himself, he is not left to act arbitrarily; for at that rate he would be altogether unaccountable: his will is regulated by desire; and desire by what pleases or displeases him. Where we are subjected to the will of another, would it be our wish, that his will <102> should be under no regulation? And where we are guided by our own will, would it be reasonable to wish, that it should be under no regulation, but be exerted without reason, without any motive, and con-

(a) Chap. 2. part 4.

trary to common sense? Thus, with regard to human conduct, there is a chain of laws established by nature, no one link of which is left arbitrary. By that wise system, man is made accountable; by it, he is made a fit subject for divine and human government: by it, persons of sagacity foresee the conduct of others: and by it, the prescience of the Deity with respect to human actions, is clearly established.

The absurd figure that a man would make acting in contradiction to motives, should be sufficient to open our eyes without an argument. What a despicable figure does a person make, upon whom the same motive has great influence at one time, and very little at another? He is a bad member of society, and cannot be rely'd on as a friend or as an associate. But how highly rational is this supposed person, compared with one who can act in contradiction to every motive? The <103> former may be termed whimsical or capricious: the latter is worse; he is absolutely unaccountable, and cannot be the subject of government, more than a lump of matter unconscious of its own motion.

Let the faculty of acting be compared with that of reasoning: the comparison will reconcile every unbiassed mind to the necessary influence of motives. A man is tied by his nature to form conclusions upon what appears to him true at the time. This indeed does not always secure him against error; but would he be more secure by a power to form conclusions contrary to what appears true? Such a power would make him a most absurd reasoner. Would he be less absurd in acting, if he had a power to act against motives, and contrary to what he thinks right or eligible? To act in that manner, is inconsistent with any notion we can form of a sensible being. Nor do we suppose that man is such a being: in accounting for any action, however whimsical, we always ascribe it to some motive; never once dreaming that there was no motive.

And after all, where would be the advantage of such an arbitrary power? Can <104> a rational man wish seriously to have such a power? or can he seriously think, that God would make man so whimsical a being? To endue man with a degree of self-command sufficient to resist every vitious motive, without any power to resist those that are virtuous, would indeed be a valuable gift; too valuable indeed for man, because it would exalt him to be an angel. But such self-command as to resist both equally, which is the present supposition, would be a great curse, as it would unqualify us for being governed either by God or by man. Better far to be led as rational creatures by the prospect of good, however erroneous our judgement may sometimes be.

While all other animals are subjected to divine government and unerringly fulfil their destination, and considering that man is the only terrestrial being who is formed to know his Maker and to worship him; will it not sound harsh that he alone should be withdrawn from divine government? The power of resisting the strongest motives, whether of religion or of morality, would render him independent of the Deity. <105>

This reasoning is too diffuse: if it can be comprehended in a single view, it will make the deeper impression. There may be conceived different systems for governing man as a thinking and rational being. One is, That virtuous motives should always prevail over every other motive. This, in appearance, would be the most perfect government: but man is not so constituted; and there is reason to doubt, whether such perfection would in his present state correspond to the other branches of his nature (*a*). Another system is, that virtuous motives sometimes prevail, sometimes vitious; and that we are always determined by the prevailing motive. This is the true system of nature; and hence great variety of character and of conduct among men. A third system is, That motives have influence; but that one can act in contradiction to every motive. This is the system I have been combating. Observe only what it resolves into. How is an action to be accounted for that is done in contradiction to every motive? It wanders from the region of com-<106>mon sense into that of mere chance. If such were the nature of man, no one could rely on another: a promise or an oath would be a rope of sand: the utmost cordiality between two friends would be no security to either against the other: the first weapon that comes in the way might be lethal. Would any man wish to have been formed according to such a model? He would probably wish to have been formed according to the model first mentioned: but that is denied him, virtuous motives sometimes prevailing, sometimes vitious; and from the wisdom of Providence we have reason to believe, that this law is of all the best fitted for man in his present state.

(*a*) See book 2. sketch 1. at the end.

To conclude this branch of the subject: In none of the works of Providence, as far as we can penetrate, is there display'd a deeper reach of art and wisdom, than in the laws of action peculiar to man as a thinking and rational being. Were he left loose to act in contradiction to motives, there would be no place for prudence, foresight, nor for adjusting means to an end: It could not be foreseen by others what a man would do the next <107> hour; nay it could not be foreseen even by himself. Man would not be capable of rewards and punishments: he would not be fitted, either for divine or for human government: he would be a creature that has no resemblance to the human race. But man is not left loose; for tho' he is at liberty to act according to his own will, yet his will is regulated by desire, and desire by what pleases and displeases. This connection preserves uniformity of conduct, and confines human actions within the great chain of causes and effects. By this admirable system, liberty and necessity, seemingly incompatible, are made perfectly concordant, fitting us for society, and for government both human and divine.

Having explained the laws that govern human actions; we proceed to what is chiefly intended in the present section, which is, to examine how far the moral sentiments handled in the foregoing sections are consistent with these laws. Let it be kept in view, that the perception of a right and a wrong in actions, is founded entirely upon the moral sense. And that upon the same sense are founded the senti-<108>ments of approbation and praise when a man does right, and of disapprobation and blame when he does wrong. Were we destitute of the moral sense, right and wrong, praise and blame, would be as little understood as colours are by one born blind.*

The formidable argument urged to prove that our moral sentiments are inconsistent with the supposed necessary influence of motives, is what fol-

---

* In an intricate subject like the present, great care should be taken to avoid ambiguities. The term *praise* has two different significations: in one sense it is opposed to *blame;* in another, to *dispraise.* In the former sense it expresses a moral sentiment: in the latter, it expresses only the approving any object that pleases me. I praise one man for his candour, and blame another for being a double-dealer. These, both of them, imply will and intention. I praise a man for being acute; but for being dull, I only dispraise him. I praise a woman for beauty; but blame not any for ugliness, I only dispraise them. None of these particulars imply will or intention.

lows. "If motives have a necessary influence on our actions, there can be no good reason to praise a man for doing right, nor to blame him for doing wrong. What <109> foundation can there be either for praise or blame, when it was not in a man's power to have acted otherwise. A man commits murder, instigated by a sudden fit of revenge: why should he be punished, if he acted necessarily, and could not resist the violence of the passion?" Here it is supposed, that a power of resistance is essential to praise and blame. But upon examination it will be found, that this supposition has not any support in the moral sense, nor in reason, nor in the common sense of mankind.

With respect to the first, the moral sense, as we have seen above, places innocence and guilt and consequently praise and blame, entirely upon will and intention. The connection between the motive and the action, so far from diminishing, enhances the praise or blame. The greater influence a virtuous motive has, the greater is the virtue of the actor, and the more warm our praise. On the other hand, the greater influence a vitious motive has, the greater is the vice of the actor, and the more violently do we blame him. As this is the cardinal point, I wish to have it considered in a general view. <110> It is essential both to human and divine government, that the influence of motives should be necessary. It is equally essential, that that necessary influence should not have the effect to lessen guilt in the estimation of men. To fulfil both ends, guilt is placed by the moral sense entirely upon will and intention: a man accordingly blames himself for doing mischief willingly and intentionally, without once considering whether he acted necessarily or not. And his sentiments are adopted by all the world: they pronounce the same sentence of condemnation that he himself does. A man put to the torture, yields to the pain, and with bitter reluctance reveals the secrets of his party: another does the same, yielding to a tempting bribe. The latter only is blamed as guilty of a crime; and yet the bribe perhaps operated as strongly on the latter, as torture did on the former. But the one was compelled reluctantly to reveal the secrets of his party; and therefore is innocent: the other acted willingly, in order to procure a great sum of money; and therefore is guilty.

With respect to reason, I observe, that <111> the moral sense is the only judge in this controversy, not the faculty of reason. I should however not be afraid of a sentence against me, were reason to be the judge. For would not reason dictate, that the less a man wavers about his duty, or, in other words, the less influence vitious motives have, the more praise-worthy he is; and the more blameable, the less influence virtuous motives have.

Nor are we led by common sense to differ from reason or from the moral sense. A man commits murder, overcome by a sudden fit of revenge which he could not resist: do we not reflect, even at first view, that the man did not desire to resist; and that he would have committed the murder, tho' he had not been under any necessity? a person of plain understanding will say, What signifies it whether the criminal could resist or no, when he committed the murder wittingly and willingly? A man gives poison privately out of revenge. Does any one doubt of his guilt, when he never once repented; tho' after administering the poison it no longer was in his power to draw back? A man may be guilty and blame-worthy, even where <112> there is external compulsion that he cannot resist. With sword in hand I run to attack an enemy: my foot slipping, I fall headlong upon him, and by that accident the sword is push'd into his body. The external act was not the effect of Will, but of accident: but my intention was to commit murder, and I am guilty. All men acknowledge, that the Deity is necessarily good. Does that circumstance detract from his praise in common apprehension? On the contrary, he merits from us the highest praise on that very account.

It is commonly said, that there can be no virtue where there is no struggle. Virtue, it is true, is best known from a struggle: a man who has never met with a temptation, can be little confident of his virtue. But the observation taken in a strict sense, is undoubtedly erroneous. A man, tempted to betray his trust, wavers; but after much doubting refuses at last the bribe. Another hesitates not a moment, but rejects the bribe with disdain: duty is obstinate, and will not suffer him even to deliberate. Is there no virtue in the lat-<113>ter? Undoubtedly more than in the former.

Upon the whole, it appears that praise and blame rest ultimately upon the disposition or frame of mind.* Nor is it obvious, that a power to act

* Malice and resentment, tho' commonly joined together, have no resemblance but in producing mischief. Malice is a propensity of nature that operates deliberately without passion: resentment is a passion to which even good-natured people are subject. A ma-

against motives, could vary in any degree these moral sentiments. When a man commits a crime, let it be supposed that he could have resisted the prevailing motive. Why then did he not resist, instead of bringing upon himself shame and misery? The answer must be, for no other can be given, that his disposition is vitious, and that he is a detestable creature. Further, it is not a little difficult to conceive, how a man can resist a prevailing motive, without having any thing in his mind that should engage him to resist it. But letting that pass, I make the following supposi-<114>tion. A man is tempted by avarice to accept a bribe: if he resist upon the principle of duty, he is led by the prevailing motive: if he resist without having any reason or motive for resisting, I cannot discover any merit in such resistance: it seems to resolve into a matter of chance or accident, whether he resist or do not resist. Where can the merit lie of resisting a vitious motive, when resistance happens by mere chance? and where the demerit of resisting a virtuous motive, when it is owing to the same chance? If a man, actuated by no principle, good or bad, and having no end or purpose in view, should kill his neighbour, I see not that he would be more accountable, than if he had acted in his sleep, or were mad.

Human punishments are perfectly consistent with the necessary influence of motives, without supposing a power to withstand them. If it be urged, That a man ought not to be punished for committing a crime when he could not resist: the answer is, That as he committed the crime intentionally and with his eyes open, he is guilty in his own opinion, and in the opinion of all men. Here is a just foun-<115>dation for punishment. And its utility is great; being intended to deter people from committing crimes. The dread of punishment is a weight in the scale on the side of virtue, to counterbalance vitious motives.

The final cause of this branch of our nature is admirable. If the necessary influence of motives had the effect either to lessen the merit of a virtuous action, or the demerit of a crime, morality would be totally unhinged. The most virtuous action would of all be the least worthy of praise; and the most vitious be of all the least worthy of blame. Nor would the evil stop

---

licious character is esteemed much more vitious than one that is irascible. Does not this shew, that virtue and vice consist more in disposition than in action?

there: instead of curbing inordinate passions, we should be encouraged to indulge them, as an excellent excuse for doing wrong. Thus, the moral sentiments of approbation and disapprobation, of praise and blame, are found perfectly consistent with the laws above mentioned that govern human actions, without necessity of recurring to an imaginary power of acting against motives.

The only plausible objection I have met with against the foregoing theory, is the remorse a man feels for a crime he sud-<116>denly commits, and as suddenly repents of. During a fit of bitter remorse for having slain my favourite servant in a violent passion, without just provocation, I accuse myself for having given way to passion; and acknowledge that I could and ought to have restrained it. Here we find remorse founded on a system directly opposite to that above laid down; a system that acknowledges no necessary connection between an action and its motive; but, on the contrary, supposes that it is in a man's power to resist his passion, and that he ought to resist it. What shall be said upon this point? Can a man be a necessary agent, when he is conscious of the contrary, and is sensible that he can act in contradiction to motives? This objection is strong in appearance; and would be invincible, were we not happily relieved of it by a doctrine laid down in Elements of Criticism (a) concerning the irregular influence of passion on our opinions and sentiments. Upon examination, it will be found, that the present case may be added to the many examples there given of that irregular influence. <117> In a peevish fit, I take exception at some slight word or gesture of my friend, which I interpret as if he doubted of my veracity. I am instantly in a flame: in vain he protests that he had no meaning, for impatience will not suffer me to listen. I bid him draw, which he does with reluctance; and before he is well prepared, I give him a mortal wound. Bitter remorse and anguish succeed instantly to rage. "What have I done? I have murdered my innocent, my best friend; and yet I was not mad—with that hand I did the horrid deed; why did not I rather turn it against my own heart?" Here every impression of necessity vanishes: my mind informs me that I was absolutely free, and that I ought to have smothered my passion. I put an opposite case. A brutal fellow treats me with great

(a) Chap. 2. part 5.

indignity, and proceeds even to a blow. My passion rises beyond the possibility of restraint: I can scarce forbear so long as to bid him draw; and that moment I stab him to the heart. I am sorry for having been engaged with a ruffian; but have no contrition nor remorse. In this case, I never once dream that I could have resisted the impulse of <118> passion: on the contrary, my thoughts and words are, "That flesh and blood could not bear the affront; and that I must have been branded for a coward, had I not done what I did." In reality, both actions were equally necessary. Whence then opinions and sentiments so opposite to each other? The irregular influence of passion on our opinions and sentiments, will solve the question. All violent passions are prone to their own gratification. A man who has done an action that he repents of and that affects him with anguish, abhors himself, and is odious in his own eyes: he wishes to find himself guilty; and the thought that his guilt is beyond the possibility of excuse, gratifies the passion. In the first case accordingly, remorse forces upon me a conviction that I might have restrained my passion, and ought to have restrained it. I will not give way to any excuse; because in a severe fit of remorse, it gives me pain to be excused. In the other case, as there is no remorse, things appear in their true light without disguise. To illustrate this reasoning, I observe, that passion warps my judgement of the actions of o-<119>thers, as well as of my own. Many examples are given in the chapter above quoted: join to these the following. My servant aiming at a partridge, happens to shoot a favourite spaniel crossing the way unseen. Inflamed with anger, I storm at his rashness, pronounce him guilty, and will listen to no excuse. When passion subsides, I become sensible that the action was merely accidental, and that the man is absolutely innocent. The nurse overlays my only child, the long-expected heir to a great estate. With difficulty I refrain from putting her to death: "The wretch has murdered my infant: she ought to be torn to pieces." When I turn calm, the matter appears to me in a very different light. The poor woman is inconsolable, and can scarce believe that she is innocent: she bitterly reproaches herself for want of care and concern. But, upon cool reflection, both she and I become sensible, that no person in sound sleep has any self-command, and that we cannot be answerable for any action of which we are not conscious. Thus, upon the whole, we discover, that any impression we occasionally have of being able to act in contra-<120>diction to motives, is the result of passion, not of sound judgement.

The reader will observe, that this section is copied from Essays on Morality and Natural Religion.[9] The ground work is the same: the alterations are only in the superstructure; and the subject is abridged in order to adapt it to its present place. The preceding parts of the Sketch were published in the second edition of the Principles of Equity.[10] But as law-books have little currency, the publishing the whole in one essay, will not, I hope, be thought improper.

APPENDIX

Upon Chance and Contingency.

I hold it to be an intuitive proposition, That the Deity is the primary cause of all things; that with consummate wisdom he formed the great plan of government, which he carries on by laws suited to the different natures of animate and in-<121>animate beings; and that these laws, produce a regular chain of causes and effects in the moral as well as the material world, admitting no events but what are comprehended in the original plan (*a*). Hence it clearly follows, that chance is excluded out of this world, that nothing can happen by accident, and that no event is arbitrary or contingent. This is the doctrine of the essay quoted; and, in my apprehension, well founded. But I cannot subscribe to what follows, "That we have an impression of chance and contingency, which consequently must be delusive." I would not willingly admit any delusion in the nature of man, unless it were made evident beyond contradiction; and I now see clearly,

---

(*a*) See Essays on Morality and Natural Religion, part 1. essay 3.

9. See *Essays on the Principles of Morality and Natural Religion,* 2nd ed., essay III, "Of Liberty and Necessity." For 3rd ed., published in 1779, Kames made several changes to essay III and incorporated passages from the present section and from the following appendix.

10. See *Principles of Equity,* 2nd ed., "Preliminary Discourse; being An investigation of the Moral Laws of Society." The "Preliminary Discourse" was excised from *Principles of Equity,* 3rd ed.

that the impression we have of chance and contingency, is not delusive, but perfectly consistent with the established plan.

The explanation of chance and contingency in the said essay, shall be given in the author's own words, as a proper text to reason upon.

In our ordinary train of thinking, it is certain that all events <122> appear not to us as necessary. A multitude of events seem to be under our power to cause or to prevent; and we readily make a distinction betwixt events that are *necessary, i.e.* that must be; and events that are *contingent, i.e.* that may be, or may not be. This distinction is void of truth: for all things that fall out either in the material or moral world, are, as we have seen, alike necessary, and alike the result of fixed laws. Yet, whatever conviction a philosopher may have of this, the distinction betwixt things necessary and things contingent, possesses his ordinary train of thought, as much as it possesses the most illiterate. We act universally upon that distinction: nay it is in truth the cause of all the labour, care, and industry, of mankind. I illustrate this doctrine by an example. Constant experience hath taught us, that death is a necessary event. The human frame is not made to last for ever in its present condition; and no man thinks of more than a temporary existence upon this globe. But the particular time of our death appears a contingent event. <123> However certain it be, that the time and manner of the death of each individual is determined by a train of preceding causes, and is no less fixed than the hour of the sun's rising or setting; yet no person is affected by this doctrine. In the care of prolonging life, we are directed by the supposed contingency of the time of death, which, to a certain term of years, we consider as depending in a great measure on ourselves, by caution against accidents, due use of food, exercise, &c. These means are prosecuted with the same diligence as if there were in fact no necessary train of causes to fix the period of life. In short, whoever attends to his own practical ideas, whoever reflects upon the meaning of the following words which occur in all languages, of things *possible, contingent, that are in our power to cause or prevent;* whoever, I say, reflects upon these words, will clearly see, that they suggest certain perceptions or notions repugnant to the doctrine above established of universal necessity.[11]

11. *Essays on the Principles of Morality and Natural Religion,* 2nd ed., pp. 149–51.

In order to show that there is no repugnance, I begin with defining *chance* and <124> *contingency.* The former is applied to events that have happened; the latter to future events. When we say a thing has happened by *chance,* we surely do not mean that *chance* was the cause; for no person ever imagined that *chance* is a thing that can act, and by acting produce events: we only mean, that we are ignorant of the cause, and that, for ought we see, it might have happened or not happened, or have happened differently. Aiming at a bird, I shoot *by chance* a favourite spaniel: the meaning is not, that chance killed the dog, but that as to me the dog's death was accidental. With respect to contingency, future events that are variable and the cause unknown, are said to be contingent; changes of the weather, for example, whether it will be frost or thaw tomorrow, whether fair or foul. In a word, chance and contingency applied to events, mean not that such events happen without any cause, but only that we are ignorant of the cause.

It appears to me, that there is no such thing in human nature as a sense that any thing happens without a cause: such a sense would be grossly delusive. It is <125> indeed true, that our sense of a cause is not always equally distinct: with respect to an event that happens regularly, such as summer, winter, rising or setting of the sun, we have a distinct sense of a cause: our sense is less distinct with respect to events less regular, such as alterations of the weather; and extremely indistinct with respect to events that seldom happen, and that happen without any known cause. But with respect to no event whatever does our sense of a cause vanish altogether, and give place to a sense of things happening without a cause.

Chance and contingency thus explained, suggest not any perception or notion repugnant to the doctrine of universal necessity; for my ignorance of a cause, does not, even in my own apprehension, exclude a cause. Descending to particulars, I take the example mentioned in the text, namely, the uncertainty of the time of my death. Knowing that my life depends in some measure on myself, I use all means to preserve it, by proper food, exercise, and care to prevent accidents. Nor is there any delusion here. I am moved to <126> use these means by the desire I have to live: these means accordingly prove effectual to carry on my present existence to the appointed period; and in that view are so many links in the great chain of causes and effects. A burning coal falling from the grate upon the floor, wakes me from a sound sleep. I start up to extinguish the fire. The motive is irresistible: nor have I reason to resist, were it in my power; for I consider the extinction of the fire by my hand, to be one of the means chosen by Providence for prolonging my life to its destined period.

Were there a chain of causes and effects established entirely independent on me, and were my life in no measure under my own power, it would indeed be fruitless for me to act; and the absurdity of knowingly acting in vain, would be a prevailing motive for remaining at rest. Upon that supposition, the *ignava ratio* of Chrysippus might take place; *cui si pareamus, nihil omnino agamus in vita.** But I act necessarily when influenced by motives; and I have no reason to forbear, consider-<127>ing that my actions, by producing their intended effects, contribute to carry on the great chain.

PART II

Progress of Morality

Having unfolded the principles of morality, the next step is, to trace out its gradual progress, from its infancy among savages to its maturity among polished nations. The history of opinions concerning the foundation of morality, falls not within my plan; and I am glad to be relieved from an article that is executed in perfection by more able hands (*a*).

An animal is brought forth with every one of its external members; and completes its growth, not by production of any new member, but by addition of matter to those originally formed. The same holds with respect to internal members; <128> the senses, for example, instincts, powers and faculties, principles and propensities: these are coeval with the individual, and are gradually unfolded, some early, some late. The external senses, being necessary for self-preservation, soon arrive at maturity. Some internal senses, of order for example, of propriety, of dignity, of grace, being of no use during infancy, are not only slow in their progress toward maturity, but require much culture. Among savages they are scarce perceptible.

---

* "The indolent principle; which if we were to follow, we should do nothing in life."
(*a*) Dr. Cudworth and Dr. Smith.

The moral sense, in its progress, differs from those last mentioned; being frequently discovered, even in childhood. It is however slow of growth, and seldom arrives at perfection without culture and experience.

The moral sense not only ripens gradually with the other internal senses mentioned, but from them acquires force and additional authority: a savage makes no difficulty to kill an enemy in cold blood: bloody scenes are familiar to him, and his moral sense is not sufficiently vigorous to give him compunction. The action appears in a different light to a person of delicate feelings; and accordingly, the moral <129> sense has much more authority over those who have received a refined education, than over savages.

It is pleasant to trace the progress of morality in members of a polished nation. Objects of external sense make the first impressions; and from them are derived a stock of simple ideas. Affection, accompanying ideas, is first directed to particular objects, such as my father, my brother, my companion. The mind, opening by degrees, takes in complex objects, such as my country, my religion, the government under which I live; and these also become objects of affection. Our connections multiply; and the moral sense, acquiring strength as the mind opens, regulates our duty to every connected object. Objects of hatred multiply as well as objects of affection, and give full scope to dissocial passions, the most formidable antagonists that morality has to encounter. But nature hath provided a remedy: the person who indulges malice or revenge, is commonly the greatest sufferer by the indulgence: men become wise by experience, and have more peace and satisfaction in fostering kindly affection: stormy pas-<130>sions are subdued, or brought under rigid discipline; and benevolence triumphs over selfishness. We refine upon the pleasures of society: we learn to submit our opinions: we affect to give preference to others; and readily fall in with whatever sweetens social intercourse: we carefully avoid causes of discord; and overlooking trivial offences, we are satisfied with moderate reparation, even for gross injuries.

A nation from its original savage state, grows to maturity like the individuals above described, and the progress of morality is the same in both. The savage state is the infancy of a nation, during which the moral sense is feeble, yielding to custom, to imitation, to passion. But a nation, like a member of a polished society, ripens gradually, and acquires a taste in the fine arts, with acuteness of sense in matters of right and wrong. Hatred and revenge, the great obstacles to moral duty, raged without control, while the privilege of avenging wrongs was permitted to individuals (*a*). But hatred and revenge yielded gradually to the pleasures of society, and to the growing authority <131> of the moral sense; and benevolent affections prevailed over dissocial passions. In that comfortable period, we hear no more of cruelty as a national character: on the contrary, the aversion we have to an enemy, is even in war exercised with moderation. Nor do the stormy passions ever again revive; for after a nation begins to decline from its meridian height, the passions that prevail are not of the violent kind, but selfish, timorous, and deceitful.

Morality however has not to this day arrived to such maturity, as to operate between nations with equal steadiness and vigour, as between individuals. Ought this to be regretted as an imperfection in our nature? I think not: had we the same compunction of heart for injuring a nation as for injuring an individual, and were injustice equally blameable as to both; war would cease, and a golden age ensue, than which a greater misfortune could not befal the human race (*b*).

In the progress from maturity to a declining state, a nation differs widely from an individual. Old age puts an end to <132> the latter: there are many causes that weaken the former; but old age is none of them, if it be not in a metaphorical sense. Riches, selfishness, and luxury, are the diseases that weaken prosperous nations: these diseases, following each other in a train, corrupt the heart, dethrone the moral sense, and make an anarchy in the soul: men stick at no expence to purchase pleasure; and they stick at no vice to supply that expence.

Such are the outlines of morality in its progress from birth to burial; and these outlines I purpose to fill up with an induction of particulars. Looking back to the commencement of civil society, when no wants were known but those of nature, and when such wants were amply provided for; we find individuals of the same tribe living innocently and cordially together: they had no irregular appetites, nor any ground for strife. In that state, moral

(*a*) See Historical Law tracts, tract 1.
(*b*) Book 2. sketch 1.

principles joined their influence with that of national affection, to secure individuals from harm. Savages accordingly, who have plenty of food and are simple in habitation and cloathing, seldom transgress the rules of morality within their <133> own tribe. Diodorus Siculus, who composed his history recently after Caesar's expedition into Britain, says, that the inhabitants dwelt in mean cottages covered with reeds or sticks; that they were of much sincerity and integrity, contented with plain and homely fare; and were strangers to the excess and luxury of rich men. In Friezeland, in Holland, and in other maritime provinces of the Netherlands, locks and keys were unknown, till the inhabitants became rich by commerce: they contented themselves with bare necessaries, which every one had in plenty. The Laplanders have no notion of theft. When they make an excursion into Norway, which is performed in the summer months, they leave their huts open, without fear that any thing will be purloined. Formerly they were entirely upright in their only commerce, that of bartering the skins of wild beasts for tobacco, brandy, and coarse cloth. But being often cheated by strangers, they begin to be more cunning. Theft was unknown among the Caribbees till Europeans came among them. When they lost any thing, they said innocently, "the Christians have <134> been here." Crantz, describing the inhabitants of Iceland before they were corrupted by commerce with strangers, says, that they lived under the same roof with their cattle; that every thing was common among them except their wives and children; and that they were simple in their manners, having no appetite but for what nature requires. In the reign of Edwin King of Northumberland, a child, as historians report, might have travelled with a purse of gold, without hazard of robbery: in our days of luxury, want is so intolerable, that even fear of death is not sufficient to deter us. All travellers agree, that the native Canadians are perfectly disinterested, abhorring deceit and lying. The Californians are fond of iron and sharp instruments; and yet are so strictly honest, that carpenter-tools left open during night, were safe. The savages of North America had no locks for their goods: they probably have learned from Europeans to be more circumspect. Procopius bears testimony (*a*), that the Sclavi, like the Huns, were innocent people, free of malice. Plan

(*a*) Historia Gothica, lib. 3.

Carpin, the Pope's am-<135>bassador to the Cham of Tartary, *anno* 1246, says, that the Tartars are not addicted to thieving; and that they leave their goods open without a lock. Nicholas Damascenus reports the same of the Celtae. The original inhabitants of the island Borneo, expelled by the Mahometans from the sea-coast to the center of the country, are honest, industrious, and kindly to each other: they have some notion of property, but not such as to render them covetous. Pagans in Siberia are numerous; and, tho' grossly ignorant especially in matters of religion, they are a good moral people. It is rare to hear among them of perjury, thieving, fraud, or drunkenness; if we except those who live among the Russian Christians, with whose vices they are tainted. Strahlenberg (*a*) bears testimony to their honesty. Having employ'd a number of them in a long navigation, he slept in the same boat with men whose names he knew not, whose language he understood not, and yet lost not a particle of his baggage. Being obliged to remain a fortnight among the Ostiacs, upon the river Oby, his baggage <136> lay open in a hut inhabited by a large family, and yet nothing was purloined. The following incident, which he also mentions, is remarkable. A Russian of Tobolski, in the course of a long journey, lodged one night in an Ostiac's hut, and the next day on the road missed his purse with a hundred rubles. His landlord's son, hunting at some distance from the hut, found the purse, but left it there. By his father's order, he covered it with branches, to secure it in case an owner should be found. After three months, the Russian returning, lodged with the same Ostiac; and mentioning occasionally the loss of his purse, the Ostiac, who at first did not recollect his face, cry'd out with joy, "Art thou the man who lost that purse? my son shall go and show thee where it lies, that thou may'st take it up with thine own hand." The Hottentots (*b*) have not the least notion of theft: tho' immoderately fond of tobacco and brandy, they are employ'd by the Dutch for tending warehouses full of these commodities. Here is an instance of probity above temptation, even among savages <137> in the first stage of social life. Some individuals are more liberally endued than others with virtuous principles: may it not be thought, that in that respect nature has

(*a*) Description of Russia, Siberia, &c.
(*b*) Kolben.

been more kind to the Hottentots than to many other tribes? Spaniards, settled on the sea-coast of Chili, carry on a commerce with neighbouring savages, for bridles, spurs, knives, and other manufactures of iron; and in return receive oxen, horses, and even children for slaves. A Spaniard carries his goods there; and after obtaining liberty to dispose of them, he moves about, and delivers his goods, without the least reserve, to every one who bargains with him. When all is sold, he intimates his departure; and every purchaser hurries with his goods to him; and it is not known that any one Indian ever broke his engagement. They give him a guard to carry him safe out of their territory, with all the slaves, horses, and cattle he has purchased. The savages of Brazil are faithful to their promises, and to the treaties they make with the Portuguese. Upon some occasions, they may be accused of error and wrong judge-<138>ment, but never of injustice nor of duplicity.

While the earth was thinly peopled, plenty of food, procured by hunting and fishing, promoted population; but as population lessens the stock of animal food, a savage nation, encreasing in numbers, must spread wider and wider for more game. Thus tribes, at first widely separated from each other, approach gradually till they become neighbours. Hence a new scene with respect to morality. Differences about their hunting-fields, about their game, about personal injuries, multiply between neighbours; and every quarrel is blown into a flame, by the aversion men naturally have to strangers. Anger, hatred, and revenge, now find vent, which formerly lay latent without an object: dissocial passions prevail without control, because among savages morality is no match for them; and cruelty becomes predominant in the human race. Ancient history accordingly is full of enormous cruelties; witness the incursions of the northern barbarians into the Roman empire; and the incursions of Genhizcan and Tamerlane into the fer-<139>tile countries of Asia, spreading destruction with fire and sword, and sparing neither man, woman, nor infant.

Malevolent passions, acquiring strength by daily exercise against persons of a different tribe, came to be vented against persons even of the same tribe; and the privilege long enjoy'd by individuals of avenging the wrongs done to them, bestow'd irresistible force upon such passions (*a*). The his-

(*a*) See Historical Law-tracts, tract 1.

tory of ancient Greece presents nothing to the reader but usurpations, as-sassinations, and other horrid crimes. The names of many famous for wick-edness, are still preserved; Atreus, for example, Eteocles, Alcmeon, Phedra, Clytemnestra. The story of Pelops and his descendents, is a chain of crim-inal horrors: during that period, parricide and incest were ordinary inci-dents. Euripides represents Medea vowing revenge against her husband Ja-son, and laying a plot to poison him. Of that infamous plot the chorus express their approbation, justifying every woman who, in like circum-stances, acts the same part. <140>

The frequent incursions of northern barbarians into the Roman empire, spred desolation and ruin through the whole. The Romans, from the high-est polish degenerating into savages, assumed by degrees the cruel and bloody manners of their conquerors; and the conquerors and conquered, blended into one mass, equalled the grossest barbarians of ancient times in ignorance and brutality. Clovis, King of the Franks, even after his conver-sion to Christianity, assassinated without remorse his nearest kinsman. The children of Clodomir, *ann.* 530, were assassinated by their two uncles. In the thirteenth century, Ezzelino de Aromano obtained the sovereignty of Padua, by massacring 12,000 of his fellow-citizens. Galeas Sforza, Duke of Milan, was assassinated *ann.* 1476 in the cathedral church of Milan, after the assassins had put up their prayers for courage to perpetrate the deed. It is a still stronger proof how low morality was in those days, that the Pope himself, Sextus IV. attempted to assassinate the two brothers, Laurent and Julien de Medicis; chusing the elevation of the host as a proper time, when the people would be busy <141> about their devotions. Nay more, that very Pope, with unparallelled impudence, excommunicated the Florentines for doing justice upon the intended assassins. The most sacred oaths were in vain employed as a security against that horrid crime. Childebert II. King of the Franks, enticed Magnovald to his court, by a solemn oath that he should receive no harm; and yet made no difficulty to assassinate him dur-ing the gaiety of a banquet. But these instances, however horrid, make no figure compared with the massacre of St. Bartholomew, where many thou-sands were inhumanly and treacherously butchered. Even so late as the fourteenth and fifteenth centuries, assassination was not held in every case to be criminal. Many solicitous applications were made to general councils of Christian clergy, to declare it criminal in every case; but without success. Ferdinand King of Aragon and Navarre, after repeated assassinations and acts of perfidy, obtained the appellation of *Great:* so little authority had the moral sense, during these dark and sanguinary ages.

But it is scarce necessary to mention <142> particular instances of the overbearing power of malevolent passions during these ages. An opinion, once universal, that the innocent may be justly involved in the same punishment with the guilty, is of itself irrefragable evidence, that morality formerly had very little influence when opposed by revenge. There is no moral principle more evident, than that punishment cannot be inflicted with justice but upon the guilty; and yet in Greece, the involving of the innocent with the guilty in the same punishment, was authorised even by positive law. By an Athenian law, a man committing sacrilege, or betraying his country, was banished with all his children (*a*). And when a tyrant was put to death, his children suffered the same fate (*b*). The punishment of treason in Macedon, was extended against the criminal's relations (*c*). Hanno, a citizen of Carthage, formed a plot to enslave his country, by poisoning the whole senate at a banquet. He was tortured to death; <143> and his children, with all his relations, were cut off without mercy, tho' they had no accession to his guilt. Among the Japanese, a people remarkably ferocious, it is the practice to involve children and relations in the punishment of capital crimes. Even Cicero, the chief man for learning in the most enlightened period of the Roman republic, and a celebrated moralist, approves that practice: "Nec vero me fugit, quam sit acerbum parentum scelera filiorum poenis lui: sed hoc praeclare legibus comparatum est, ut caritas liberorum amiciores parentes reipublicae redderet" (*d*).* In Britain, every one knows, that murder was retaliated, not only upon the criminal and his relations, but upon his whole clan; a practice so common as to be distin-

---

* "I am sensible of the hardship of punishing the child for the crime of the parent: this, however, is a wise enactment of our laws; for hereby the parent is bound to the interest of the state by the strongest of all ties, the affection to his offspring."

(*a*) Meursius de legibus Atticis, lib. 2. cap. 2.

(*b*) Eod. lib. 2. cap. 15.

(*c*) Quintus Curtius, lib. 6. cap. 11.

(*d*) Ep. 12. ad Brutum.

guished by a peculiar name, that of *deadly feud*. As late as the days of King Edmund, a law <144> was made in England, prohibiting deadly feud, except between the relations of the person murdered and the murderer himself.

I embrace the present opportunity to honour the Jews, by observing, that they were the first people we read of, who had correct notions of morality with respect to the present point. The following law is express: "The fathers shall not be put to death for the children, neither shall the children be put to death for the fathers: every man shall be put to death for his own sin (*a*)." Amaziah, King of Judah, gave strict obedience to that law, in avenging his father's death: "And it came to pass as soon as the kingdom was confirmed in his hand, that the slew his servants which had slain the king his father. But the children of the murderers he slew not; according to that which is written in the book of the law of Moses (*b*)." There is an elegant passage in Ezekiel to the same purpose (*c*): "What mean ye, that ye use this proverb concerning the land of Israel, say-<145>ing, The fathers have eaten sour grapes, and the children's teeth are set on edge? As I live, saith the Lord God, ye shall not have occasion any more to use this proverb in Israel. The soul that sinneth, it shall die: the son shall not bear the iniquity of the father, neither shall the father bear the iniquity of the son; the righteousness of the righteous shall be upon him, and the wickedness of the wicked shall be upon him." Among the Jews however, as among other nations, there are instances without number, of involving innocent children and relations in the same punishment with the guilty. Such power has revenge, as to trample upon conscience, and upon the most express laws. Instigated with rage for Nabal's ingratitude, King David made a vow to God, not to leave alive of all who pertained to Nabal any that pisseth against the wall. And it was not any compunction of conscience that diverted him from his cruel purpose, but Nabal's beautiful wife, who pacified him (*d*). But such contradiction between principle and practice, is not peculiar to the Jews. We find <146> examples of it in the laws of the Roman empire.

(*a*) Deuteronomy, xxiv. 16.
(*b*) 2 Kings, chap. 14.
(*c*) Chap. 18.
(*d*) 1 Samuel, chap. 25.

The true principle of punishment is laid down in an edict of the Emperors Arcadius and Honorius (*a*). "Sancimus, ibi esse poenam, ubi et noxia est. Propinquos, notos, familiares, procul a calumnia submovemus, quos reos sceleris societas non facit. Nec enim adfinitas vel amicitia nefarium crimen admittunt. Peccata igitur suos teneant auctores: nec ulterius progrediatur metus quam reperiatur delictum. Hoc singulis quibusque judicibus intimetur."* These very Emperors, with respect to treason, which touched them nearer than other crimes, talk a very different language. After observing, that will and purpose alone without an ouvert act, is treason, subjecting the criminal to capital <147> punishment and to forfeiture of all that belongs to him, they proceed in the following words (*b*). "Filii vero ejus, quibus vitam Imperatoria specialiter lenitate concedimus, (paterno enim deberent perire supplicio, in quibus paterni, hoc est, hereditarii criminis exempla metuuntur), a materna, vel avita, omnium etiam proximorum hereditate ac successione, habeantur alieni: testamentis extraneorum nihil capeant: sint perpetuo egentes et pauperes, infamia eos paterna semper comitetur, ad nullos prorsus honores, ad nulla sacramenta perveniant: sint postremo tales, ut his, perpetua egestate sordentibus, sit et mors solatium et vita supplicium."† <148>

Human nature is not so perverse, as without veil or disguise to punish a person acknowledged to be innocent. An irregular bias of imagination, which extends the qualities of the principal to its accessories, paves the way

---

* "We ordain, that the punishment of the crime shall extend to the criminal alone. We hold his relations, his friends, and his acquaintances, unsuspected; for intimacy, friendship, or connection, are no proof or argument of guilt. The consequences of the crime shall pursue only its perpetrator. Let this statute be intimated to all our judges."

† "By a special extension of our imperial clemency, we allow the sons of the criminal to live; altho' in strict justice, being tainted with hereditary guilt, they ought to suffer the punishment of their father. But it is our will, that they shall be incapable of all inheritance, either from the mother, the grandfather, or any of their kindred; that they shall be deprived of the power of inheriting by the testament of a stranger; that they shall be abandoned to the extreme of poverty and perpetual indigence; that the infamy of their father shall ever attend them, incapable of honours, and excluded from the participation of religious rites; that such, in fine, shall be the misery of their condition, that life shall be a punishment, and death a comfort."

(*a*) l. 22. Cod. De poenis.

(*b*) l. 5. Cod. ad leg. Jul. majest.

to that unjust practice (*a*). That bias, strengthened by indignation against an atrocious criminal, leads the mind hastily to conclude, that all his connections are partakers of his guilt. In an enlightened age, the clearness of moral principles fetters the imagination from confounding the innocent with the guilty. There remain traces however of that bias, tho' not carried so far as murder. The sentence pronounced against Ravilliac for assassinating Henry IV. of France, ordains, "That his house be erazed to the ground, and that no other building be ever erected upon that spot." Was not this in imagination punishing a house for the proprietor's crime? <149>

Murder and assassination are not only destructive in themselves, but, if possible, still more destructive in their consequences. The practice of shedding blood unjustly and often wantonly, blunts conscience, and paves the way to every crime. This observation is verified in the ancient Greeks: their cruel and sanguinary character, rendered them little regardful of the strict rules of justice. Right was held to depend on power, among men as among wild beasts: it was conceived to be the will of the gods, that superior force should be a lawful title to dominion; "for what right can the weak have to what they cannot defend?" Were that maxim to obtain, a weak man would have no right to liberty nor to life. That impious doctrine was avowed by the Athenians, and publicly asserted by their ambassadors in a conference with the Melians, reported by Thucydides (*b*). Many persons act as if force and right were the same; but a barefac'd profession of such a doctrine is uncommon. In the Eumenides, a tragedy of Eschylus, Orestes is arraigned in the Areopagus for killing his <150> mother. Minerva, president of the court, decrees in favour of Orestes: and for what reason? "Having no mother myself, the murder of a mother toucheth not me."* In the tragedy of Electra, Orestes, consulting the Delphic oracle about means to avenge

---

* Athens, from the nature of its government, as established by Solon, was rendered uncapable of any regular or consistent body of laws. In every case, civil and criminal, the whole people were judges in the last resort. And what sort of judges will an ignorant multitude make, who have no guide but passion and prejudice? It is vain to make good laws, when such judges are the interpreters. Anacharsis, the Scythian, being present at an assembly of the people, said, "It was singular, that in Athens, wise men pleaded causes, and fools determined them."

(*a*) Elements of Criticism, chap. 2. sect. 5.

(*b*) Lib. 5.

his father's murder, was enjoined by Apollo to forbear force, but to employ fraud and guile. Obedient to that injunction, Orestes commands his tutor to spread in Argos the news of his death, and to confirm the same with a solemn oath. In Homer, even the great Jupiter makes no difficulty to send a lying dream to Agamemnon, chief of the Greeks. Dissimulation is recommended by the goddess Minerva (a). Ulysses de-<151>clares his detestation at using freedom with truth (b): and yet no man deals more in feigned stories (c). In the 22d book of the Iliad, Minerva is guilty of gross deceit and treachery to Hector. When he flees from Achilles, she appears to him in the shape of his brother Deiphobus, exhorts him to turn upon Achilles, and promises to assist him. Hector accordingly, returning to the fight, darts his lance; which rebounds from the shield of Achilles, for by Vulcan it was made impenetrable. Hector calls upon his brother for another lance; but in vain, for Deiphobus was not there. The Greeks in Homer's time must have been strangely deformed in their morals, when such a story could be relished.* A nation begins not <152> to polish nor to advance in morality, till writing be common; and writing was not known among the Greeks at the siege of Troy. Nor were the morals of that people, as we see, much purified for a long time after writing became common. When Plautus wrote, the Roman system of morals must have been extremely impure. In his play termed *Menaechmi,* a gentleman of fashion having accidentally got into his hands a lady's robe with a gold clasp; instead of returning them to the owner, endeavours to sell them without shame or remorse. Such a scene would not be endured at present, except among pickpockets. Both the Greeks and Carthaginians were held by the Romans to be artful and cunning. The Romans continued a plain people, with much simplicity of manners, when the nations mentioned had made great progress in the arts of

---

* Upon the story of Jupiter being deceived by Juno in the 14th book of the Iliad, Pope says, "That he knows not a bolder fiction in all antiquity, nor one that has a greater air of impiety." Pope it would seem was little acquainted with antiquity: for such acts of impiety were common among the Greeks; and in particular the incident mentioned in the text, is not only more impious, but also a more gross violation of the laws of morality.

(a) Odyssey, book 13.
(b) Book 14.
(c) Book 14. book 15.

life; and it is a sad truth, that morality declines in proportion as a nation polishes. But if the Romans were later than the Greeks and Carthaginians in the arts of life, they soon surpassed them in every sort of immorality. For this change of manners, they were indebted to their rapid con-<153>quests. The sanguinary disposition both of the Greeks and Romans, appears from another practice, that of exposing their infant children, which continued till humanity came in some measure to prevail. The practice continues in China to this day, the populousness of the country throwing a veil over the cruelty; but from the humanity of the Chinese, I conjecture, that the practice is rare. The Jews, a cloudy and peevish tribe much addicted to bloodshed, were miserably defective in moral principles. Take the following examples out of an endless number recorded in the books of the Old Testament. Jael, wife of Heber, took under her protection Sisera, general of the Canaanites, and engaged her faith for his security. She put him treacherously to death when asleep; and was applauded by Deborah the prophetess for the meritorious action (*a*). That horrid deed would probably have appeared to her in a different light, had it been committed against Barac, general of the Israelites. David, flying from Saul, took refuge with Achish, King of Gath; and, tho' protected by that King, made <154> war against the King's allies, saying, that it was against his own countrymen of Judah. "And David saved neither man nor woman alive to bring tidings to Gath. And Achish believed David, saying, He hath made his people Israel utterly to abhor him: therefore he shall be my servant for ever" (*b*). This was a complication of ingratitude, lying, and treachery. Ziba, by presents to King David and by defaming his master Mephibosheth, procured from the King a gift of his master's inheritance; tho' Mephibosheth had neither trimmed his beard, nor washed his cloaths, from the day the King departed till he returned in peace. "And it came to pass, when Mephibosheth was come to Jerusalem to meet the king, that the king said unto him, Wherefore wentest thou not with me, Mephibosheth? And he answered, My lord, O king, my servant deceived me; for thy servant said, I will saddle me an ass, that I may ride thereon, and go to the king; because thy servant is lame,

(*a*) Judges, iv. 5.
(*b*) 1 Samuel, xxvii. 11.

and he hath slandered thy servant unto my lord the king. But my lord the king is <155> as an angel of God: do therefore what is good in thine eyes. For all my father's house were but dead men before my lord the king: yet didst thou set thy servant among them that did eat at thine own table: what right therefore have I to cry any more unto the king?" David could not possibly atone for his rashness, but by restoring to Mephibosheth his inheritance, and punishing Ziba in an exemplary manner. But hear the sentence: "And the king said unto him, Why speakest thou any more of thy matters? I have said, Thou and Ziba divide the land" (*a*). The same king, after pardoning Shimei for cursing him, and swearing that he should not die; yet upon deathbed enjoined his son Solomon to put Shimei to death: "Now therefore hold him not guiltless; but his hoary head bring thou down to the grave with blood" (*b*). I wish not to be misapprehended, as intending to censure David in particular. If the best king the Jews ever had, was so miserably deficient in morality, what must be thought of the na-<156>tion in general? When David was lurking to avoid the wrath of Saul, he became acquainted with Nabal, who had a great stock of cattle. "He discharged his followers," says Josephus (*c*), "either for avarice, or hunger, or any pretext whatever, to touch a single hair of them; preaching still on the text of doing justice to all men, in conformity to the will of God, who is not pleased with any man that covets or lays violent hands on the goods of his neighbour." Our author proceeds to acquaint us, that Nabal having refused to supply David with provisions, and having sent back the messengers with a scoffing answer, David in rage made a vow, that he would destroy Nabal with his house and family. Our author observes, that David's indignation against Nabal, was not so much for his ingratitude, as for the virulence of an insolent outrage against one who had never injured him. And what was the outrage? It was, says our author, that Nabal enquiring who the said David was, and being told that he was one of the sons of Jesse, "Yes, yes," says <157> Nabal, "your run-away servants look upon themselves to be brave fellows, I warrant you." Strange looseness of morals! I mean not David,

(*a*) 2 Samuel, xix. 24.
(*b*) 1 Kings, ii. 9.
(*c*) Antiquities, book 6.

who was in wrath, but Josephus writing sedately in his closet. He every where celebrates David for his justice and piety, composes for him the very warm exhortation mentioned above: and yet thinks him not guilty of any wrong, in vowing to break every rule of justice and humanity, upon so slight a provocation as a scoffing expression, such as no man of temper will regard.

European nations, who originally were fierce and sanguinary like the Greeks and Jews, had the same cloudy and uncorrect notions of right and wrong. It is scarce necessary to give instances, the low state of morality during the dark ages of Christianity being known to all. In the time of Louis XI. of France, promises and engagements were utterly disregarded, till they were sanctified by a solemn oath: nor were such oaths long regarded; they lost their force, and were not relied on more than simple promises. All faith among men seemed to be at an end. Even <158> those who appeared the most scrupulous about character, were however ready to grasp at any subterfuge to excuse their breach of engagement. And it is a still clearer proof of self-deceit, that such subterfuges were frequently prepared beforehand, in order to furnish an excuse. It was a common practice some ages ago, to make private protestations, which were thought sufficient to relieve men in conscience from being bound by a solemn treaty. The Scotch nation, as an ally of France, being comprehended in a treaty of peace between the French King and Edward I. of England, the latter ratified publicly the treaty, after having secretly protested before notaries against the article that comprehended Scotland.[12] Charles, afterward Emperor of Germany, during his minority, gave authority to declare publicly his accession to a treaty of peace, between his grandfather Maximilian and the King of France: but at the same time protested privately, before a notary and witnesses, "That, notwithstanding his public accession to the said treaty, it was not his intention to be bound by every article of it; and particularly, that the clause <159> reserving to the King of France the sovereignty of certain territories in the Netherlands, should not be binding." Is it possible Charles could be so blind as not to see, that such a protestation, if sufficient to relieve from an engagement, must destroy all faith among men? Francis I. of France, while prisoner in Spain, engaged Henry VIII. of England in a

12. "The Scotch nation . . . that comprehended Scotland": added in 2nd edition.

treaty against the Emperor, submitting to very hard terms in order to gain Henry's friendship. The King's ministers protested privately against some of the articles; and the protest was recorded in the secret register of the parliament of Paris, to serve as an excuse in proper time, for breaking the treaty. At the marriage of Mary Queen of Scotland to the Dauphin of France, the King of France ratified every article insisted on by the Scotch parliament, for preserving the independence of the nation, and for securing the succession of the crown to the house of Hamilton; confirming them by deeds in form and with the most solemn oaths. But Mary previously had been persuaded to subscribe privately three deeds, in which, failing heirs of her body, she gifted the king-<160>dom of Scotland to the King of France declaring all promises to the contrary that had been extorted from her by her subjects, to be void.[13] What better was this than what was practised by Robert King of France in the tenth century, to free his subjects from the guilt of perjury? They swore upon a box of relics, out of which the relics had been privately taken. Correa, a Portuguese general, made a treaty with the King of Pegu; and it was agreed, that each party should swear to observe the treaty, laying his hand upon the sacred book of his religion. Correa swore upon a collection of songs; and thought that by that vile stratagem he was free from his engagement. The inhabitants of Britain were so loose formerly, that a man was not reckoned safe in his own house, without a mastiff to protect him from violence. Mastiffs were permitted even to those who dwelt within the king's forests; and to prevent danger to the deer, there was in England a court for *lawing* or *expeditation* of mastives, i.e. for cutting off the claws of their fore-feet to prevent them from run-<161>ning (*a*). The trial and condemnation of Charles I. in a pretended court of justice, however audacious and unconstitutional, was an effort toward regularity and order. In the preceding age, the king would have been taken off by assassination or poison. Every prince in Europe had an officer, whose province it was to secure his master against poison. A lady was appointed to that office by Queen Elisabeth of England; and the form was

(*a*) Carta de Foresta, cap. 6. [[The Carta de Foresta, or charter concerning the forest, was granted by King John of England in 1215, at the same time as the Magna Carta. It was later ratified and expanded upon by Henry III.]]

13. "Francis I. of . . . to be void": added in 2nd edition.

to give to each of the servants a mouthful to eat of the dish he brought in. Poison must have been frequent in those days, to make such a regulation necessary. To vouch still more clearly the low ebb of morality during that period, seldom it happened that a man of figure died suddenly, or of an unusual disease, but poison was suspected. Men conscious of their own vitious disposition, are prone to suspect others. The Dauphin, son to Francis I. of France, a youth of about eighteen, having overheated himself at play, took a great draught of iced water, and died of a pleurisy in five days. The death was sudden, but none is more <162> natural. The suspicion however of poison was universal; and Montecuculi, who attended the young prince, was formally condemned to death for it, and executed; for no better reason, than that he had at all times ready access to the prince.

Considering the low state of morality where dissocial passions bear rule, as in the scenes now display'd, one would require a miracle to recover mankind out of so miserable a state. But, as observed above (*a*), Providence brings order out of confusion. The intolerable distress of a state of things where a promise, or even an oath, is a rope of sand, and where all are set against all (*b*), made people at last sensible, that they must either renounce society altogether, or qualify themselves for it by checking their dissocial passions. Finding from experience, that the gratification of social affections exceeds greatly that of cruelty and revenge; men endeavoured to acquire a habit of self-command, and of restraining their stormy passions. The necessity of fulfilling every moral duty was recognised: men listened to conscience, the voice of God in their <163> hearts: and the moral sense was cordially submitted to, as the ultimate judge in all matters of right and wrong. Salutary laws and steady government contributed to perfect that glorious revolution: private conviction alone would not have been effectual, not at least in many ages.

From that revolution is derived what is termed *the law of nations,* meaning certain regulations dictated by the moral sense in its maturity. The laws of our nature refine gradually as our nature refines. From the putting an enemy to death in cold blood, improved nature is averse, tho' such practice

(*a*) Book 2. sketch 1.
(*b*) Hobbes.

was common while barbarity prevailed. It is held infamous to use poisoned weapons, tho' the moral sense made little opposition while rancour and revenge were ruling passions. Aversion to strangers is taught to vary its object, from individuals, to the nation that is our enemy: I bear enmity against France; but dislike not any one Frenchman, being conscious that it is the duty of subjects to serve their king and country.* In distributing justice, we make no distinction be-<164>tween natives and foreigners: if any partiality be indulged, it is in favour of the helpless stranger.

But cruelty is not the only antagonist to morality. There is another, less violent indeed, but more cunning and undermining; and that is the hoarding-appetite. Before money was introduced, that appetite was extremely faint: in the first stage of civil society, men are satisfied with plain necessaries; and having these in plenty, they think not of providing against want. But money is a species of property, so universal in operation, and so permanent in value, as to rouse the appetite for hoarding: love of money excites industry; and the many beautiful productions of industry, magnificent houses, splendid gardens, rich garments, inflame the appetite to an extreme. The people of Whidah, in Guinea, are much addicted to pilfering. Bozman was told by the king, "That his subjects were <165> not like those of Ardrah, who on the slightest umbrage will poison an European. This, says he, you have no reason to apprehend here: but take care of your goods; for so expert are my people at thieving, that they will steal from you while you are looking on."[14] In the thirteenth century, so obscured was the moral sense by rapacity and avarice, that robbery on the highway, and the coining false money, were in Germany held to be privileges of great lords. Cicero some where talks of banditti who infested the roads near Rome, and made travelling extremely dangerous. In the days of Henry III. of England, the chronicle of Dunstable reports, that the country was in great disorder by theft and robbery, that men were not secure in their own houses, and that whole villages were often plundered by bands of robbers, tho' the kingdom

* In one of our ill-concerted descents upon France during the late war, signal humanity appeared, in forbearing to burn a manufactory of sails and ropes, belonging to the King; because it would have destroy'd an adjoining building of the same kind belonging to a private manufacturer.

14. "The people of . . . are looking on": added in 2nd edition.

was otherwise at peace. Many of the King's own household were found to be robbers; and excused themselves, that having received no wages from the King, they were obliged to rob for subsistence.[15] That perjury was common in the city of London, especially among jury-<166>men, makes a preamble in more than one statute of Henry VII. In *the Dance of Death,* translated from the French in the said king's reign with additions adapted to English manners, a juryman is introduced, who, influenced by bribes, had frequently given a false verdict. And the sheriff was often suspected as accessory to the crime, by returning for jurymen persons of a bad character. Carew, in his account of Cornwall, says, that it was an ordinary article in an attorney's bill, to charge *pro amicitia vicecomitis.** Perjury in jurors of the city of London is greatly complained of. Stow informs us, that, in the year 1468, many jurors of that city were punished; and papers fixed on their heads declaring their offence of being corrupted by the parties to the suit. He complains of that corruption as flagrant in the reign of Elisabeth, when he wrote his account of London. Fuller, in his English Worthies, mentions it as a proverbial saying, "That London juries hang half, and save half." Grafton, in his Chronicle, mentions, that the chancellor of the Bishop of London being indicted <167> for murder, the Bishop wrote a letter to Cardinal Wolsey, begging his interposition for having the prosecution stopt, "because London juries were so corrupted, that they would find Abel guilty of the murder of Cain." Mr. Hume, in the first volume of his history of England (page 417. edition 1762.) cites many instances from Madox of bribes given for perverting justice. In that period, the morals of the low people were in other particulars equally loose. We learn from Strype's annals (*a*), that in the county of Somerset alone, forty persons were executed in one year for robbery, theft, and other felonies, thirty-five burnt in the hand, thirty-seven whipped, one hundred and eighty-three discharged tho' most wicked and desperate persons; and yet that the fifth part of the felonies committed in that county were not brought to trial, either from cunning in the felons, indolence in the magistrate, or foolish lenity in the people;

* "For the friendship of the sheriff."
(*a*) Vol. 4.
15. "Cicero some where . . . rob for subsistence": added in 2nd edition.

that other counties were in no better condition, and many in a worse; and that commonly there were three or four hundred able-bodied vagabonds in every <168> county, who lived by theft and rapine. Harrison computes, that in the reign of Henry VIII. seventy-two thousand thieves and rogues were hanged; and that in Elisabeth's time there were only hanged yearly between three and four hundred for theft and robbery. At present, there are not forty hanged in a year for these crimes. The same author reports, that in the reign of Elisabeth, there were computed to be in England ten thousand gypsies. In the year 1601, complaints were made in parliament, of the rapine of the justices of peace; and a member said, that this magistrate was an animal, who, for half a dozen of chickens, would dispense with a dozen of penal statutes. The low people in England are greatly improved in their morals since the days of Elisabeth. Laying aside London, there are few places in the world where the common people are more orderly and honest. But we must not conclude, that England has gained much in point of morality. It has lost more by the luxury and loose manners of its nobles, than it has gained by good discipline among their inferiors. The undisciplined manners of our forefathers in <169> Scotland, made a law necessary, that whoever intermeddled irregularly with the goods of a deceased person, should be subjected to pay all his debts, however extensive. A due submission to legal authority, has in effect abrogated that severe law; and it is now scarce ever heard of.[16]

To control the hoarding-appetite, which when inflamed is the bane of civil society, the God of nature has provided two efficacious principles; the

16. "The low people . . . ever heard of": added in 2nd edition. In the 1st edition, Kames places the anecdote from Bosman about Whiddah here and adds: "The Caribbeans, who know no wants but what nature inspires, are amaz'd at the industry of the Europeans in amassing wealth. Listen to one of them expostulating with a Frenchman in the following terms: 'How miserable are thou, to expose thy person to tedious and dangerous voyages, and to suffer thyself to be oppressed with anxiety about futurity! An inordinate appetite for wealth is thy bane; and yet thou art no less tormented in preserving the goods thou hast acquired, than in acquiring more: fear of robbery or shipwreck suffers thee not to enjoy a quiet moment. Thus thou growest old in thy youth, thy hair turns gray, thy forehead is wrinkled, a thousand ailments afflict thy body, a thousand distresses surround thy heart, and thou movest with a painful hurry to the grave. Why art thou not content with what thy own country produceth? Why not contemn superfluities, as we do?'" [2:335].

moral sense, and the sense of property. The hoarding-appetite, it is true, is more and more inflamed by beautiful productions in the progress of art: but, on the other hand, the senses mentioned, arrived at maturity, have a commanding influence over the actions of men; and, when cherished in a good government, are a sufficient counterbalance to the hoarding-appetite. The ancient Egyptians enjoy'd for ages the blessings of good government; and moral principles were among them carried to a greater degree of refinement than at present even in our courts of equity. It was made the duty of every one, to succour those who were unjustly attacked: even passengers were not exempted. A regula-<170>tion among them, that a man could not be imprisoned for debt, was well suited to the tenor of their laws and manners: it could not have taken place but among an honest and industrious people. In old Rome, tho' remarkable for temperance and austerity of manners, a debtor could be imprisoned, and even sold as a slave, for payment of the debt; but the Patricians were the creditors, and the poor Plebeians were held in woful subjection.* <171> The moderation of the inhabitants

---

* A bankrupt in England who pays three fourths of his debt, and obtains a certificate of his good behaviour, is discharged of all the debts contracted by him before his bankruptcy. Such regulation was perhaps not unsuitable to the moderation and frugality of the period when it was made. But luxury and external show, have now become our ruling passions; and to supply our extravagance, money must be procured at any rate. Trade in particular has degenerated into a species of gaming; men venturing their all, in hopes of a lucky hit to elevate them above their neighbours. And did they only venture their own, the case would not be deplorable: they venture all they can procure upon credit; and by that means, reduce to beggary many an innocent family: with respect to themselves, they know the worst, which is to be clear'd from their debts by a certificate. The morals of our people are indeed at so low an ebb, as to require the most severe laws against bankruptcy. When a man borrows a sum, it is implied in the covenant, that all his effects present and future shall lie open to the creditor; for which reason, it is contradictory to justice, that the creditor should be forc'd to discharge the debt without obtaining complete payment. Many debtors, it is true, deserve favour; but it ought to be left to the humanity of creditors, and not be forc'd from them by law. A debtor, at the same time, may be safely left to the humanity of his creditors: for if he have conducted his affairs with strict integrity and with any degree of prudence, there will scarce be found one man so hard-hearted, as to stand out against the laudable and benevolent intentions of his fellow-creditors. Nay, if he have any regard to character, he dare not stand out: he would be held as a monster, and be abhorred by all the world. To leave a bankrupt thus to the mercy of his creditors, would produce the most salutary effects. It would excite men to be strictly just in their dealings, and put an end to gaming, so destructive to credit; be-

of Hamburgh, and their public spirit kept in vigour by a free government, preserve morality among them entire from taint or <172> corruption. I give an illustrious instance. Instead of a tax upon trade or riches, every merchant puts privately into the public chest, what he thinks ought to be his contribution: the total sum seldom falls short of expectation; and among that numerous body of men, not one is suspected of contributing less than his proportion. But luxury has not yet got footing in that city. A climate not kindly and a soil not fertile, enured the Swiss to temperance and to virtue. Patriotism continues their ruling passion: they are fond of serving their country; and are honest and faithful to each other: a law-suit among them is a wonder; and a door is seldom shut unless to keep out cold.

The hurtful effects of the hoarding-appetite upon individuals, make no figure compared with what it has upon the public, in every state enriched by conquest or by commerce; which I have had more than one opportunity to mention. Overflowing riches unequally distributed, multiply artificial wants beyond all bounds: they eradicate patriotism: they foster luxury, sensuality, and selfishness, which are commonly gratified at the expence <173> even of justice and honour. The Athenians were early corrupted by opulence; to which every thing was made subservient. "It is an oracle," says the chorus in the Agamemnon of Eschylus, "that is not purchased with money." During the infancy of a nation, vice prevails from imbecillity in the moral sense: in the decline of a nation, it prevails from the corruption of affluence.

In a small state, there is commonly much virtue at home, and much violence abroad. The Romans were to their neighbours more baneful than famine or pestilence; but their patriotism produced great integrity at home. An oath, when given to fortify an engagement with a fellow-citizen, was more sacred at Rome than in any other part of the world (a). The censorian office cannot succeed but among a virtuous people; because its rewards and

---

cause misbehaviour in any of these particulars would set the whole creditors against their debtor, and leave him no hope of favour. In the late bankrupt-statute for Scotland, accordingly, the clause concerning the certificate was wisely left out, as unsuitable to the depraved manners of the present time.

(a) [[Montesquieu,]] L'Esprit des loix, liv. 8. ch. 13.

punishments have no influence but upon those who are ashamed of vice.*
As soon <174> as Asiatic opulence and luxury prevailed in Rome, selfishness, sensuality, and avarice, formed the character of the Romans; and the
censorian power was at an end. Such relaxation of morals ensued, as to
make a law necessary, prohibiting the custody of an infant to be given to
the heir, for fear of murder. And for the same reason, it was held unlawful
to make a covenant *de hereditate viventis.* These regulations prove the Romans to have been grossly corrupt. Our law is different in both articles;
because it entertains not the same bad opinion of the people whom it governs.† Domitius Enobarbus and Appius Pulcher were consuls of Rome in
<175> the 699th year; and Memmius and Calvinus were candidates for suc-
ceeding them in that office. It was agreed among these four worthy gentlemen, that they should mutually assist each other. The consuls engaged
to promote the election of Memmius and Calvinus: and they, on the other
hand, subscribed a bond, obliging themselves, under a penalty of about
L. 3000 Sterling, to procure three augurs, who should attest, that they were
present in the comitia when a law passed investing the consuls with military
command in their provinces; and also obliging themselves to produce three
persons of consular rank, to depose, that they were in the number of those
who signed a decree, conferring on the consuls the usual proconsular ap-
pointments. And yet the law made in the comitia, and the decree in the
senate, were pure fictions. Infamous as this transaction was, Memmius, to
answer some political purpose, was not ashamed to divulge it to the senate.
This same Memmius, however, continued to be Cicero's correspondent,
and his professed friend. *Proh tempora! proh mores!* But the passion for

---

* In the fifteenth century, the French clergy from the pulpit censured public transactions, and even the conduct of their king, as our British clergy did in the days of Charles
I. and II. They assumed the privilege of a Roman censor; but they were not men of such
authority as to do any good in a corrupted nation.

† In the beginning of the present century, attorneys and agents were so little rely'd
on for honesty and integrity, as to be disqualified by the court of session from being
factors on the estates of bankrupts. (Act of sederunt 23d November 1710.) At present,
the factors chosen are commonly of that profession, writers or agents; and it appears
from experience, that they make the best factors. Such improvement in morals in so short
a time, has not many parallels. [[Note added in 2nd edition.]]

power and riches was at <176> that time prevalent; and the principles of morality were very little regarded.

It cannot be dissembled, that selfishness, sensuality, and avarice, must in England be the fruits of great opulence, as in every other country; and that morality cannot maintain its authority against such undermining antagonists. Customhouse-oaths have become so familiar among us, as to be swallowed without a wry face; and is it certain, that bribery and perjury in electing parliament-members, are not approaching to the same cool state? In the infancy of morality, a promise makes but a slight impression: to give it force, it is commonly accompanied with many ceremonies (*a*); and in treaties between sovereigns, even these ceremonies are not relied on without a solemn oath. When morality arrives at maturity, the oath is thought unnecessary; and at present, morality is so much on the decline, that a solemn oath is no more relied on, than a simple promise was originally. Laws have been made to prevent such immorality, but in vain: because none but patriots have an interest to support them; and <177> when patriotism is banished by corruption, there is no remaining spring in government to make them effectual. The statutes made against gaming, and against bribery and corruption in elections, have no authority over a degenerate people. Nothing is studied, but how to evade the penalties; and supposing statutes to be made without end for preventing known evasions, new evasions will spring up in their stead. The misery is, that such laws, if they prove abortive, are never innocent with regard to consequences; for nothing is more subversive of morality as well as of patriotism, than a habit of disregarding the laws of our country.* <178>

(*a*) See Historical Law tracts, tract 2.

* Lying and perjury are not in every case equally criminal; at least are not commonly reckoned so. Lying or perjury, in order to injure a man, is held highly criminal; and the greater the hurt, the greater the crime. To relieve from punishment, few boggle at a lie or at perjury; sincerity is not even expected; and hence the practice of torture. Many men are not scrupulous about oaths, when they have no view but to obtain justice to themselves: the Jacobites, that they might not be deprived of their privileges as British subjects, made no great difficulty to swallow oaths to the present government, tho' in them it was perjury. It is dangerous to withdraw the smallest peg in the moral edifice; for the whole will totter and tumble. Men creep on to vice by degrees. Perjury in order to support a friend, has become customary of late years; witness fictitious qualifications

But pride sometimes happily interposes to stem the tide of corruption. The poor are not ashamed to take a bribe from the rich; nor weak states from those that are powerful, disguised only under the name of *subsidy* or *pension*. Both France and England have been in the practice of securing the alliance of neighbouring princes by pensions; and it is natural in the ministers of a pensioned prince, to receive a gratification for keeping their master to his engagement. England never was at any time so inferior to France, as to suffer her king openly to accept a pension from the French king, whatever private transactions might be between the kings themselves. But the ministers of England <179> thought it no disparagement, to receive pensions from France. Every minister of Edward IV. of England received a pension from Louis XI.; and they made no difficulty of granting a receipt for the sum. The old Earl of Warwick, says Commines, was the only exception: he took the money, but refused a receipt. Cardinal Wolsey had a pension both from the Emperor and from the King of France: and his master Henry was vain to find his minister so much regarded by the first powers in Europe. During the reigns of Charles II. and of his brother James, England made so despicable a figure, that the ministers accepted pensions from Louis XIV. A king deficient in virtue, is never well served. King Charles, most disgracefully, accepted a pension from France: what scruple could his ministers have? Britain, governed by a king eminently virtuous and patriotic, makes at present so great a figure, that even the lowest minister would disdain a pension from any foreign prince. Men formerly were so blind, as not to see that a pension creates a bias in a minister, against his master and his country. At present, men clearly see, that a foreign <180> pension to a minister is no better than a bribe; and it would be held so by all the world.

In a nation enriched by conquest or commerce, where selfish passions always prevail, it is difficult to stem the tide of immorality: the decline of virtue may be retarded by wholesome regulations; but no regulations will

---

in the electors of parliament-men, which are made effectual by perjury: yet such is the degeneracy of the present times, that no man is the worse thought of upon that account. We must not flatter ourselves that the poison will reach no farther: a man who boggles not at perjury to serve a friend, will in time become such an adept, as to commit perjury in order to ruin a friend when he becomes an enemy.

ever restore it to its meridian vigour. Marcus Aurelius, Emperor of Rome, caused statues to be made of all the brave men who figured in the Germanic war. It has long been a practice in China, to honour persons eminent for virtue, by feasting them annually at the Emperor's expence. A late Emperor made an improvement: he ordered reports to be sent him annually, of men and women who when alive had been remarkable for public spirit or private virtue, in order that monuments might be erected to their memory. The following report is one of many that were sent to the Emperor. "According to the order of your Majesty, for erecting monuments to the honour of women, who have been celebrated for continence, for filial piety, or for purity of manners, the viceroy <181> of Canton reports, that in the town of Sinhoei, a beautiful young woman, named *Leang,* sacrificed her life to save her chastity. In the fifteenth year of our Emperor Canghi, she was dragg'd by pirates into their ship; and having no other way to escape their brutal lust, she threw herself headlong into the sea. Being of opinion, that to prefer honour before life is an example worthy of imitation, we purpose, according to your Majesty's order, to erect a triumphal arch for that young woman, and to engrave her story upon a large stone, that it may be preserved in perpetual remembrance." At the foot of the report is written, *The Emperor approves.* Pity it is, that such regulations should ever prove abortive, for their purpose is excellent. But they would need angels to carry them on. Every deviation from a just selection enervates them; and frequent deviations render them a subject of ridicule. But how are deviations to be prevented, when men are the judges? Those who distribute the rewards have friends or flatterers; and those of greater merit will be neglected. Like the censorian power in <182> Rome, such regulations, after many abuses, will sink into contempt.

Two errors, which infested morality in dark times, have occasioned much injustice; and I am not certain, that they are yet entirely eradicated. The first is an opinion, That an action derives its quality of right and wrong from the event, without regard to intention. The other is, That the end justifies the means; or, in other words, That means otherwise unlawful, may be lawfully employ'd to bring about a good end. With an account of these two errors, I shall close the present historical sketch.

That intention is the circumstance which qualifies an action and its author, to be criminal or innocent, is made evident in the first part of the present sketch; and is now admitted to be so by every moral writer. But rude and barbarous nations seldom carry their thoughts beyond what falls under their external senses: they conclude an action to be right that happens to do good, and an action to be wrong that happens to do harm; without ever thinking of motives, of Will, of intention, or of any circumstance that is not <183> obvious to eye-sight. From many passages in the Old Testament it appears, that the external act only, with its consequences, was regarded. Isaac, imitating his father Abraham, made his wife Rebecca pass for his sister. Abimelech, King of the Philistines, having discovered the imposture, said to Isaac, "What is this thou hast done unto us? One of the people might lightly have lien with thy wife, and thou shouldst have brought guiltiness upon us" (*a*). Jonathan was condemned to die for transgressing a prohibition he had never heard of (*b*). A sin of ignorance, *i.e.* an action done without ill intention, required a sacrifice of expiation (*c*). Saul, defeated by the Philistines, fell on his own sword: the wound not being mortal, he prevailed on a young Amalekite, to pull out the sword, and to dispatch him with it. Josephus (*d*) says, that David ordered the criminal to be delivered up to justice as a regicide.

The Greeks appear to have wavered greatly about intention, sometimes holding it essential to a crime, and sometimes <184> disregarding it as a circumstance of no moment. Of these contradictory opinions, we have pregnant evidence in the two tragedies of Oedipus; the first taking it for granted, that a crime consists entirely in the external act and its consequences; the other holding intention to be indispensable. Oedipus had killed his father Laius, and married his mother Jocasta; but without any criminal intention, being ignorant of his relation to them. And yet history informs us, that the gods punished the Thebans with pestilence, for suffering a wretch so grossly criminal to live. Sophocles, author of both tragedies, puts the following words in the mouth of Tiresias the prophet.

(*a*) Genesis, chap. 26.
(*b*) 1 Samuel, xiv. 44.
(*c*) Leviticus, chap. 4.
(*d*) Book 3. of Antiquities.

———— Know then,
That Oedipus, in shameful bonds united,
With those he loves, unconscious of his guilt,
Is yet most guilty.

And that doctrine is espoused by Aristotle in a later period; who holding
Oedipus to have been deeply criminal, tho' without intention, is of opinion, that a more proper subject for tragedy never was brought upon the
stage. Nay as a philo-<185>sopher he talks currently of any involuntary
crime. Orestes, in Euripides, acknowledges himself to be guilty in killing
his mother; yet asserts with the same breath, that his crime was inevitable,
a necessary crime, a crime commanded by religion.

In Oedipus Coloneus, the other tragedy mentioned, a very different
opinion is maintained. A defence is made for that unlucky man, agreeable
to sound moral principles; that, having had no bad intention, he was entirely innocent; and that his misfortunes ought to be ascribed to the wrath
of the gods.

Thou who upbraid'st me thus for all my woes,
Murder and incest, which against my will
I had committed; so it pleas'd the gods,
Offended at my race for former crimes.
But I am guiltless: can'st thou name a fault
Deserving this? For, tell me, was it mine,
When to my father, Phoebus did declare,
That he should one day perish by the hand
Of his own child; was Oedipus to blame,
Who had no being then? If, born at length
To wretchedness, he met his sire unknown,
And slew him; that involuntary deed
Can'st thou condemn? And for my fatal marriage,
Dost thou not blush to name it? was not she
Thy sister, she who bore me, ignorant <186>
And guiltless woman! afterwards my wife,
And mother to my children? What she did, she did unknowing.
But, not for that, nor for my murder'd father,
Have I deserv'd thy bitter taunts: for, tell me,

Thy life attack'd, wouldst thou have staid to ask
Th' assassin, if he were thy father? No;
Self-love would urge thee to revenge the insult.
Thus was I drove to ill by th' angry gods;
This, should my father's soul revisit earth,
Himself would own, and pity Oedipus.

Again, in the fourth act, the following prayer is put up for Oedipus by the chorus.

———— O grant,
That not oppress'd by tort'ring pain,
Beneath the stroke of death he linger long;
But swift with easy steps, descend to Styx's drear abode;
For he hath led a life of toil and pain;
May the just gods repay his undeserved woe.

The audience was the same in both plays. Did they think Oedipus to be guilty in the one play, and innocent in the other? If they did not, how could both plays be relished? if they did, they must have been grossly stupid.

The statues of a Roman Emperor were held so sacred, that to treat them with any <187> contempt was high treason. This ridiculous opinion was carried so far out of common sense, that a man was held guilty of high treason, if a stone thrown by him happened accidentally to touch one of these statues. And the law continued in force till abrogated by a rescript of Severus Antoninus (a).

In England, so little was intention regarded, that casual homicide, and even homicide in self-defence, were capitally punished. It requires strong evidence to vouch so absurd a law; and I have the strongest, viz. the act 52° Henry III. cap. 26. converting the capital punishment into a forfeiture of moveables. The same absurdity continued much longer to be law in Scotland. By act 19. parl. 1649, renewed act 22. parl. 1661, the capital punishment is converted to imprisonment, or a fine to the wife and children. In a period so late as the Restoration, strange blindness it was not to be sensible, that homicide in self-defence, being a lawful act justified by the strict-

(a) l. 5. ad leg. Jul. Majest.

est rules of morality, subjects not a man to punishment, <188> more than the defending his property against a robber; and that casual homicide, meaning homicide committed innocently without ill intention, may subject him to reparation, but never to any punishment, mild or severe.

The Jesuits in their doctrines seem to rest on the external act, disregarding intention. It is with them a matter of perfect indifference, from what motive men obey the laws of God; consequently that the service of those who obey from fear of punishment, is no less acceptable to the Deity, than of those who obey from a principle of love.[17]

The other error mentioned above, is, That the end justifies the means. In defence of that proposition, it is urged, that the character of the means is derived from the end; that every action must be right which contributes to a good end; and that every action must be wrong which contributes to an ill end. According to this reasoning, it is right to assassinate a man who is a declared or concealed enemy to his country. It is right to rob a rich man in order to relieve a person in want. What becomes then of <189> property, which by all is held inviolable? It is totally unhinged. The proposition then is untenable as far as light can be drawn from reason. At the same time, the tribunal of reason may be justly declined in this case.[18] Reason is the only touchstone of truth and falsehood: but the moral sense is the only touchstone of right and wrong. And to maintain, that the qualities of right and wrong are discoverable by reason, is no less absurd than that truth and falsehood are discoverable by the moral sense. The moral sense dictates, that on no pretext whatever it is lawful to do an act of injustice, or any wrong (*a*): and men, conscious that the moral sense governs in matters of right and wrong, submit implicitly to its dictates. Influenced however by the reason-

(*a*) See the first part of this Sketch, Sect. 3. at the end.

17. In the 1st edition the following note is added here: "External show made a great figure, when nothing was regarded but what is visible. By acuteness of judgement, and refinement of taste, the pleasures of society prevail, and forms and ceremonies are disregarded. External show, however, continues to stand its ground in several instances. It occasions, in particular, many an ill-sorted match: a young man is apt to be captivated with beauty or dress; a young woman with equipage or a title" [2:347].

18. "According to this reasoning . . . in this case": added in 2nd edition. In the 1st edition: "But those who reason thus, ought first to consider, whether reasoning be at all applicable to the present subject" [2:397].

ing mentioned, men, during the nonage of the moral sense, did wrong currently in order to bring about a good end; witness pretended miracles and forged writings, urged without reserve by every sect of Christians against their antagonists. And I am sorry to observe, that the error is not entirely eradi-<190>cated: missionaries employed in converting infidels to the true faith, are little scrupulous about the means: they make no difficulty to feign prodigies in order to convert those who are not moved by argument. Such pious frauds tend to sap the very foundations of morality. <191>

Principles and Progress of Theology

As no other science can vie with theology, either in dignity or importance, it justly claims to be a favourite study with every person endued with true taste and solid judgement. From the time that writing was invented, natural religion has employ'd pens without number; and yet in no language is there found a connected history of it. The present work will only permit a slight sketch: which I shall glory in, however imperfect, if it excite any one of superior talents to undertake a complete history. <192>

CHAPTER I.

Existence of a Deity.

That there exist beings, one or many, powerful above the human race, is a proposition universally admitted as true, in all ages, and among all nations. I boldly call it universal, notwithstanding what is reported of some gross savages; for reports that contradict what is acknowledged to be general among men, require more able vouchers than a few illiterate voyagers. Among many savage tribes, there are no words but for objects of external sense: is it surprising, that such people are incapable to express their religious perceptions, or any perception of internal sense? and from their silence can it be fairly presumed, that they have no such perception?* <193>

* In the language even of Peru, there is not a word for expressing an abstract idea, such as *time, endurance, space, existence, substance, matter, body.* It is no less defective in expressing moral ideas, such as *virtue, justice, gratitude, liberty.* The Yameos, a tribe on

790

The conviction that men have of superior powers in every country where there are words to express it, is so well vouched, that in fair reasoning it ought to be taken for granted among the few tribes where language is deficient. Even the grossest idolatry affords evidence of that conviction. No nation can be so brutish as to worship a stock or a stone, merely as such: the visible object is always imagined to be connected with some invisible power; and the worship paid to the former, is as representing the latter, or as in some manner connected with it. Every family among the ancient Lithuanians, entertained a real serpent as a household god; and the same practice is at present universal among the negroes in the kingdom of Whidah: it is not the serpent that is worshipped, but some deity imagined to reside in it. The ancient Egyptians were not idiots, to pay divine honours to a bull or a cat, <194> as such: the divine honours were paid to a deity, as residing in these animals. The sun is to man a familiar object; being frequently obscured by clouds, and totally eclipsed during night, a savage naturally conceives it to be a great fire, sometimes flaming bright, sometimes obscured, and sometimes extinguished. Whence then sun-worship, once universal among savages? Plainly from the same cause: it is not properly the sun that is worshipped, but a deity who is supposed to dwell in that luminary.

Taking it then for granted, that our conviction of superior powers has been long universal, the important question is, From what cause it proceeds. A conviction so universal and so permanent, cannot proceed from chance; but must have a cause operating constantly and invariably upon all men in all ages. Philosophers, who believe the world to be eternal and self-existent, and imagine it to be the only deity tho' without intelligence, endeavour to account for our conviction of superior powers, from the terror that thunder and other elementary convulsions raise in savages; and thence conclude that <195> such belief is no evidence of a deity. Thus Lucretius,

> Praeterea, cui non animus formidine divum
> Contrahitur? cui non conripunt membra pavore,

---

the river Oroonoko described by Condamine, use the word *poettarraroincouroac* to express the number three, and have no word for a greater number. The Brasilian language is nearly as barren.

      Fulminis horribili cum plaga torrida tellus
      Contremit, et magnum percurrunt murmura coelum? (*a*)*

And Petronius Arbiter,

      Primus in orbe deos fecit timor: ardua coelo
      Fulmina quum caderent discussaque moenia flammis,
      Atque ictus flagraret Athos.†

    It will readily be yielded to these gentlemen, that savages, grossly igno-
rant of causes and effects, are apt to take fright at every unusual appearance,
and to think that some malignant being is the cause. <196> And if they
mean only, that the first perception of deity among savages is occasioned
by fear, I heartily subscribe to their opinion. But if they mean, that such
perceptions proceed from fear solely, without having any other cause, I wish
to be informed from what source is derived the belief we have of benevolent
deities. Fear cannot be the source: and it will be seen anon, that tho' malevolent deities were first recognised among savages, yet that in the progress
of society, the existence of benevolent deities was universally believed. The
fact is certain; and therefore fear is not the sole cause of our believing the
existence of superior beings.

    It is beside to me evident, that the belief even of malevolent deities, once
universal among all the tribes of men, cannot be accounted for from fear
solely. I observe, first, That there are many men, to whom an eclipse, an
earthquake, and even thunder, are unknown: Egypt, in particular, tho' the
country of superstition, is little or not at all acquainted with the two latter;
and in Peru, tho' its government was a theocracy, thunder is not known.[1]

---

  * What man can boast that firm undaunted soul,
      That hears, unmov'd, when thunder shakes the pole;
      Nor shrinks with fear of an offended pow'r,
      When lightnings flash, and storms and tempests roar?

  † When dread convulsions rock'd the lab'ring earth,
      And livid clouds first gave the thunder birth,
      Instinctive fear within the human breast
      The first ideas of a God impress'd.

(*a*) Lib. 5.
1. "and in Peru . . . is not known": added in 2nd edition.

Nor do such appearances strike <197> terror into every one who is acquainted with them. The universality of the belief, must then have some
cause more universal than fear. I observe next, That if the belief were
founded solely on fear, it would die away gradually as men improve in the
knowledge of causes and effects: instruct a savage, that thunder, an eclipse,
an earthquake, proceed from natural causes, and are not threatenings of an
incensed deity; his fear of malevolent beings will vanish; and with it his
belief in them, if founded solely on fear. Yet the direct contrary is true: in
proportion as the human understanding ripens, our conviction of superior
powers, or of a Deity, turns more and more firm and authoritative; which
will be made evident in the chapter immediately following.

Philosophers of more enlarged views and of deeper penetration, may be
inclined to think, that the operations of nature and the government of this
world, which loudly proclaim a Deity, may be sufficient to account for the
universal belief of superior powers. And to give due weight to the argument, I shall relate a conversation between a Greenlander and a Danish
mis-<198>sionary, mentioned by Crantz in his history of Greenland. "It is
true," says the Greenlander, "we were ignorant Heathens, and knew little
of a God, till you came. But you must not imagine, that no Greenlander
thinks about these things. A kajak (*a*), with all its tackle and implements,
cannot exist but by the labour of man; and one who does not understand
it, would spoil it. But the meanest bird requires more skill than the best
kajak; and no man can make a bird. There is still more skill required to
make a man: by whom then was he made? He proceeded from his parents,
and they from their parents. But some must have been the first parents:
whence did they proceed? Common report says, that they grew out of the
earth: if so, why do not men still grow out of the earth? And from whence
came the earth itself, the sun, the moon, the stars? Certainly there must be
some being who made all these things, a being more wise than the wisest
man." The reasoning here from effects to their causes is stated with great
precision; and <199> were all men equally penetrating with the Greenlander, such reasoning might perhaps be sufficient to account for the conviction of a Deity, universally spred among savages. But such penetration

(*a*) A Greenland boat.

is a rare quality among savages; and yet the conviction of superior powers is universal, not excepting even the grossest savages, who are altogether incapable of reasoning like our Greenland philosopher. Natural history has made so rapid a progress of late years, and the finger of God is so visible to us in the various operations of nature, that we do not readily conceive how even savages can be ignorant: but it is a common fallacy in reasoning, to judge of others by what we feel in ourselves. And to give juster notions of the condition of savages, I take liberty to introduce the Wogultzoi, a people in Siberia, exhibiting a striking picture of savages in their natural state. That people were baptized at the command of Prince Gagarin, governor of the province; and Laurent Lange, in his relation of a journey from Petersburg to Pekin *ann.* 1715, gives the following account of their conversion. "I had curiosity," says he, "to <200> question them about their worship before they embraced Christianity. They said, that they had an idol hung upon a tree, before which they prostrated themselves, raising their eyes to heaven, and howling with a loud voice. They could not explain what they meant by howling; but only, that every man howled in his own fashion. Being interrogated, Whether, in raising their eyes to heaven, they knew that a god is there, who sees all the actions, and even the thoughts of men; they answered simply, That heaven is too far above them to know whether a god be there or not; and that they had no care but to provide meat and drink. Another question being put, Whether they had not more satisfaction in worshipping the living God, than they formerly had in the darkness of idolatry; they answered, We see no great difference, and we do not break our heads about such matters." Judge how little capable such ignorant savages are, to reason from effects to their causes, and to trace a Deity from the operations of nature. It may be added with great certainty, that could they be <201> made in any degree to conceive such reasoning, yet so weak and obscure would their conviction be, as to rest there without moving them to any sort of worship; which however among savages goes hand in hand with the conviction of superior powers.

If fear be a cause altogether insufficient for our conviction of a Deity, universal among all tribes; and if reasoning from effects to their causes can have no influence upon ignorant savages; what other cause is there to be laid hold of? One still remains, and imagination cannot figure another: to make this conviction universal, the image of the Deity must be stamp'd upon the mind of every human being, the ignorant equally with the knowing: nothing less is sufficient. And the original perception we have of Deity, must proceed from an internal sense, which may be termed the *sense of Deity.*

Included in the sense of Deity, is the duty we are under to worship him. And to enforce that duty, the principle of devotion is made a part of our nature. All men accordingly agree in worshipping superior beings, however they may differ <202> in the mode of worship. And the universality of such worship, proves devotion to be an innate principle.*

The perception we have of being accountable agents, arises from another branch of the sense of Deity. We expect approbation from the Deity when we do right; and dread punishment from him when guilty of any wrong; not excepting the most occult crimes, hid from every mortal eye. From what cause can dread proceed in that case, but from conviction of a superior being, avenger of wrongs? The dread, when immoderate, disorders the mind, and makes every unusual misfortune pass for a punishment inflicted by an invisible hand. "And they said one to another, We are verily guilty concerning our brother, in that we saw the anguish of his soul, when he besought us, and we would not hear: therefore is this distress come upon us. And Reuben answered them, saying, Spake I not unto you, saying, Do not <203> sin against the child; and ye would not hear? therefore behold also his blood is required" (*a*). Alphonsus King of Naples, was a cruel and tyrannical prince. He drove his people to despair with oppressive taxes, treacherously assassinated several of his barons, and loaded others with chains. During prosperity, his conscience gave him little disquiet; but in adversity, his crimes star'd him in the face, and made him believe that his distresses proceeded from the hand of God, as a just punishment. He was terrified to distraction, when Charles VIII. of France approached with a numerous army: he deserted his kingdom; and fled to hide himself from the face of God and of man.

* See this principle beautifully explained and illustrated in a sermon upon the love of God, by Doctor Butler Bishop of Durham, a writer of the first rank. [[Note added in 2nd edition.]]

(*a*) Genesis, xlii. 21. 22.

But admitting a sense of Deity, is it evidence to us that a Deity actually exists? It is complete evidence. So framed is man as to rely on the evidence of his senses (*a*); which evidence he may reject in words; but he cannot reject in thought, whatever bias he may have to scepticism. And experience confirms our belief; for <204> our senses, when in order, never deceive us.

The foregoing sense of Deity is not the only evidence we have of his existence: there is additional evidence from other branches of our nature. Inherent in the nature of man are two passions, devotion to an invisible Being, and dread of punishment from him, when one is guilty of any crime. These passions would be idle and absurd, were there no Deity to be worshipped or to be dreaded. Man makes a capital figure; and is the most perfect being that inhabits this earth: and yet were he endued with passions or principles that have no end nor purpose, he would be the most irregular and absurd of all Beings. These passions both of them, direct us to a Deity, and afford us irresistible evidence of his existence.

Thus our Maker has revealed himself to us, in a way perfectly analogous to our nature: in the mind of every human creature, he has lighted up a lamp, which renders him visible even to the weakest sight. Nor ought it to escape observation, that here, as in every other case, the conduct of Providence to man, is uniform. It <205> leaves him to be directed by reason, where liberty of choice is permitted; but in matters of duty, he is provided with guides less fallible than reason: in performing his duty to man, he is guided by the moral sense; in performing his duty to God, he is guided by the sense of Deity. In these mirrors, he perceives his duty intuitively.

It is no slight support to this doctrine, that if there really be a Deity, it is highly presumable, that he will reveal himself to man, fitted by nature to adore and worship him. To other animals, the knowledge of a Deity is of no importance: to man, it is of high importance. Were we totally ignorant of a Deity, this world would appear to us a mere chaos: under the government of a wise and benevolent Deity, chance is excluded; and every event appears to be the result of established laws: good men submit to whatever happens, without repining; knowing that every event is ordered by

(*a*) See Essays on Morality and Natural Religion, part 2. sect. 3.

divine Providence: they submit with entire resignation; and such resignation is a sovereign balsam for every misfortune. <206>

The sense of Deity resembles our other senses, which are quiescent till a proper object be presented. When all is silent about us, the sense of hearing lies dormant; and if from infancy a man were confined to a dark room, he would be as ignorant of his sense of seeing, as one born blind. Among savages, the objects that rouse the sense of Deity, are uncommon events above the power of man. A savage, if acquainted with no events but what are familiar, has no perception of superior powers; but a sudden eclipse of the sun, thunder rattling in his ears, or the convulsion of an earthquake, rouses his sense of Deity, and directs him to some superior being as the cause of these dreadful effects. The savage, it is true, errs in ascribing to the immediate operation of a Deity, things that have a natural cause: his error however is evidence that he has a sense of Deity, no less pregnant, than when he more justly attributes to the immediate operation of Deity, the formation of man, of this earth, of all the world.

The sense of Deity, like the moral sense, makes no capital figure among savages; the perceptions of both senses being in <207> them faint and obscure. But in the progress of nations to maturity, these senses become more and more vigorous, so as among enlightened nations to acquire a commanding influence; leaving no doubt about right and wrong, and as little about the existence of a Deity.

The obscurity of the sense of Deity among savages, has encouraged some sceptical philosophers to deny its existence. It has been urged, That God does nothing by halves; and that if he had intended to make himself known to men, he would have afforded them conviction equal to that from seeing or hearing. When we argue thus about the purposes of the Almighty, we tread on slippery ground, where we seldom fail to stumble. What if it be the purpose of the Deity, to afford us but an obscure glimpse of his being and attributes? We have reason from analogy to conjecture, that this may be the case. From some particulars mentioned above (*a*), it appears at least probable, that entire submission to the moral sense, would be ill-suited to man in his present state; and would prove more hurtful than <208> ben-

(*a*) Book 2. sketch 1.

eficial. And to me it appears evident, that to be conscious of the presence of the Great God, as I am of a friend whom I hold by the hand, would be inconsistent with the part that Providence has destined me to act in this life. Reflect only on the restraint one is under, in presence of a superior, suppose the King himself: how much greater our restraint, with the same lively impression of God's awful presence! Humility and veneration would leave no room for other passions: man would be no longer man; and the system of our present state would be totally subverted. Add another reason: Such a conviction of future rewards and punishments as to overcome every inordinate desire, would reduce us to the condition of a traveller in a paltry inn, having no wish but for day-light to prosecute his journey. For that very reason, it appears evidently the plan of Providence, that we should have but an obscure glimpse of futurity. As the same plan of Providence is visible in all, I conclude with assurance, that a certain degree of obscurity, weighs nothing against the sense of Deity, more than against the moral sense, or against a future <209> state of rewards and punishments. Whether all men might not have been made angels, and whether more happiness might not have resulted from a different system, lie far beyond the reach of human knowledge. From what is known of the conduct of Providence, we have reason to presume, that our present state is the result of wisdom and be-nevolence. So much we know with certainty, that the sense we have of Deity and of moral duty, correspond accurately to the nature of man as an im-perfect being; and that these senses, were they absolutely perfect, would convert him into a very different being.

A doctrine espoused by several writers ancient and modern, pretends to compose the world without a Deity; that the world, composed of animals, vegetables, and brute matter, is self-existent and eternal; and that all events happen by a necessary chain of causes and effects. It will occur even at first view, that this theory is at least improbable: can any supposition be more improbable than that the great work of planning and executing this uni-verse, beautiful in all its parts, and bound together by the most perfect laws, should be a <210> blind work, performed without intelligence or contri-vance? It would therefore be a sufficient answer to observe, that this doc-trine, though highly improbable, is however given to the public, like a foundling, without cover or support. But affirmatively I urge, that it is fundamentally overturned by the knowledge we derive of Deity from our own nature: if a Deity exist, self-existence must be his peculiar attribute; and we cannot hesitate in rejecting the supposition of a self-existent world, when it is so natural to suppose that the whole is the operation of a self-existent Being, whose power and wisdom are adequate to that great work. I add, that this rational doctrine is eminently supported from contemplating the endless number of wise and benevolent effects, display'd every where on the face of this globe; which afford complete evidence of a wise and benevolent cause. As these effects are far above the power of man, we necessarily ascribe them to a superior Being, or in other words to the Deity (a).[2]

Some philosophers there are, not indeed so hardened in scepticism as to deny the <211> existence of a Deity: They acknowledge a self-existent Being; and seem willing to bestow on that Being power, wisdom, and every other perfection. But then they maintain, that the world, or matter at least,

---

(a) First sketch of this third book, sect. 1.

2. In the 1st edition this paragraph is as follows: "A theory espoused by several writers ancient and modern, must not be overlooked; because it pretends to compose the world without a Deity; which would reduce the sense of a Deity to be delusive, if it have any existence. The theory is, That the world, composed of animals, vegetables, and brute matter, is self-existent and eternal; and that all events happen by a necessary chain of causes and effects. In this theory, tho' wisdom and benevolence are conspicuous in every part, yet the great work of planning and executing the whole, is understood to have been done blindly without intelligence or contrivance. It is scarce necessary to remark, that this theory, assumed at pleasure, is highly improbable, if not absurd; and yet that it is left naked to the world without the least cover or support. But what I chiefly insist on is, that the endless number of wise and benevolent effects, display'd every where on the face of this globe, afford to us complete evidence of a wise and benevolent cause; and as these effects are far above the power of man, we necessarily ascribe them to some superior being, or in other words to the Deity. And this is sufficient to remove the present objection against the existence of a sense of a Deity. But I am not satisfied with this partial victory. I proceed to observe, that nothing more is required but the proof a Deity, to overturn the supposition of self-existence in a world composed of many heterogeneous parts, and of a chain of causes and effects framed without intelligence or foresight, tho' full of wisdom and contrivance in every part. For if a Deity exist, wise and powerful above all other beings, self-existence ought to be his peculiar attribute; and no person of rationality will have any hesitation in rejecting the self-existence of such a world, when so natural a supposition lies in view, as that the whole is the operation of the truly self-existing being, whose power and wisdom are fully adequate to that arduous task" [2:360–61].

must also be self-existent. Their argument is, that *ex nihilo nihil fit*, that it is inconsistent for any thing to be made out of nothing, out of a *nonens*. To consider nothing or a *nonens* as a material or substance out of which things can be formed, like a statue out of stone or a sword out of iron, is I acknowledge a gross absurdity. But I perceive no absurdity nor inconsistence in supposing that matter was brought into existence by Almighty power; and the popular expression, that God made the world out of nothing, has no other meaning. It is true, that in the operations of men nothing can be produced but from antecedent materials; and so accustomed are we to such operations, as not readily to conceive how a thing can be brought into existence without antecedent materials, or made out of nothing, as commonly expressed. But will any man in sober sense venture to set bounds to Almighty power, where he cannot point out a clear incon-<212>sistence? It is indeed difficult to conceive a thing so remote from common apprehension; but is there less difficulty in conceiving matter to exist without a cause, and to be intitled to the awful appellation of self-existent, like the Lord of the Universe, to whom a more exalted appellation cannot be given? Now, if it be within the utmost verge of possibility for matter to have been created, I conclude with the highest probability, that it owes its existence to Almighty power. The necessity of one self-existent being is intuitively certain; but I perceive no necessity, nor indeed probability, that there should be more than one. Difficulties about the creation of matter, testify our ignorance; but to argue from our ignorance that a thing cannot be, has always been held very weak reasoning. Our faculties are adapted to our present state, and perform their office in perfection. But to complain that they do not reach the origin of things, is no less absurd than to complain that we cannot ascend to the moon in order to be acquainted with its inhabitants. At the same time, it is a comfortable reflection, that the question, whether matter was created or no, is <213> a pure speculation, and that either side may be adopted without impiety. To me it appears more simple and more natural to hold it to be a work of creation, than to be self-existent, and consequently independent of the Almighty either to create or to annihilate. I chearfully make the former an article of my Creed; but without anathemising those who adopt the latter. I would however have it understood, that I limit my concession to matter in its original rude state. I cannot possibly carry my complaisance so far as to comprehend the world in its present perfection. That immense machine composed of parts without number so artfully combined as to fulfil the intention of the maker, must be the production of a great being, omniscient as well as omnipotent. To assign blind fatality as the cause, is an insufferable absurdity.[3]

Many gross and absurd conceptions of Deity that have prevailed among rude nations, are urged by some writers as an objection against a sense of Deity. That objection shall not be overlooked; but it will be answered to better purpose, after these gross and absurd conceptions are ex-<214>amined in the chapter immediately following.

The proof of a Deity from the innate sense here explained, differs materially from what is contained in essays on morality and natural religion (a). The proof there given is founded on a chain of reasoning, altogether independent on the innate sense of Deity. Both equally produce conviction; but as sense operates intuitively without reasoning, the sense of Deity is made a branch of human nature, in order to enlighten those who are incapable of a long chain of reasoning; and to such, who make the bulk of mankind, it is more convincing, than the most perspicuous reasoning to a philosopher. <215>

CHAPTER II.

Progress of Opinions with respect to Deity.

The sense of Deity, like many other delicate senses, is in savages so faint and obscure as easily to be biassed from truth. Among them, the belief of many superior beings, is universal. And two causes join to produce that belief. The first is, that being accustomed to a plurality of visible objects, men, mountains, trees, cattle, and such like, they are naturally led to imagine a like plurality in things not visible; and from that slight bias, slight indeed but natural, is partly derived the system of Polytheism, universal among savages. The other is, that savages know little of the connection

(a) Part 2. sect. 7.
3. Paragraph added in 3rd edition.

between causes and effects, and still less of the order and government of
the world: every event that is not familiar, appears to them singular and
extraordinary; and if such event exceed human power, it is <216> without
hesitation ascribed to a superior being. But as it occurs not to a savage, nor
to any person who is not a philosopher, that the many various events exceeding human power and seemingly unconnected, may all proceed from
the same cause; they are readily ascribed to different beings. Pliny ascribes
Polytheism to the consciousness men have of their imbecillity: "Our powers are confined within narrow bounds: we do not readily conceive powers
in the Deity much more extensive: and we supply by number what is wanting in power."* Polytheism, thus founded, is the first stage in the progress
of theology; for it is embraced by the rudest savages, who have neither
capacity nor inclination to pierce deeper into the nature of things.

This stage is distinguishable from others, by a belief that all superior
beings are malevolent. Man, by nature weak and helpless, is prone to fear,
dreading <217> every new object and every unusual event. Savages, having
no protection against storms, tempests, nor other external accidents, and
having no pleasures but in gratifying hunger, thirst, and animal love; have
much to fear, and little to hope. In that disconsolate condition, they attribute the bulk of their distresses to invisible beings, who in their opinion
must be malevolent. This seems to have been the opinion of the Greeks in
the days of Solon; as appears in a conversation between him and Croesus
King of Lydia, mentioned by Herodotus in the first book of his history.
"Croesus," said Solon, "you ask me about human affairs; and I answer as
one who thinks, that all the gods are envious and disturbers of mankind."
The negroes on the coast of Guinea, dread their deities as tyrants and oppressors: having no conception of a good deity, they attribute the few blessings they receive, to the soil, to the rivers, to the trees, and to the plants.
The Lithuanians continued Pagans down to the fourteenth century; and
worshipped in gloomy woods, where their deities were held to reside. Their
worship probably was prompted by fear, <218> which is allied to gloomi-
ness. The people of Kamskatka acknowledge to this day many malevolent

---

* Plurality of heads or of hands in one idol, is sometimes made to supply plurality
of different idols. Hence among savages the grotesque figure of some of their idols.

deities, having little or no notion of a good deity. They believe the air, the water, the mountains, and the woods to be inhabited by malevolent spirits, whom they fear and worship. The savages of Guiana ascribe to the devil even their most common diseases; nor do they ever think of another remedy, but to apply to a sorcerer to drive him away. Such negroes as believe in the devil, paint his images white. Beside the Esquimaux, there are many tribes in the extensive country of Labrador, who believe the Deity to be malevolent, and worship him out of fear. When they eat, they throw a piece of flesh into the fire as an offering to him; and when they go to sea in a canoe, they throw something on the shore to render him propitious. Sometimes, in a capricious fit, they go out with guns and hatchets to kill him; and on their return boast that they have done so.[4]

Conviction of superior beings, who, like men, are of a mixed nature, sometimes doing good, sometimes mischief, constitutes the second stage.[5] This came <219> to be the system of theology in Greece. The introduction of writing among the Greeks while they were little better than savages, produced a compound of character and manners, that has not a parallel in any other nation. They were acute in science, skilful in fine arts, extremely deficient in morals, gross beyond conception in theology, and superstitious to a degree of folly; a strange jumble of exquisite sense and absurd nonsense. They held their gods to resemble men in their external figure, and to be corporeal. In the 21st book of the Iliad, Minerva with a huge stone beats Mars to the ground, whose monstrous body covered seven broad acres. As corporeal beings, they were supposed to require the nourishment of meat, drink, and sleep. Homer mentions more than once the inviting of gods to a feast: and Pausanias reports, that in the temple of Bacchus at Athens, there were figures of clay, representing a feast given by Amphyction to Bacchus and other deities. The inhabitants of the island Java are not so gross in their conceptions, as to think that the gods eat the offerings presented to them: but it is their opinion, <220> that a deity brings his mouth near the offering,

---

4. "Beside the Esquimaux . . . have done so": added in 2nd edition.

5. In the 1st edition this is referred to as the third stage. It would appear that in the 1st edition the belief that all superior beings are malevolent, described in the previous paragraph, constitutes a second stage.

sucks out all its savour, and leaves it tasteless like water.* The Grecian gods, as described by Homer, dress, bathe, and anoint, like mortals. Venus, after being detected by her husband in the embraces of Mars, retires to Paphos,

> Where to the pow'r an hundred altars rise,
> And breathing odours scent the balmy skies:
> Conceal'd she bathes in consecrated bow'rs,
> The Graces unguents shed, ambrosial show'rs,
> Unguents that charm the gods! She last assumes
> Her wond'rous robes; and full the goddess blooms.
>
> ODYSSEY, *book* 8.

Juno's dress is most poetically described, Iliad, book 14. It was also universally believed, that the gods were fond of women, and had many children by them. The ancient Germans thought more sensibly, that the gods were too high to resemble men in any degree, or to be confined within the walls of a temple. The Greeks seem to have thought, that the gods did not much exceed themselves in <221> knowledge. When Agesilaus journeyed with his private retinue, he usually lodged in a temple; making the gods witnesses, says Plutarch, of his most secret actions. The Greeks thought, that a god, like a man, might know what passed within his own house; without knowing any thing passing at a distance. "If it be true," says Aristotle, (Rhetoric, book 2.) "that even the gods do not know every thing, there is little reason to expect great knowledge among men." Agamemnon in Eschylus, putting off his travelling habit and dressing himself in splendid purple, is afraid of being seen and envied by some jealous god. We learn from Seneca, that people strove for the seat next to the image of the deity, that their prayers might be the better heard. But what we have chiefly to remark upon this head, is, that the Grecian gods were, like men, held capable of doing both good and ill. Jupiter, their highest deity, was a ravisher of women, and a notorious adulterer. In the second book of the Iliad, he sends a lying dream to deceive Agamemnon. Mars seduces Venus by <222>

---

* All Greek writers, and those in their neighbourhood, form the world out of a chaos. They had no such exalted notion of a deity as to believe, that he could make the world out of nothing.

bribes to commit adultery (*a*). In the Rhesus of Euripides, Minerva, disguised like Venus, deceives Paris by a gross lie. The ground-work of the tragedy of Xuthus is a lying oracle, declaring Ion, son of Apollo and Creusa, to be the son of Xuthus. Orestes in Euripides, having slain his mother Clytemnestra, excuses himself as having been misled by Apollo to commit the crime. "Ah!" says he, "had I consulted the ghost of my father, he would have dissuaded me from a crime that has proved my ruin, without doing him any good." He concludes with observing, that having acted by Apollo's command, Apollo is the only criminal. In a tragedy of Sophocles, Minerva makes no difficulty to cheat Ajax, promising to be his friend, while underhand she is serving Ulysses, his bitter enemy. Mercury, in revenge for the murder of his son Myrtilus, entails curses on Pelops the murderer, and on all his race.* In ge-<223>neral, the gods, every where in Greek tragedies, are partial, unjust, tyrannical, and revengeful. The Greeks accordingly have no reserve in abusing their gods. In the tragedy of Prometheus, Jupiter, without the least ceremony, is accused of being an usurper. Eschylus proclaims publicly on the stage, that Jupiter, a jealous, cruel, and implacable tyrant, had overturned every thing in heaven; and that the other gods were reduced to be his slaves. In the Iliad, book 13. Menelaus addresses Jupiter in the following words: "O Father Jove! in wisdom, they say, thou excellest both men and gods. Yet all these ills proceed from thee; for the wicked thou dost aid in war. Thou art a friend to the Trojans, whose souls delight in force, who are never glutted with blood." The gods were often treated with a sort of contemptuous familiarity, and employed in very low offices. Nothing is more common, than to introduce them as actors in Greek tragedies; frequently for trivial purposes: Apollo comes upon the stage most courteously to acquaint the audience with the subject of the play. Why is this not urged by our <224> critics, as classical authority against the rule of Horace, *Nec deus intersit nisi dignus vindice nodus.*† Homer makes very useful ser-

---

* The English translator of that tragedy, observes it to be remarkable in the Grecian creed, that the gods punish not only the persons guilty, but their innocent posterity.

† Nor let a god in person stand display'd,
  Unless the labouring plot deserve his aid.
                    FRANCIS.

(*a*) Odyssey, book 8.

vants of his gods. Minerva, in particular, is a faithful attendant upon Ulysses. She acts the herald, and calls the chiefs to council (*a*). She marks the place where a great stone fell that was thrown by Ulysses (*b*). She assists Ulysses to hide his treasure in a cave (*c*), and helps him to wrestle with the beggar (*d*). Ulysses being tost with cares in bed, she descends from heaven to make him fall asleep (*e*). This last might possibly be squeez'd into an allegory, if Minerva were not frequently introduced where there is no place for an allegory. Jupiter, book 17. of the Iliad, is introduced comforting the steeds of Achilles for the death of Patroclus. Creusa keeps it a profound secret from her husband, that she had a child by Apollo. <225> It was held as little honourable in Greece to commit fornication with a god as with a man. It appears from Cicero (*f*), that when Greek philosophers began to reason about the deity, their notions were wonderfully crude. One of the hardest morsels to digest in Plato's philosophy, was a doctrine, That God is incorporeal; which by many was thought absurd, for that, without a body, he could not have senses, nor prudence, nor pleasure. The religious creed of the Romans seems to have been little less impure than that of the Greeks. It was a ceremony of theirs, in besieging a town, to evocate the tutelar deity, and to tempt him by a reward to betray his friends and votaries. In that ceremony, the name of the tutelar deity was thought of importance; and for that reason, the tutelar deity of Rome was a profound secret.* Appian

(*a*) Odyssey, book 8.
(*b*) Book 8.
(*c*) Book 13.
(*d*) Book 18.
(*e*) Book 20.
(*f*) Lib. 1. De natura deorum.
* The form of the *evocatio* follows. "Tuo ductu, inquit, Pythie Apollo, tuoque numine instinctus, pergo ad delendam urbem Veios: tibique hinc decimam partem praedae voveo. Te simul, Juno Regina, quae nunc Veios colis, precor, ut nos victores in nostram tuamque mox feturam urbem sequare: ubi te, dignum amplitudine tua, templum accipiat." *Titus Livius, lib.* 5. *cap.* 21.—[*In English thus:* "Under thy guidance and divine inspiration, O Pythian Apollo, I march to the destruction of *Veii;* and to thy shrine I devote a tenth of the plunder. Imperial Juno, guardian of Veii, deign to prosper our victorious arms, and a temple shall be erected to thy honour, suitable to the greatness and majesty of thy name."]—But it appears from Macrobius, that they used a form of evocation even when the name of the tutelar deity was unknown to them. "Si deus, si

of Alexandria, <226> in his book of the Parthian war, reports, that Anthony, reduced to extremity by the Parthians, lifted up his eyes to heaven, <227> and besought the gods, that if any of them were jealous of his former happiness, they would pour their vengeance upon his head alone, and suffer his army to escape. The story of Paris and the three goddesses gives no favourable impression, either of the morals or religion of the Romans. Juno and her two sister-deities submit their dispute about beauty to the shepherd Paris, who conscientiously pronounces in favour of Venus. But

> ——— *manet alta mente repostum*
> *Judicium Paridis, spretaeque injuria formae.* [6]

Juno, not satisfied with wreaking her malice against the honest shepherd, declares war against his whole nation. Not even Eneas, tho' a fugitive in foreign lands, escapes her fury. Their great god Jupi-<228>ter is introduced on the stage by Plautus, to deceive Alcmena, and to lie with her in the shape of her husband. Nay, it was the opinion of the Romans, that this play made much for the honour of Jupiter; for in times of national troubles and calamities, it was commonly acted to appease his anger;—a pregnant instance of the gross conceptions of that warlike people in morality, as well as in religion.

A division of invisible beings into benevolent and malevolent, without

---

dea est, cui populus civitasque Carthaginiensis est in tutela, teque maxime ille qui urbis hujus populique tutelam recipisti, precor, venerorque, veniamque a vobis peto, ut vos populum civitatemque Carthaginiensem deseratis, loca, templa, sacra, urbemque eorum relinquiatis, absque his abeatis, eique populo, civitatique metum, formidinem, oblivionem injiciatis, proditique Romam ad me meosque veniatis, nostraque vobis loca, templa, sacra, urbs, acceptior probatiorque sit, mihique populoque Romano militibusque meis praepositi sitis, ut sciamus intelligamusque. Si ita feceritis, voveo vobis templa ludosque facturum." *Saturnal. lib.* 3. *cap.* 9.—[*In English thus:* "That divinity, whether god or goddess, who is the guardian of the state of Carthage, that divinity I invoke, I pray and supplicate, that he will desert that perfidious people. Honour not with thy presence their temples, their ceremonies, nor their city; abandon them to all their fears, leave them to infamy and oblivion. Fly hence to Rome, where, in my country, and among my fellow citizens, thou shalt have nobler temples, and more acceptable sacrifices; thou shalt be the tutelar deity of this army, and of the Roman state. On this condition, I here vow to erect temples and institute games to thine honour."]

6. "Deep in her heart remain the beauty of Paris and the outrage to her slighted beauty": Virgil, *Aeneid,* bk. I, ll. 26–27.

any mixture of these qualities, makes the third stage.[7] The talents and feelings of men, refine gradually under good government: social amusements begin to make a figure: benevolence is highly regarded; and some men are found without gall. Having thus acquired a notion of pure benevolence, and finding it exemplified in some eminent persons, it was an easy step in the progress of theological opinions, to bestow the same character upon some superior beings. This led men to distinguish their gods into two kinds, essentially different, one entirely benevolent, another entirely malevolent; and the difference between good and ill, which are diametrical-<229>ly opposite, favoured that distinction. Fortunate events out of the common course of nature, were accordingly ascribed to benevolent deities; and unfortunate events of that kind to malevolent. In the time of Pliny the elder, malevolent deities were worshipped at Rome. He mentions a temple dedicated to *Bad Fortune,* another to the disease termed a *Fever.* The Lacedemonians worshipped *Death* and *Fear;* and the people of Cadiz *Poverty* and *Old Age;* in order to deprecate their wrath. Such gods were by the Romans termed *Averrunci,* as putting away evil.

Conviction of one supreme benevolent Deity, and of inferior deities, some benevolent, some malevolent, is the fourth stage.[8] Such conviction, which gains ground in proportion as morality ripens, arises from a remarkable difference between gratitude and fear. Willing to show my gratitude for some kindness proceeding from an unknown hand, several persons occur to my conjectures; but I always fix at last upon one person as the most likely. Fear is of an opposite nature: it expands itself upon every suspicious person, and blackens them all. <230> Thus, upon providential good fortune above the power of man, we naturally rest upon one benevolent Deity as the cause; and to him we confine our gratitude and veneration. When, on the other hand, we are struck with an uncommon calamity, every thing that possibly may be the cause raises terror. Hence the propensity in savages to multiply objects of fear; but to confine their gratitude and veneration to a single object. Gratitude and veneration, at the same time, are of such a nature, as to raise a high opinion of the person who is their

7. In 1st edition, the fourth stage.
8. In 1st edition, the fifth stage.

object; and when a single invisible being is understood to pour out blessings with a liberal hand, good men, inflamed with gratitude, put no bounds to the power and benevolence of that being. And thus one supreme benevolent Deity comes to be recognised among the more enlightened savages. With respect to malevolent deities, as they are supposed to be numerous, and as there is no natural impulse for elevating one above another; they are all of them held to be of an inferior rank, subordinate to the supreme Deity.

Unity in the supreme being hath, a-<231>mong philosophers, a more solid foundation, namely, unity of design and of order in the creation and government of this world.* At the same time, the passion of gratitude, which leads even savages to the attribute of unity in the supreme being, prepares the mind for relishing the proof of that unity, founded on the unity of his works.

The belief of one supreme benevolent Deity, and of subordinate deities benevolent and malevolent, is and has been more universal than any other religious creed. I confine myself to a few instances; for a complete enumeration would be endless. The different savage tribes in Dutch Guiana, agree pretty much in their articles of faith. They hold the existence of one supreme Deity, whose chief attribute is be-<232>nevolence; and to him they ascribe every good that happens. But as it is against his nature to do ill, they believe in subordinate malevolent beings, like our devil, who occasion thunder, hurricanes, earthquakes, and who are the authors of death, diseases, and of every misfortune. To these devils, termed in their language *Yowahoos,* they direct every supplication, in order to avert their malevolence; while the supreme Deity is entirely neglected: so much more powerful among savages, is fear than gratitude. The North-American savages have all of them a notion of a supreme Deity, creator and governor of the world; and of inferior deities, some good, some ill. These are supposed to have bodies, and to live much as men do, but without being subjected to

---

* All things in the universe are evidently of a piece. Every thing is adjusted to every thing; one design prevails through the whole: and this uniformity leads the mind to acknowledge one author; because the conception of different authors without distinction of attributes or operations, serves only to perplex the imagination, without bestowing any satisfaction on the understanding. *Natural history of Religion, by David Hume, Esquire.*

any distress. The same creed prevails among the negroes of Benin and Congo, among the people of New Zeland, among the inhabitants of Java, of Madagascar, of the Molucca islands, and of the Caribbee islands. The Chingulese, a tribe in the island of Ceylon, acknowledge one God creator of the universe, with subordinate deities who act as his deputies: agricul-<233>ture is the peculiar province of one, navigation of another. The creed of the Tonquinese is nearly the same. The inhabitants of Otaheite, termed *King George's island,* believe in one supreme Deity; and in inferior deities without end, who preside over particular parts of the creation. They pay no adoration to the supreme Deity, thinking him too far elevated above his creatures to concern himself with what they do. They believe the stars to be children of the sun and moon, and an eclipse to be the time of copulation. The Naudowessies are the farthest remote from our Colonies of any of the North Americans whom we are in any degree acquainted with. They acknowledge one supreme being or giver of life, to whom they look up as the source of good, and from whom no evil can proceed. They acknowledge also a bad spirit of great power, by whom all the evils that befal mankind are inflicted. To him they pray in their distresses; begging that he will either avert their troubles or mitigate them. They acknowledge beside good spirits of an inferior degree, who in their particular departments contribute to the happiness of mor-<234>tals. But they seem to have no notion of a spirit divested of matter. They believe their gods to be of the human form, but of a nature more excellent than man. They believe in a future state; and that their employments will be similar to what they are engaged in here, but without labour or fatigue; in short, that they shall live for ever in regions of plenty, and enjoy in a higher degree every gratification they delight in here.[9] According to Arnobius, certain Roman deities presided over the various operations of men. Venus presided over carnal copulation; Puta assisted at pruning trees; and Peta in requesting benefits: Nemestrinus was god of the woods, Nodutus ripened corn, and Terensis helped to thresh it; Vibilia assisted travellers; orphans were under the care of Orbona, and dying persons, of Naenia; Ossilago hardened the bones of infants; and Mellonia protected bees, and bestow'd sweetness on their honey. The inhabitants of

9. "The Naudowessies are . . . delight in here": added in 3rd edition.

the island of Formosa recognise two supreme deities in company; the one a male, god of the men, the other a female, goddess of the women. The bulk of their inferior deities are the <235> souls of upright men, who are constantly doing good, and the souls of wicked men, who are constantly doing ill. The inland negroes acknowledge one supreme being, creator of all things; attributing to him infinite power, infinite knowledge, and ubiquity. They believe that the dead are converted into spirits, termed by them *Imanini,* or protectors, being appointed to guard their parents and relations. The ancient Goths and several other northern nations, acknowledged one supreme being; and at the same time worshipped three subordinate deities; Thor, reputed the same with Jupiter; Oden, or Woden, the same with Mars; and Friga, the same with Venus.* Socrates taking the cup of poison from the executioner, held it up toward heaven, and pouring out some of it as an oblation to the supreme Deity, pronounced the following prayer: "I implore the immortal God that my translation hence may be happy." Then turning <236> to Crito, said, "O Crito! I owe a cock to Esculapius, pay it." From this incident we find that Socrates, soaring above his countrymen, had attained to the belief of a supreme benevolent Deity. But in that dark age of religion, such purity is not to be expected from Socrates himself, as to have rejected subordinate deities, even of the mercenary kind.

Different offices being assigned to the gods, as above mentioned, proper names followed of course. And when a god was ascertained by a name, the busy mind would naturally proceed to trace his genealogy.

As unity in the Deity was not an established doctrine in the countries where the Christian religion was first promulgated, Christianity could not fail to prevail over Paganism; for improvements in the mental faculties lead by sure steps, tho' slow, to one God.

The fifth stage is,[10] the belief of one supreme benevolent Deity, as in that immediately foregoing, with many inferior benevolent deities, and one only who is malevolent. As men improve in natural knowledge and become

* Regnator omnium Deus, caetera subjecta atque parentia; *Tacitus de moribus Germanorum, cap.* 39. [*In English thus:* "One God the ruler of all; the rest inferior and subordinate."]

10. In 1st edition, the sixth stage.

skilful in tracing <237> causes from effects, they find much less malice and
ill-design than was imagined: humanity at last prevails, which with improved knowledge banish the suspicion of ill-design, in every case where
an event can be explained without it. In a word, a settled opinion of good
prevailing in the world, produced conviction among some nations, less ignorant than their neighbours and less brutal, that there is but one malevolent subordinate deity, and good subordinate deities without number. The
ancient Persians acknowledged two principles; one all good and all powerful, named *Hormuz,* and by the Greeks corruptly *Oromazes;* the other
evil, named *Ahariman,* and by the Greeks *Arimanes.* Some authors assert,
that the Persians held these two principles to be co-eternal: others that
Oromazes first subsisted alone, that he created both light and darkness, and
that he created Arimanes out of darkness. That the latter was the opinion
of the ancient Persians, appears from their Bible, termed the *Sadder;* which
teaches, That there is one God supreme over all, many good angels, and
but one evil spirit. Plutarch acquaints us, that Hormus <238> and Ahariman, ever at variance, formed each of them creatures of their own stamp;
that the former created good genii, such as goodness, truth, wisdom, justice;
and that the latter created evil genii, such as infidelity, falsehood, oppression, theft. This system of theology, commonly termed the *Manichean system,* is said to be also the religious creed of Pegu, with the following addition, that the evil principle only is to be worshipped; which is abundantly
probable, as fear is a predominant passion in barbarians. The people of
Florida believe a supreme benevolent Deity, and a subordinate deity that
is malevolent: neglecting the former, who, they say, does no harm, they
bend their whole attention to soften the latter, who, they say, torments them
day and night. The inhabitants of Darien acknowledge but one evil spirit,
of whom they are desperately afraid. The Hottentots, mentioned by some
writers as altogether destitute of religion, are on the contrary farther advanced toward its purity, than some of their neighbours. Their creed is,
That there is a supreme being, who is goodness itself; of whom they have
no occasion to <239> stand in awe, as he is incapable by his nature to hurt
them; that there is also a malevolent spirit, subordinate to the former, who
must be served and worshipped in order to avert his malice. The Epicurean
doctrine with respect to the gods in general, That being happy in themselves

they extend not their providential care to men, differs not widely from what the Hottentot believes with respect to the supreme being.

Having traced the sense of deity, from its dawn in the grossest savages to its approaching maturity among enlightened nations, we proceed to the last stage of the progress, which makes the true system of theology; and that is, conviction of a supreme being, boundless in every perfection, without subordinate deities, benevolent or malevolent. Savages learn early to trace the chain of causes and effects, with respect to ordinary events: they know that fasting produces hunger, that labour occasions weariness, that fire burns, that the sun and rain contribute to vegetation. But when they go beyond such familiar events, they lose sight of cause and effect: the changes of weather, <240> of winds, of heat and cold, impress them with a notion of chance: earthquakes, hurricanes, storms of thunder and lightning, which fill them with terror, are ascribed to malignant beings of greater power than man. In the progress of knowledge light begins to break in upon them: they discover, that such phenomena, however tremendous, come under the general law of cause and effect; and that there is no ground for ascribing them to malignant spirits. At the same time, our more refined senses ripen by degrees: social affections come to prevail, and morality makes a deep impression. In maturity of sense and understanding, benevolence appears more and more; and beautiful final causes are discovered in many of nature's productions, that formerly were thought useless, or perhaps hurtful: and the time may come, we have solid ground to hope that it will come, when doubts and difficulties about the government of Providence, will all of them be cleared up; and every event be found conducive to the general good. Such views of Providence banish malevolent deities; and we settle at last in a most <241> comfortable opinion; either that there are no such beings; or that, if they exist and are permitted to perpetrate any mischief, it is in order to produce greater good.* Thus, through a long maze of errors, man arrives at true religion, acknowledging but one Being, supreme in power, intelligence, and benevolence, who created all other be-

* The Abyssinians think that the ascribing to the devil the wicked acts of which the Portugueze declare him to be guilty, is falling into the error of the Manichees, who admit two principles, one good, one evil. [[Note added in 2nd edition.]]

ings, to whom all other beings are subjected, and who directs every event to answer the best purposes. This system is true theology.*

Having gone through the different stages of religious belief, in its gradual progress toward truth and purity, I proceed to a very important article, The history of tutelar deities. The belief of tutelar deities preceded indeed several of the <242> stages mentioned, witness the tutelar deities of Greece and Rome; but as it is not connected with any one of them exclusive of the rest, the clearness of method required it to be postponed to all of them. This belief, founded on selfishness, made a rapid progress after property in the goods of fortune was established. The Greeks, the Romans, and indeed most nations that were not mere savages, appropriated to themselves tutelar deities, who were understood to befriend them upon all occasions; and, in particular, to fight for them against their enemies. The Iliad of Homer is full of miraculous battles between the Greeks and Trojans, the tutelar deities mixing with the contending parties, and partaking of every disaster, death only excepted, which immortals could not suffer. The *lares, penates,* or household-gods, of Indostan, of Greece, and of Rome, bear witness, that every family, perhaps every person, was thought to be under the protection of a tutelar deity. Alexander ab Alexandro gives a list of tutelar deities. Apollo and Minerva were the tutelar deities of Athens; Bacchus and Hercules of the Boeotian Thebes; Juno <243> of Carthage, Samos, Sparta, Argos, and Mycené; Venus of Cyprus; Apollo of Rhodes and of Delphos; Vulcan of Lemnos; Bacchus of Naxus; Neptune of Tenedos, &c. The poets testify, that even individuals had tutelar deities:

> Mulciber in Trojam, pro Troja stabat Apollo:
> Aequa Venus Teucris, Pallas iniqua fuit.
> Oderat Aeneam, propior Saturnia Turno;
> Ille tamen Veneris numine tutus erat.

---

* Pliny seems to relish the doctrine of unity in the Deity; but is at a loss about forming any just conception of him, sometimes considering the world to be our only deity, sometimes the sun.

Saepe ferox cautum petiit Neptunus Ulyssem;
Eripuit patruo saepe Minerva suo (*a*).*

Though the North-American savages recognise a supreme Being, wise and benevolent, and also subordinate benevolent beings who are intrusted with the government of the world; yet as the great distance of these subordinate beings and the full occupation they have in general go-<244>vernment, are supposed to make them overlook individuals, every man has a tutelar deity of his own, termed *Manitou,* who is constantly invoked during war to give him victory over his enemies. The Natches, bordering on the Missisippi, offer up the skulls of their enemies to their god, and deposite them in his temple. They consider that being as their tutelar deity, who assists them against their enemies, and to whom therefore the skull of an enemy must be an acceptable offering. Tho' they worship the sun, who impartially shines on all mankind; yet such is their partiality, that they consider them-selves as his chosen people, and that their enemies are his enemies.

A belief so absurd shews woful imbecillity in human nature. Is it not obvious, that the great God of heaven and earth governs the world by in-flexible laws, from which he never can swerve in any case, because they are the best possible in every case? To suppose any family or nation to be an object of his peculiar love, is no less impious, than to suppose any family or nation to be an object of his peculiar hatred: they equally arraign Prov-idence of <245> partiality. Even the Goths had more just notions of the Deity. Totila, recommending to his people justice and humanity, says, "Quare sic habete, ea quae amari ab hominibus solent ita vobis salva fore, si justiciae reverentiam servaveritis. Si transitis in mores alios, etiam Deum

---

*   The rage of Vulcan, and the martial maid,
     Pursu'd old Troy; but Phoebus' love repay'd.
     Aeneas safe, defy'd great Juno's hate,
     For Venus guards her favour'd offspring's fate:
     In vain Ulysses Neptune's wrath assails,
     O'er winds and waves Minerva's power prevails.

(*a*) Ovid. Trist. lib. 1. eleg. 2.

ad hostes transiturum. Neque enim ille, aut omnibus omnino hominibus, aut uni alicui genti, addicit se socium."*

That God was once the tutelar deity of the Jews, is true; but not in the vulgar acceptation of that term, importing a deity chosen by a people to be their patron and protector. The orthodox faith is, "That God chose the Jews as his peculiar people, not from any partiality to them, but that there might be one nation to keep alive the knowledge of one supreme <246> Deity; which should be prosperous while they adhered to him, and un-prosperous when they declined to idolatry; not only in order to make them persevere in the true faith, but also in order to exemplify to all nations the conduct of his Providence." It is certain, however, that the perverse Jews claimed God Almighty as their tutelar deity in the vulgar acceptation of the term. And this error throws light upon an incident related in the Acts of the Apostles. There was a prophecy firmly believed by the Jews, that the Messiah would come among them in person to restore their kingdom. The Christians gave a different sense to the prophecy, namely, that the kingdom promised was not of this world. And they said, that Christ was sent to pave the way to their heavenly kingdom, by obtaining forgiveness of their sins. At the same time, as the Jews held all other nations in abhorrence, it was natural for them to conclude, that the Messiah would be sent to them only, God's chosen people: for which reason, even the apostles were at first doubt-ful about preaching the gospel <247> to any but to the Jews (a). But the apostles reflecting, that it was one great purpose of the mission, to banish from the Jews their grovelling and impure notion of a tutelar deity, and to proclaim a state of future happiness to all who believe in Christ, they pro-ceeded to preach the gospel to all men: "Then Peter opened his mouth, and said, Of a truth I perceive, that God is no respecter of persons: but in every nation, he that feareth him, and worketh righteousness, is accepted with

---

* "Be assured of this, that while ye preserve your reverence for justice, ye will enjoy all the blessings which are estimable among mankind. If ye refuse to obey her dictates, and your morals become corrupted, God himself will abandon you, and take the part of your enemies. For although the benevolence of that power is not partially confined to tribe or people, yet in the eye of his justice all men are not equally the objects of his approbation."

(a) See the 10th and 11th chapters of the Acts of the Apostles.

him" (*a*). The foregoing reasoning, however, did not satisfy the Jews: they could not digest the opinion, that God sent his Messiah to save all nations, and that he was the God of the Gentiles as well as of the Jews. They stormed against Paul in particular, for inculcating that doctrine (*b*).

Considering that religion in its purity was established by the gospel, is it not amazing, that even Christians fell back to <248> the worship of tutelar deities? They did not indeed adopt the absurd opinion, that the supreme Being was their tutelar deity; but they held, that there are divine persons subordinate to the Almighty, who take under their care nations, families, and even individuals; an opinion that differs not essentially from that of tutelar deities among the Heathens. That opinion, which flatters self-love, took root in the fifth century, when the deification of saints was introduced, similar to the deification of heroes among the ancients. People are fond of friends to be their intercessors; and with regard to the Deity, deified saints were thought the properest intercessors. Temples were built and dedicated to them; and solemn rites of worship instituted to render them propitious. It was imagined, that the souls of deified saints are at liberty to roam where they list, and that they love the places where their bodies are interred; which accordingly made the sepulchres of the saints a common rendezvous of supplicants. What paved the way to notions so absurd, was the gross ignorance that clouded the Christian world, after the northern barbarians became ma-<249>sters of Europe. In the seventh century, the bishops were so illiterate, as to be indebted to others for the shallow sermons they preached; and the very few of that order who had any learning, satisfied themselves with composing insipid homilies, collected from the writings of Augustin and Gregory. In the ninth century, matters grew worse and worse; for these saints, held at first to be mediators for Christians in general, were now converted into tutelar deities in the strictest sense. An opinion prevailed, that such saints as are occupied about the souls of Christians in general, have little time for individuals; which led every church, and every private Christian, to elect for themselves a particular saint, to be their patron or tutelar deity. That practice made it necessary to deify saints

(*a*) Acts of the Apostles, x. 34.
(*b*) Acts of the Apostles, chap. 13.

without end, in order to furnish a tutelar deity to every individual. The dubbing of saints, became a new source of abuses and frauds in the Christian world: lying wonders were invented, and fabulous histories composed, to celebrate exploits that never were performed, and to glorify persons who never had a being. And thus religion among <250> Christians, sunk down to as low a state as it had been among Pagans.

There still remains upon hand, a capital branch of our history; and that is idolatry, which properly signifies the worshipping visible objects as deities. But as idolatry evidently sprung from religious worship, corrupted by the ignorant and brutish; it will make its appearance with more advantage in the next chapter, of which religious worship is the subject.

We have thus traced with wary steps, the gradual progress of theology through many stages, corresponding to the gradual openings and improvements of the human mind. But tho' that progress, in almost all countries, appears uniform with respect to the order of succession, it is far otherwise with respect to the quickness of succession: nations, like individuals, make a progress from infancy to maturity; but they advance not with an equal pace, some making a rapid progress toward perfection in knowledge and in religion, while others remain ignorant barbarians. The religion of Hindostan, if we credit history or tradition, had advanced to a considerable degree of purity and refinement, at a <251> very early period. The Hindostan Bible, termed *Chatahbhade* or *Shastah,* gives an account of the creation, lapse of the angels, and creation of man; instructs us in the unity of the Deity, but denies his prescience, as being inconsistent with free-will in man; all of them profound doctrines of an illuminated people, to establish which a long course of time must have been requisite, after wandering through errors without number. Compared with the Hindows in theology, even the Greeks were mere savages. The Grecian gods were held to be little better than men, and their history, as above mentioned, corresponds to the notion entertain'd of them.

In explaining the opinions of men with respect to Deity, I have confined my view to such opinions as are suggested by principles or biasses that make a part of common nature; omitting many whimsical notions, no better than dreams of a roving imagination. The plan delineated, shows wonderful uniformity in the progress of religion through all nations. That irregular and whimsical notions are far otherwise, is not wonderful. Take the fol-<252>lowing specimen. The Kamskatkans are not so stupidly ignorant, as to be altogether void of curiosity. They sometimes think of natural appearances.—Rain, say they, is some deity pissing upon them; and they imagine the rainbow to be a party-coloured garment, put on by him in preparing for that operation. They believe wind to be produced by a god shaking with violence his long hair about his head. Such tales will scarce amuse children in the nursery. The inhabitants of the island Celebes formerly acknowledged no gods but the sun and the moon, which were held to be eternal. Ambition for superiority made them fall out. The moon being wounded in flying from the sun, was delivered of the earth.

Hitherto of the gradual openings of the human mind with respect to Deity. I close this section with an account of some unsound notions concerning the conduct of Providence, and concerning some speculative matters. I begin with the former.

In days of ignorance, the conduct of Providence is very little understood. Far from having any notion, that the govern-<253>ment of this world is carried on by general laws, which are inflexible because they are the best possible, every important event is attributed to an immediate interposition of the Deity. As the Grecian gods were thought to have bodies like men, and like men to require nourishment; they were imagined to act like men, forming short-sighted plans of operation, and varying them from time to time, according to exigencies. Even the wise Athenians had an utter aversion at philosophers who attempted to account for effects by general laws: such doctrine they thought tended to fetter the gods, and to prevent them from governing events at their pleasure. An eclipse being held a prognostic given by the gods of some grievous calamity, Anaxagoras was accused of Atheism for attempting to explain the eclipse of the moon by natural causes: he was thrown into prison, and with difficulty was relieved by the influence of Pericles. Protagoras was banished Athens for maintaining the same doctrine. Procopius overflows with signal interpositions of Providence; and Agathias, beginning at the battle of Marathon, sagely main-<254>tains, that from that time downward, there was not a battle lost but by an immediate judgement of God, for the sins of the commander, or of his army, or of one person or other. Our Saviour's doctrine with respect to those who suffered by the fall of the tower of Siloam, ought to have opened their eyes; but superstitious eyes are never opened by instruction. At the same time, it is deplorable that such belief has no good influence on manners: on the contrary, never doth wickedness so much abound as in dark times. A curious fact is related by Procopius (a) with respect to that sort of superstition. When Rome was besieged by the Goths and in danger of destruction, a part of the town-wall was in a tottering condition. Belisarius, proposing to fortify it, was opposed by the citizens, affirming, that it was guarded by St. Peter. Procopius observes, that the event answered expectation; for that the Goths, during a tedious siege, never once attempted that weak part. He adds, that the wall remained in the same ruinous state at the time of his writing. Here is a curious conceit—Peter created a tutelar <255> deity, able and willing to counteract the laws by which God governs the material world. And for what mighty benefit to his votaries? Only to save them five or fifty pounds in rebuilding the crazy part of the wall.

It is no less inconsistent with the regular course of Providence, to believe, as many formerly did, that in all doubtful cases the Almighty, when appealed to, never fails to interpose in favour of the right side. The inhabitants of Constantinople, ann. 1284, being split into parties about two contending patriarchs, the Emperor ordered a fire to be made in the church of St. Sophia, and a paper for each party to be thrown into it; never doubting, but that God would save from the flames the paper given in for the party whose cause he espoused. But, to the utter astonishment of all beholders, the flames paid not the least regard to either. The same absurd opinion gave birth to the trial by fire, by water, and by single combat. And it is not a little remarkable, that such trials were common among many nations that had no intercourse one with another: even the <256> enlightened people of Indostan try crimes by dipping the hand of a suspected person in boiling oil. In cases of doubtful proof, they recur in the kingdom of Siam, as in many other countries, to artificial proofs. One is to walk barefoot through fire. As the Siamites are accustomed to walk barefooted, their soles become hard; and those who have skill have a good chance to escape without burning. The art is to set down their feet on the fire with all their weight, which

(a) Historia Gothica, lib. 1.

excludes the air, and prevents the fire from burning. Another proof is by water. The accuser and accused are thrown into a pond; and he who keeps the longest under water is declared to be in the right.[11]—Such uniformity is there with respect even to superstitious opinions. Pope Gregory VII. insisting that the Kings of Castile and Aragon should lay aside their Gothic liturgy for the Romish, the matter was put to trial by single combat; and two champions were chosen to declare by victory the opinion of God Almighty. The Emperor Otho I. observing the law-doctors to differ about the right of representation in land-estates, appointed a duel; and the <257> right of representation gain'd the victory. If any thing can render such a doctrine palatable, it is the believing in a tutelar deity, who with less absurdity may interpose in behalf of a favourite opinion, or of a favourite people. Appian gravely reports, that when the city of Rhodes was besieged by Mithridates, a statue of the goddess Isis was seen to dart flames of fire upon a bulky engine, raised by the besiegers to overtop the wall.

Historians mention an incident that happened in the island Celebes, founded on a belief of the same kind with that above mentioned. About two centuries ago, some Christian and some Mahometan missionaries made their way to that island. The chief king, struck with the fear of hell taught by both, assembled a general council; and stretching his hands towards heaven, addressed the following prayer to the supreme being. "Great God, from thee I demand nothing but justice, and to me thou owest it. Men of different religions have come to this island, threatening eternal punishment to me and my people if we disobey thy laws. What are thy laws? <258> Speak, O my God, who art the author of nature: thou knowest the bottom of our hearts, and that we can never intentionally disobey thee. But if it be unworthy of thy essence to employ the language of men, I call upon my whole people, the sun which gives me light, the earth which bears me, the sea which surrounds my empire, and upon thee thyself, to bear witness for me, that in the sincerity of my heart I wish to know thy will; and this day I declare, that I will acknowledge as the depositaries of thy oracles, the first ministers of either religion that shall land on this island."

It is equally erroneous to believe, that certain ceremonies will protect

---

11. "In cases of . . . in the right": added in 3rd edition.

one from mischief. In the dark ages of Christianity, the signing with the figure of a cross, was held not only to be an antidote against the snares of malignant spirits, but to inspire resolution for supporting trials and calamities: for which reason no Christian in those days undertook any thing of moment, till he had used that ceremony. It was firmly believed in France, that a <259> gold or silver coin of St. Louis, hung from the neck, was a protection against all diseases: and we find accordingly a hole in every remaining coin of that king, for fixing it to a ribband. In the minority of Charles VIII. of France, the three estates, ann. 1484, supplicated his Majesty, that he would no longer defer the being anointed with the holy oil, as the favour of Heaven was visibly connected with that ceremony. They affirmed, that his grandfather Charles VII. never prospered till he was anointed; and that Heaven afterward fought on his side, till the English were expelled out of his kingdom.* The high <260> altar of St. Margaret's church in the island of Icolmkill, was covered with a plate of blue marble finely veined; which has suffered from a superstitious conceit, that the smallest bit of it will preserve a ship from sinking. It has accordingly been carried off piece-meal; and at present there is scarce enough left to make an experiment. In the Sadder, certain prayers are enjoined when one sneezes or pisses, in order to chase away the devil. Cart-wheels in Lisbon, are composed of two clumsy boards nailed together in a circular form. Tho' the noise is intolerable, the axles are never greased; the noise, say they, frightens the devil from hurting their oxen.

Nay, so far has superstition been carried, as to found a belief, that the

---

* That ridiculous ceremony is kept up to this day: such power has custom. Take the following sample of it; "The Grand Prior of St. Remi opens the holy phial, and gives it to the Archbishop, who with a golden needle takes some of the precious oil, about the size of a grain of wheat, which he mixes with consecrated ointment. The King then prostrates himself before the altar on a violet-coloured carpet, embroidered with fleurs de lys, while they pray. Then the King rises, and the Archbishop anoints him on the crown of the head, on the stomach, on the two elbows, and on the joints of the arms. After the several anointings, the Archbishop of Rheims, the Bishops of Laon and Beauvais close the openings of the shirt; the High Chamberlain puts on the tunic and the royal mantle; the King then kneels again, and is anointed in the palms of his hands." Is this farce less ludicrous than that of an English King curing the King's evil with a touch? [[Note added in 2nd edition.]]

devil by magic can control the course of Providence. A Greek bishop having dreamed that a certain miracle had failed by magic, <261> the supposed magician and his son were condemned to die, without the least evidence but the dream. Montesquieu collects a number of circumstances, each of which, tho' all extremely improbable, ought to have been clearly made out, in order to prove the crime (*a*). The Emperor Theodore Lascaris, imagining magic to be the cause of his distemper, put the persons suspected to the trial of holding a red-hot iron without being burnt. In the capitularies of Charlemagne, in the canons of several councils, and in the ancient laws of Norway, punishments are enacted against those who are supposed able to raise tempests, termed *Tempestarii.* During the time of Catharine de Medicis, there was in the court of France a jumble of politics, gallantry, luxury, debauchery, superstition, and Atheism. It was common to take the resemblance of enemies in wax, in order to torment them by roasting the figure at a slow fire, and pricking it with needles. If an enemy happened in one instance of a thousand to pine and die, the charm was established for ever. Sorcery and witchcraft were so <262> universally believed in England, that in a preamble to a statute of Henry VIII. ann. 1511, it is set forth, "That smiths, weavers, and women, boldly take upon them great cures, in which they partly use sorcery and witchcraft." The first printers, who were Germans, having carried their books to Paris for sale, were condemned by the parliament to be burnt alive as sorcerers; and did not escape punishment but by a precipitate flight. It had indeed much the appearance of sorcery, that a man could write so many copies of a book, without the slightest variation.

Superstition flourishes in times of danger and dismay. During the civil wars of France and of England, superstition was carried to extravagance. Every one believed in magic, charms, spells, sorcery, witchcraft, &c. The most absurd tales past current as gospel truths. Every one is acquainted with the history of the Duchess of Beaufort, who was said to have made a compact with the devil, to procure Henry IV. of France for her lover. This ridiculous story was believed through all France; and is reported as a truth by <263> the Duke de Sully. Must not superstition have been at a high

(*a*) L'Esprit des loix, lib. 12. ch. 5.

pitch, when that great man was infected with it? James Howel, eminent for knowledge and for the figure he made during the civil wars of England, relates as an undoubted truth an absurd fiction concerning the town of Hamelen, that the devil with a bagpipe enticed all the rats out of the town, and drowned them in a lake; and because his promised reward was denied, that he made the children suffer the same fate. Upon a manuscript doubting of the existence of witches, he observes, "that there are some men of a mere negative genius, who cross and puzzle the clearest truths with their *but, yet, if:* they will flap the lie in truth's teeth, tho' she visibly stands before their face without any vizard. Such perverse cross-grain'd spirits are not to be dealt with by arguments, but palpable proofs: as if one deny that the fire burns, or that he hath a nose on his face. There is no way to deal with him, but to pull him by the tip of the one and put his finger into the other."

In an age of superstition, men of the <264> greatest judgement are infected: in an enlightened age, superstition is confined among the vulgar. Would one imagine that the great Louis of France is an exception. It is hard to say, whether his vanity or his superstition was the most eminent. The Duke of Luxembourg was his favourite and his most successful general. In order to throw the Duke out of favour, his rivals accused him of having a compact with the devil. The King permitted him to be treated with great brutality, on evidence no less foolish and absurd, than that on which old women were some time ago condemned as witches.[12]

There are many examples of the attributing extraordinary virtue to certain things, in themselves of no significancy. The Hungarians were possessed of a golden crown, sent from heaven with the peculiar virtue, as they believed, of bestowing upon the person who wore it, an undoubted title to be their king.

But the most extraordinary effort of absurd superstition, is a persuasion, that one may control the course of Providence, by making a downright bargain with God Almighty to receive from him *quid pro* <265> *quo.* A herd of Tartars in Siberia, named by the Russians *Baravinskoi,* have in every hut a wooden idol about eighteen inches high; to which they address their prayers for plenty of game in hunting, promising it, if successful, a new

---

12. This and the previous paragraph added in 2nd edition.

coat or a new bonnet: a sort of bargain abundantly brutish; and yet more excusable in mere savages, than what is made with the Virgin Mary by enlightened Roman Catholics; who, upon condition of her relieving them from distress, promise her a waxen taper to burn on her altar. Philip II. of Spain made a vow, that, upon condition of gaining the battle of St. Quintin, he would build the monastery of Escurial; as if an establishment for some idle monks, could be a motive with the great God to vary the course of his Providence.* <266> Beside the absurdity of thinking that such vows can have the effect to alter the established laws of Providence; they betray a most contemptible notion of the Deity, as if his favours, like a horse or a cow, could be purchased with money.

But however loose and disjointed events appear to the ignorant, when viewed as past or as passing; future events take on a very different appearance. The doctrine of prognostics, is evidently founded upon a supposition that future events are unalterably fixed; for otherwise that doctrine would appear absurd, even to the ignorant. No bias in human nature has greater influence, than curiosity about futurity; which in dark ages governs without control: men with no less folly than industry have ransacked the earth, the sea, the air, and even the stars, for prognostics of future events. The Greeks had their oracles, the Romans their augurs, and all the world their omens. The Grecian oracles and the Roman auguries, are evidently built upon their belief of tutelar deities; and the numberless omens that influence weak people in every country, seem to rest <267> upon the same foundation.†

---

* Having gained the battle of St. Quintin on the festival of St. Laurence, Philip reckoned himself obliged to the saint for this victory, as much as to God Almighty; and accordingly, he not only built the monastery he had vowed, but also a church for the saint and a palace for himself, all under one roof: and what is not a little ludicrous, the edifice is built in resemblance of a gridiron, which, according to the legend, was the instrument of Laurence's martyrdom.

† It is no wonder that the Romans were superstitiously addicted to omens and auguries: like mere savages, they put no value upon any science but that of war; and, for that reason, they banished all philosophers, as useless members of society. Thus, that nation, so fierce and so great in war, surrendered themselves blindly to superstition, and became slaves to imaginary evils. Even their gravest historians were deeply tainted with that disease.

Ancient histories are stuffed with omens, prodigies, and prognostics: Livy overflows with fooleries of that kind. Endless are the adverse omens reported by Appian of Alexandria, that are said to have given warning of the defeat of Crassus by the Parthians; and no fewer in number are those which happened at the death of the Emperor Hadrian, if we believe Spartianus. Lampridius, with great gravity, recites the omens which prognosticated that Alexander Severus would be Emperor: he was born the same day on which Alexander the Great died: he was brought forth in a temple dedicated to Alexander the Great: he was named *Alexander;* and an old woman gave to his mother, a pigeon's egg of a purple colour produced on his birthday. A comet is an infallible prognostic of the <268> death of a king. But of what king? Why, of the king who dies next. Suetonius, with the solemnity of a pulpit-instructor, informs us, that the death of the Emperor Claudius was predicted by a comet; and of Tiberius, by the fall of a tower during an earthquake.* Such opinions, having a foundation in our nature, take fast hold of the mind, when envigorated by education and example. Even philosophy is not sufficient to eradicate them but by slow degrees: witness Tacitus, the most profound of all historians, who cannot forbear to usher in the death of the Emperor Otho, with a foolish account of a strange unknown bird appearing at that time. He indeed, with decent reserve, mentions it only as a fact reported by others; but from the glow of his narrative it is evident, that the story had made an impression upon him. When Onosander wrote his military institutions, which was in the fourth century, the intrails of an animal sacrificed were still depended on as a prognostic of good or bad <269> fortune. And in chap. 15. he endeavours to account for the misfortunes that sometimes happened after the most favourable prognostics; laying the blame, not upon the prognostic, but upon some cross accident that was not foreseen by the tutelar deity. The ancient Germans drew many of their omens from horses: "Proprium gentis, equorum presagia ac monitus experiri. Publice aluntur iisdem nemoribus ac lucis, candide, et nullo mortali opere contacti, quos pressos sacro curru, sacerdos, ac rex, vel princeps civitatis, comitantur, hinnitusque ac fremitus observant.

---

* Charlemagne, tho' an eminent astronomer for his time, was afraid of comets and eclipses. [[Note added in 2nd edition.]]

Nec ulli auspicio major fides, non solum apud plebem, sed apud proceres, apud sacerdotes" (*a*).* There is scarce a thing seen or imagined, <270> but what the inhabitants of Madagascar consider as a prognostic of some future event. The Hindows rely on the augury of birds, precisely as the old Romans did. Tho' there is not the slightest probability, that an impending misfortune was ever prevented by such prognostics; yet the desire of knowing future events is so deeply rooted in our nature, that omens will always prevail among the vulgar, in spite of the clearest light of philosophy.†

With respect to prophecies in particular, one apology may be made for them, that no other prognostic of futurity is less apt to do mischief. What Procopius (*b*) observes of the Sybilline oracles, is equally applicable to all prophecies, "That it is above the sagacity of man to explain any of them before the event happen. Matters are there handled, not in any <271> order, nor in a continued discourse: but after mentioning the distresses of Africa, for example, they give a slight touch at the Persians, the Romans, the Assyrians; then returning to the Romans, they fall slap-dash upon the calamities of Britain." A curious example of this observation, is a book of prophecies composed in Scotland by Thomas Learmont, commonly called *Thomas the Rhymer,* because the book is in rhyme. Plutarch in the life of Cicero reports, that a spectre appeared to Cicero's nurse, and foretold, that the child would become a great support to the Roman state; and most innocently he makes the following reflection, "This might have passed for an idle tale, had not Cicero demonstrated the truth of the prediction." At that rate, if a prediction happen to prove true, it is a real prophecy; if otherwise,

---

* "It is peculiar to that people, to deduce omens and presages from horses. These animals are maintained at the public expence, in groves and forests, and are not allowed to be polluted with any work for the use of man; but being yoked in the sacred chariot, the priest, and the king, or chief of the state, attend them, and carefully observe their neighings. The greatest faith is given to this method of augury, both among the vulgar and the nobles."

† Is it not mortifying to human pride, that a great philosopher [*Bacon*] should think like the vulgar upon this subject? With respect to rejoicings in London upon the marriage of the daughter of Henry VII. of England to James IV. of Scotland, he says, "not from any affection to the Scots, but from a secret instinct and inspiration of the advantages that would accrue from the match."

(*a*) Tacitus De moribus Germanorum, cap. 10.

(*b*) Gothica Historia, lib. 1.

it is an idle tale. There have been prophecies not altogether so well guarded as the Sybilline oracles. Napier, inventor of the logarithms, found the day of judgement to be predicted in the Revelation; and named the very day, which unfortunately he survived. He made another predic-<272>tion, but prudently named a day so distant as to be in no hazard of blushing a second time. Michel Stifels, a German clergyman, spent most of his life in attempting to discover the day of judgement; and at last announced to his parishioners, that it would happen within a year. The parishioners, resolving to make the best of a bad bargain, spent their time merrily, taking no care to lay up provisions for another year; and so nice was their computation, as at the end of the year to have not a morsel remaining, either of food or of industry. The famous Jurieu has shewn great ingenuity in explaining prophecies; of which take the following instance. In his book, intitled *Accomplishment of the prophecies,* he demonstrates, that the beast in the Apocalypse, which held the *poculum aureum plenum abominationum,** is the Pope; and his reason is, that the initial letters of these four Latin words compose the word *papa;* a very singular prophecy indeed, that is a prophecy in Latin, but in no other language. The candid reader will advert, that such prophecies as relate to our Saviour and <273> tend to ascertain the truth of his mission, fall not under the foregoing reasoning; for they do not anticipate futurity, by producing foreknowledge of future events. They were not understood till our Saviour appeared among men; and then they were clearly understood as relative to him.

There is no end of superstition in its various modes. In dark times, it was believed universally, that by certain forms and invocations, the spirits of the dead could be called upon to reveal future events. A lottery in Florence, gainful to the government and ruinous to the people, gives great scope to superstition. A man who purposes to purchase tickets, must fast six and thirty hours, must repeat a certain number of Ave Maries and Pater Nosters, must not speak to a living creature, must not go to bed, must continue in prayer to the Virgin and to saints, till some propitious saint appear and declare the numbers that are to be successful. The man, fatigued with fasting, praying, and expectation, falls asleep. Occupied with the thoughts he

---

* "The golden cup full of abominations."

had when awake, he dreams that a saint appears, and mentions the lucky numbers. If he be disappointed, he < 274 > is vexed at his want of memory; but trusts in the saint as an infallible oracle. Again he falls asleep, again sees a vision, and again is disappointed.

Lucky and unlucky days, which were so much rely'd on as even to be marked in the Greek and Roman calendars, make an appendix to prophecies. The Tartars never undertake any thing of moment on a Wednesday, being held by them unlucky. The Nogayan Tartars hold every thirteenth year to be unlucky: they will not even wear a sword that year, believing that it would be their death; and they maintain, that none of their warriors ever returned who went upon an expedition in one of these years. They pass that time in fasting and prayer, and during it never marry. The inhabitants of Madagascar have days fortunate and unfortunate with respect to the birth of children: they destroy without mercy every child that is born on an unfortunate day.

There are unlucky names as well as unlucky days. Julien Cardinal de Medicis, chosen Pope, was inclined to keep his own name. But it being observed to him by the cardinals, says Guichardin, that the popes < 275 > who retained their own name had all of them died within the year, he took the name of Clement, and was Clement VII. As John was held an unlucky name for a king, John heir to the Crown of Scotland was persuaded to change his name into Robert; and he was Robert III.[13]

I close this important article with a reflection that will make an impression upon every rational person. The knowledge of future events, as far as it tends to influence our conduct, is inconsistent with a state of activity, such as Providence has allotted to man in this life. It would deprive him of hopes and fears, and leave him nothing to deliberate upon, nor any end to prosecute. In a word, it would put an end to his activity, and reduce him to be merely a passive being. Providence therefore has wisely drawn a veil over future events, affording us no light for prying into them but sagacity and experience.

These are a few of the numberless absurd opinions about the conduct of Providence, that have prevailed among Christians, and still prevail

13. Paragraph added in 2nd edition.

among some of them. Many opinions no less absurd have <276> prevailed about speculative points. I confine myself to one or two instances; for to make a complete list would require a volume. The first I shall mention, and the most noted, is transubstantiation; a doctrine in which it is asserted, first, that the bread and wine in the sacrament are converted into the body and blood of our Saviour; next, that his body and blood exists wholly and entirely in every particular sacrament administered in the Christian world even at the same instant of time. This article of faith, tho' it has not the least influence on practice, is reckoned so essential to salvation, as to be placed above every moral duty. The following text is appealed to as its sole foundation. "And as they were eating, Jesus took bread, and blessed it, and brake it, and gave it to the disciples, and said, Take, eat; this is my body. And he took the cup, and gave thanks, and gave it to them, saying, Drink ye all of it: for this is my blood of the new testament, which is shed for many for the remission of sins. But I say unto you, I will not drink henceforth of this fruit of the vine, until that day when I drink <277> it new with you in my Father's kingdom" (a). That this is a metaphor, must strike every one: the passage cannot even bear a literal meaning, considering the final clause; for surely the most zealous Roman Catholic believes not, that Christians are to drink new wine with their Saviour in the kingdom of heaven. At the same time, it is not so much as insinuated, that there was here any miraculous transubstantiation of the bread and wine into the body and blood of our Saviour; nor is it insinuated, that the apostles believed they were eating the flesh of their master, and drinking his blood. St. John, the favourite apostle, mentions not a word of this ceremony, which he certainly would not have omitted, had he imagined it an essential article of faith.

But supposing transubstantiation were clearly expressed in this text, yet men of understanding will be loth to admit a meaning that contradicts their five senses. They will reflect, that no man now living ever saw the original books of the New Testament; nor are they certain, that the <278> editions we have, are copied directly from the originals. Every remove from them is liable to errors, which may justly create a suspicion of texts that contradict

(a) St. Matthew, xxvi. 26. &c.

reason and common sense. Add, that the bulk of Christians have not even a copy from the original to build their faith upon; but only a translation into another language. But the second branch of this article is obvious to a still stronger objection than of its contradicting our senses: it is a direct inconsistence, as we cannot even conceive it possible that the same body or thing can be in two different places at the same time.[14]

And this leads to what chiefly determined me to select that instance. God and nature have bestowed upon us the faculty of reason, for distinguishing truth from falsehood. If by reasoning with candor and impartiality, we discover a proposition to be true or false, it is not in our power to remain indifferent: we must judge, and our belief must be regulated by our judgement. I say more, to judge is a duty we owe our Maker; for to what purpose has he bestow'd reason upon us, but in order to direct our judge-<279>ment? At the same time, we may depend on it as an intuitive truth, that God will never impose any belief on us, contradictory, not only to our reason, but to our senses.

The following objection however will perhaps relish more with people of plain understanding. Transubstantiation is a very extraordinary miracle, reiterated every day and in every corner of the earth, by priests not always remarkable either for piety or for morality. Now I demand an answer to the following plain question: To what good end or purpose is such a profusion of miracles subservient? I see none. But I discover a very bad one, if they have any influence; which is, that they accustom the Roman Catholics to more cruelty and barbarity, than even the grossest savages are ever guilty of: some of these indeed devour the flesh of their enemies; but none of them the flesh of their friends, especially of their greatest friend. But to do justice to people of that religion, I am confident, that this supposed miracle has no influence whatever upon their manners: to me it <280> appears impossible for any man seriously to believe, that the bread and wine used at the Lord's supper, is actually converted into the body and blood of our Saviour. The Romish church requires the belief of transubstantiation; and a zealous Catholic, out of pure obedience, thinks he believes it. Convince once a man that salvation depends on belief, and he will believe any

14. "But the second . . . the same time": added in 3rd edition.

thing; that is, he will imagine that he believes: *Credo quia impossible est.**
<281> That our first reformers, who were prone to differ from the Romish
faith, should adopt this doctrine, shows the supreme influence of superstition. The Lutherans had not even the excuse of inattention: after serious
examination, they added one absurdity more; teaching, that the bread and
wine are converted into the body and blood of our Saviour, and yet remain
bread and wine as at first; which is termed by them *consubstantiation.* I am
persuaded, that at this time not a single man of them harbours such a
thought.

Many persons, impenetrable by a serious argument, can discover falsehood when put in a ridiculous light. It requires, I am sensible, a very delicate
hand to attack a grave subject with ridicule as a test of truth; and for that
reason, I forbear to offer any thing of my own. But I will <282> set before
my readers some excerpts from a book of absolute authority with Roman
Catholics. Tho' transubstantiation be there handled in the most serious
manner, with all the ceremonies and punctilios that naturally flow from it,
yet in my judgement it is happily contrived to give it a most ridiculous
appearance. The book is the Roman Missal, from which the following is a
literal translation.

> Mass may be deficient in the matter, in the form, in the minister, or in the
> action. First, in the matter. If the bread be not of wheat, or if there be so
> great a mixture of other grain that it cannot be called wheat-bread, or if

---

* A traveller describing the Virgin Mary's house at Loretto, has the following reflection. "When there are so many saints endued with such miraculous powers, so many
relics, and so many impregnated wells, each of them able to cure the most dangerous
diseases; one would wonder, that physicians could live there, or others die. But people
die here as elsewhere; and even churchmen, who preach upon the miracles wrought by
relics, grow sick and die like other men." It is one thing to believe: it is another thing to
fancy that we believe. In the year 1666 a Jew named *Sabatai Levi* appeared at Smyrna,
pretending to be the true Messiah, and was acknowledged to be so by many. The Grand
Signior, for proof of his mission, insisted for a miracle; proposing that he should present
himself as a mark to be shot at, and promising to believe that he was the Messiah, if he
remained unwounded. Sabatai, declining the trial, turned Mahometan to save his life.
But observe the blindness of superstition: tho' Sabatai was seen every day walking the
streets of Constantinople in the Turkish habit, many Jews insisted that the true Sabatai
was taken up into heaven, leaving only behind him his shadow; and probably they most
piously fancied that they believed so.

any way corrupted, it does not make a sacrament. If it be made with rose-water, or any other distilled water, it is doubtful whether it make a sacrament or not. Tho' corruption have begun, or tho' it be leavened, it makes a sacrament, but the celebrator sins grievously.

If the celebrator, before consecration, observe that the host is corrupted, or is not of wheat, he must take another host: if after consecration, he must still <283> take another and swallow it, after which he must also swallow the first, or give it to another, or preserve it in some place with reverence. But if he have swallowed the first before observing its defects, he must nevertheless swallow also the perfect host; because the precept about the perfection of the sacrament, is of greater weight than that of taking it fasting. If the consecrated host disappear by an accident, as by wind, by a miracle, or by some animal, another must be consecrated.

If the wine be quite sour or putrid, or made of unripe grapes, or be mixed with so much water as to spoil the wine, it is no sacrament. If the wine have begun to sour or to be corrupted, or be quite new, or not mixed with water, or mixed with rose-water or other distilled water, it makes a sacrament, but the celebrator sins grievously.

If the priest, before consecration, observe that the materials are not proper, he must stop, if proper materials cannot be got; but after consecration, he must proceed, to avoid giving scandal. If proper materials can be pro-<284>cured by waiting, he must wait for them, that the sacrifice may not remain imperfect.

Second, in form. If any of the words of consecration be omitted, or any of them be changed into words of a different meaning, it is no sacrament: if they be changed into words of the same meaning, it makes a sacrament; but the celebrator sins grievously.

Third, in the minister. If he does not intend to make a sacrament, but to cheat; if there be any part of the wine, or any wafer that he has not in his eye, and does not intend to consecrate; if he have before him eleven wafers, and intends to consecrate only ten, not determining what ten he intends: in these cases the consecration does not hold, because intention is requisite. If he think there are ten only, and intends to consecrate all before him, they are all consecrated; therefore priests ought always to have such intention. If the priest, thinking he has but one wafer, shall, after the consecration, find two sticking together, he must take them both. And he must take off all the re-<285>mains of the consecrated matter; for they all belong to the same sacrifice. If in consecrating, the intention be not actual by wandering of mind, but virtual in approaching the altar, it makes a sacrament: tho' priests should be careful to have intention both virtual and actual.

Beside intention, the priest may be deficient in disposition of mind. If he be suspended, or degraded, or excommunicated, or under mortal sin, he makes a sacrament, but sins grievously. He may be deficient also in disposition of body. If he have not fasted from midnight, if he have tasted water, or any other drink or meat, even in the way of medicine, he cannot celebrate nor communicate. If he have taken meat or drink before midnight, even tho' he have not slept nor digested it, he does not sin. But on account of the perturbation of mind, which bars devotion, it is prudent to refrain.

If any remains of meat, sticking in the mouth, be swallowed with the host, they do not prevent communicating, provided they be swallowed, not as meat, <286> but as spittle. The same is to be said, if in washing the mouth a drop of water be swallowed, provided it be against our will.

Fourth, in the action. If any requisite be wanting, it is no sacrament; for example, if it be celebrated out of holy ground, or upon an altar not consecrated, or not covered with three napkins: if there be no wax candles; if it be not celebrated between day-break and noon; if the celebrator have not said mattins with lauds; if he omit any of the sacerdotal robes; if these robes and the napkins be not blessed by a bishop; if there be no clerk present to serve, or one who ought not to serve, a woman, for example; if there be no chalice, the cup of which is gold, or silver, or pewter; if the vestment be not of clean linen adorned with silk in the middle, and blessed by a bishop; if the priest celebrate with his head covered; if there be no missal present, tho' he have it by heart.

If a gnat or spider fall into the cup after consecration, the priest must swallow it with the blood, if he can: other-<287>wise, let him take it out, wash it with wine, burn it, and throw it with the washings into holy ground. If poison fall into the cup, the blood must be poured on tow or on a linen cloth, remain till it be dry, then be burnt, and the ashes be thrown upon holy ground. If the host be poisoned, it must be kept in a tabernacle till it be corrupted.

If the blood freeze in winter, put warm cloths about the cup: if that be not sufficient, put the cup in boiling water.

If any of Christ's blood fall on the ground by negligence, it must be licked up with the tongue, and the place scraped: the scrapings must be burnt, and the ashes buried in holy ground.

If the priest vomit the eucharist, and the species appear entire, it must be licked up most reverently. If a nausea prevent that to be done, it must be kept till it be corrupted. If the species do not appear, let the vomit be burnt, and the ashes thrown upon holy ground.

As the foregoing article has beyond intention swelled to an enormous size, I shall add but one other article, which shall be <288> extremely short; and that is the creed of Athanasius. It is a heap of unintelligible jargon; and yet we are appointed to believe every article of it, under the pain of eternal damnation. As it enjoins belief of rank contradictions, it seems purposely calculated to be a test of slavish submission to the tyrannical authority of a proud and arrogant priest.* <289>

CHAPTER III.

Religious Worship.

In the foregoing chapter are traced the gradual advances of the sense of Deity, from its imperfect state among savages to its maturity among enlightened nations; displaying to us one great being, to whom all other beings owe their existence, who made the world, and who governs it by perfect laws. And our perception of Deity, arising from that sense, is fortified by an intuitive proposition, that there necessarily must exist some being who had no beginning. Considering the Deity as the author of our existence, we owe him gratitude; considering him as governor of the world, we owe him obedience: and upon these duties is founded the obligation we are under to worship him. Further, God made man for society, and implanted in his nature the moral sense to direct his conduct in <290> that state. From these premises, may it not with certainty be inferred to be the will of God,

* Bishop Burnet seems doubtful whether this creed was composed by Athanasius. His doubts, in my apprehension, are scarce sufficient to weigh against the unanimous opinion of the Christian church.

that men should obey the dictates of the moral sense in fulfilling every duty of justice and benevolence? These moral duties, it would appear, are our chief business in this life; being enforced not only by a moral but by a religious principle.

Morality, as laid down in a former sketch, consists of two great branches, the moral sense which unfolds the duty we owe to our fellow-creatures, and an active moral principle which prompts us to perform that duty. Natural religion consists also of two great branches, the sense of Deity which unfolds our duty to our Maker, and the active principle of devotion which prompts us to perform our duty to him. The universality of the sense of Deity proves it to be innate; the same reason proves the principle of devotion to be innate; for all men agree in worshipping superior beings, whatever difference there may be in the mode of worship.

Both branches of the duty we owe to God, that of worshipping him, and that of obeying his will with respect to our <291> fellow-creatures, are summed up by the Prophet Micah in the following emphatic words. "He hath shewed thee, O man, what is good: and what doth the Lord require of thee, but to do justly, to love mercy, and to walk humbly with thy God?" The two articles first mentioned, are moral duties regarding our fellow-creatures: and as to such, what is required of us is to do our duty to others; not only as directed by the moral sense, but as being the will of our Maker, to whom we owe absolute obedience. That branch of our duty is reserved for a second section: at present we are to treat of religious worship, included in the third article, the walking humbly with our God. <292>

SECTION I

Religious Worship respecting the Deity singly.[15]

The obligation we are under to worship God, or to walk humbly with him, is, as observed above, founded on the two great principles of gratitude and obedience; both of them requiring fundamentally a pure heart, and a well-disposed mind. But heart-worship is alone not sufficient: there are over and

---

15. In the 1st edition this section is entitled simply "Religious Worship."

above required external signs, testifying to others the sense we have of these
duties, and a firm resolution to perform them. That such is the will of God,
will appear as follows. The principle of devotion, like most of our other
principles, partakes of the imperfection of our nature: yet, however faint
originally, it is capable of being greatly invigorated by cultivation and exercise. Private exercise is not sufficient. Nature, and consequently the God
of nature, require public exercise or public worship: for devotion is com-
municative, like <293> joy or grief (a); and by mutual communication in
a numerous assembly, is greatly invigorated. A regular habit of expressing
publicly our gratitude and resignation, never fails to purify the mind, tending to wean it from every unlawful pursuit. This is the true motive of public
worship; not what is commonly inculcated, That it is required from us, as
a testimony to our Maker of our obedience to his laws: God, who knows
the heart, needs no such testimony.* <294>

The setting apart one day in seven for public worship is not a pious
institution merely, but highly moral. With regard to the latter, all men are
equal in the presence of God; and when a congregation pray for mercy and
protection, every one must be inflamed with good-will and brotherly love
to every one.

In the next place, the serious and devout tone of mind inspired by public
worship, suggests naturally self-examination. Retired from the bustle of the

---

* Arnobius (*Adversus gentes, lib.* 1.) accounts rationally for the worship we pay to the
Deity: "Huic omnes ex more prosternimur, hunc collatis precibus adoramus, ab hoc
justa, et honesta, et auditu ejus condigna, deposcimus. Non quo ipse desideret supplices
nos esse, aut amet substerni tot millium venerationem videre. Utilitas haec nostra est, et
commodi nostri rationem spectans. Nam quia proni ad culpas, et ad libidinis varios ap-
petitus, vitio sumus infirmitatis ingenitae, patitur se semper nostris cogitationibus con-
cipi: ut dum illum oramus, et mereri ejus contendimus munera, accipiamus innocentiae
voluntatem, et ab omni nos labe delictorum omnium amputatione purgemus."—[*In
English thus:* "It is our custom, to prostrate ourselves before him; and we ask of him such
gifts only as are consistent with justice and with honour, and suitable to the character of
the Being whom we adore. Not that he receives pleasure or satisfaction from the humble
veneration of thousands of his creatures. From this we ourselves derive benefit and advantage; for being the slaves of appetite, and prone to err from the weakness of our
nature, when we address ourselves to God in prayer, and study by our actions to merit
his approbation, we gain at least the wish, and the inclination, to be virtuous."]

(a) Elements of Criticism, vol. 1. p. 180. edit. 5.

world in the day of rest, the errors we have been guilty of are recalled to memory: we are afflicted for these errors, and are firmly resolved to be more on our guard in time coming. In short, Sunday is only a day of rest from worldly concerns, in order to be more use-<295>fully employed upon those that are internal. Sunday accordingly is a day of account; and a candid account every seventh day, is the best preparation for the great day of account. A person who diligently follows out this preparatory discipline, will seldom be at a loss to answer for his conduct, called upon by God or man. This consideration leads me necessarily to condemn a practice authorised among Christians with very few exceptions, that of abandoning to diversion and merriment what remains of Sunday after public worship, parties of pleasure, dancing, gaming, any thing that trifles away the time without a serious thought; as if the purpose were to cancel every virtuous impression made at public worship.

Unhappily, this salutary institution can only be preserved in vigour during the days of piety and virtue. Power and opulence are the darling objects of every nation; and yet in every nation possessed of power and opulence virtue subsides, selfishness prevails, and sensuality becomes the ruling passion. Then it is, that the most sacred institutions, first, lose their hold, <296> next, are disregarded, and at last are made a subject for ridicule.[16]

I shall only add upon the general head, that lawgivers ought to avoid with caution the enforcing public worship by rewards and punishments: human laws cannot reach the heart, in which the essence of worship consists: they may indeed bring on a listless habit of worship, by separating the external act from the internal affection, than which nothing is more hurtful to true religion. The utmost that can be safely ventured, is to bring public worship under censorian powers, as a matter of police, for preserving good order, and for preventing bad example.

The religion of Confucius, professed by the *literati* and persons of rank in China and Tonquin, consists in a deep inward veneration for the God or King of heaven, and in the practice of every moral virtue. They have neither temples, nor priests, nor any settled form of external worship: every one adores the supreme Being in the manner he himself thinks best. This

---

16. This and the previous two paragraphs added in 3rd edition.

is indeed the most refined system of religion that ever took place among men; but <297> it is not fitted for the human race: an excellent religion it would be for angels; but is far too refined even for sages and philosophers.

Proceeding to deviations from the genuine worship required by our Maker, and gross deviations there have been, I begin with that sort of worship which is influenced by fear, and which for that reason is universal among savages. The American savages believe, that there are inferior deities without end, most of them prone to mischief; they neglect the supreme Deity because he is good; and direct their worship to soothe the malevolent inferior deities from doing harm. The inhabitants of the Molucca islands, who believe the existence of malevolent beings subordinate to the supreme benevolent Being, confine their worship to the former, in order to avert their wrath; and one branch of their worship is, to set meat before them, hoping that when the belly is full, there will be less inclination to mischief. The worship of the inhabitants of Java is much the same. The negroes of Benin worship the devil, as Dapper expresses it, and sacrifice to him both men <298> and beasts. They acknowledge indeed a supreme Being, who created the universe, and governs it by his providence: but they regard him not: "for," say they, "it is needless, if not impertinent, to invoke a being, who, good and gracious, is incapable of injuring or molesting us." Gratitude, it would appear, is not a ruling principle among savages.[17]

The austerities and penances that are practised in almost all religions, spring from the same root. One way to please invisible malignant powers, is to make ourselves as miserable as possible. Hence the horrid penances of the Faquirs in Hindostan, who outdo in mortification whatever is reported of the ancient Christian anchorites. Some of these Faquirs continue for life in one posture: some never lie down: some have always their arms raised above their head: and some mangle their bodies with knives and scourges. The town of Jagrenate in Hindostan is frequented by pilgrims, some of them from places 300 leagues distant; and they travel, not by walking or riding, but by measuring the road with the <299> length of their bodies; in which mode of loco-motion, some of them consume years before they complete their pilgrimage. A religious sect made its way some centuries ago

17. "Gratitude, it would . . . principle among savages": added in 2nd edition.

into Japan, termed *Bubsdoists,* from *Bubs,* the founder. This sect has prevailed over the ancient sect of the Sintos, chiefly by its austerity and mor-
tifications. The spirit of this sect inspires nothing but excessive fear of the
gods, who are painted prone to vengeance and always offended. These sec-
taries pass most of their time in tormenting themselves, in order to expiate
imaginary faults; and they are treated by their priests with a degree of despotism and cruelty, that is not parallelled but by the inquisitors of Spain.
Their manners are fierce, cruel, and unrelenting, derived from the nature
of their superstition. The notion of invisible malevolent powers, formerly
universal, is not to this hour eradicated, even among Christians; for which
I appeal to the fastings and flagellations among Roman-Catholics, held by
them to be an essential part of religion. People infected with religious horrors, are never seriously convinced that an upright heart and sound <300>
morality make the essence of religion. The doctrine of the Jansenists concerning repentance and mortification, shows evidently, however they may
deceive themselves, that they have an impression of the Deity as a malevolent being. They hold the guilt contracted by Adam's fall to be a heinous
sin, which ought to be expiated by acts of mortification, such as the torturing and macerating the body with painful labour, excessive abstinence,
continual prayer and contemplation. Their penances, whether for original
or voluntary sin, are carried to extravagance; and those who put an end to
their lives by such severities, are termed the sacred victims of repentance,
consumed by the fire of divine love. Such suicides are esteemed peculiarly
meritorious in the eye of Heaven; and it is thought, that their sufferings
cannot fail to appease the anger of the Deity. That celibacy is a state of
purity and perfection, is a prevailing notion in many countries: among the
Pagans, a married man was forbidden to approach the altar, for some days
after knowing his wife; and this ridiculous notion of pollution, contributed
to introduce celi-<301>bacy among the Roman-Catholic priests.* The Emperor Otho, *anno* 1218, became a signal penitent: but instead of atoning
for his sins by repentance and restitution, he laid himself down to be trod-
den under foot by the boys of his kitchen; and frequently submitted to the

* Fasting and celibacy were by Zoroaster condemned with abhorrence, as a criminal
rejection of the best gifts of Providence.

discipline of the whip, inflicted by monks. The Emperor Charles V. toward the end of his days, was sorely depressed in spirit with fear of hell. Monks were his only companions, with whom he spent his time in chanting hymns. As an expiation for his sins, he in private disciplined himself with such severity, that his whip, found after his death, was tinged with his blood. Nor was he satisfied with these acts of mortification: timorous and illiberal solicitude still haunting him, he aimed at something extraordinary, at some new and singular act of piety, to display his zeal, and to merit the favour of Heaven. The act he fixed on, was as wild as any that supersti-<302>tion ever suggested to a distempered brain: it was to celebrate his own obsequies. He ordered his tomb to be erected in the chapel of the monastery: his domestics marched there in funeral procession, holding black tapers: he followed in his shroud: he was laid in his coffin with much solemnity: the service of the dead was chanted; and he himself joined in the prayers offered up for his *requiem,* mingling his tears with those of his attendants. The ceremony closed with sprinkling holy water upon the coffin; and the assistants retiring, the doors of the chapel were shut. Then Charles rose out of the coffin, and stole privately to his apartment.

The history of ancient sacrifices is not so accurate, as in every instance to ascertain upon what principle they were founded, whether upon fear, upon gratitude for favours received, or to solicit future favour. Human sacrifices undoubtedly belong to the present head: for being calculated to deprecate the wrath of a malevolent deity, they could have no other motive but fear; and indeed they are a <303> most direful effect of that passion.* It is needless to lose time in mentioning instances, which are well known to those who are acquainted with ancient history. A number of them are collected in Historical Law-tracts (*a*): and to these I take the liberty of adding, that the Cimbrians, the Germans, the Gauls, particularly the Druids, practised human sacrifices; for which we have the authority of Julius Caesar, Strabo, and other authors. A people on the bank of the Missisippi, named *Tensas,* worship the sun; and, like the Natches their neighbours, have a

---

* The Abbé de Boissy derives human sacrifices from the history of Abraham preparing to sacrifice his son Isaac, which, says he, was imitated by others. A man who is so unlucky at guessing had better be silent. [[Note added in 2nd edition.]]

(*a*) Tract 1.

temple for that luminary, with a sacred fire in it, continually burning. The temple having been set on fire by thunder, was all in flames when some French travellers saw them throw children into the fire, one after another, to appease the incensed deity. The Prophet Micah (*a*), in a passage partly quoted above, inveighs bitterly against <304> such sacrifices: "Wherewith shall I come before the Lord, and bow myself before the high God; shall I come before him with burnt-offerings, with calves of a year old? will the Lord be pleased with thousands of rams, or with ten thousands of rivers of oil? shall I give my first-born for my transgression, the fruit of my body for the sin of my soul? He hath shewed thee, O man, what is good: and what doth the Lord require of thee, but to do justly, to love mercy, and to walk humbly with thy God?"

The ancient Persians acknowledged Oromazes and Arimanes as their great deities, authors of good and ill to men. But I find not that Arimanes, the evil principle, was ever an object of any religious worship. The Gaures, who profess the ancient religion of Persia, address no worship but to one God, all-good and all-powerful.

Next, of worshipping the Deity in the character of a mercenary being. Under that head come sacrifices and oblations, whether prompted by gratitude for favours received, or by self-interest to pro-<305>cure future favours: which, for the reason mentioned, I shall not attempt to distinguish. As the deities of early times were thought to resemble men, it was a natural endeavour in men to conciliate their favour by such offerings as were the most relished by themselves. It is probable, that the first sacrifices of that kind, were of sweet-smelling herbs, which in the fire emitted a flavour that might reach the nostrils of a deity, even at a distance. The burning incense to their gods, was practised in Mexico and Peru; and at present is practised in the peninsula of Corea. An opportunity so favourable for making religious zeal a fund of riches to the priesthood, is seldom neglected. There was no difficulty to persuade ignorant people, that the gods could eat as well as smell: what was offered to a deity for food, being carried into the temple, was understood to be devoured by him.

With respect to the Jewish sacrifices of burnt-offerings, meat-offerings,

(*a*) Chap. 6.

sin-offerings, peace-offerings, heave-offerings, and wave-offerings, these were appointed by God himself, in order to keep that stiff-<306>necked people in daily remembrance of their dependence on him, and to preserve them if possible from idolatry. But that untractable race did not adhere to the purity of the institution: they insensibly degenerated into the notion that their God was a mercenary being; and in that character only, was the worship of sacrifices performed to him. The offerings mentioned were liberally bestowed on him, not singly as a token of their dependence, but chiefly in order to avert his wrath, or to gain his favour.*

The religious notions of the Greeks were equally impure: they could not think of any means for conciliating the favour of their gods, more efficacious than gifts. Homer paints his gods as excessively mercenary. In the fourth book of the Iliad, Jupiter says, "Of these cities, honoured the most by the soul of <307> Jove, is sacred Troy. Never stands the altar empty before me, oblations poured forth in my presence, favour that ascends the skies." Speaking in the fifth book of a warrior, known afterward to be Diomedes, "Some god he is, some power against the Trojans enraged for vows unpaid: destructive is the wrath of the gods." Diomedes prays to Minerva, "With thine arm ward from me the foe: a year-old heifer, O Queen, shall be thine, broad-fronted, unbroken, and wild: her to thee I will offer with prayer, gilding with gold her horns." Precisely of the same kind, are the offerings made by superstitious Roman-Catholics to the Virgin Mary, and to saints. Electra, in the tragedy of that name, supplicates Apollo in the following terms:

> ———— O! hear Electra too,
> Who, with unsparing hand, her choicest gifts
> Hath never fail'd to lay before thy altars;
> Accept the little All that now remains
> For me to give.

* There is no mention in ancient authors of fish being offered to the gods in sacrifice. The reason I take to be, that the most savoury food of man was reckoned the most agreeable to their gods; that savages never thought of fish till land-animals became scarce; and that the matter as well as form of sacrifices were established in practice, long before men had recourse to fish for food.

The people of Hindostan, as mentioned above, atone for their sins by austere pe-<308>nances; but they have no notion of presenting gifts to the Deity, nor of deprecating his wrath by the flesh of animals. On the contrary, they reckon it a sin to slay any living creature; which reduces them to vegetable food. This is going too far; for the Deity could never mean to prohibit animal food, when originally man's chief dependence was upon it. The abstaining however from animal food, shows greater humanity in the religion of Hindostan, than of any other known country. The inhabitants of Madagascar are in a stage of religion, common among many nations, which is, the acknowledging one supreme benevolent deity, and many malevolent inferior deities. Most of their worship is indeed addressed to the latter; but they have so far advanced before several other nations, as to offer sacrifices to the supreme Being, without employing either idols or temples.

Philosophy and sound sense in polished nations, have purified religious worship, by banishing the profession, at least, of oblations and sacrifices. The Being that made the world, governs it by laws that are inflexible, because they <309> are the best; and to imagine that he can be moved by prayers, oblations, or sacrifices, to vary his plan of government, is an impious thought, degrading the Deity to a level with ourselves: "Hear O my people, and I will testify against thee: I am God, even thy God. I will take no bullock out of thy house, nor he goat out of thy fold: for every beast of the forest is mine, and the cattle upon a thousand hills. Will I eat the flesh of bulls, or drink the blood of goats? Offer unto God thanksgiving, and pay thy vows to the Most High. Call upon me in the day of trouble: I will deliver thee, and thou shalt glorify me" (*a*). "Thou desirest not sacrifice, else would I give it; thou delightest not in burnt-offering. The sacrifices of God are a broken spirit: a broken and a contrite heart, O God, thou wilt not despise" (*b*). "For I desired mercy, and not sacrifice; and the knowledge of God more than burnt-offerings" (*c*). In dark ages, there is

(*a*) Psalm 50.
(*b*) Psalm 51.
(*c*) Hosea vi. 6.

great shew of reli-<310>gion, with little heart-worship: in ages of philos-ophy, warm heart-worship, with little shew.* <311>

This is a proper place for the history of idolatry; which, as will anon appear, sprung from religious worship corrupted by men of shallow un-derstanding and gross conceptions, upon whom things invisible make little impression.

Savages, even of the lowest class, have an impression of invisible powers, tho' they cannot form any distinct notion of them. But such impression is too faint for the exercise of devotion. Whether inspired with love to a good being, or impressed with fear of an ill being, savages are not at ease without some sort of visible object to fix their attention. A great stone served that purpose originally; a very low <312> instrument indeed of religious wor-ship; but not altogether whimsical, if it was introduced, which is highly probable, in the following manner. It was an early and a natural custom among savages, to mark with a great stone the place where their worthies were interred; of which we have hints every where in ancient history, par-

---

* Agathias urges a different reason against sacrifices. "Ego nullam naturam esse ex-istimo, cui voluptati sint foedata sanguine altaria, et animantium lanienae. Quod si qua tamen est cui ista sint cordi, non ea mitis et benigna est aliqua, sed fera ac rabida, qualem pavorem poetae fingunt, et Metum, et Bellonam, et Malam Fortunam, et Discordiam, quam indomitam appellant."—[*In English thus:* "I cannot conceive, that there should exist a superior being, who takes delight in the sacrifice of animals, or in altars stained with blood. If such there be, his nature is not benevolent, but barbarous and cruel. Such indeed were the gods whom the poets have created: such were Fear and Terror, the god-dess of War, of Evil Fortune, and of Discord."]—Arnobius batters down bloody sac-rifices with a very curious argument. "Ecce si bos aliquis, aut quodlibet ex his animal, quod ad placandas caeditur mitigandasque numinum furias, vocem hominis sumat, elo-quaturque his verbis: Ergone, O Jupiter, aut quis alius deus es, humanum est istud et rectum, aut aequitatis alicujus in aestimatione ponendum, ut cum alius peccaverit, ego occidar, et de meo sanguine fieri tibi patiaris satis, qui nunquam te laeserim, nunquam sciens aut nesciens, tuum numen majestatemque violarim, animal, ut scis, mutum, na-turae meae simplicitatem sequens, nec multiformium morum varietatibus lubricum?"— [*In English thus:* "What if the ox, while he is led out to slaughter to appease the fancied wrath of an offended deity, should assume the human voice, and in these words astonish his conductors: Are these, O merciful God, are these the dictates of humanity, or of justice, that for the crime of another I should forfeit my life. I have never by my will offended thee, and, dumb as I am, and uninformed by reason, my actions, according to the simplicity of my nature, cannot have given thee displeasure, who hast made me as I am."]—If this argument were solid, it would be equally conclusive against animal food.

ticularly in the poems of Ossian. "Place me," says Calmar mortally wounded, "at the side of a stone of remembrance, that future times may hear my fame, and the mother of Calmar rejoice over the stone of my renown." Superstition in later times having deified these worthies, their votaries, rejoicing as formerly over the stones dedicated to them, held these stones to be essential in every act of religious worship performed to their new deities.* Tradition points out many <313> stones in different parts of the world, that were used in religious worship. The sun was worshipped at Emesa in Syria by the name of *Elagabalus,* and under the form of a black conical stone, which, as universally believed, had fallen from heaven on that sacred place.[18] A large stone worshipped by the Pessenuntians, a people of Phrygia, under the name of *Idaea mater,* was, upon a solemn embassy to that people, brought to Rome: it being contained in the Sybilline books, that unless the Romans got possession of that goddess, they never would prevail over Hannibal. And Pausanias mentions many stones in Greece, dedicated to different divinities; particu-<314>larly thirty square stones in Achaia, on which were engraved the names of as many gods. In another place, he mentions a very ancient statue of Venus in the island Delos, which, instead of feet, had only a square stone. This may appear a puzzling circumstance in the history of Greece, considering that all the Grecian gods were originally mortals, whom it was easy to represent by statues: but in that early period, the Greeks knew no more of statuary than the most barbarous nations. It is perhaps not easy to gather the meaning of savages, with respect to such stones: the most natural conjecture is, that a great stone,

---

* Frequent mention is made of such stones in the poems of Ossian. "But remember, my son, to place this sword, this bow, and this horn, within that dark and narrow house marked with one gray stone." p. 55. "Whose fame is in that dark-green tomb? Four stones with their heads of moss stand there, and mark the narrow house of death." p. 67. "Let thy bards mourn those who fell. Let Erin give the sons of Lochlin to earth, and raise the mossy stones of their fame; that the children of the north hereafter may behold the place where their fathers fought." p. 78. "Earth here incloses the loveliest pair on the hill: grass grows between the stones of the tomb." p. 208. In the same poems we find stones made instruments of worship. The spirit of Loda is introduced threatening Fingal: " 'Fly to thy land,' replied the form: 'receive the wind and fly. The blasts are in the hollow of my hand: the course of the storm is mine. The King of Sora is my son: he bends at the stone of my power.' " p. 200.

18. "The sun was . . . that sacred place": added in 2nd edition.

dedicated to the worship of a certain deity, was considered as belonging to him. This notion of property had a double effect: the worshippers, by connection of ideas, were led from the stone to the deity: and the stone tended to fix their wandering thoughts. It was probably imagined, over and above, that some latent virtue communicated to the stone, made it holy or sacred. Even among enlightened people, a sort of virtue or sanctity is conceived to reside in the place of worship: why not also in a <315> stone dedicated to a deity? The ancient Ethiopians, in their worship, introduced the figure of a serpent as a symbol of the deity: two sticks laid cross represented Castor and Pollux, Roman divinities: a javelin represented their god Mars; and in Tartary formerly, the god of war was worshipped under the symbol of an old rusty sabre. The ancient Persians used consecrated fire, as an emblem of the great God. Tho' the negroes of Congo and Angola have images without number, they are not however idolaters in any proper sense: their belief is, that these images are only organs by which the deities signify their will to their votaries.

If the use that was made of stones and of other symbols in religious worship, be fairly represented, it may appear strange, that the ingenious Greeks sunk down into idolatry, at the very time they were making a rapid progress in the fine arts. Their improvements in statuary, one of these arts, was the cause. They began with attempting to carve heads of men and women, representing their deified heroes; which were placed upon the stones dedicated to these heroes. In the progress <316> of the art, statues were executed complete in every member; and at last, statues of the gods were made, expressing such dignity and majesty, as insensibly to draw from beholders a degree of devotion to the statues themselves. Hear Quintilian upon that subject. "At quae Polycleto defuerunt, Phidiae atque Alcameni dantur. Phidias tamen diis quam hominibus efficiendis melior artifex traditur: in ebore vero, longe citra aemulum, vel si nihil nisi Minervam Athenis aut Olympium in Elide Jovem fecisset, cujus pulchritudo adjecisse aliquid etiam receptae religioni videtur; adeo majestas operis deum aequavit."*

---

* "The deficiencies of Polycletus were made up in Phidias and Alcamenes. Phidias is reckoned to have had more skill in forming the statues of gods than of men. In works of ivory he was unrivalled, altho' there had been no other proofs of his excellence than

Here is laid a foundation for idolatry: let us trace its progress. Such statues as are represented by Quintilian, serve greatly to enflame <317> devotion; and during a warm fit of the religious passion, the representation is lost, and the statue becomes a deity; precisely as where King Lear is represented by Garrick: the actor vanishes; and, behold! the King himself. This is not singular. Anger occasions a metamorphosis still more extraordinary: if I happen to strike my gouty toe against a stone, the violence of the pain converts the stone for a moment into a voluntary agent; and I wreak my resentment on it, as if it really were so. It is true, the image is only conceived to be a deity during the fervour of devotion; and when that subsides, the image falls back to its original representative state. But frequent instances of that kind, have at last the effect among illiterate people, to convert the image into a sort of permanent deity: what such people see, makes a deep impression; what they see not, very little. There is another thing that concurs with eye-sight, to promote this delusion: devotion, being a vigorous principle in the human breast, will exert itself upon the meanest object, when none more noble is in view.

The ancient Persians held the conse-<318>crated fire to be an emblem only of the great God: but such veneration was paid to that emblem, and with so great ceremony was it treated, that the vulgar came at last to worship it as a sort of deity. The priests of the Gaures watch the consecrated fire day and night: they keep it alive with the purest wood, without bark: they touch it not with sword nor knife: they blow it not with bellows, nor with the mouth: even the priest is prohibited to approach it, till his mouth be covered with fine linen, lest it be polluted with his breath: if it happen to go out, it must be rekindled by striking fire from flint, or by a burning glass.

The progress of idolatry will more clearly appear, from attending to the religion of the Greeks and Romans. The Greeks, as mentioned above, made use of stones in divine worship, long before idolatry was introduced: and we learn from Varro, that for a hundred and seventy years after Numa, the Romans had no statues nor images in their temples. After statues of the

---

the statue of Minerva at Athens, and the Jupiter Olympius in Elis. Its beauty seems to have added to the received religion; the majestic statue resembling so much the god himself."

gods became fashionable, they acquired by degrees more and more respect. The Greek and Roman writers talk of di-<319>vine virtue being communicated to statues; and some Roman writers talk familiarly, of the *numen* of a deity residing in his statue. Arnobius, in his book against the Gentiles, introduces a Gentile delivering the following opinion. "We do not believe, that the metal which composes a statue, whether gold, or silver, or brass, is a god. But we believe, that a solemn dedication brings down the god to inhabit his image; and it is the god only that we worship in that image." This explains the Roman ceremony, of inviting to their side the tutelar deities of towns besieged by them, termed *evocatio tutelarium deorum.* The Romans, cruel as they were, overflowed with superstition; and as they were averse from combating the tutelar deities even of their enemies, they endeavoured to gain these deities by large promises, and assurance of honourable treatment. As they could not hope that a statue would change its place, their notion must have been, that by this ceremony, the tutelar deity might be prevailed upon to withdraw its *numen,* [19] and leave the statue a dead lump of matter. When Stilpo was banished by the Areopagus of Athens, <320> for affirming, that the statue in the temple of Minerva, was not the goddess, but a piece of matter carved by Phidias; he surely was not condemned for saying, that the statue was made by Phidias, a fact universally known: his heresy consisted in denying that the *numen* of Minerva resided in the statue. Augustus, having twice lost his fleet by storm, forbade Neptune to be carried in procession along with the other gods; imagining he had avenged himself of Neptune, by neglecting the favourite statue in which his *numen* resided.

When saints in the Christian church were deified, even their images became objects of worship; from a fond imagination, that such worship draws down into the images the souls of the saints they represent; which is the same belief that Arnobius, in the passage above mentioned, ascribes to the Gentiles; and is not widely different from the belief of the Pagan Tartars and Ostiacs, by and by to be mentioned. In the eleventh century, there was a violent dispute about images in the Greek church; many asserting, that in the images of our Saviour and of the saints, there resides an inherent

19. The *numen* of a deity is his or her power, or spirit.

sanctity which is <321> a proper object of worship; and that Christians
ought not to confine their worship to the persons represented, but ought
also to extend it to their images.

As ignorant and savage nations can form no conception of Deity but of
a being like a man, only superior in power and greatness; many images have
been made of the Deity conformable to that conception. It is easy to make
some resemblance of a man; but how is power and greatness to be represented? To perform this with success, would require a Hogarth. Savages go
more bluntly to work: they endeavour to represent a man with many heads,
and with a still greater number of hands. The northern Tartars seem to
have no deities but certain statues or images coarsely formed out of wood,
and bearing some distant resemblance to the human figure. To palliate so
gross an absurdity as that a god can be fabricated by the hands of man, they
imagine this image to be endued with a soul: to say whence that soul came
would puzzle the wisest of them. That soul is conceived to be too elevated
for dwelling constantly in a piece of matter: they be-<322>lieve that it re-
sides in some more honourable place; and that it only visits the image or
idol, when it is called down by prayers and supplications. They sacrifice to
this idol, by rubbing its mouth with the fat of fish, and by offering it the
warm blood of some beast killed in hunting. The last step of the ceremony
is, to honour the soul of the idol with a joyful shout, as a sort of convoy
to it when it returns home. The Ostiacs have a wooden idol, termed *The
Old Man of Oby,* who is guardian of their fishery: it hath eyes of glass, and
a head with short horns. When the ice dissolves, they crowd to this idol,
requesting that he will be propitious to their fishery. If unsuccessful, he is
loaded with reproaches: if successful, he is entitled to a share of the capture.
They make a feast for him, rubbing his snout with choice fat; and when
the entertainment is over, they accompany the soul of the idol a little way,
beating the air with their cudgels. The Ostiacs have another idol, that is
fed with milk so abundantly, as to come out on both sides of the spoon,
and to fall down upon the vesture; which however is never washed, so little
is clean-<323>ness thought essential to religion by that people. It is indeed
strangely absurd, to think, that invisible souls require food like human creatures; and yet the same absurdity prevailed in Greece.

The ancient Germans, a sober and sensible people, had no notion of representing their gods by statues, or of building temples to them. They worshipped in consecrated groves (*a*). The Egyptians, from a just conception that an invisible being can have no resemblance to one that is visible, employ'd hieroglyphical figures for denoting metaphorically the attributes of their gods; and they employ'd, not only the figures of birds and beasts, but of vegetables; leeks, for example, and onions. This metaphorical adjunct to religion, innocent in itself, sunk the Egyptians into the most groveling idolatry. As hieroglyphical figures, composed frequently of heterogeneous parts, resemble not any being human or divine; the vulgar, losing sight of the emblematic signification understood by poets and philosophers only, took up with the plain figures as real <324> divinities. How otherwise can it be accounted for, that the ox, the ape, the onion, were in Egypt worshipped as deities? Plutarch, it is true, in his chapter upon Isis and Osiris observes, that the Egyptians worshipped the bull, the cat, and other animals; not as divinities, but as representatives of them, like an image seen in a glass; or, as he expresses it in another part of the same chapter, "just as we see the resemblance of the sun in a drop of water." But that this must be understood of Philosophers only, will be probable from what is reported by Diodorus Siculus, that in a great famine, the Egyptians ventured not to touch the sacred animals, tho' they were forc'd to devour one another.[20] A snake of a particular kind, about a yard long, and about the thickness of a man's arm, is worshipped by the Whidans in Guinea. It has a large round head, piercing eyes, a short pointed tongue, and a smooth skin, beautifully speckled. It has a strong antipathy to all the venomous kind; in other respects, innocent and tame. To kill these snakes being a capital crime, they travel about unmolested, even into bedchambers. They occa-<325>sioned, ann. 1697, a ridiculous persecution. A hog, teased by one of them, tore it with his tusks till it died. The priests carried their complaint to the king;

(*a*) Tacitus, De moribus Germanorum, cap. 9.

20. "But that this . . . devour one another": added in 2nd edition. In 1st edition: "However this be, the Egyptian worship is an illustrious instance of the influence of devotion: how powerful must it be in its purity, when even in a wrong direction, it can force its way against every obstacle of common sense! And such respect was paid to these animals, if we can trust Diodorus Siculus, that in a great famine, the Egyptians ventured not to touch the sacred animals, tho' they were forced to devour one another" [2:419].

and no one presuming to appear as counsel for the hogs, orders were issued for slaughtering the whole race. At once were brandished a thousand cutlasses; and the race would have been extirpated, had not the king interposed, representing to the priests, that they ought to rest satisfied with the innocent blood they had spilt. Rancour and cruelty never rage more violently, than under the mask of religion.

It is amazing how prone even the most polished nations were to idolatry. A statue of Hercules was worshipped at Tyre, not as a representative of the Deity but as the Deity himself. And accordingly, when Tyre was besieged by Alexander, the Deity was fast bound in chains, to prevent him from deserting to the enemy. The city of Ambracia being taken by the Romans, and every statue of their gods being carried to Rome; the Ambracians complained bitterly, that not a single divinity was left them to worship. How much more rational are the Hindostan <326> bramins, who teach their disciples, that idols are emblems only of the Deity, intended merely to fix the attention of the populace!

The first statues in Greece and Tuscany were made with wings, to signify the swift motion of the gods. These statues were so clumsy, as scarce to resemble human creatures, not to talk of a divinity. But the admirable statues executed in later times, were imagined to resemble most accurately the deities represented by them: whence the vulgar notion, that gods have wings, and that angels have wings.

I proceed to what in the history of idolatry may be reckoned the second part. Statues, we have seen, were at first used as representatives only of the Deity; but came afterward to be metamorphosed into Deities. The absurdity did not stop there. People, not satisfied with the visible deities erected in temples for public worship, became fond to have private deities of their own, whom they worshipped as their tutelar deities; and this practice spread so wide, that among many nations every family had household-gods cut in wood or stone. Every family in Kam-<327>skatka has a tutelar deity in the shape of a pillar, with the head of a man, which is supposed to guard the house against malevolent spirits. They give it food daily, and anoint the head with the fat of fish. The Prophet Isaiah (*a*) puts this species

(*a*) Chap. 44.

of deification in a most ridiculous light: "He burneth part thereof in the fire: with part thereof he roasteth flesh: of the residue he maketh a god, even his graven image: he falleth down, worshipping, and praying to it, and saith, Deliver me, for thou art my god." Multiplication could not fail to sink household-gods into a degree of contempt: some slight hope of good from them, might produce some cold ceremonial worship; but there could be no real devotion at heart. The Chinese manner of treating their household-gods, will vouch for me. When a Chinese does not obtain what he prays for, "Thou spiritual dog," he will say, "I lodge thee well, thou art beautifully gilded, treated with perfumes and burnt-offerings; and yet thou withholdest from me the necessaries of life." Sometimes they fasten a cord to the idol, <328> and drag it through the dirt. The inhabitants of Ceylon treat their idols in the same manner. Thor, Woden, and Friga, were the great deities of the Scandinavians. They had at the same time inferior deities, who were supposed to have been men translated into heaven for their good works. These they treated with very little ceremony, refusing to worship them if they were not propitious; and even punishing them with banishment; but restoring them after a time, in hopes of amendment. Domestic idols are treated by the Ostiacs with no greater reverence than by the people mentioned. But they have public idols, some particularly of brass, which are highly reverenced: the solidity of the metal is in their imagination connected with immortality; and great regard is paid to these idols, for the knowledge and experience they must have acquired in an endless course of time.

When by philosophy and improvement of the rational faculty, the Pagan religion in Rome was sinking into contempt, little regard was had to tutelar deities, to auguries, or to prophecies. Ptolemy King of Egypt, being thrust out of his kingdom <329> by a powerful faction, applied to the senate of Rome to be restored. Lentulus proconsul of Syria was ambitious to be employ'd; but he had enemies who made violent opposition. They brought religion into the quarrel, alledging a Sybilline oracle, prophesying that Ptolemy should be restored but not by an army. Cicero, in a letter still extant, gave Lentulus the following advice, that with his Syrian army he should invade Egypt, beat down all opposition, and when the country was quieted, that Ptolemy should be at hand to take possession. And this the great Cicero thought might be piously done without contradicting the oracle.[21]

Saints, or tutelar deities, are sometimes not better treated among Roman Catholics, than among Pagans. "When we were in Portugal," says Captain Brydone, "the people of Castelbranco were so enraged at St. Antonio, for suffering the Spaniards to plunder their town, contrary, as they affirmed, to his express agreement with them, that they broke many of his statues to pieces; and one that had been more revered than the rest, they took the head off, <330> and in its stead placed one of St. Francis. The great St. Januarius himself was in imminent danger, during the last famine at Naples. They loaded him with abuse and invective; and declared point-blank, that if he did not procure them corn by such a time, he should be no longer their saint." The tutelar saint of Cattania, at the foot of Mount Etna, is St. Agatha. A torrent of lava burst over the walls, and laid waste great part of that beautiful city. Where was St. Agatha at that time? The people say, that they had given her just provocation; but that she has long ago been reconciled to them, and has promised never to suffer the lava to hurt them again. At the foot of Mount Etna, a statue of a saint is placed as a memorial, for having prevented the lava from running up the mountain of Taurominum, and destroying that town; the saint having conducted the lava down a low valley to the sea.

Let a traveller once deviate from the right road, and there is no end of wandering. Porphyrius reports, that in Anubis, an Egyptian city, a real man was worshipped as a god; which is also as-<331>serted by Minutius Foelix, in his apology for the Christians. A thousand writers have said, that the Tartars believe their high-priest, termed *Dalai Lama*, to be immortal. But that is a mistake: his death is published through the whole country; and couriers intimate it even to the Emperor of China: his effigy is taken down from the portal of the great church, and that of his successor is put in its stead. The system of the metempsychosis, adopted in that country, has occasion'd the mistake. They believe, that the holy spirit, which animates a Dalai Lama, passes upon his death into the body of his successor. The spirit therefore is believed to be immortal, not the body. The Dalai Lama,

21. Paragraph added in 2nd edition.

however, is the object of profound veneration. The Tartar Princes are daily sending presents to him, and consulting him as an oracle: they even undertake a pilgrimage in order to worship him in person. In a retired part of the temple, he is shown covered with precious stones, and sitting cross-legged. They prostrate themselves before him at a distance, for they are not permitted to kiss his toe. The priests make traffic even of his excre-<332>ments, which are greedily purchased at a high price, and are kept in a golden box hanging from the neck, as a charm against every misfortune. Like the cross of Jesus, or the Virgin's milk, we may believe, there never will be wanting plenty of that precious stuff to answer all demands: the priests out of charity will furnish a quota, rather than suffer votaries to depart with their money for want of goods to purchase. The person of the Japan Pope, or Ecclesiastical Emperor, is held so sacred, as to make the cutting his beard, or his nails a deadly sin. But absurd laws are never steadily executed. The beard and the nails are cut in the nighttime, when the Pope is supposed to be asleep; and what is taken away by that operation, is understood to be stolen from him, which is no impeachment upon his Holiness.

That the Jews were idolaters when they sojourned in the land of Goshen, were it not presumable from their commerce with the Egyptians, would however be evident from the history of Moses. Notwithstanding their miraculous deliverance from the Egyptian king, notwithstanding the daily <333> miracles wrought among them in the wilderness; so addicted were they to a visible deity, that, during even the momentary absence of Moses conversing with God on the mount, they fabricated a golden calf, and worshipped it as their god. "And the Lord said unto Moses, Go, get thee down: for thy people which thou broughtest out of the land of Egypt, have corrupted themselves: they have turned aside quickly out of the way which I commanded them: they have made them a molten calf, have worshipped it, have sacrificed thereunto, and said, 'These be thy gods, O Israel, which have brought thee up out of the land of Egypt'" (a). The history of the Jews, shows how difficult it is to reclaim from idolatry a brutish nation, addicted to superstition, and fettered by inveterate habit. What profusion

(a) Exod. xxxii. 7.

of blood, to bring that obstinate and perverse people to the true religion! all in vain. The book of Judges, in particular, is full of reiterated relapses, from their own invisible God, to the visible gods of other na-<334>tions. And in all probability, their anxious desire for a visible king, related in the first book of Samuel, arose from their being deprived of a visible god. There was a necessity for prohibiting images (*a*); which would have soon been converted into deities visible: and it was extremely prudent, to supply the want of a visible god, with endless shews and ceremonies; which accordingly became the capital branch of the Jewish worship.

It appears to me from the whole history of the Jews, that a gross people are not susceptible but of a gross religion; and without an enlightened understanding, that it is vain to think of eradicating superstition and idolatry. And after all the covenants made with the Jews, after all the chastisements and all the miracles lavish'd on them, that they were not however reclaimed from the most groveling idolatry, is evident from the two golden calves fabricated by Jeroboam, saying, "Behold thy gods, O Israel, which brought thee up out of the land of E-<335>gypt" (*b*). The people also of Judah fell back to idol-worship under Rehoboam, son of Solomon (*c*). Jehu, king of the ten tribes, did not tolerate the worship of other gods (*d*); but he continued to worship the two golden calves fabricated by Jeroboam (*e*). Down to the days of King Hezekiah, the Jews worshipped the brazen serpent erected by Moses in the wilderness. The Jews seem indeed to have been a very perverse people: the many promises and threatenings announced by their prophets, and the many miracles wrought among them, had no permanent effect to restrain them from idolatry; and yet, during their captivity in Babylon, several of them submitted to be burnt alive, rather than to join in idol-worship (*f*). Captivity cured them radically of idolatry; and from that period to this day, they have not been guilty of a single relapse. Xiphilin, in his abridgement of Dion Cassius, relating <336> their war with

(*a*) Deuteronomy, xvi. 22.
(*b*) 1 Kings, xii. 28.
(*c*) 1 Kings, xiv. 23.
(*d*) 2 Kings, x. 25.
(*e*) 2 Kings, x. 29.
(*f*) Daniel, chap. 3.

Pompey many centuries after the Babylonish captivity, gives the following account of them. "Their customs are quite different from those of other nations. Beside a peculiar manner of living, they acknowledge none of the common deities: they acknowledge but one, whom they worship with great veneration. There never was an image in Jerusalem; because they believe their God to be invisible and ineffable. They have built him a temple of great size and beauty, remarkable in the following particular, that it is open above, without any roof."

There lies no solid objection against images among an enlightened people, when used merely to rouse devotion; but as images tend to pervert the vulgar, they ought not to be admitted into churches. Pictures are less liable to be misapprehended; and the Ethiopians accordingly indulge pictures in their churches, tho' they prohibit statues. The general council of Frankfort permitted the use of images in churches; but strictly prohibited any worship to be addressed to them. So prone <337> however to idolatry are the low and illiterate, that the prohibition lost ground both in France and in Germany; and idol-worship became again general.

It is probable, that the sun and moon were early held to be deities, and that they were the first visible objects of worship. Of all the different kinds of idolatry, it is indeed the most excusable. Upon the sun depends health, vigour, and chearfulness: during his retirement, all is dark and dismal; when he performs his majestic round, to bless his subjects and to bestow fecundity, can a mere savage withhold gratitude and veneration! Hear an old Pagan bard upon that subject. "O thou who rollest above, round as the shield of my fathers! Whence are thy beams, O sun, thy everlasting light? Thou comest forth in thy awful beauty, and the stars hide their face: thou movest alone, for who can be a companion of thy course! The oaks of the mountain fall: the mountains decay with years: the ocean shrinks and grows again: the moon herself is lost in heaven: but thou art for ever the same, rejoicing in the brightness of thy <338> course. When tempests darken the world, when thunder rolls, and lightning flies, thou lookest in thy beauty from the clouds, and laughest at the storm" (a). Worship to the sun as a real deity, was in former times universal; and prevails in many countries

(a) Ossian.

even at present. The American savages worship the sun as sovereign of the universe, known by the name of *Ariskoui* among the Hurons, and of *Agriskoué* among the Iroquois. They offer him tobacco, which they term *smoking the sun:* the chief man in the assembly lights the calumet, and offers it thrice to the rising sun; imploring his protection, and recommending the tribe to his care. The chief proceeds to smoke; and every one smokes in his turn. This ceremony is performed on important occasions only: less matters are reserved for their Manitou. The Missisippi people offer to the sun the first of what they take in hunting; which their commander artfully converts to his own use. The Apalachites, bordering on Florida, worship the sun; but sacrifice nothing to <339> him that has life: they hold him to be the parent of life, and think that he can take no pleasure in the destruction of any living creature: their devotion is exerted in perfumes and songs. The Mexicans, while a free people, presented to the sun a share of their meat and drink. The inhabitants of Darien, believe in the sun as their god, and in the moon as his wife, paying them equal adoration. The people of Borneo worship the sun and moon as real divinities. The Samoides worship both, bowing to them morning and evening in the Persian manner.

But if the sun and moon were the first objects of idolatry, knowledge and reflection reformed many from the error of holding these luminaries to be deities. "That original intelligence," say the Magians, "who is the first principle of all things, discovers himself to the mind and understanding only: but he hath placed the sun as his image in the visible universe; and the beams of that bright luminary, are but a faint copy of the glory that shines in the higher heavens." The Persians, as Herodotus reports, had neither temples, nor altars, <340> nor images: for, says that author, they do not think, like the Greeks, that there is any resemblance between gods and men. The Gaures, who to this day profess the ancient religion of Persia, celebrate divine worship before the sacred fire, and turn with peculiar veneration toward the rising sun, as the representative of God; but they adore neither the sun, nor the sacred fire. They are professed enemies to every image of the Deity cut with hands: and hence the havock made by the ancient Persians, upon the statues and temples of the Grecian gods. Such sublimity of thought was above the reach of other uninspired nations, excepting only the Hindows and Chinese.

I close the history of idolatry with a brief recapitulation of the outlines. Admitting the sun and moon to have been the first objects of idolatry, yet as Polytheism was once universal, they make only two of the many gods that were every where worshipped. We have seen, that the sacred fire was employ'd in the worship of the sun, and that images were employ'd in the worship of other deities. Images were originally used for the sole purpose of animating devotion: such was their use in <341> Persia and Hindostan; and such was their use in every country among philosophers. The Emperor Julian, in an epistle to Theodore concerning the images of the gods, says, "We believe not that these images are gods: we only use them in worshipping the gods." In the progress toward idolatry, the next step is, to imagine, that a deity loves his image, that he makes it his residence, or at least communicates some virtue to it. The last step is, to fancy the image itself to be a deity; which gained ground imperceptibly as statuary advanced toward perfection. It would be incredible that men of sense should ever suffer themselves to be impressed with so wild a delusion, were it not the overbearing influence of religious superstition. *Credo quia impossible est,* is applicable to idolatry as well as to transubstantiation. The worshipping of the sun and moon as deities, is idolatry in the strictest sense. With respect to images, the first step of the progress is not idolatry: the next is mixed idolatry: and the last is rank idolatry.

So much upon idolatry. I proceed to what approaches the nearest to it, which is worship addressed to deified mortals. The <342> ancient gods were exalted so little above men, that it was no hard task for the imagination to place in heaven, men who had made a figure on earth. The Grecian heaven was entirely peopled with such men, as well as that of many other nations. Men are deified every day by the Romish church, under the denomination of saints: persons are frequently selected for that honour who scarce deserved a place on earth, and some who never had a place there. The Roman Catholics copy the Pagans, in worshipping these saints in quality of tutelar deities. One branch of the office bestow'd on them, is to explain the wants of their votaries to the King of heaven, and to supplicate for them. The mediatorial office prevails with respect to earthly potentates, as well as heavenly: being struck with awe and timidity in approaching those exalted above us, we naturally take hold of some intermediate person to solicit with us.

In approaching the Almighty, the mind, sinking down into humility and profound veneration, stops short, relying upon some friend in heaven to intercede in its behalf. Temples among the Cochin-Chinese are constructed with a deep and dark niche, <343> which is their *sanctum sanctorum*. They hold, that no representation, whether by painting or sculpture, can be made of God, who is invisible. The niche denotes his incomprehensibility; and the good men placed by them in heaven, are believed to be their intercessors at the throne of grace. The prayers of the Chingulese are seldom directed to the supreme being, but to his vicegerents. Intercessors, at the same time, contribute to the ease of their votaries: a Roman Catholic need not assume a very high tone, in addressing a tutelar saint chosen by himself.

False notions of Providence have prompted groveling mortals to put confidence in mediators and intercessors of a still lower class, namely, living mortals, who by idle austerities have acquired a reputation for holiness. Take the following instance, the strongest of the kind that can be figured. Louis XI. of France, sensible of the approach of death, sent for a hermit of Calabria, named *Francisco Martarillo;* and throwing himself at the hermit's feet in a flood of tears, entreated him to intercede with God, that his life might be prolonged; as if the voice of a Calabrian friar, <344> says Voltaire, could alter the course of Providence, by preserving a weak and perverse soul in a worn-out body.

Having discussed the persons that are the objects of worship, the next step in order is, to take under view the forms and ceremonies employ'd in religious worship. Forms and ceremonies illustrate a prince in his own court: they are necessary in a court of law for expediting business; and they promote seriousness and solemnity in religious worship. At the same time, in every one of these a just medium ought to be preserved between too many and too few. With respect to religious worship in particular, superfluity of ceremonies quenches devotion, by occupying the mind too much upon externals. The Roman Catholic worship is crowded with ceremonies: it resembles the Italian opera, which is all sound, and no sentiment. The presbyterian form of worship is too naked: it is proper for philosophers more than for the populace. This is fundamentally the cause of the numerous secessions from the church of Scotland that have made a figure of late: people dislike the established forms, <345> when they find less animation in public worship than is desired; and without being sensible of the real cause, they chuse pastors for themselves, who supply the want of ceremonies by loud speaking, with much external fervor and devotion.* <346>

The frequent ablutions or washings among the Mahometans and others, as acts of devotion, show the influence that <347> the slightest resemblances have on the ignorant. Because purification, in several languages, is a term applicable to the mind as well as to the body, shallow thinkers, misled

---

* External show figures greatly in dark times, when nothing makes an impression but what is visible. A German traveller (Hentzner) talking of Queen Elisabeth, thus describes the solemnity of her dinner. "While she was at prayers, we saw her table set out in the following solemn manner. A gentleman entered the room bearing a rod, and along with him another who had a table-cloth, which, after they had both kneeled three times with the utmost veneration, he spread upon the table, and after kneeling again, they both retired. Then came two others, one with the rod again, the other with a salt-cellar, a plate and bread; when they had kneeled, as the others had done, and placed what was brought upon the table, they too retired with the same ceremonies performed by the first. At last came an unmarried lady, (we were told she was a Countess), and along with her a married one, bearing a tasting knife; the former was dressed in white silk; who when she had prostrated herself three times, in the most graceful manner, approached the table, and rubbed the plates with bread and salt, with as much awe as if the Queen had been present: when they had waited there a little while, the yeomen of the guard entered, bareheaded, cloathed in scarlet, with a golden rose upon their backs, bringing in at each turn a course of twenty-four dishes, served in plate most of it gilt; these dishes were received by a gentleman in the same order they were brought, and placed upon the table, while the lady-taster gave to each of the guard a mouthful to eat, of the particular dish he had brought, for fear of any poison. During the time that this guard, which consists of the tallest and stoutest men that can be found in all England, were bringing dinner, twelve trumpets and two kettle-drums made the hall ring for half an hour together. At the end of this ceremonial, a number of unmarried ladies appeared, who, with particular solemnity, lifted the meat off the table, and conveyed it into the Queen's inner and more private chamber, where, after she had chosen for herself, the rest goes to the ladies of the court." Forms were greatly regarded among the old Romans, dresses appropriated to different ranks; lictors, axes, bundles of rods, and other ensigns of power; military merit rewarded with triumphs, ovations, crowns of gold, of leaves, &c. &c. Such appearances strike the multitude with respect and awe: they are indeed despised by men of plain sense; but they regain their credit with philosophers. Excessive courage, the exertion of which is visible, was the heroism of the last age: "I shall never esteem a king," said the great Gustavus Adolphus, "who in battle does not expose himself like a private man." By acuteness of judgement and refinement of taste, we cling to the substance and disregard forms and ceremonies. External show, however, continues to prevail in many instances. A young man is apt to be captivated with beauty or dress: a young woman, with equipage or a title. And hence, many an ill-sorted match. [[Note added in 2nd edition.]]

by the double meaning, imagine that the mind, like the body, is purified by water.

The sect of Ali use the Alcoran translated into the Persian language, which is their native tongue. The sect of Omar esteem this to be a gross impiety; being persuaded, that the Alcoran was written in Arabic, by the Angel Gabriel, at the command of God himself. The Roman Catholics are not then the only people who profess to speak nonsense to God Almighty; or, which is the same, who profess to pray in an unknown tongue.

At meals, the ancients poured out some <348> wine as a libation to the gods: Christians pronounce a short prayer, termed a *grace*.

The gross notion of Deity entertained by the ancients, is exemplified in their worshipping and sacrificing on high places; in order, as they thought, to be more within sight. Jupiter in Homer praises Hector for sacrificing to him frequently upon the top of Ida; and Strabo observes, that the Persians, who used neither images nor altars, sacrificed to the gods in high places. Balak carried Balaam the prophet to the top of Pisgah and other mountains, to sacrifice there, and to curse Israel. The votaries of Baal always worshipped in high places. Even the sage Tacitus was infected with that absurdity. Speaking of certain high mountains where the gods were worshipped, he expresses himself thus: *Maxime coelo appropinquare, precesque mortalium a Deo nusquam propius audiri.**

Ceremonies that tend to unhinge morality, belong more properly to the following section, treating of the connection between religion and morality. <349>

It is now full time to take under consideration an objection to the sense of Deity hinted above, arguing from the gross conceptions of deity among many nations, that this sense cannot be innate. The objection is not indeed directly stated in the following passage, borrowed from a justly-celebrated author; but as it perhaps may be implied, the passage shall be fairly transcribed. "The universal propensity to believe invisible intelligent power, being a general attendant on human nature, if not an original instinct, may be considered as a kind of stamp which the Deity has set upon his work;

---

* "As approaching nearer to heaven, the prayers of mortals are there more distinctly heard."

and nothing surely can more dignify mankind, than to be the only earthly being who bears the stamp or image of the universal Creator. But consult this image as it commonly is in popular religions: How is the Deity disfigured! what caprice, absurdity, and immorality, are attributed to him (*a*)!" A satisfactory answer to the objection implied in this passage, will occur, upon recollecting the progress of men and nations from infancy to maturity. Our external <350> senses, necessary for self-preservation, soon arrive at perfection: the more refined senses of propriety, of right and wrong, of Deity, of being accountable creatures, and many others of the same kind, are of slower growth: the sense of right and wrong in particular and the sense of Deity, seldom reach perfection but by good education and much study. If such be the case among enlightened nations, what is to be expected from savages who are in the lowest stage of understanding? To a savage of New Holland, whose sense of deity is extremely obscure, one may talk without end of a being who created the world, and who governs it by wise laws; but in vain, for the savage will be never the wiser. The same savage hath also a glimmering of the moral sense, as all men have; and yet in vain will you discourse to him of approbation and disapprobation, of merit and demerit: of these terms he has no clear conception. Hence the endless aberrations of rude and barbarous nations, from pure religion as well as from pure morality. Of the latter, there are many instances collected in the preceding tract; and of the former, still more in the <351> present tract. The sense of deity in dark times has indeed been strangely distorted, by certain biasses and passions that enslave the rude and illiterate: but these yield gradually to the rational faculty as it ripens, and at last leave religion free to sound philosophy. Then it is, that men, listening to the innate sense of deity purified from every bias, acquire a clear conviction of one supreme Deity who made and governs the world.

The foregoing objection then weighs not against the sense of deity more than against the moral sense. If it have weight, it resolves into a complaint against Providence for the weakness of the sense of deity in rude and illiterate nations. If such complaint be solidly founded, it pierces extremely deep: why have not all nations, even in their nascent state, the sense of deity

(*a*) Natural History of Religion.

and the moral sense in purity and perfection? why do they not possess all the arts of life without necessity of culture or experience? why are we born poor and helpless infants, instead of being produced complete in every member, internal and external, as Adam and Eve were? The plan of Providence is far a-<352>bove the reach of our weak criticisms: it is but a small portion that is laid open to our view; can we pretend to judge of the whole? I venture only to suggest, that as, with respect to individuals, there is a progress from infancy to maturity; so there is a similar progress in every nation, from its savage state to its maturity in arts and sciences. A child that has just conceptions of the Deity and of his attributes, would be a great miracle; and would not such knowledge in a savage be equally so? Nor can I discover what benefit a child or a savage could reap from such knowledge; provided it remained a child or a savage in every other respect. The genuine fruits of religion, are gratitude to the Author of our being, veneration to him as the supreme being, absolute resignation to the established laws of his providence, and chearful performance of every duty: but a child has not the slightest idea of gratitude nor of veneration, and very little of moral duties; and a savage, with respect to these, is not much superior to a child. The formation and government of the world, as far as we know, are excellent: we have great reason to presume the same <353> with respect to what we do not know; and every good man will rest satisfied with the following reflection, That we should have been men from the hour of our birth, complete in every part, had it been conformable to the system of unerring Providence. <354>

SECTION II

Morality considered as a branch of duty to our Maker.

Having travelled long on a rough road, not a little fatiguing, the agreeable part lies before us; which is, to treat of morality as a branch of religion. It was that subject which induced me to undertake the history of natural religion; a subject that will afford salutary instruction; and will inspire true piety, if instruction can produce that effect.

Bayle states a question, Whether a people may not be happy in society and be qualified for good government, upon principles of morality singly, without any sense of religion. The question is ingenious, and may give opportunity for subtile reasoning; but it is useless, because the fact supposed cannot happen. The principles of morality and of religion are equally rooted in our nature: they are indeed weak <355> in children and in savages; but they grow up together, and advance toward maturity with equal steps. Where the moral sense is entire, there must be a sense of religion; and if a man who has no sense of religion live decently in society, he is more indebted for his conduct to good temper than to sound morals.

We have the authority of the Prophet Micah, formerly quoted, for holding, that religion, or, in other words, our duty to God, consists in doing justice, in loving mercy, and in walking humbly with him. The last is the foundation of religious worship, discussed in the foregoing section: the two former belong to the present section. And if we have gratitude to our Maker and Benefactor, if we owe implicit obedience to his will as our rightful sovereign, we ought not to separate the worship we owe to him, from justice and benevolence to our fellow-creatures; for to be unjust to them, to be cruel or hard-hearted, is a transgression of his will, no less gross than a total neglect of religious worship. "Master, which is the great commandment in the law? Jesus said unto him, Thou shalt love the Lord thy God with all thy <356> heart, with all thy soul, and with all thy mind. This is the first and great commandment. And the second is like unto it, Thou shalt love thy neighbour as thyself. On these two commandments hang all the law and the prophets" (a). "Then shall the King say unto them on his right hand, Come, ye blessed of my Father, inherit the kingdom prepared for you. For I was hungry, and ye gave me meat: I was thirsty, and ye gave me drink: I was a stranger, and ye took me in: naked, and ye cloathed me: sick, and ye visited me: in prison, and ye came unto me. Then shall the righteous answer, saying, Lord, when saw we thee hungry, and fed thee? or thirsty, and gave thee drink? When saw we thee a stranger, and took thee in? or naked, and cloathed thee? When saw we thee sick, or in prison, and came unto thee? And the King shall answer, Verily I say unto you, in as much as ye have done it unto one of the least of these my brethren, ye have done

(a) Matthew, xxii. 36.

it unto me" (*a*). "Pure religion <357> and undefiled before God, is this, To visit the fatherless and widow in their affliction; and to keep himself unspotted from the world" (*b*). "Hostias et victimas Domino offeram quas in usum mei protulit, ut rejiciam ei suum munus? Ingratum est; cum sit litabilis hostia bonus animus, et pura mens, et sincera conscientia. Igitur qui innocentiam colit, Domino supplicat; qui justitiam, Deo libat; qui fraudibus abstinet, propitiat Deum; qui hominem periculo subripit, optimam victimam caedit. Haec nostra sacrificia, haec Dei sacra sunt. Sic apud nos religiosior est ille, qui justior" (*c*).* The laws of <358> Zaleucus, lawgiver to the Locrians, who lived before the days of Pythagoras, are introduced with the following preamble. "No man can question the existence of Deity who observes the order and harmony of the universe, which cannot be the production of chance. Men ought to bridle their passions, and to guard against every vice. God is pleased with no sacrifice but a sincere heart; and differs widely from mortals, whose delight is splendid ceremonies and rich offerings. Let justice therefore be studied; for by that only can a man be acceptable to the Deity. Let those who are tempted to do ill, have always before their eyes the severe judgements of the gods against wicked men. Let them always keep in view the hour of death, that fatal hour which is attended with bitter remorse for transgressing the rules of justice. If a bad disposition incline you to vice, pray to Heaven at the foot of the altar, to mend your heart."

Morality is thus included in religion. Some nations, however, leave not this proposition to reasoning or conviction, but ingross many moral duties in their re-<359>ligious creed. In the 67th chapter of the Sadder, a lie is declared to be a great sin, and is forbid even where it tends to bring about

---

* "Shall I offer to God for a sacrifice those creatures which his bounty has given me for my use? It were ingratitude to throw back the gift upon the giver. The most acceptable sacrifice is an upright mind, an untainted conscience, and an honest heart. The actions of the innocent ascend to God in prayer; the observance of justice is more grateful than incense; the man who is sincere in his dealings, secures the favour of his Creator; and the delivery of a fellow-creature from danger or destruction, is dearer in the eyes of the Almighty than the sacrifice of blood."

(*a*) Matthew, xxv. 34.
(*b*) James, i. 27.
(*c*) Minucius Foelix.

good. So much purer is the morality of the ancient Persians than of the present Jesuits. The religion of the people of Pegu, inculcates charity, forbids to kill, to steal, or to injure others. Attend to the consequence: that people, fierce originally, have become humane and compassionate. In a sacred book of the ancient Persians, it is written, "If you incline to be a saint, give good education to your children; for their virtuous actions will be imputed to you." The people of Japan pay great respect to their parents; it being an article in their creed, That those who fail in duty to their parents, will be punished by the gods. In these two instances, religion tends greatly to connect parents and children in the most intimate tie of cordial affection. The reverence the Chinese have for their ancestors and the ceremonies performed annually at their tombs, tend to keep them at home, and prevent their wandering into foreign countries.

Ancient Persia was fertile and populous: <360> at present it is barren and thin of inhabitants. Sir John Chardin accounts for the difference. The climate of Persia is so dry, that scarce a shower falls during summer: even grass will not grow without being watered. This defect of climate was remedied by the ancient inhabitants, termed *Gaures;* among whom it was a religious act, to cultivate waste land and to plant trees for fruit. It was a maxim in the sacred book of that religion, That he who cultivates the ground with care and diligence, acquires a greater stock of religious merit, than can be acquired by ten thousand prayers. The religion, on the contrary, of the present Mahometan inhabitants, leads them to take no care for tomorrow: they grasp at present enjoyment, and leave all the rest to fate.[22]

Superstitious rites in some religions, are successfully employ'd to enforce certain moral duties. The Romans commonly made their solemn covenants in the capitol, before the statue of Jupiter; by which solemnity he was understood to guarantee the covenant, ready to pour out vengeance upon the transgressor. When an oath enters into any engagement, the <361> Burates, a people in Grand Tartary, require it to be given upon a mountain, held to be sacred: they are firmly persuaded, that the person who swears a falsehood, will not come down alive. The Essenes, a Jewish sect, bound themselves by a solemn oath, to shun unlawful gain, to be faithful to their promises, not

---

22. Paragraph added in 2nd edition.

to lie, and never to harm any one. In Cochin-China, the souls of those who have been eminent for arts or arms, are worshipped. Their statues are placed in the temples; and the size of a statue is proportioned to the merit of the person represented. If that be impartially executed, there cannot be a nobler incitement to public spirit. The Egyptians did not reach the thought of honouring virtue after death; but they dishonoured vice, by excluding it from the Elysian fields.

The salutary influence of religion on morality, is not confined to pure religion, whether by its connection with morality in general, or by inculcating particular moral duties. There are many religious doctrines, doubtful or perhaps erroneous, that contribute also to enforce morality. Some followers of Confucius ascribe im-<362>mortality to the souls of the just only; and believe that the souls of the wicked perish with their bodies. The native Hindows are gentle and humane: the metempsychosis or transmigration of souls, is an article in their creed; and hence the prohibition to destroy any living creature, because it might disturb the soul of an ancestor.[23] In the second chapter of the Sadder, it is written, that a man whose good works are more numerous than his sins, will go to paradise; otherwise that he will be thrust into hell, there to remain for ever. It adds, that a bridge erected over the great abyss where hell is situated, leads from this earth to paradise; that upon the bridge there stands an angel, who weighs in a balance the merits of the passengers; that the passenger whose good works are found light in the balance, is thrown over the bridge into hell; but that the passenger whose good works preponderate, proceeds in his journey to paradise, where there is a glorious city, gardens, rivers, and beautiful virgins, whose looks are a perpetual feast, but who must not be enjoy'd. In the fourth chapter of the Sadder, good works are zealously recommended in the <363> following parable. Zeradusht, or Zoroaster, being in company with God, saw a man in hell who wanted his right foot. "Oh my Creator," said Zoroaster, "who is that man who wants the right foot? God answered, He was the king of thirty-three cities, reigned many years, but never did any good, except once, when, seeing a sheep ty'd where it could not reach its food, he with his right foot pushed the food to it; upon which account

23. "The native Hindows . . . of an ancestor": added in 2nd edition.

that foot was saved from hell." In Japan, those of the Sinto religion believe, that the souls of good men are translated to a place of happiness, next to the habitation of their gods. But they admit no place of torment; nor have they any notion of a devil, but what animates the fox, a very mischievous animal in that country. What then becomes of the souls of ill men? Being denied entrance into heaven, they wander about to expiate their sins. Those of the Bubsdo religion believe, that in the other world, there is a place of misery as well as of happiness. Of the latter there are different degrees, for different degrees of virtue; and yet, far from envying the happier lot of others, every <364> inhabitant is perfectly satisfied with his own. There are also different degrees of misery; for justice requires, that every man be punished according to the nature and number of his sins. *Jemma O* is the severe judge of the wicked: their vices appear to him in all their horror, by means of a mirror, named *the mirror of knowledge.* When souls have expiated their sins, after suffering long in the prison of darkness, they are sent back into the world, to animate serpents, toads, and such vile animals as resembled them in their former existence. From these they pass into the bodies of more innocent animals; and at last are again suffered to enter human bodies; after the dissolution of which, they run the same course of happiness or misery as at first. The people of Benin, in Africa, believe a man's shadow to be a real being, that gives testimony after death for or against him; and that he accordingly is made happy or miserable in another world. The Negroes hold that their own country is delicious above all others; and it is the belief of several of their tribes, that where-ever they die, they will return to their own country. <365> This is a perpetual source of comfort, and inspires them with humanity above the other tribes.[24] A religious belief in ancient Greece, that the souls of those who are left above ground without rites, have not access to Elysium, tended to promote humanity; for those who are careful of the dead, will not be altogether indifferent about the living.

Immense are the blessings that proceed from the union of pure religion with sound morality: but however immense, I boldly affirm, that they scarce counterbalance the manifold evils that proceed from impure religion,

---

24. "The Negroes hold . . . the other tribes": added in 2nd edition.

indulging and even encouraging gross immoralities. A few glaring instances shall be selected. The first I shall mention is, the holding religion to consist in the belief of points purely speculative, such as have no relation to good works. The natural effect of that doctrine is, to divorce religion from morality, in manifest contradiction to the will of God. What avails it, for example, to the glory of God or to the happiness of men, whether the conception of the Virgin Mary was maculate or immaculate? The following few instances, selected from a great <366> number, are controversies of that kind, which for ages miserably afflicted the Christian church, and engendered the bitterest enmity, productive of destruction and slaughter among brethren of the same religion. In the fifth century, it was the employment of more than one general council, to determine, whether *the mother of God,* or *the mother of Christ,* is the proper epithet of the Virgin Mary. In the sixth century, a bitter controversy arose whether Christ's body was corruptible. In the seventh century, Christians were divided about the volition of Christ, whether he had one or two Wills, and how his Will operated. In the eighth and ninth centuries, the Greek and Latin churches divided about the Holy Ghost, whether he proceeded from the Father and Son, or only from the Father. In the eleventh century, there arose a warm contest between the Greek and Latin churches about using unleavened bread in the eucharist. In the fourteenth century, it was controverted between Pope John XXII. and the divines of his time, whether souls in their intermediate state see God, or only the human nature of Christ. Franciscans have suffered death in multitudes about the <367> form of their hood. It was disputed between the Dominicans and Franciscans, whether Christ had any property. The Pope pronounced the negative proposition to be a pestilential and blasphemous doctrine, subversive of Catholic faith. Many councils were held at Constantinople, to determine what sort of light it was that the disciples saw on Mount Tabor: it was solemnly pronounced, to be the eternal light with which God is encircled; and which may be termed his energy or operation, but is distinct from his nature and essence. A heap of propositions in the creed of St. Athanasius, as far as intelligible, are merely speculative, such as may be adopted or rejected, without the least danger to religion, or to morality; and yet we are commanded to believe every one of them, under the pain of eternal damnation. An endless number of such propositions, adopted by the Romish church, clearly evince, that Christianity was in that church held to consist entirely in belief, without any regard to good works.* Whether the Alcoran be eternal, <368> or whether it were created, is a dispute that has occasioned much effusion of Mahometan blood. The Calif Mamoun, with many doctors, held it to have been created; but the greater number insisted, that being the word of God, it must like him be eternal. This opinion is embraced by the present Mahometans, who hold all who deny it to be infidels. One great maxim of the Brahmines contained in their ancient books, is, that it is better to sit than to walk, better to lie than to sit, better to sleep than to wake, better to die than to live. This is directly subversive of industry, and consequently of morality.[25] There is among men great uniformity of opinion in matters of importance. Religious differences are generally about trifles, where liberty ought to be indulged without reserve (a); and yet upon these trifles are founded the bitterest enmities. It ought therefore to be a fundamental law in every church, to abstain from loading <369> its creed with articles that are not essential; for such articles tend to eradicate brotherly love, and to convert into bitter enemies, men who are fundamentally of the same faith. This leads me naturally to say a few words on religion as a branch of education, of all the most important branch. Avoiding all the points disputed among the different sects of Christians, and leaving mysteries to the future sagacity of your children if they shall be inclined to pry into them, let them know that there is a God over all who loves the good, and is an enemy to evil-doers; that this great Being, tho' invisible to us, is witness to all our words and actions, and that even our secret thoughts are not hid from him. Take every opportunity to inculcate this great truth, till it make so deep an impression as to be the great regulator of their conduct. With respect to every intended action, train them up into the habit of enquiring first how it will appear in the sight of their Maker at the great day of judgement.

---

* The great weight that was laid upon orthodoxy, appears from a triumphal arch erected over the tomb of Charlemagne, upon which was the following inscription: "Here lies the body of Charles, a great and orthodox emperor." And yet that orthodox Emperor could not write his name. [["And yet that . . . write his name": added in 2nd edition.]]

(a) Elements of Criticism, vol. 2. p. 493. edit. 5.

25. "One great maxim . . . consequently of morality": added in 2nd edition.

This is true religion, the main support of virtue. It is all that is requisite in point of education; leaving to those who have penetration and leisure to form a more complete system.[26] <370>

In the next place shall be mentioned, certain articles of faith that tend to sap the very foundation of one or other moral duty. What, for example, can more effectually promote cruelty, than the creed of the Idaans, a people in the island of Borneo, That every person they put to death must attend them as a slave in the other world? This belief makes them prone to war, and occasions assassinations without end. According to the creed of the savages in Canada, the killing and burning enemies are what chiefly entitle them to be happy in another world; and that he who destroys the greatest number, will be the most happy. At the same time, they have no notion of greater happiness there, than plenty of game, great abundance of all things without labour, and full gratification of every sensual appetite. The Scandinavians had no notion of greater bliss in another world, than to drink beer out of the skull of an enemy, in the hall of Woden their tutelar deity: can hatred and revenge indulged in this world be more honourably rewarded? The doctrine of tutelar deities is equally productive of ha-<371>tred and revenge: relying on a superior power who espouses all my quarrels, I put no bounds to my resentment, and every moral duty in opposition is trampled under foot. The following creed of the inhabitants of the Marian or Ladrone islands, is a great encouragement to cowardice. Heaven, according to that creed, is a region under the earth, filled with cocoa-trees, sugar-canes, and variety of other delicious fruits. Hell is a vast furnace, constantly red hot. Their condition in the other world depends not on good or bad actions, but on the manner of their death. Those who die a natural death, go straight to heaven: they may sin freely, if they can but secure their persons against violence. But war and bloodshed are their aversion, because those who suffer a violent death go straight to hell. In many ancient nations, a goddess was worshipped, whose province it was to promote animal love without regard to matrimony. That goddess was in Greece termed *Aphrodité,* in Rome *Venus,* and in Babylon *Mylitta.* To her was sacrificed, in some countries, the virginity of young women; which, it

26. "This leads me . . . more complete system": added in 2nd edition.

was believed, did se-<372>cure their chastity for ever after. Justin mentions a custom in the island of Cyprus, of sending young women at stated times to the sea-shore; where they prostituted themselves as a tribute to Venus, that they might be chaste the rest of their lives. His words are, "Pro reliqua pudicitiae libamenta Veneri solituras" (*a*).[27] In other nations, a small number only were prostituted, in order to secure to the remainder, a chaste and regular life. This explains a custom among the Babylonians, which, far from being thought a religious act, is held as a proof of abandoned debauchery. The custom was, That every woman once in her life should prostitute herself in the temple of the goddess Mylitta. Herodotus reports, that thereby they became proof against all temptation. And Aelian observes the same of the Lydian ladies. *Credat Judeus Apella.* Margaret Poretta, who in the fourteenth century made a figure among the Beguines, preached a doctrine not a little favourable to incontinence. She undertook to demonstrate, "That the soul, when absorbed in the love of God, is free from the <373> restraint of law, and may freely gratify every natural appetite, without contracting guilt"; a cordial doctrine for a lady of pleasure. That crazy person, instead of being laugh'd at, was burnt alive at Paris. In the fifteenth century, a sect termed *brethren and sisters of the free spirit,* held, That modesty is a mark of inhering corruption; and that those only are perfect, who can behold nakedness without emotion. These fanatics appeared at public worship, without the least covering. Many tenets professed by the Jesuits, open a door to every immorality. "Persons truly wicked and void of the love of God, may expect eternal life in heaven; provided only they be impressed with fear of divine anger, and avoid heinous crimes through the dread of future punishment." Again, "Persons may transgress with safety, who have any plausible argument for transgressing. A judge, for example, may decide for the least probable side of a question, and even against his own opinion, provided he be supported by any tolerable authority." Again, "Actions intrinsically evil and contrary to <374> divine law, may however be innocently performed, by those who can join, even ideally, a good end to the performance. For example, an ecclesiastic may safely commit simony by

(*a*) Lib. 18. cap. 5.
27. "They made offerings to Venus in the name of the remainder of their chastity."

purchasing a benefice, if to the unlawful act, he join the innocent purpose of procuring to himself a subsistence. A man who runs another through the body for a slight affront, renders the action lawful, if his motive be honour, not revenge." A famous Jesuit taught, that a young man may wish the death of his father, and even rejoice at his death, provided the wish proceed, not from hatred, but from fondness of his father's estate. And another Jesuit has had the effrontery to maintain, that a monk may lawfully assassinate a calumniator, who threatens to charge his order with scandalous practices. Among the negroes of Sanguin on the river Sestro in Guinea, it is an article of faith that dextrous robbery is no less lawful than beneficial.[28]

The Quakers, a sect generated during the civil wars in the reign of Charles I. contracted such an aversion to war as to declare it unlawful even in self-defence; <375> a doctrine that soars high above morality and is contradictory to human nature. But by what magic has a tenet so unnatural subsisted so long? The Quakers exclude pride, admitting no difference of rank but considering all men as their brethren. And they exclude vanity by simplicity and uniformity of dress. Thus by humility and temperance they have preserved their institutions alive. But these passions cannot always be kept in subjection: vanity is creeping in, especially among the females, who indulge in silks, fine linen, bone-lace, &c. Vanity and pride will reach the males; and the edifice will totter and fall.[29]

A doctrine that strikes at the root of every moral duty, as well as of religion itself, is, That God will accept a composition for sin; a doctrine that prevailed universally during the days of ignorance. Compositions for crimes were countenanced by law in every country (a); and men, prone to indulge their passions, flatter'd themselves, that they might compound with God for sinning against him, as with their neighbours for injuring them: those <376> who have no notion of any motive but interest, naturally think it to be equally powerful with the Deity. An opinion prevailed universally in the Christian church, from the eighth century down to the Reformation, that liberal donations to God, to a saint, to the church, would procure par-

---

(a) Historical Law tracts, tract 1.

28. "Among the negroes . . . lawful than beneficial": added in 2nd edition.

29. Paragraph added in 2nd edition.

don even for the grossest sins. During that period, the building churches and monasteries was in high vogue. This absurd or rather impious doctrine, proved a plentiful harvest of wealth to the clergy; for the great and opulent, who are commonly the boldest sinners, have the greatest ability to compound for their sins. There needs nothing but such an opinion, to annihilate every duty, whether moral or religious; for what wicked man will think either of restitution or of reformation, who can purchase a pardon from Heaven with so little trouble? Louis XI. of France was remarkably superstitious, even in a superstitious age. To ingratiate himself with the Virgin Mary, he surrendered to her the county of Boulogne with great solemnity. Voltaire remarks, that godliness consists, not in making the Virgin a Countess, but in abstaining from <377> sin. Composition for sins is a doctrine of the church of Rome, boldly professed without disguise. A book of rates, published by authority of the Pope, contains stated prices for absolutions, not excepting the most heinous sins. So true is the observation of Aeneas Silvius, afterward Pope Paul II. "Nihil est quod absque argento Romana curia det: ipsa manuum impositio, et Spiritus Sancti dona, venduntur; nec peccatorum venia nisi nummatis impenditur."* Of all the immoral atonements for sin, human sacrifices are the most brutal; deviating no less from the purity of religion, than from the fundamental principles of morality. They wore out of use as kindly affections prevailed; and will never again be restored, unless we fall back to the savage manners of our forefathers. Composition for crimes, once universal, is now banished from every enlightened nation. Composition for sins, was once <378> equally universal; and I wish it could be said, that there are now no remains of that poisonous opinion among Christians: the practice of the church of Rome will not permit it to be said. Were men deeply convinced, as they ought to be, that sincere repentance and reformation of manners are the only means for obtaining pardon, they would never dream of making bargains with the Almighty, and of compounding with him for their sins.

In the practice of religion, the laying too great weight on forms, cere-

---

* "There is nothing to be obtained from the court of Rome but by the force of money: even the ceremony of consecration, and the gifts of the Holy Ghost, are sold; and the remission of sins is bestowed only on those who can pay for it."

monies, and other external arbitrary acts, tends to the corruption of morals.
That error has infected every religion. The Sadder, the Bible of the Gaures,
prohibits calumny and detraction, lying, stealing, adultery, and fornication.
It however enervates morality and religion, by placing many trifling acts
on a level with the most important duties. It enjoins the destruction of five
kinds of reptiles, frogs, mice, ants, serpents, and flies that sting. It teaches,
that to walk barefoot profanes the ground. Great regard for water is en-
join'd: it must not be used during night; and when set upon the fire, a third
part <379> of the pot must be empty, to prevent boiling over. The Bramins
have wofully degenerated from their original institutions, thinking that religion consists in forms and ceremonies. As soon as an infant is born, the
word *Oum* must be pronounced over it; otherwise it will be eternally miserable: its tongue must be rubbed with consecrated meal: the third day of
the moon, it must be carried into open air, with its head to the north. The
inhabitants of Formosa believe in hell; but it is only for punishing those
who fail to go naked in certain seasons, or who wear cotton instead of silk.
In the time of Ghenhizcan, it was held in Tartary a mortal sin, to put a
knife into the fire, to whip a horse with his bridle, or to break one bone
with another; and yet these pious Tartars held treachery, robbery, murder
to be no sins. A faction in Aegina, a Greek commonwealth, treacherously
assassinated seven hundred of their fellow-citizens. They cut off the hands
of a miserable fugitive, who had laid hold of the altar for protection, in
order to murder him without the precincts of the temple. Their treacherous
assassinations <380> made no impression: but tho' they refrained from
murder in the temple, yet by profaning it with blood, says Herodotus, they
offended the gods, and contracted inexpiable guilt. Would one believe, that
a tribunal was established by Charlemagne more horrible than the inquisition itself? It was established in Westphalia, to punish with death every
Saxon who eat meat in lent. It was established in Flanders and in French-
county, the beginning of the seventeenth century. Smollet in his travels into
Italy observes, that it is held more infamous to transgress the slightest ceremonial institution of the church of Rome, than to transgress any moral
duty; that a murderer or adulterer will be easily absolved by the church,
and even maintain his character in society; but that a man who eats a pigeon
on a Saturday, is abhorred as a monster of reprobation. During the twelfth

and thirteenth centuries, long curled hair, of which men of fashion in England were extremely vain, suffered a violent persecution. Anselm, Archbishop of Canterbury, pronounced the sentence of excommunication against those who indulged in that dress; and was cele-<381>brated by his brethren of the clergy, tho' at that time excommunication was a dreadful punishment. William of Malmsbury relates in lively colours an incident that shows the gross superstition of that age. "A certain knight, who was very proud of his long luxuriant hair, dreamed that a person suffocated him with its curls. As soon as he awoke from his sleep, he cut his hair to a decent length. The report of this spread over all England; and almost all the knights reduced their hair to the proper standard. But this reformation was not of long continuance. For in less than a year all who wished to appear fashionable, returned to their former wickedness, and contended with the ladies in length of hair. Those to whom nature had denied that ornament, supplied the defect by art." What can be more grossly superstitious than the form used in Roman-Catholic countries of baptizing a church-bell? The priest, assisted by some of his brethren, mumbles over some prayers, and sprinkles the outside with holy water, while they wash the inside with the same precious liquor. The priest next draws seven crosses on the outside, and four on the inside, with consecrated oil. Then <382> a censer full of frankincense is put under the bell to smoke it. And the whole concludes with prayer.[30]

Listen to a celebrated writer upon this subject. "It is certain, that in every religion, however sublime, many of the votaries, perhaps the greatest number, will still seek the divine favour, not by virtue and good morals, which alone can be acceptable to a perfect being, but either by frivolous observances, by intemperate zeal, by rapturous ecstasies, or by the belief of mysterious and absurd opinions. When the old Romans were attacked with a pestilence, they never ascribed their sufferings to their vices, or dreamed of repentance and amendment. They never thought that they were the general robbers of the world, whose ambition and avarice made desolate the earth, and reduced opulent nations to want and beggary. They only created a dictator in order to drive a nail into a door; and by that means they thought

---

30. "Smollet in his . . . concludes with prayer": added in 2nd edition.

that they had sufficiently appeased their incensed deity" (*a*). <383> Thus, gradually, the essentials of religion wear out of mind, by the attention given to forms and ceremonies: these intercept and exhaust the whole stock of devotion, which ought to be reserved for the higher exercises of religion. The neglect or transgression of mere punctilios, are punished as heinous sins; while sins really heinous are suffered to pass with impunity. The Jews exalted the keeping their sabbath holy, above every other duty; and it was the general belief, that the strict observance of that day was alone sufficient to atone for every sin. The command of resting that day, was taken so literally, that they would not on that day defend themselves even against an assassin. Ptolomy, son of Lagus, entered Jerusalem on the Jewish sabbath, in a hostile manner without resistance. Nor did experience open the eyes of that foolish people. Xiphilin, relating the siege of Jerusalem by Pompey, says, that if the Jews had not rested on the sabbath, Pompey would not have been successful. Every Saturday he renewed his batteries; and having on that day made a breach, he marched into the town without opposi- <384>tion. One cannot help smiling at an Amsterdam Jew, who had no check of conscience for breaking open a house and carrying off money; and yet being stopped in his flight by the sabbath, he most piously rested, till he was apprehended, and led to the gallows. Nor are the Jews to this day cured of that frenzy. In some late accounts from Constantinople, a fire broke out in a Jew's house on Saturday: rather than profane the sabbath, he suffered the flames to spread, which occasioned the destruction of five hundred houses.* We laugh at the Jews, and we <385> have reason; and yet there are many well-meaning Protestants, who lay the whole of religion upon punctual attendance at public worship. Are the Roman Catholics less superstitious with respect to the place of worship, than the Jews are with

---

* "And there was a woman which had a spirit of infirmity eighteen years, and was bowed together. And Jesus laid his hands on her, and immediately she was made straight, and glorified God. And the ruler of the synagogue with indignation said unto the people, There are six days in which men ought to work: in them therefore come and be healed, and not on the sabbath-day. The Lord then said, Thou hypocrite, doth not each one of you on the sabbath loose his ox or his ass from the stall, and lead him away to watering? and ought not this woman, whom Satan hath bound, be loosed from this bond on the sabbath-day?" *Luke,* xiii. 11.

(*a*) Natural History of Religion, by David Hume, Esq.

respect to the day of worship? In the year 1670, some Arabians, watching an opportunity, got into the town of Dieu when the gates were opened in the morning. They might easily have been expelled by the cannon of the citadel; but the Portuguese governor was obliged to look on without firing a gun, being threatened with excommunication, if the least mischief should be done to any of the churches. The only doctrines inculcated from the Romish pulpit down to the Reformation, were the authority of holy mother-church; the merit of the saints, and their credit in the court of heaven; the dignity and glory of the blessed Virgin; the efficacy of relics; the intolerable fire of purgatory; and the vast importance of indulgences. Relying on such pious acts for obtaining remission of sin, all orders of men rushed headlong in-<386>to vice;* nor was there a single attempt to stem the current of immorality; for the traffic of indulgences could not but flourish in proportion to the growth of sin. And thus was religion set in direct opposition to morality. St. Eloy, bishop of Noyon in the seventh century, and canonized by the church of Rome, delivers the following doctrine. "He is a good Christian who goes frequently to church; who presents his oblations upon the altar; who tastes not the fruit of his own industry till part be consecrated to God; who, when the holy festivals approach, lives chastely even with his own wife for several days; and who can repeat the creed and the Lord's prayer. Redeem then your souls from destruction, while you have the means in your power: offer presents and tithes to churchmen: come more frequently to <387> church: humbly implore the patronage of saints. If you observe these things, you may, in the day of judgement, go with confidence to the tribunal of the eternal Judge, and say, Give to us, O Lord, for we have given unto thee." A modern author subjoins a proper observation. "We see here a very ample description of a good Christian, in which there is not the least mention of the love of God, resignation to his will, obedience to his laws, nor of justice, benevolence, or charity." Gross ignorance and wretched superstition prevailed so much even in the fourteenth century, that people reckoned themselves secure of salvation, if at

---

* An ingenious writer pleasantly observes, "That a croisade was the South-Sea project of former times: by the latter, men hoped to gain riches without industry: by the former, they hoped to gain heaven without repentance, amendment of life, or sanctity of manners." *Sir David Dalrymple, a Judge in the Court of Session.*

the day of judgement they could show any connection with monks. Many at the point of death, made it their last request, to be admitted into the mendicant order, or to be interred in their burial-place. Religion need not associate with morality, if such silly practices be sufficient for obtaining the favour of God. Is this less absurd than the Hindostan belief, That the water of the Ganges hath a sanctifying virtue; and that those who die on its banks, are not only exempted <388> from future punishment, but are wafted straight to paradise?

Forms and ceremonies are visible acts, which make a deep impression on the vulgar. Hence their influence in reasoning and in morality, as we have seen in the two sketches immediately foregoing; and hence also their influence in religion. Forms and ceremonies are useful at public worship: but they ought not to take place of essentials. People however, governed by what they see and hear, are more addicted to external acts of devotion, than to heart worship, which is not known but by reflection.

It will be no excuse for relying so much on forms and ceremonies, that they are innocent. In themselves they may be innocent; but not so in their consequences. For they have by such reliance a vigorous tendency to relax the obligations of morality. "La pure morale," says M. Rousseau, "est si chargée de devoirs séveres que si on la surcharge encore de formes indif-férentes, c'est presque toujours aux dépends de l'essentiel. On dit que c'est le cas de la plupart des moines, qui, soumis à mille regles inutiles, ne savent <389> ce que c'est qu'honneur et vertu."[31] Religious rites that contradict not any passion, are keenly embraced, and punctually performed; and men, flattering themselves that they have thus been punctual in their duty to God, give vent to their passions against men. "They pay tithes of mint, and anise, and cummin; but omit the weightier matters of the law, judgement, mercy, and faith" (a). Upon such a man religion sits extremely light. As he seldom exercises any act of genuine devotion, he thinks of the Deity with

(a) Matthew, xxiii. 23.

31. "Pure morality is so burdened with strict duties that if in addition it is overbur-dened with unimportant formalities, it is nearly always at the expense of what is essential. They say that this is the case for most monks, who, subjected to a thousand useless rules, do not know what honour and virtue are" (Julie, ou la nouvelle Héloïse, pt. IV, letter 10, p. 375).

ease and familiarity: how otherwise is it accountable, that the plays, termed *Mysteries,* could be relished, where mean and perhaps dissolute persons are brought on the stage, acting Jesus Christ, the Virgin Mary, and even God himself? These objects of worship were certainly no more regarded than the Grecian gods, who frequently made part of the *Dramatis personae* in Greek plays. Many other facts might be urged, to prove the low ebb of religion in those days: I select one or two, which probably will afford some amusement to <390> the reader. Bartolus, a famous lawyer, in order to shew the form of proceeding in a court of justice, imagines a process between the devil and mankind. The devil cites mankind to appear at the tribunal of Jesus Christ, claiming them as belonging to him by Adam's fall. He swells in rage, demanding whether any one dare appear in their behalf. Against the Virgin Mary offering herself as their advocate, the devil makes two objections; first, That being the mother of the Judge, her influence would be too great; second, That a woman is debarred from being an advocate: and these objections are supported by numberless quotations from the *Corpus Juris.* The Virgin, on her part, quotes texts permitting women to appear for widows, orphans, and for persons in distress. She is allowed to plead for mankind, as coming under the last article. The devil urges prescription, as having been in possession of mankind ever since the fall. The Virgin answers, That a *mala-fide possessor*[32] cannot acquire by prescription. Prescription being repelled, the parties go to the merits of the case, which are learnedly discussed with texts from the <391> Pandects. The memoirs of the French academy of Belles Lettres (*a*) has the following story: A monk returning from a house which he durst not visit in day-light, had a river to cross. The boat was overturned by Satan, and the monk was drowned when he was beginning to invocate the Virgin Mary. Two devils having laid hold of his soul, were stopped by two angels. "My Lords," said the devils, "true it is and not a fable, that God died for his friends; but this monk was an enemy to God, and we are carrying him to hell." After much altercation, it was proposed by the angels, to refer the dispute to the Virgin

(*a*) Vol. 18.

32. That is, one who possesses property upon a title which he knows or should know to be invalid.

Mary. The devils were willing to accept of God for judge, because he would judge according to law. "But from the Virgin Mary," said they, "we expect no justice: she would break to atoms every gate of hell, rather than suffer one to remain there a moment who pays any worship to her image. She may say, that black is white, and that puddled water is pure—God never contradicts her. The day on which God <392> made his mother, was a fatal day to us."

People who profess the same religion, and differ only in forms and cere-monies, may justly be compared to neighbouring states, who are commonly bitter enemies to each other, if they have any difference. At the same time, dissocial passions never rage so furiously, as under the mask of religion; for in that case they are held to be meritorious, as exerted in the cause of God. This observation is but too well verified in the disputes among Christians. However low religion was in the dark ages, yet men fought for forms and ceremonies as *pro aris et focis.* In the Armenian form of baptism, the priest says at the first immersion, *In name of the Father;* at the second, *In name of the Son;* at the third, *In name of the Holy Ghost.* This form is bitterly condemned by the Romish church, which appoints the three persons of the Trinity to be joined in the same expression, in token of their union. Strahlenberg gives an account of a Christian sect in Russia, which differs from the established Greek church in the following particulars: First, In public worship they re-<393>peat *Halleluia* but twice; and it is a mortal sin to repeat it thrice. Second, In celebrating mass, not five but seven loaves ought to be used. Third, The cross stamped upon a mass-loaf ought to have eight corners. Fourth, In signing with the cross at prayers, the end of the ring-finger must be joined to the end of the thumb, and the two inter-mediate fingers be held out at full length. How trifling are these differences! and yet for these, all who dissent from them are held unclean, and no better than Pagans: they will not eat nor drink with any of the established church; and, if a person of that church happen to sit down in a house of theirs, they wash and purify the seat.* There are few sects founded upon more

---

* Christians, occupied too much with external forms, have corrupted several of the fine arts. They have injured architecture, by erecting magnificent churches in the ugly form of a cross. And they have injured painting, by withdrawing the best hands from

trivial differences than the Turkish and Persian Mahometans. The epithets given to the <394> Persians by the Turks are, "Forsaken of God, Abominable, Blasphemers of the Holy Prophet"; and so bitter is their enmity to the Persians, That the schools of the seraglio are open to young men of all nations, those of Persia alone excepted. The Persians are held to be such apostates from the true faith, as to be utterly past recovery: they receive no quarter in war, being accounted unworthy of life or slavery: nor do the Persians yield to the Turks in hatred. Whether coffee be or be not prohibited in the Alcoran, has produced much controversy in the Mahometan church, and consequently much persecuting zeal. A mufti, not fond of coffee, declared it to have an inebriating quality, and therefore to be virtually prohibited by Mahomet. Another mufti, fond of coffee for its exhilarating virtue, declared it lawful; "because," said he, "all things are lawful that are not expressly prohibited in the Alcoran." The coffee-houses in Constantinople were for a long period alternately opened and shut, according to the taste of the reigning mufti; till coffee at last, surmounting all obstacles, came to be an established Maho-<395>metan liquor. Religion thus runs wild, whenever it loses sight of its true ends, worshipping God, and enforcing justice to man. The Hindows hate the Mahometans for eating the flesh of cows: the Mahometans hate the Hindows for eating the flesh of swine. The aversion that men of the same religion have at each other for the most trivial differences, converts them frequently into brutal savages. Suppose, for example, that a man, reduced to the extremity of hunger, makes a greedy meal of a dead horse, a case so deplorable would wring every heart. And yet, let this be done in Lent, or on a meagre day—Behold! every zealot is instantly metamorphosed into a devil incarnate. In the records of St. Claude, a small district of Burgundy, is engrossed a sentence against a poor gentleman named *Claude Guillon.* The words are: "Having considered the process, and taken advice of the doctors of law, we declare the said Claude Guillon duly convicted for having carried away and boiled a piece of a dead horse, and of having eat the same on the 31st March, being Saturday." And he was beheaded according-<396>ly 28th July 1629; notwith-

---

proper subjects, and employing them on the legendary martyrdom of pretended saints, and other such disagreeable subjects.

standing a defence above all exception, That he committed that irregularity to preserve his life. How was it possible for the monsters to persuade themselves, that this sentence was agreeable to God, who is goodness itself!

No less prejudicial to morality than the relying too much on forms and ceremonies, is the treating some sins with great severity; neglecting others equally heinous, or perhaps more so. In a book of rates for absolution, mentioned above, no just distinction is made among sins; some venial sins being taxed at a higher rate than many of the deepest dye. For example, the killing father, mother, brother, sister, or wife, is taxed at five gross; and the same for incest with a mother or sister. The lying with a woman in the church is taxed at six gross; and, at the same time, absolution for usury is taxed at seven gross, and for simony at no less than sixteen gross.*

A maxim adopted by many pious persons, has a smiling appearance, but in its consequences is hurtful both to religion <397> and morality; which is, That to testify our veneration for the Deity, and zeal for his service, the performing public and private worship, and the fulfilling moral duties, are not alone sufficient; that over and above we are bound to fast, to do penance, to honour the priesthood, and to punish the enemies of God, *i.e.* those who differ from us in principle or practice. This maxim, which may be termed *the doctrine of supererogation,* is finely illustrated by an author mentioned above.

> The duties which a man performs as a friend or parent, seem merely owing to his benefactor or children; nor can he be wanting to these duties without breaking through all the ties of nature and morality. A strong inclination may prompt him to the performance: a sentiment of order and moral beauty joins its force to these natural ties: and the whole man is drawn to his duty without any effort or endeavour. Even with regard to the virtues which are more austere, and more founded on reflection, such as public spirit, filial duty, temperance, or integrity: the mo-<398>ral obligation, in our apprehension, removes all pretence to religious merit: and the virtuous conduct is esteemed no more than what we owe to society, and to ourselves. In all this, a superstitious man finds nothing which he has properly performed for the sake of his Deity, or which can peculiarly recommend

---

* A gross is the third part of a ducat.

him to the divine favour and protection. He considers not, that the most
genuine method of serving the Divinity is, by promoting the happiness
of his creatures. He still looks out for some more immediate service of the
supreme Being: and any practice recommended to him, which either
serves to no purpose in life, or offers the strongest violence to his natural
inclinations; that practice he will the more readily embrace, on account
of those very circumstances, which should make him absolutely reject it.
It seems the more purely religious, that it proceeds from no mixture of
any other motive or consideration. And if for its sake he sacrifices much
of his ease and quiet, his claim of merit appears still to rise upon him, in
proportion to the zeal <399> and devotion which he discovers. In restoring
a loan, or paying a debt, his divinity is no wise beholden to him; because
these acts of justice are what he was bound to perform, and what many
would have performed, were there no God in the universe. But if he fast
a day, or give himself a sound whipping, this has a direct reference, in his
opinion, to the service of God. No other motive could engage him to such
austerities. By these distinguished marks of devotion, he has now acquired
the divine favour; and may expect in recompense, protection and safety
in this world, and eternal happiness in the next (a).

My yoke is easy, saith our Saviour, and my burden is light. So they really
are. Every essential of religion is founded on our nature, and to a pure heart
is pleasant in the performance: what can be more pleasant, than gratitude
to our Maker, and obedience to his will in comforting our fellow-creatures?
But enthusiasts are not easily persuaded, that to make ourselves happy in
the exer-<400>cises of piety and benevolence, is the most acceptable service to God that we can perform. In loading religion with unnecessary articles of faith and practice, they contradict our Saviour, by making his yoke
severe, and his burden heavy.* Law, who writes on Christian perfection,
enjoins such unnatural austerity of manners, as to be subversive both of
religion and morality: loose education is not more so. Our passions, when
denied proper exercise, are apt to break their fetters, and to plunge us into
every extravagance: like the body, which squeezed in one part, swells the

---

* An old woman walking with others to a sacrament, was observed to pick out the
worst bits of the road: "I never can do enough," said she, "for sweet Jesus."
(a) Natural History of Religion.

more in another. In the same way of thinking, the pious Jeremy Taylor, treating of mortification, prescribes it as the indispensable duty of a Christian, to give no indulgence even to the most innocent emotions; because, says he, the most indifferent action becomes sinful, when there is no other motive for the performance but barely its being pleasant. <401> Could a malevolent deity contrive any thing more severe against his votaries?

In the same spirit of supererogation, holidays have been multiplied without end, depriving the working poor of time, that would be more usefully employed in providing bread for themselves and families. Such a number of holidays, beside contradicting Providence which framed us more for action than contemplation, have several poisonous effects with respect to morality. The moral sense has great influence on the industrious, who have no time for indulging their irregular appetites: the idle, on the contrary, lie open to every temptation. Men likewise are apt to assume great merit from a rigid observance of holidays and other ceremonies; and having thus acquired, in their opinion, the favour of God, they rely on his indulgence in other matters which they think too sweet for sinners.

Monastic institutions are an improvement upon holidays: the whole life of a monk is intended to be a holiday, dedicated entirely to the service of God. The idleness of the monastic state among Christians, opens a wide door to immorality. <402>

In the third section, penances are handled as a mode of worship, for obtaining pardon of sin. But they are sometimes submitted to by the innocent, in order to procure from the Almighty still more favour than innocence alone is entitled to; in which view, they are evidently a work of supererogation. They seem to have no bad effect with respect to religion as distinguished from morality: the body is indeed tortured unnecessarily; but if enthusiasts voluntarily submit to bodily distresses, they have themselves only to blame. With respect to morality, their bad tendency is not slight. Those who perform extraordinary acts of devotion, conceive themselves peculiarly entitled to the favour of God. Proud of his favour, they attach themselves to him alone, and turn indifferent about every other duty. The favourite of a terrestrial potentate, assumes authority; and takes liberties that private persons dare not venture upon: shall a favourite of Heaven be less indulged? The Faquirs in Hindostan submit to dreadful penances; and,

holding themselves secure of God's favour, they are altogether indifferent about the duty they <403> owe to a neighbour. So much are they above common decency, as to go about naked, not even concealing what modesty hides. The penances enjoined in the Romish church, such as fasting and flagellation, have evidently the same bad tendency.* With respect to fasting in particular, to what good purpose it can serve, except to gluttons, is not readily conceived. Temperance in eating and drinking is essential to health: too much or too little are equally noxious, though their effects are different.†
Fasting therefore ought never to be enjoined to the temperate as a religious duty, because it cannot <404> be acceptable to a benevolent Deity. Listen to a great prophet on that subject: "Behold, ye fast for strife and debate, and to smite with the fist of wickedness; ye shall not fast as ye do this day, to make your voice to be heard on high. Is it such a fast that I have chosen? a day for a man to afflict his soul? Is it to bow down his head as a bulrush, and to spread sackcloth and ashes under him? Wilt thou call this a fast, and an acceptable day to the Lord? Is not this the fast that I have chosen, to loose the bands of wickedness, to undo the heavy burdens, and to let the oppressed go free, and that ye break every yoke? Is it not to deal thy bread to the hungry; and that thou bring the poor that are cast out to thy house? when thou seest the naked, that thou cover him, and that thou hide not thyself from thine own flesh?" (a)

The most extraordinary penance of all is celibacy considered as a religious duty. Many fathers of the church declare against matrimony. St. Jerom in particular says, That the end of matrimony is eternal <405> death; that the earth, indeed, is filled by it, but heaven by virginity. The intemperate zeal of many primitive Christians led them to abstain from matrimony,

---

* A sect of Christians, styled *Flagellantes,* held, that flagellation is of equal virtue with baptism and the other sacraments; that it will procure forgiveness of sin; that the old law of Christ is to be abolished; and a new law substituted, enjoining the baptism of blood to be administered by whipping.

† The Baron de Manstein observes, that the frequent lents enjoined by the Greek church, contribute greatly to promote diseases in the Russian armies. They are forbidden to touch flesh three-fourths of the year. The synod, it is true, grants a dispensation to soldiers during war; but such is the superstition of the people, that few take the benefit of the dispensation. [[Note added in 2nd edition.]]

(a) Isaiah, lviii, 4. &c.

and even from conjugal caresses, if they had the misfortune to be married; believing that the carnal appetite is inconsistent with pure religion. Edward the Confessor was sainted, for no better reason than the abstaining from matrimonial duties. Jovinian, in the fourth century, taught, that all who observe the laws of piety and virtue laid down in the gospel, have an equal title to happiness in another life: consequently, that those who pass their days in celibacy and mortification, are in no respect more acceptable to God than those who live virtuously in marriage without mortification. He published his opinions in a book, against which Jerom wrote a bitter and abusive treatise, still extant. These opinions were condemned by the church, and by St. Ambrose, in a council at Milan; and Jovinian was banished by the Emperor Honorius. Such ridiculous self-denial was not confined to Christians. Strabo mentions a sect among the Thracians, who made a vow of perpetual vir-<406>ginity; and were much respected on that account. Garcilasso mentions virgins in Peru consecrated to the sun: a vestal guilty of frailty was buried alive, her lover hanged, and the inhabitants of the town where she lived put to the sword. Among all the absurd acts of mortification, celibacy is the strongest instance of superstition triumphing over common sense; for what can be more inconsistent with common sense, not to talk of religion, than an endeavour to put an end to the human species? Barbeyrac, *De la Moriae des Peres,* gives examples of fathers of the church who wished to extinguish by celibacy the human species, and to hasten the day of judgment.[33] Some glimpses of reason have abated the zeal of enthusiasts for celibacy; but have not totally extirpated it; for celibacy of the clergy remains to this day a law in the Romish church. It cannot, however, seriously be thought the will of our benevolent God, that his priests should be denied the exercise of natural powers, bestowed on all for a most valuable purpose. This impious restraint, which contradicts the great law of *Increase and multiply,* has opened the door to gross de-<407>bauchery in the pastors of the Romish church, though ecclesiastics ought, of all men, to be the most circumspect in their conduct. Men restrained from what is necessary and proper, are more prone than others to break out into gross irregulari-

---

33. "Barbeyrac . . . day of judgment": added in 2nd edition.

ties.* Marriage is warmly recommended in the laws of Zoroaster. Children are said to be a bridge that conducts men to heaven; and a man who has no children, is held to be under the power of Ahriman. The prayer of a priest who has no children, is held disagreeable to Ormusd.

The celibacy of the clergy was countenanced by the Pope; and enforced from a political consideration, That it united the whole clergy into one compact body, un-<408>der his spiritual Majesty. How short-sighted is man! It was justly esteemed at the time to be the corner-stone of Papal power; and yet became the chief cause of its downfal. Celibacy precipitated the Romish clergy into adultery, fornication, cunning, dissimulation, and every secret vice. Will men of such manners be listened to, when they preach purity to others? There was no medium, but either to reform their own manners, or to give every indulgence to the laity. But ignorance and superstition in the latter, made the former think themselves secure. The restoration of learning broke the charm. Men beginning to think for themselves, were provoked at the dissolute lives of their pastors; and raised a loud cry against them. Reformers were burnt as heretics; and clergymen were held to be emissaries from Satan, to establish his throne upon earth. Knox, that violent reformer, believed seriously that Cardinal Beaton was *a conjured enemy to Christ Jesus.* Providence brings good out of ill. Had not the clergy been dissolute, poor Christians might have laboured under ignorance <409> and ecclesiastic thraldom to this hour. Our reformers, beginning with their pastors, extended insensibly their hatred to the doctrines taught by their pastors. Every article of faith was sifted: the chaff was separated from the corn: and a reformation was established upon the scriptures, rejecting every innovation of the Romish church.

There is not mentioned in history a more impudent disregard of moral

---

* An ingenious writer, mentioned above, makes the following observation: "The celibacy of ecclesiastics was originally introduced by some superstitious refinements on the law of God and nature. Could men have been kept alive without eating or drinking as well as without marriage, the same refinements would have prohibited ecclesiastics from eating and drinking, and thereby have elevated them so much nearer to the state of angels. In process of time, this fanatical interdiction became an instrument of worldly wisdom: and thus, as frequently happens, what weak men began, politicians completed." *Sir David Dalrymple.*

principles, than a privilege assumed by the Bishop of Rome to disengage
men from their oaths and promises: it is not a greater stretch to disengage
them from every duty, whether of morality or of religion. The barons of
Valentia, dreading a persecution against the industrious Moors, their tenants, obtained the following clause to be inserted in their king's coronation-
oath: "That he should not expel the Moriscos, nor force them to be baptized; that he should never desire to be relieved from the oath by a
dispensation from the Pope, nor accept a dispensation if offered." The Emperor Charles V. took this oath solemnly in presence of his nobles; and yet
accepted a dispensation < 410 > from the Pope, absolving him from the oath,
and from the guilt of perjury in breaking it. Augustus King of Poland, in
the treaty of Altramstadt, renounced the kingdom of Poland to his competitor Stanislaus. The defeat of the King of Sweden at Poltowa was an
inviting opportunity to renew his pretensions. A solemn treaty stood in his
way; but the Pope removed that obstacle, by annulling the treaty, and setting him at liberty. The Pope has been known to bestow that wonderful
privilege upon others. Pope Pascal II. having, with a solemn oath, renounced the right of investitures, empowered the cardinals to declare his
oath null. Bishops also, imitating their superior, have assumed the privilege
of dispensing with moral duties. Instances are not rare, of curates being
authorized by their bishop to entertain concubines, paying for each a regular tax of a crown yearly. Nay, in some provincial synods, they are enjoined
to keep concubines, in order to prevent scandal. Common prostitutes, li-
censed in the city of Leghorn, have a church peculiar to themselves, and
must not enter into any other. They follow their trade with the utmost
< 411 > freedom; except in passion-week, during which they must forbear
sinning, under pain of banishment (a).

(a) Sir David Dalrymple, in his Annals of Scotland, vol. II. page 16th, has the following paragraph: "Thus did Edward chastise the Scots for their breach of faith. It is
remarkable, that in the preceding year he himself procured a papal bull, absolving him
from the oath which he had taken for maintaining the privileges of his people. But the
Scots, without papal authority, violated their oaths, and were punished as perjured men.
It is a truth not to be disguised, that in those times the common notions of right and
wrong were, in some sort, obliterated. Conscience, intoxicated with indulgencies, or
stupified by frequent absolution, was no longer a faithful monitor amidst the temptations

The power of bestowing kingdoms, assumed by the Bishop of Rome, was an encroachment on the rules of justice, no less bold. Christian princes, not many ages ago, esteemed the Pope's gift to be their best title of property. In 1346, the Venetians requested the Pope's permission to carry on commerce in Asia, and to purchase there pepper and cinnamon. The <412> Pope not only granted their request, but pronounced anathemas upon any who should dare to interfere in that commerce. Ferdinand and Isabella of Spain applied to Pope Alexander VI. to vest in them the property of America, discovered under their auspices by Columbus. The Pope having formerly granted to the kings of Portugal their discoveries in the East-Indies, both grants were held sacred; and it came to be strenuously disputed, under which of the grants the Molucca islands were comprehended. Both grants proceed upon a narrative, of the power bestowed by Almighty God on the Pope, as successor to St. Peter and vicar of Christ. To imagine that the Almighty would bestow such powers on the Bishop of Rome, or on any human being, shews gross ignorance of the common rights of mankind, and of the government of Providence.

The grossest of all deviations, not only from sound morality, but from pure religion, and the most extensive in its baneful effects, is a doctrine embraced by established churches, not many excepted, That, because heretics are odious in the sight of God, it is the duty of the ortho-<413>dox to extirpate them, root and branch. Observe the consequence: people who differ from the established church are held to be obstinate sinners, deserving punishment here as well as hereafter. The religion of every country is changeable; and the religion at present dominant may soon be under depression; which of course subjects all mankind to the rigour of persecution. An invention more effectual for extirpating the human race, is not within the reach of imagination: the horror of human sacrifices is as nothing in comparison.

Persecution for differences in religion can never take place but where the

---

of interest, ambition, and national animosities." This author, a few pages after, very ingeniously observes, that, in those days, an oath or promise on the honour of knighthood, was the only thing relied on; because the Pope did not pretend to interpose in a point of honour. [[Note added in 3rd edition.]]

ministers of religion are formed into a class, totally distinct from the rest
of the people. They made not a distinct class among the old Romans; who,
far from having any notion of persecution, adopted the gods of every nation they conquered.[34] A learned writer (a) observes, that, as the number
of their gods increased with their conquests, it is possible that they might
have worshipped all the gods in the world. <414> Their belief in tutelar
deities produced that effect. Titus Livius mentions a sect of Bacchanals
spread through Italy. They performed their ceremonies during night; men
and women mixing in the dark, after intemperate eating and drinking.
Never did wicked wretches deserve more exemplary punishment; yet listen
to the following decree of the Roman senate, breathing the true spirit of
toleration. "Ne qua Bacchanalia Romae, neve in Italia essent. Si quis tale
sacrum, solenne, et necessarium duceret, nec sine religione et piaculo se id
omittere posse; apud Praetorem urbanum profiteretur; Praetor senatum
consuleret. Si ei permissum esset, quum in senatu centum non minus essent; ita id sacrum faceret, dum ne plus quinque sacrificio interessent; neu
qua pecunia communis, neu quis magister sacrorum, aut sacerdos esset."*
The Jews were prone to per-<415>secution, because their priests formed a
distinct body. It is true, they believed in tutelar deities: their hatred, however, of neighbouring nations prevailed to make them hold in abhorrence
the worship of every other god. Even among themselves they were abundantly disposed to war; and nothing kept within bounds the Pharisees, the
Saduccees, and the Essenes, their three sects, but terror of the Roman
power. The Christian religion implies toleration in its very nature and principles; and yet became prone to persecution above all others. Christian sects
were enflamed against each other to a degree of brutality; the most opposite

---

* "Let there be no Bacchanalian ceremonies performed in the city, nor within Italy.
If there be any person who reckons it a matter of conscience to perform these rites, and
that he ought not to omit them, let him state his opinion to the city Praetor, who shall
thereupon consult the senate. If liberty be granted him by the senate when no fewer than
a hundred senators are present, let him perform the sacrifice, but privately, in presence
of no greater number than five persons. Let there be no public fund for them, nor any
who shall preside as priest or master of the rites."

(a) Morinus.

34. In the 1st edition this paragraph begins: "The old Romans, far from having any
notion of perfection, adopted the gods of every nation they conquered" [2:464].

to peace and brotherly love, inculcated in the gospel. It was propagated by
the orthodox, that Arius expired in a common jakes, and that his entrails
burst out. The same is related of Huneric King of the Vandals, <416> a
zealous Arian; with the following addition, that being possessed with the
devil, whom he had glutted with the blood of many martyrs, he tore his
flesh with his teeth, and ended his wretched life in the most excrutiating,
though justly deserved torments. The falsehoods every where spread, during the fourteenth century, against the Jews, such as their poisoning the
public fountains, killing Christian infants, and drinking their blood, with
many other falsehoods of the same stamp, were invented, and greedily swallowed, through the influence of religious hatred. Through the same influence a law was once made in England, that a Christian marrying a Jew
should be burnt alive.[35] The greater part of persecutions have been occasioned in the same manner; for men are not so desperately wicked, as to
approve of persecution, unless when blinded by intemperate zeal. The same
religious hatred produced the assassination of the Duke of Guise, and of
two Henries, Kings of France; produced the gunpowder plot; and produced the most horrid deed that ever was perpetrated <417> among men,
the massacre of St. Bartholomew.*

There is no occasion to be particular on the massacre of St. Bartholomew, the circumstances of which are universally known. I shall mention
another, which happened in Lisbon, 6th April 1506, the effect entirely of
bigotry. The day mentioned being Sunday, certain persons in the church
of St. Dominic, observing that a crucifix in one of the chapels was more
than ordinary luminous, the priest cried out, a miracle! a miracle: A new
convert, who had been a Jew, saying slightly that it was but the sun shining
on the crucifix, he was dragged instantly out of the church, and burnt. The
friars, with vehement speeches, encouraged the rabble assembled about the

---

* Monsieur de Tavannes, afterwards Mareschal of France, was a great partisan of the
Queen-mother; and so active in the massacre, as with his own hand to murder no fewer
than seventeen Hugenots. Having on death-bed made a full confession of his sins,
"What," said the priest, "not a word of St. Bartholomew?" "Of St. Bartholomew!" answered the penitent; "the service I did that memorable day to God and the church, is
alone a sufficient atonement for all my transgressions."

35. "Through the same . . . be burnt alive": added in 2nd edition.

fire to more mischief; while <418> other friars ran about the streets bawling out, heresy, heresy, with crucifixes in their hands. Above 500 men gathered together, and slew every new convert they could find, and burnt them to ashes. Next morning they murdered above 1000 men, women, and children, dragging them from the altars, to which they had fled as a sanctuary. The same fury continued the third day, on which above 400 persons more were massacred.[36]

No false principle in religion has shed more innocent or rather virtuous blood, than that of persecuting heretics; *i.e.* those who differ in any article from the religion established by law. The doctrine of burning heretics, is in effect the professing to burn men eminently virtuous; for they must be so, when they submit to be burnt alive, rather than be guilty even of dissimulation. The Mahometan practice of converting people by the sword, if not more rational, is at least more manly. Louis IX. of France, one of its best princes, would have been a greater blessing to his people had he been less pious: he had an implacable aversion to heretics; against whom he thought it more proper to em-<419>ploy racks and gibbets, than argument. Torquemada, that infernal inquisitor of Spain, brought into the inquisition, in the space of fourteen years, no fewer than 80,000 persons; of whom 6000 were condemned to the flames, and burnt alive with the greatest pomp and exultation. Of that vast number, there was perhaps not a single person, who was not more pure in religion, as well as in morals, than their outrageous persecutor. *Hunter,* a young man about nineteen years of age, was one of the unhappy victims to the zeal of Queen Mary of England for Popery. Having been inadvertently betrayed by a priest to deny transubstantiation, he absconded, to keep out of harm's way. Bonner, that archhangman of Popery, threatened ruin to the father, if he did not deliver up the young man. Hunter, hearing of his father's danger, made his appearance, and was burnt alive, instead of being rewarded for his filial piety. A woman of Guernsey was brought to the stake, without regard to her big belly; which bursting by the torture, she was delivered in the midst of the flames. One of the guards snatched the infant from <420> the fire: but the magistrate who attended the execution ordered it to be thrown back; being

36. Paragraph added in 3rd edition.

resolved, he said, that nothing should survive which sprung from a parent so obstinately heretical. Father Paul (*a*) computes that, in the Netherlands alone, from the time that the edict of Charles V. was promulgated against the reformers, fifty thousand persons were hanged, beheaded, buried alive, or burnt, on account of religion. Some Faquirs, crazed with opium and fanaticism, have been known, with poisoned daggers, to fall upon uncircumcised Europeans, and to put every one to death whom they could master. In the last century, a Faquir at Surate murdered, within the space of a minute, seventeen Dutch sailors with seventeen stabs of a dagger. We think with horror of human sacrifices among the ancient Pagans; and yet we behold them every day among Christians, rendered still more horrid by the most atrocious torments that religious hatred can devise. < 421 >

The great motive to such cruelties, is the superstitious and absurd notion, that heretics are God's enemies; which makes it thought an acceptable service to God, not only to persecute them by fire and sword in this world, but to deliver them over to Satan in the world to come. Another circumstance enflames religious hatred; which is, that neighbours are either intimate friends or bitter enemies. This holds with a slight variation in sects of the same religion: however minute their differences are, they cannot be intimate friends; and therefore are bitter enemies: the nearer they approach to unison, if not entirely so, the greater in proportion is their mutual hatred. Such hatred, subduing the meek spirit of Christianity, is an additional cause for persecution. Blind zeal for what is believed to be the only true religion, never discovers error nor innocence in those who differ, but perverseness and criminal obstinacy. Two religions totally different, like two countries in opposite parts of the globe, produce no mutual enmity. At the siege of Constantinople by the Turks, anno 1453, the Emperor, in order to procure assistance from < 422 > the princes of the Latin church, ordered mass to be celebrated in one of his churches according to the form used in Rome. The people with great indignation protested, that they would rather see the Turks in their churches, than the hat of a cardinal.

The history of the Waldenses, though well known, cannot be too often repeated. In the twelfth century, a merchant of Lyons, named *Peter Valdo,*

(*a*) [[Paolo Sarpi,]] Council of Trent, Book 5.

dissatisfied with the pomp and ceremonies of the Romish church, ill suited
in his opinion to the humility of a Christian, retired to a desert in the high
country of Provence, with several poor people his disciples. There he became their spiritual guide, instructing them in certain doctrines, the same
that were afterwards adopted by the Protestants. Their incessant labour
subdued the barren soil, and prepared it for grain as well as for pasture. The
rent which in time they were enabled to pay for land that afforded none
originally, endeared them to their landlords. In 250 years, they multiplied
to the number of 18,000, occupying thirty villages, beside hamlets, the
work of their own hands. Priests they had none, nor any disputes about
religion; neither had <423> they occasion for a court of justice, as brotherly
love did not suffer them to go to law: they worshipped God in their own
plain way, and their innocence was secured by incessant labour. They had
long enjoyed the sweets of peace and mutual affection, when the reformers
of Germany and Geneva sent ministers among them; which unhappily laid
them open to religious hatred, the most unrelenting of all furies. In the year
1540, the parliament of Provence condemned nineteen of them to be burnt
for heresy, their trees to be rooted up, and their houses to be razed to the
ground. The Waldenses, terrified at this sentence, applied in a body to Cardinal Sadolet, bishop of Carpentras; who received them kindly, and obtained from Francis I. of France, a pardon for the persons under sentence
of death, on condition of abjuring heresy. The matter lay over five years;
when the parliament, irritated at their perseverance, prevailed on the King
to withdraw his pardon. The sentence was executed with great rigour; and
the parliament, laying hold of that opportunity, broke through every restraint of law, and commenced a violent persecution <424> against the whole
tribe. The soldiers began with massacring old men, women, and children,
all having fled who were able to fly; and proceeded to burn their houses,
barns, and corn. There remained in the town of Cabriere sixty men and thirty
women; who having surrendered upon promise of life, were butchered all
of them without mercy. Some women who had taken refuge in a church,
were dragged out, and burnt alive. Twenty-two villages were reduced to ashes;
and that populous and flourishing district became once more a desart.

   To conceive this horrid scene in all its deformity, the people persecuted
ought to be compared with the clergy their persecutors; for the civil mag-

istrate was the hand only that executed their vengeance: on the one side, an industrious honest people, pure in their morals, and no less pure in their religion: on the other, proud pampered priests, abandoned without shame to every wickedness, impure in their morals, and still more impure in their religion—the world never furnished such another contrast. Had the scene been reversed, to make these wretches suffer per-<425>secution from the Waldenses—but that people were too upright and too religious for being persecutors. The manners of the Christian clergy in general, before the Reformation, enlivens the contrast. The doctrine promulgated during the dark times of Christianity, That God is a mercenary being, and that every person however wicked may obtain pardon of his sins by money, made riches flow into the hands of the clergy in a plentiful stream. And riches had the same effect upon the Christian clergy that they have upon all men, which is, to produce pride, sensuality, and profligacy: these again produced dissipation of money, which prompted avarice, and every invention for recruiting exhausted treasures.* Even as early as the eighth century, the Christian clergy, tempted by opulence, abandoned themselves to pleasure, without moderation; and far exceeded the laity in luxury, glut-<426>tony, and lust. When such were the pastors, what must have been the flock! Rejoice, O Scotland, over the poverty and temperance of thy pastors. During that period, the clergy could read, and, like parrots, they could mumble prayers in Latin: in every other respect, they rivalled the laity in ignorance. They were indeed more cunning than the laity; and understood their interest better, if to covet riches at the expence of probity, deserve that name. Three articles were established that made religion an easy service. First, That faith is the essence of religion, without regard to good works; and hence the necessity of being strictly orthodox, which the church only could determine. Second, Religious worship was reduced to a number of external ceremonies and forms, which, being declared sufficient for salvation, absolved Christians from every moral duty. Remark, that a priest is always the chief person in ceremonial worship. The third article, That God is a mer-

---

* In the eleventh and twelfth centuries, many of the clergy became merchants; and, being free of taxes, engrossed all. In the Netherlands particularly, there was a great cry, that monasteries were converted into shops and warehouses, and the mansions of secular priests into tap-houses and inns.

cenary being, is mentioned above, with its necessary consequences. These articles brought about a total neglect, both in clergy and laity, not only of morality, but of every <427> essential religious duty. In fine, there never was a religion that deviated more from just principles, than that professed by Christians during the dark ages. Persecution reached none but the sincerely pious and virtuous. What a glorious tolerating sentiment doth Arnobius (a) throw out, and what profusion of blood would have been prevented, had it been adopted by all Christians! "Da veniam, Rex summe, tuos persequentibus famulos: et quod tuae benignitatis est proprium, fugientibus ignosce tui nominis et religionis cultum. Non est mirum, si ignoraris: majoris est admirationis, si sciaris."* The following parable against persecution was communicated to me by Dr. Franklin of Philadelphia, a man who makes a figure in the learned world.

And it came to pass after these things, that Abraham sat in the door of his tent, about the going down of the sun. And behold a <428> man bent with age, coming from the way of the wilderness leaning on a staff. And Abraham arose, and met him, and said unto him, Turn in, I pray thee, and wash thy feet, and tarry all night; and thou shalt arise early in the morning, and go on thy way. And the man said, Nay; for I will abide under this tree. But Abraham pressed him greatly: so he turned, and they went into the tent: and Abraham baked unleavened bread, and they did eat. And when Abraham saw that the man blessed not God, he said unto him, Wherefore dost thou not worship the most high God, creator of heaven and earth? And the man answered and said, I do not worship thy God, neither do I call upon his name; for I have made to myself a god, which abideth always in mine house, and provideth me with all things. And Abraham's zeal was kindled against the man, and he arose, and fell upon him, and drove him forth with blows into the wilderness. And God called unto Abraham, saying, Abraham, where is the stranger? And Abraham answered and said, Lord, he would not worship thee, <429> neither would he call upon thy name; therefore have I driven him out from before my face into the wilderness. And God said, Have I borne with him these hundred ninety and eight years, and nourished

---

* "Forgive, Almighty power, the persecutors of thy servants; and, in the peculiar benevolence of thy nature, pardon those men whose unhappiness it is to be strangers to thy name and worship. Ignorant as they are of thee, we cannot wonder at the impiety of their actions."

(a) Lib. I. Adversus Gentes.

him, and clothed him, notwithstanding his rebellion against me; and couldst not thou, who art thyself a sinner, bear with him one night?

The historical style of the Old Testament is here finely imitated; and the moral must strike every one who is not sunk in stupidity and superstition. Were it really a chapter of Genesis, one is apt to think, that persecution could never have shown a bare face among Jews or Christians. But alas! that is a vain thought. Such a passage in the old Testament, would avail as little against the rancorous passions of men, as the following passages in the New Testament, though persecution cannot be condemned in terms more explicit. "Him that is weak in the faith, receive you, but not to doubtful disputations. For one believeth that he may eat all things; another, who is weak, eateth herbs. Let not him that eateth, despise him that eateth not; and let not him which <430> eateth not, judge him that eateth. Who art thou that judgest another man's servant? to his own master he standeth or falleth. One man esteemeth one day above another; another esteemeth every day alike. Let every man be fully persuaded in his own mind. But why dost thou judge thy brother? or why dost thou set at nought thy brother? for we shall all stand before the judgement-seat of Christ, every one to give an account of himself to God. I know, that there is nothing unclean of itself: but to him that esteemeth any thing unclean, to him it is unclean. The kingdom of God is not meat and drink, but righteousness and peace, and joy in the Holy Ghost. Let us therefore follow after the things which make for peace, and things wherewith one may edify another" (*a*). Our Saviour himself declared against persecution in the most express terms. The Jews and Samaritans were of the same religion; but some trivial differences in the ceremonial part of worship, rendered them odious to each <431> other. Our Saviour being refused lodging in a village of Samaria, because he was travelling to Jerusalem, his disciples James and John said, "Lord, wilt thou that we command fire to come down from heaven, and consume them, even as Elias did?" But he rebuked them, and said, "The Son of Man is not come to destroy men's lives, but to save them" (*b*).*

(*a*) Epistle of Paul to the Romans, chap. 14.

(*b*) Luke ix. 54.

* Toleration in religion, though obvious to common understanding, was not however the production of reason, but of commerce. The advantage of toleration for promoting

It gives me real concern, that even the hot fire of persecution did not altogether purify our Reformed clergy from that satanical spirit. No sooner were the Dissenters settled in New England, where they fled to avoid persecution, than they set on foot a persecution against the Quakers, no less furious than what they them-<432>selves had suffered at home. Nor did the Reformed clergy in Scotland lose sight of the same magisterial authority that had been assumed by their predecessors of the Romish church, on the ridiculous pretext of being ambassadors to men from Jesus Christ. Upon a representation, anno 1646, from the commission of the kirk of Scotland, James Bell and Colin Campbell, bailies of Glasgow, were committed to prison by the parliament, merely for having said, that kirkmen meddled too much in civil matters. Could a despotic prince have exerted a more arbitrary act? but the church was all-powerful in those days.* <433>

---

commerce, was early discovered by the Portuguese. They were too zealous Catholics to think of so bold a measure in Portugal; but it was permitted in Goa, and the inquisition in that town was confined to Roman Catholics. There is a singular example of toleration in the Knights of Malta. That fraternity was instituted to make perpetual war against the Turks; and yet of late years they have erected a mosque for their Turkish prisoners.

* The Christian religion is eminent for a spirit of meekness, toleration, and brotherly love; and yet persecution never raged so furiously in any other religion. Such opposition between practice and principle, is a singular phenomenon in the history of man. Let us try to account for it. In the Pagan religion I discover few traces of persecution. Tutelar deities were universal; and, far from imposing these deities on others, every nation valued itself on being the only favourite of its own deity. Priests by profession have ever been ambitious of imposing on the laity peculiar forms of worship and peculiar religious tenets; but the Greeks and Romans had none such. The Jews had priests by profession; and they were beside a gloomy people naturally inclined to persecution: they hated their neighbours and were hated by them. The Mahometan religion was sown in a fertile soil. The Arabians were warlike; but ignorant and easily deluded by a warm imagination. The Koran is finely contrived to impose upon such a people. The ambition of Mahomet corresponded to the warlike genius of his countrymen; who were taught to convert all men to his religion, by the simple but effectual argument of fire and sword. This spirit of persecution accompanied that of conquest. The latter is now extinguished by luxury and sensuality; and there scarce remains any vestige of the former.

Among an illiterate and credulous people, directed by the light of nature to worship the Deity, but without any established form, every innovation is peaceably and cordially admitted. When Christianity was introduced into Britain, the Druids, as appears from Ossian, had lost all authority. The people were prepared for the new religion; and there could be no persecution where there was none to oppose. Upon that plain people, the Christian religion had its genuine effect: it softened their manners, and produced a spirit

I would do justice to every church, not excepting that of Rome; and it is doing <434> that church no more but justice to acknowledge, that the spirit of persecution was <435> not more eminent in it, than zeal for making

---

of meekness and brotherly love. Never was practice more concordant with principle. The scene is very different where a new religion is introduced in opposition to one long established. Zeal for a new religion inflames its converts; and as violent passions are infectious, those who adhere to the established worship are by degrees equally inflamed. Mutual hatred and persecution are the never failing consequences. This was the case in the countries where the Christian religion was first promulgated.

When that religion began to make a figure, the Roman empire was finely prepared for its reception. The fables of Paganism, which pass current as important truths in days of ignorance, were now exploded as childish and ridiculous. The despotism of the Roman government, and successive irruptions of barbarians, had sunk the Roman people, had filled them with superstitious terrors, and disposed them to embrace any religion that promised happiness either here or in another world. Luckily, the new religion was that of Jesus Christ. The meek spirit of the gospel would in time have prevailed over a religion that was grossly idolatrous: but, unhappily, the zeal of the new converts, and their abhorrence of idolatry, was not confined to argument, but was vented with all the violence of religious hatred. Here, the Man got the better of the Christian. Those of the established religion became equally violent, through the infection of passion; and mutual persecution knew no bounds.

This appears to be a fair account of the mutual persecution between Christians and Pagans. But persecution did not stop there: it raged among different sects of Christians no less than formerly against the common enemy. This requires to be accounted for. Acuteness and subtility formed the character of the Greeks. Every man eminent for learning had his followers: in philosophy many sects were formed, and much disputation and wrangling ensued. The Christian religion was early introduced into Greece; and its votaries were infected with the spirit of the nation: the slightest differences occasioned disputes; and sects were formed upon the slightest differences. In the gospel, eternal happiness is promised to those who believe in Jesus Christ. The true sense was perverted by the bulk of Christians; and salvation was annexed to the mere act of belief, without regard to good works. Men are prone to such a doctrine: they conceive belief to be an easy matter, as it puts no restraint upon their passions: they are extremely willing to believe, provided they be left free to act as they please. Thus as the whole of religion was understood to rest upon belief, the most minute differences in belief, became of the highest importance. That Christ was a divine person sent by God to correct and reform mankind, is the belief of the Arians. This is not believing in Christ, say the orthodox. "You must believe, that he is the Son of God, and equal to the Father." This was a capital dispute. But the spirit of disputation did not rest there: every trifle was made a subject of wrangling; and hence persecution without end. Violent passions were thus encouraged among Christians; and even the most unmanly vices were meritorious to promote the interest of one sect against another. It became a maxim, that ill may be done in order to bring about good; and accordingly every deceit was put in practice by clergymen, not

converts. The former is retiring out <436> of the world; and I wish it most profound rest, never again to awake. People begin to be ashamed of it, as of a garment long out of fashion. Let the other continue for amusement: it is innocent; and if it do no good, it is not productive of so much harm. <437>

The desire of making converts proceeds from two different causes. In superstitious zealots, it proceeds from an opinion, that all who differ from them are in the road to damnation: for which reason, there is a rage of making converts among Roman Catholics; who, without ceremony, deliver over to the flames of hell, every person who is not of their communion. The other cause is more natural: every man thinks himself in the right, especially in matters of consequence; and, for that reason, he is happy to find others of his opinion (a). With respect to the first cause, I beg attention to the following considerations; not with any hope of converting zealots, but to prevent, if possible, others from becoming such. In none of the works of God is variety more happily blended with uniformity, than in the formation of man. Uniformity prevails in the human face with respect to eyes, nose, mouth, and other capital parts: variety prevails in the expressions

---

excepting forgery, in support of their own sect. Such practices were common as early as the third century. The persecuting spirit continues in vigour among the Roman Catholics, against those who deny the infallibility of their sovereign pontiff. It is high treason to disregard his authority; and rebels are persecuted with fire and sword in this world, and with eternal damnation in the next. No sooner had Protestants renounced the Papal authority, than they gave vent to persecution against one another. America was the refuge of many dissenters from the church of England, to avoid persecution at home. But scarce were they established there, when they raised a violent persecution against Quakers, the most innocuous of all sects.

Zeal for a new religion is immoderate. It cools gradually, and at last vanishes where that religion has been long established, and is peaceably submitted to. Then it is, that a salutary truth is discovered, that people of different religions, nay even of different sects, may live peaceably together. In England and Holland, men are permitted to worship God their own way, provided they give no disturbance to society. Holland has given to mankind a glorious example, not only of universal toleration, but of permitting men, without regard to difference of religion, to enjoy all the privileges of a citizen. Even the Jews in Surinam are admitted to bear a part in the government. And that laudable example is copied by Britain with respect to the Roman Catholics in the island Grenade. [[Note added in 2nd edition.]]

(a) Elements of Criticism, vol. 2. p. 493. edit. 5.

of these parts, serving to distinguish one person from another, without hazard of error. In like manner, the minds of men are uniform <438> with respect to their passions and principles; but the various tones and expressions of these, form different characters without end. A face destitute of a nose or of a mouth, is monstrous: a mind destitute of the moral sense, or of a sense of religion, is no less so. But variety of expression in different faces is agreeable, because we relish variety; and a similar variety in the expressions or tones of passion, ought to be equally agreeable. Endless differences in temper, in taste, and in mental faculties, that of reason in particular, produce necessarily variety in sentiment and in opinion. Can God be displeased with such variety, when it is his own work? He requires no uniformity, except with respect to an upright mind and clear conscience, which are indispensable. Here at the same time is discovered an illustrious final cause. Different countenances in the human race, not only distinguish one person from another, but promote society, by aiding us to chuse a friend, an associate, a partner for life. Differences in opinion and sentiment have still more beneficial effects: they rouse the attention, give exercise to the understanding, and sharpen the reasoning facul-<439>ty. With respect to religion in particular, perfect uniformity, which furnisheth no subject for thinking nor for reasoning, would produce langour in divine worship, and make us sink into cold indifference. How foolish then is the rage of making proselytes? Let every man enjoy his native liberty, of thinking as well as of acting; free to act as he pleases, provided only he obey the rules of morality; equally free to think as he pleases, provided only he acknowledge the Great God as his maker and master, and perceive the necessary connection of religion with morality. Strict uniformity in other matters, may be compared to a spring-day, calm and serene; neither so hot as to make us drop a garment, nor so cold as to require an addition; no wind to ruffle, nor rain to make shelter necessary. We enjoy the sweet scene for a moment: we walk, we sit, we muse—but soon fall asleep. Agitation is the element of man, and the life of society. Let us not attempt to correct the works of God: the attempt will betray us into absurd errors. This doctrine cannot be better illustrated than by a con-<440>versation, reported by the Jesuit Tachard, between the King of Siam, and a French ambassador, who, in his master's name, urged that king to embrace the Christian religion. "I am surprised," said his Majesty of Siam, "that the King of France, my good friend, should interest himself so warmly in what concerns God only. He hath given to his creatures different minds and different inclinations, which naturally lead them to differ in opinion. We admire variety in the material world: why not equally admire it in matters of religion? Have we not then reason to believe, that God takes pleasure in all the different forms of worship? Had it been the intention of God to produce uniformity in religion, he would have formed all men with the same mind." Bernier introduces some Gentiles of Hindostan defending their religion much in the same manner: "That they did not pretend their law to be universal; that they did not hold ours to be false, as, for ought they knew, it might be a good law for us; and <441> that God probably made many roads to heaven."

With respect to the other cause above mentioned, the desire of putting people in the right road: To reason others into our religious principles, is natural; but it is not always prudent. I wish my neighbour to be of my opinion, because I think my opinion right: but is there no danger of undermining his religious principles, without establishing better in their stead? Ought I not to restrain my desire of making converts, when the attempt may possibly reduce them to abandon religion altogether, as a matter of utter uncertainty? If a man of clear understanding has, by some unhappy means, been led into error, that man may be set right by fair reasoning: but beware of endeavouring to convert people of low parts, who are indebted for their creed to parents, to education, or to example: it is safer to let them rest as they are.

At any rate, let us never attempt to gain proselytes by rewards, or by terror: what other effect can such motives produce, but dissimulation and lying, parents of every secret crime. The Empress of <442> Russia uses a method for converting her Pagan subjects of Kamskatka, no less agreeable than effectual; which is, to exempt from taxes for ten years, such of them as profess the Christian religion. This practice may be political; but it tends not to advance religion, and is destructive of morality. Terror, on the other hand, may be equally effectual, but is not altogether so agreeable. The people of Rum, one of the Hebrides, were Papists till the beginning of the present century, when in one day they were all proselyted to the Protestant faith. Maclean of Coll, their chieftain, went to the island with a Protestant minister, and ordered all the inhabitants to appear on Sunday at public worship. They came, but refused to hear a Protestant minister. The chieftain reasoned with them: but finding that his reasonings made no impression, he laid hold of the most forward; and having made a deep impression on him with his cane, pushed him into the church. The rest followed like meek lambs; and from that day have continued firm Protestants. The Protestantism of Rum is <443> styled by their Popish neighbours the faith of the *yellow stick*.

To apply any means for making proselytes, other than fair reasoning, appears to me a strange perversion. Can God be pleased with using rewards or punishments, or can any rational man justify them? What then should move any one to put them in practice? I should be utterly at a loss to answer the question, but for a fact mentioned more than once above, that the rude and illiterate judge by sight only, not by reflection. They lay weight on the external visible act, without thinking of intention, which is not visible. In truth, the bulk of mankind rest upon the external profession of religion; they never think of the heart, nor consider how that stands affected. What else is it but the external act merely that moves the Romish missionaries to baptize the infants of savages even at the moment of expiring? which they prosecute with much pious ardour. Their zeal merits applause, but not their judgment. Can any rational person seriously believe, that the dipping a savage or an infant in water will make either of them a Chri-<444>stian, or that the want of this ceremony will precipitate them into hell? The Lithuanians, before their conversion to Christianity, worshipped serpents, every family entertaining one as a household god. Sigismundus, in his commentaries of Muscovy, reports the following incident. A converted Christian having persuaded a neighbour to follow his example, and, in token of his conversion, to kill his serpent, was surprised, at his next visit, to find his convert in the deepest melancholy, bitterly lamenting that he had murdered his god, and that the most dreadful calamities would befal him. Was this person a Christian more than nominally? At the end of the last century, when Kempfer was in Japan, there remained but about fifty Japan Christians, who were locked up in prison for life. These poor people knew no more of the Christian religion, but the names of our Saviour and of the Virgin Mary; and yet so zealous Christians were they, as rather to die miserably in jail, than to renounce the name of Christ, and be set at liberty. The inhabitants of the island Annaboa in the gulf of Guinea have been converted by the Portuguese to Chri-<445>stianity. No more is required of them, as Bosman observes, but to repeat a *Pater Noster,* and *Ave Maria,* confess to the priest, and bring offerings to him.[37]

I cannot with satisfaction conclude this sketch, without congratulating my present countrymen of Britain upon their knowledge of the intimate connection that true religion has with morality. May the importance of that connection, always at heart, excite us to govern every action of our lives by the united principles of morality and religion:—what a happy people would we be! <446> <447>

---

37. "The inhabitants of . . . offerings to him": added in 2nd edition.

Sketches concerning SCOTLAND

১০১ SKETCH I ১০১

Scotch Entails considered in Moral and Political Views[1]

Man is by nature a hoarding animal; and to secure what is acquired by honest industry, the sense of property is made a branch of human nature (*a*). During the infancy of nations, when artificial wants are unknown, the hoarding appetite makes no figure. The use of money produced a great alteration in the human heart. Money having at command the goods of fortune, introduced inequality of rank, luxury, and artificial wants without end. No bounds are <448> set to hoarding, where an appetite for artificial wants is indulged: love of money becomes the ruling passion: it is coveted by many, in order to be hoarded; and means are absurdly converted into an end.

The sense of property, weak among savages, ripens gradually till it arrives at maturity in polished nations. In every stage of the progress, some new power is added to property; and now, for centuries, men have enjoyed every

---

(*a*) Book 1. Sketch 2.

1. An entail is a means of settling property on a number of people in succession, so as to prevent any one of them from selling or mortgaging that property. Kames discusses entails in *Historical Law-Tracts,* Tract 1, "History of Property."

power over their own goods, that a rational mind can desire (*a*): they have
the free disposal during life, and even after death, by naming an heir. These
powers are sufficient for accomplishing every rational purpose: they are sufficient for commerce, and they are sufficient for benevolence. But the artificial wants of men are boundless: not content with the full enjoyment
of their property during life, nor with the prospect of its being enjoyed by
a favourite heir, they are anxiously bent to preserve it to themselves for ever.
A man who has amassed a great estate in land, is miserable at the <449>
prospect of being obliged to quit his hold: to soothe his diseased fancy, he
makes a deed securing it for ever to certain heirs; who must without end
bear his name, and preserve his estate entire. Death, it is true, must at last
separate him from his idol: it is some consolation, however, that his will
governs and gives law to every subsequent proprietor. How repugnant to
the frail state of man are such swollen conceptions! Upon these, however,
are founded entails, which have prevailed in many parts of the world, and
unhappily at this day infest Scotland. Did entails produce no other mischief
but the gratification of a distempered appetite, they might be endured,
though far from deserving approbation: but, like other transgressions of
nature and reason, they are productive of much mischief, not only to commerce, but to the very heirs for whose sake alone it is pretended that they
are made.

Considering that the law of nature has bestowed on man every power
of property that is necessary either for commerce or for benevolence, how
blind was it in the English legislature to add a most irrational <450> power,
that of making an entail! But men will always be mending; and, when a
lawgiver ventures to tamper with the laws of nature, he hazards much mischief. We have a pregnant instance above, of an attempt to mend the laws
of God in many absurd regulations for the poor; and that the law authorising entails is another instance of the same kind, will be evident from what
follows.

The mischievous effects of English entails were soon discovered: they
occasioned such injustice and oppression, that even the judges ventured to
relieve the nation from them by an artificial form, termed *fine and recovery.*

(*a*) Historical Law-tracts, Tract. 3.

And yet, though no moderate man would desire more power over his estate than he has by common law, the legislature of Scotland enabled every land-proprietor to fetter his estate for ever; to tyrannize over his heirs; and to reduce their property to a shadow, by prohibiting them to alien, and by prohibiting them to contract debt, were it even to redeem them from death or slavery. Thus, many a man, fonder of his estate than of his wife and children, grudges the use of it to his natural heirs, reducing them to <451> the state of mere liferenters. Behold the consequences. A number of noblemen and gentlemen among us lie in wait for every parcel of land that comes to market. Intent upon aggrandizing their family, or rather their estate, which is the favourite object, they secure every purchase by an entail; and the same course will be followed, till no land be left to be purchased. Thus every entailed estate in Scotland becomes in effect a mortmain, admitting additions without end, but absolutely barring alienation; and if the legislature interpose not, the period is not distant, when all the land in Scotland will be locked up by entails, and withdrawn from commerce.

The purpose of the present essay, is to set before our legislature, coolly and impartially, the destructive effects of a Scotch entail. I am not so sanguine as to hope, that men, who convert means into an end, and avariciously covet land for its own sake, will be prevailed upon to regard, either the interest of their country, or of their posterity: but I would gladly hope, that the legislature may be roused to give at-<452>tention to a national object of no slight importance.

I begin with effects of a private or domestic nature. To the possessor, an entail is a constant source of discontent, by subverting that liberty and independence, which all men covet with respect to their goods as well as their persons. What can be more vexatious to a proprietor of a great land-estate, than to be barred from the most laudable acts, suitable provisions, for example, to a wife or children? not to mention numberless acts of benevolence, that endear individuals to each other, and sweeten society. A great proportion of the land in Scotland is in such a state that, by laying out a thousand pounds or so, an intelligent proprietor may add a hundred pounds yearly to his rent-roll. But an entail effectually bars that improvement: it affords the proprietor no credit; and supposing him to have the command of money independent of the estate, he will be ill-fated if he have not means to employ it more profitably for his own interest. An entail, at the same time, is no better than a trap for an improvident possessor: to avoid altogether the contracting <453> debt, is impracticable; and if a young man be guided more by pleasure than by prudence, which commonly is the case of young men, a vigilant and rapacious substitute, taking advantage of a forfeiting clause, turns him out of possession, and delivers him over to want and misery.

I beg indulgence for introducing a case, which, though particular, may frequently happen. A gentleman, who has a family-seat finely situated, but in the state of nature, is tempted to lay out great sums upon improvements and embellishments, having a numerous issue to benefit by his operations. They all fail; and a stranger, perhaps his enemy, becomes the heir of entail. Fond, however, of his darling seat, he is willing to preserve all entire, upon procuring to his heirs a reasonable sum for his improvements; which is refused. Averse to lay waste the work of his own hands, he restricts his demand to the real value of the growing timber—All in vain. Provoked at the obstinacy of the heir of entail, he cuts down every tree, dismantles the place; and with a sad heart abandons his beloved habitation. In a bare country <454> like Scotland, is it not cruel to deter proprietors by an entail, from improving their land, and embellishing their family-seats? Is it not still more cruel, to force a proprietor, who has no heir of his own blood, to lay all waste, instead of leaving behind him a monument of his taste and industry?[2]

But an entail is productive of consequences still more dismal, even with respect to heirs. A young man upon whom the family-estate is entailed without any power reserved to the father, is not commonly obsequious to advice, nor patiently submissive to the fatigues of education: he abandons himself to pleasure, and indulges his passions without control. In one word, there is no situation more subversive of morals, than that of a young man, bred up from infancy in the certainty of inheriting an opulent fortune.

The condition of the other children, daughters especially, is commonly deplorable. The proprietor of a large entailed estate leaves at his death children who have acquired a taste for sumptuous living. The sons drop off

---

2. Paragraph added in 2nd edition.

one by one, and a number of daughters remain, with a <455> scanty pro-vision, or perhaps with none at all. A collateral male heir succeeds, who, after a painful search, is discovered in some remote corner, qualified to pro-cure bread by the spade or the plough, but entirely unqualified for behaving as master of an opulent fortune. By such a metamorphosis, the poor man makes a ludicrous figure; while the daughters, reduced to indigence, are in a situation much more lamentable than are the brats of beggars.

Our entails produce another domestic evil, for which no proper remedy is provided. The sums permitted in most entails to younger children, how-ever adequate when the entail is made, become in time too scanty, by a fall in the value of money, and by increase of luxury; which is peculiarly hard upon daughters of great families: the provisions destined for them will not afford them bread; and they cannot hope to be suitably matched, without a decent fortune. If we adhere to entails, nunneries ought to be provided.

But the domestic evils of an entail make no figure, compared with those that respect the public. These in their full ex-<456>tent would fill a volume: they are well known; and it may be sufficient to keep them in view by some slight hints.

As observed above, few tenants in tail can command money for im-provements, however profitable. Such discouragement to agriculture, hurt-ful to proprietors of entailed estates, is still more so to the public. It is now an established maxim, That a state is powerful in proportion to the product of its land: a nation that feeds its neighbours, can starve them. The quantity of land that is locked up in Scotland by entails, has damped the growing spirit of agriculture. There is not produced sufficiency of corn at home for our own consumpt: and our condition will become worse and worse by new entails, till agriculture and industry be annihilated. Were the great en-tailed estates in Scotland split into small properties of fifty or a hundred pounds yearly rent, we should soon be enabled, not only to supply our own markets, but to spare for our neighbours.

In the next place, our entails are no less subversive of commerce than of agriculture. There are numberless land e-<457>states in Scotland of one, two, or three hundred pounds yearly rent. Such an estate cannot afford bare necessaries to the proprietor, if he pretend to live like a gentleman. But he has an excellent resource: let him apply to any branch of trade, his estate will afford him credit for what money he wants. The profit he makes, pays the interest of the money borrowed, with a surplus; and this surplus, added to the rent of his estate, enables him to live comfortably. A number of land-proprietors in such circumstances, would advance commerce to a great height. But alas! there are not many who have that resource: such is the itch in Scotland for entailing, as even to descend lower than one hundred pounds yearly. Can one behold with patience, the countenance that is given to selfish wrong-headed people, acting in direct opposition to the prosperity of their country? Commerce is no less hurt in another respect: when our land is withdrawn from commerce by entails, every prosperous trader will desert a country where he can find no land to purchase; for to raise a family, by acquiring an estate in land, is the <458> ultimate aim of every merchant, and of every man who accumulates money.

Thirdly, An entail is a bitter enemy to population. Population depends greatly on the number of land-proprietors. A very small portion of land, managed with skill and industry, affords bread to a numerous family; and the great aim of the frugal proprietor, is to provide a fund for educating his children, and for establishing them in business. A numerous issue, at the same time, is commonly the lot of the temperate and frugal; because luxury and voluptuousness enervate the body, and dry up the sources of procreation. This is no chimera or fond imagination: traverse Europe; compare great capitals with distant provinces; and it will be found to hold universally, that children abound much more among the industrious poor, than among the luxurious rich. But if division of land into small properties, tend to population; depopulation must be the necessary consequence of an entail, the avowed intent of which is to unite many small properties in one great estate; and consequently, to <459> reduce land-proprietors to a small number.

Let us, in the fourth place, take under consideration the children of land-holders with respect to education and industry; for, unless men be usefully employed, population is of no real advantage to a state. In that respect, great and small estates admit no comparison. Children of great families, accustomed to affluence and luxury, are too proud for business; and, were they even willing, are incapable to drudge at a laborious employment. At the same time, the father's hands being tied up by his entail from affording them suitable provisions, they become a burden on the family, and on the state, and can do no service to either, but by dying. Yet there are men so blind, or so callous, as to be fond of entails. Let us try whether a more pleasing scene will have any effect upon them. Children of small land-holders are from infancy educated in a frugal manner; and they must be industrious, as they depend on industry for bread. Among that class of men, education has its most powerful influence: and upon that class a nation chiefly relies, for <460> its skilful artists and manufacturers, for its lawyers, physicians, divines, and even for its generals and statesmen.

And this leads to consider, in the fifth place, the influence that great and small estates have on manners. Gentlemen of a moderate fortune, con-nected with their superiors and inferiors, improve society, by spreading kindly affection through the whole members of the state. In such only re-sides the genuine spirit of liberty, abhorrent equally of servility to superiors, and of tyranny to inferiors. The nature of the British government creates a mutual dependence of the great and small on each other. The great have favours to bestow: the small have many more, by their privilege of electing parliament-men; which obliges men of high rank to affect popularity, how-ever little feeling they may have for the good of their fellow creatures. This connection produces good manners at least, between different ranks, and perhaps some degree of cordiality. Accumulation of land into great estates, produces opposite manners: when all the land in Scotland is swallowed up by a number of grandees, and few gentlemen of the middle <461> rank are left; even the appearance of popularity will vanish, leaving pride and insolence on the one hand, and abject servility on the other. In a word, the distribution of land into many shares, accords charmingly with the free spirit of the British constitution; but nothing is more repugnant to that spirit, than overgrown estates in land.

In the sixth place, Arts and sciences can never flourish in a country, where all the land is engrossed by a few. Science will never be cultivated by the dispirited tenant, who can scarce procure bread; and still less, if possible, by the insolent landlord, who is too self-sufficient for instruction. There will be no encouragement for arts: great and opulent proprietors, fostering ambitious views, will cling to the seat of government, which is far removed from Scotland; and if vanity make them sometimes display their grandeur at their country-seats, they will be too delicate for any articles of luxury but what are foreign. The arts and sciences being thus banished, Scotland will be deserted by every man of spirit who can find bread elsewhere. <462>

In the seventh place, Such overgrown estates will produce an irregular and dangerous influence with respect to the House of Commons. The parliament-boroughs will be subdued by weight of money; and, with respect to county-elections, it is a chance if there be left in a county as many qualified landholders as to afford a free choice. In such circumstances, will our constitution be in no danger from the ambitious views of men elevated above others by their vast possessions? Is it unlikely, that such men, taking advantage of public discord, will become an united body of ambitious oppressors, overawing their sovereign as well as their fellow-subjects? Such was the miserable condition of Britain, while the feudal oligarchy subsisted: such at present is the miserable condition of Poland: and such will be the miserable condition of Scotland, if the legislature do not stretch out a saving hand.

If the public interest only were to be regarded, entails ought to be destroyed root and branch. But a numberless body of substitutes are interested, many of whom would be disinherited, if the tenants in tail had power. To reconcile as <463> much as possible these opposite interests, it is proposed that the following articles be authorised by a statute. First, That the act of parliament 1685 be repealed with respect to all future operations.[3] Second, That entails already made and completed, shall continue effectual to such substitutes as exist at the date of the act proposed; but shall not benefit any substitute born after it. Third, That power be reserved to every proprietor, after the act 1685 is at an end, to settle his estate upon what heirs he thinks proper, and to bar these heirs from altering the order of succession; these powers being inherent in property at common law.

At the same time, the prohibiting entails will avail little, if trust-deeds be permitted in their utmost extent, as in England. And therefore, in order to re-establish the law of nature with respect to land-property, a limitation of trust-deeds is necessary. My proposal is, That no trust-deed, directing or limiting the succession of heirs to a land-estate, shall be effectual beyond the life of the heirs in existence at the time. <464>

---

3. This was the act of parliament that introduced entails into Scots law.

Government of Royal Boroughs in Scotland

By a royal borough is in Scotland understood, an incorporation that hold their lands of the crown, and are governed by magistrates of their own naming. The administration of the annual revenues of a royal borough, termed the *common good,* is trusted to the magistrates; but not without control. It was originally subjected to the review of the Great Chamberlain; and accordingly the chap. 39. § 45. of the *Iter Camerarii,* contains the following articles, recommended to the Chamberlain, to be inquired into. "Giff there be an good assedation and uptaking of the common good of the burgh, and giff faithful compt be made thereof to the community of the burgh; and giff no compt is made, he whom and in quhaes hands it is come, and how it passes by the community." In pur-<465>suance of these instructions, the Chamberlain's precepts for holding the ayr, or circuit, is directed to the provost and bailies, enjoining them "to call all those who have received any of the town's revenues, or used any office within the burgh, since the last chamberlain-ayr, to answer such things as shall be laid to their charge." *Iter Camer. Cap.* 1. And in the third chapter, which contains the forms of the chamberlain-ayr, the first thing to be done after fencing the court, is, to call the bailies and serjeants to be challenged and accused from the time of the last ayr.

This office, dangerous by excess of power, being suppressed, the royal boroughs were left in a state of anarchy. There being now no check or control, the magistracy was coveted by noblemen and gentlemen in the neighbourhood; who, under the name of office-bearers, laid their hands on the revenues of the borough, and converted all to their own profit. This corruption was heavily complained of in the reign of James V.; and a remedy

was provided by act 26. parl. 1535, enacting, 1st, That none be quali-
<466>fied to be provost, bailie, or alderman, but an indwelling burgess.
2dly, "That no inhabitant purchase lordship out of burgh, to the terror of
his comburgesses. And, 3dly, That all provosts, bailies, and aldermen of
boroughs, bring yearly to the chequer, at a day certain, the compt-books
of their common-good, to be seen and considered by the Lords Auditors,
giff the same be spended for the common well of the burgh, or not, under
the penalty of losing their freedom. And that the saids provosts, bailies, and
aldermen, warn yearly, fifteen days before their coming to the chequer, all
those who are willing to come for examining the said accounts, that they
may impugn the same, in order that all murmur may cease in that behalf."
And to enforce these regulations, a brieve was issued from the chancery,
commanding the magistrates to present their accounts to the exchequer,
and summoning the burgesses to appear and object to the same.

A defect in this statute made it less effectual than it was intended to
be. Magistrates, to avoid the penalty, brought the count-books of their
common-good <467> to the exchequer; but they brought no rental of the
common-good to found a charge against them. This defect was remedied
by act 28. parl. 1693, containing the following preamble. "That the royal
boroughs, by the mal-administration of their magistrates, have fallen under
great debts and burdens, to the diminution of their dignity, and the dis-
abling of them to serve the crown and government as they ought; and that
the care, oversight, and control, of the common-good of boroughs, belong
to their Majesties by virtue of their prerogative-royal; therefore, for preventing the like abuses and misapplications in all time thereafter, their Majesties statute and ordain, That every burgh-royal shall, betwixt and the first
of November next, bring to the Lords of Treasury and Exchequer an exact
account of charge and discharge, subscribed by the magistrates and town-
clerk, of their whole public-good and revenues, and of the whole debts and
incumbrances that affect the same." This completed the remedy, by putting
means into the hands of the Barons of Exchequer to control the ac-
<468>counts enjoined by the former statute to be yearly given in.

The foregoing regulations are kept in observance. Every year a precept
issues from the exchequer, signed by one of the Barons, addressed to the
director of the chancery, requiring him to make out a brieve for every royal

borough. The brieve is accordingly made out, returned to the exchequer, and sent to the several sheriffs, to be served in all the royal boroughs within their bounds, as directed by the statute. These brieves are accordingly so served by the sheriffs; and particularly it is a constant form in most of the royal boroughs, to issue a proclamation, fifteen days before the day named for appearance in exchequer, warning the inhabitants to repair there, in order to object to the public accounts of the town: and further, in order to give them opportunity to frame objections, the book and counts are laid open for these fifteen days, to be inspected by all the inhabitants.

We learn from the records of exchequer, that, from the year 1660 to the year 1683, accounts were regularly given in to ex-<469>chequer, in obedience to the statute. The town of Edinburgh only having failed for some short time, Captain Thomas Hamilton merchant there, by an action in exchequer, compelled the magistrates to produce upon oath their treasurer's accounts, which were accordingly audited. And we also learn, that, from the Restoration down to the Union, a clerk to the borough-roll was appointed by the crown, whose proper business it was to examine and audite the accounts of the boroughs.

Notwithstanding the foregoing salutary regulations, and the form constantly practised to make them effectual, the boroughs of late years have forborn to present their accounts in exchequer; hoping that they would be overlooked by the English court of exchequer, established in Scotland after the Union; which accordingly happened. This neglect in the court of exchequer is greatly to be regretted, because it reduces the royal boroughs, by the mal-administration of their magistrates, to the same miserable condition that is so loudly complained of in the statutes above mentioned. It is undoubtedly in the power of the Barons to restore good <470> government to the boroughs, by compelling the magistrates to account yearly in the court of exchequer, according to the foregoing regulations: no more is necessary, but to signify publicly that they are resolved to put these regulations in execution.

How beneficial that step would be to this country in general, and to the royal boroughs in particular, will appear from considering, first, the unhappy consequences that result from suffering magistrates to dispose of the town's revenues, without any check or control; and next, the good effects that must result from a regular and careful management, under the inspection of the King's judges.

The unhappy consequences of leaving magistrates without any check or control, are too visible to be disguised. The revenues of a royal borough are seldom laid out for the good of the town, but in making friends to the party who are in possession of the magistracy; and in rioting and drunkenness, for which every pretext is laid hold of, particularly that of hospitality to strangers. Such mismanagement tends to idleness, and corruption of man-<471>ners; which accordingly are remarkable in most royal boroughs. Nor is the contagion confined within the town: it commonly spreads all around.

Another consequence no less fatal, of leaving magistrates to act without control, is a strong desire in every licentious burgess, of stepping into the magistracy, for his own sake, and for that of his friends. Hence the factions and animosities that prevail in almost all the royal boroughs; which are violently and indecently pursued, without the least regard to the good of the community.

The greatest evil of all, respects the choice of their representatives in parliament. A habit of riot and intemperance, makes them fit subjects to be corrupted by every adventurer who is willing to lay out money for purchasing a seat in parliament. Hence the infamous practice of bribery at elections, which tends not only to corrupt the whole mass of the people, but, which is still more dreadful, tends to fill the House of Commons with men of dissolute manners, void of probity and honour.

But, turning from scenes so dismal, let <472> us view the beautiful effects that result from an administration regularly carried on, as directed by the statutes above mentioned. The revenues of the royal boroughs are supposed to be above L. 40,000 yearly. And were this sum, or the half of it, prudently expended, for promoting arts and industry among the numerous inhabitants of royal boroughs; the benefit, in a country so narrow and poor as Scotland, would be immense: it would tend to population, it would greatly increase industry, manufactures, and commerce, beside augmenting the public revenue. In the next place, as there would be no temptation for designing men to convert the burden of magistracy into a benefit, faction and discord would vanish; and there would be no less solicitude to shun the burden, than at present is seen to obtain it. None would submit to the burden but the truly patriotic, men who would chearfully bestow their time, and perhaps their money, upon the public; and whose ambition it would be to acquire a character, by promoting industry, temperance, and honesty, among their fellow-citizens. <473>

And when the government of the royal boroughs comes to be in so good hands, bribery, which corrupts the very vitals of our constitution, will be banished of course. And considering the proper and constitutional dependence of the royal boroughs upon the king's judges, we may have reasonable assurance, that few representatives will be chosen, but who are friends to their country and to their sovereign. <474>

Plan for improving and preserving in order the Highways in Scotland

PREFACE.

Highways have in Scotland become a capital object of police, by the increase of inland commerce, upon which bad roads are a heavy tax. Happily for our country, no person is ignorant of this truth; and we see with pleasure the fruits of their conviction in various attempts, public and private, to establish this valuable branch of police upon the best footing. As this is no easy task, it may reasonably be hoped, that men interested will seriously apply to it, and will freely produce such hints as occur to them. In the latter view, the following plan is offered to the public: and if, from the various proposals that have been or shall be published, an effective plan can be framed, such as completely to answer its purpose, it <475> may safely be pronounced, that it will produce more benefit to this country, than has been produced by any other single improvement since the union of the two kingdoms.

1. The justices of peace, commissioners of supply, the sheriff or stewart depute, and the first magistrate of royal boroughs, shall be commissioners for making and repairing highways, bridges, and ferries, in the several shires and stewartries. All the powers given by law to the justices of peace, and commissioners of supply, with respect to highways, bridges, and ferries, shall be transferred to them; and any two shall be a quorum, except where a greater number is required by this act.

2. The sheriff or stewart depute shall appoint the first day of meeting of the said commissioners, as soon as may conveniently be after the date of the act, by an intimation at each parish-church upon a Sunday, at the close of the forenoon service. And the last Tuesday of March shall yearly thereafter be a day of meeting at the head borough of the shire or stewartry, in place of the first or third Tuesday of May <476> appointed by former acts. The commissioners shall appoint a preses, convener, and clerk: and they shall be impowered to adjourn themselves from time to time.

3. The commissioners, at their first meeting, shall divide the shire or stewartry into two or more districts, as they see convenient. And if they cannot overtake this work at that meeting, they shall appoint proper persons to form a plan of the intended divisions, which plan shall be reported to the commissioners at their next meeting, in order to be approved or altered by them. This being settled, the commissioners shall appoint the heritors in these several districts, or any three of them, to meet on a certain day and place, to make lists of the whole public roads within their respective districts, and to settle the order of reparation, beginning with those that are the most frequented. The proceedings of these district meetings must be reported to the commissioners at their next meeting; who are empowered to settle the order of reparation, in case of variance among the heritors; and also to add any road that may have been omitted. And they shall record a scheme or plan of the <477> whole roads in the shire, thus enlisted, with their resolutions thereupon, to be seen in the clerk's hands *gratis*. But upon any just cause appearing in the course of administration, the commissioners shall be empowered to alter or vary this plan, provided it be at a meeting previously appointed for that purpose, and where three fifths at least of the commissioners are present.

4. If the sheriff or stewart neglect to appoint the first meeting of the commissioners, he shall incur a penalty of L. 100, upon a summary complaint to the court of session by any one heritor of the shire, with costs of suit; the one half of the penalty to the plaintiff, and the other half to be applied by the commissioners for the purposes of this act. If the commissioners fail to meet at the day appointed by the sheriff or stewart, or fail to divide the shire or stewartry into districts, within six months of their first meeting, the sheriff or stewart depute, under the foresaid penalty, shall be

bound to do that work himself; and also to appoint the heritors in the several districts, or any three of them, to make lists of the public roads as <478> above mentioned, and to report their resolutions to him; and he is empowered to settle the order of reparation, in case of variance among the heritors. If the heritors fail to meet, and to make a list of the roads as aforesaid, this work shall be performed by the sheriff or stewart depute himself. And he shall be indemnified of whatever expences he is at in prosecuting the said work, out of the sums that are to be levied by authority of this act, in manner after mentioned, with an additional sum for his own trouble, to be named by the circuit judges.

5. No person shall act as a commissioner upon this statute, but who has an estate within the county of L. 200 Scots valuation, or is heir-presumptive to such an estate, or is named a commissioner *virtute officii,* under the penalty of L. 20 Sterling *toties quoties,* to be prosecuted before any competent court, by a popular action, with costs of suit; the one half to the plaintiff, the other half to the purposes of this act.

6. Whereas the sum of 10 d. directed by the act 1669 to be imposed upon each L. 100 of valued rent, is insufficient for the <479> purposes therein expressed; and whereas the six days statute-work for repairing the highways is in many respects inconvenient; therefore, instead of the 10 d. and instead of the statute-work, the commissioners, together with the heritors possessed of L. 200 Scots of valued rent, five, whether commissioners or heritors, making a quorum, shall annually, upon the said last Tuesday of March, assess each heritor in a sum not exceeding[1]   upon each L. 100 valued rent; the assessment imposed on the heritors to be levied by the collector of supply, along with the cess, and by the same legal remedies. The heritors are entitled to relieve themselves of the one half of the said assessment, by laying the same upon their tenants, in proportion to the rent they pay; an heritor being always considered as a tenant of the land he has in his natural possession.

7. With respect to boroughs of royalty, regality, and barony, and large trading villages, the commissioners are empowered to levy from each house-

---

1. There is a space in the text here, where Kames should have indicated how much more than 10 pence in each 100 pounds of valued rent would support his scheme.

holder, a sum not exceeding 2 s. yearly, more or less in proportion to the assessment of the shire, to be paid within forty days after notice <480> given, under the penalty of double, besides expence of process. Provided, that any of these householders who have country-farms, by which they contribute to relieve their landlords as above mentioned, shall be exempted from this part of the assessment.

8. If the commissioners and heritors neglect to assess their shire, or name so small a sum as to be an elusory assessment, insufficient to answer the purposes of this act, the court of justiciary, or the circuit-judges, are in that case empowered and required to lay on the highest assessment that is made lawful by this act. In case of a total omission, the commissioners and heritors who, by neglecting to convene without a good cause of absence, have occasioned the said omission, shall be subjected each of them to a penalty of L. 20 Sterling. And to make these penalties effectual, the trustees for fisheries and manufactures are appointed to sue for the same before the court of session, and to apply the same, when recovered, to any useful purpose within the shire, especially to the purposes of this act. And to preserve the said fines entire for the public <481> service, the trustees shall be entitled to costs of suit.

9. The sums levied as aforesaid shall be laid out annually upon the highways, bridges, and ferries, for making, repairing, or improving the same; proceeding regularly with the reparation according to the scheme or plan ordered as above to be settled in each shire and stewartry.

10. With respect to roads that are not the first in order, and for which there is no interim provision by this act during reparation of the more frequented roads, the commissioners are empowered to exact from cottars and day-labourers their statute-work, according to the acts presently in force, to be applied to these secondary roads. The statute-work is not to be demanded unless for this purpose; and is to cease totally after the highways have, by means of the present act, been once totally repaired.

11. The commissioners and heritors, at all their meetings, shall bear their own charges.

12. The clause in the act 1661, empowering heritors, at the sight of the sheriff, to cast about highways for their con-<482>venience, shall be repealed; and it shall be declared unlawful, in time coming, to turn about or

change any highway, unless for the benefit of the public, as by shortening it, carrying it through firmer ground, or making it more level; and to that purpose the commissioners shall be empowered to turn about highways, as also to widen the same, not exceeding thirty feet, free of ditches. But the commissioners shall have no power to carry a road through any house, garden, orchard, or pleasure-ground.

13. The commissioners shall have power to take from the adjacent lands, stones, sand, gravel, or other materials for making the highways, paying always for the damage done.

14. With respect to highways that bound the properties of neighbouring heritors, which it may be found necessary to alter or widen, the commissioners shall be empowered to adjudge to one heritor any small bits of ground cut off from the other by the road so altered; and if land cannot be given for land, to make a compensation in money, valuing the land at the current price of the market. <483>

15. In order to prevent water stagnating on the highways, the commissioners shall be empowered to make ditches or drains through neighbouring grounds; and such ditches or drains shall be preserved entire by the proprietors of the land, or at their charges.

16. As the foresaid assessment, after repairing the highways, may not be sufficient for building bridges or making ferries, where rivers are large; any five of the commissioners may, for building bridges or making ferries, establish a pontage or toll; so much for horses, so much for horned cattle, and so much for sheep, and the double for each beast in a wheel-carriage. Upon the credit of the toll, the said commissioners may borrow money, to be employed wholly upon the bridge or ferry where the toll is gathered.

But before borrowing, an estimate must be made of the expence of the work. After the work is finished, the sum bestowed on it must be ascertained: an accurate account must be kept of the gradual payment of this sum by the toll; and when it is completely paid, the commissioners must declare the bridge or ferry to be free. <484>

17. The determinations of the commissioners shall be final, unless complained of in manner following.

18. If any heritor apprehend that undue preference is given to a certain highway, or conceive himself aggrieved by any order or sentence of the

commissioners, it shall be lawful for him, within forty days of the act complained of, to enter a complaint in the court of session; and the judgement
upon such complaint shall be final. But such complaint shall only be effectual for damages, and shall not stay execution of the work. At the same
time, no complaint shall be admitted till security be given to pay full costs,
in case the plaintiff be found in the wrong.

19. Former laws concerning highways, bridges, or ferries, to continue in
force, unless as far as altered by this act.

20. An annual state of what is done by virtue of this act, made by the
commissioners, or their clerk, shall, before the last Tuesday of March, be
laid before the trustees for fisheries and manufactures, in order to be made
a part of their annual report to the King; and these trustees shall direct
proper persons to inspect what <485> work is done upon the high-roads,
and in what manner. Upon any misapplication or embezzlement of the
money levied, any neglect in levying, or any wrong done to the public contrary to the intention of this act, the trustees are required to set on foot and
prosecute what redress is competent in law or equity, provided the prosecution be commenced within a year after the offence.

Query, Ought not broad wheels to be required?   <486>

Considerations that support the preceding Plan.

The laws in Scotland relating to this branch of public police, are numerous;
some enacted while Scotland was a separate kingdom, some after its union
with England. It is not the purpose of this essay to enter into a detail of
the various regulations established by these laws: they are generally known;
and in the late abridgement of our statute-law, they are all recapitulated
with brevity and precision.[2] It shall suffice cursorily to observe, that the acts
made during the reign of Charles II. form the ground-work of our regulations concerning highways: the later acts are little more than explanatory
of the former.

It seems to have been the plan of the legislature, that highways should

2. Kames refers to his own *Statute Law of Scotland Abridged.*

be repaired by those who are employed in husbandry; and accordingly, the six days <487> annual labour is, in the statutes of Charles II. imposed upon them only.

This was a measure not ill suited to the state of Scotland at that period. During the last century, we had little inland commerce to require good roads, except that of corn carried to market; and for that reason, it was natural to impose upon husbandmen the burden of repairing highways. These persons, at the same time, passing the whole summer in idleness, unless when called to perform personal services to capricious and unfeeling landlords, could not think it a hardship to have some part of their time employed in serving themselves instead of their landlords.

That annual labour upon highways, limited to a few days, should be required from men in that condition, appears not unjust. And why may we not suppose the legislature at that time capable of such enlarged views, as to prefer this method for repairing highways, in order to bring on gradually a habit of labour and industry? But the condition of Scotland at present differs widely from what it was in the reign of Charles II.; and the regulations for repairing highways which were <488> then proper, have, by alteration of circumstances, become both unjust and inexpedient.

Unjust they have become in a high degree. Inland commerce, which begins to flourish in Scotland, is greatly promoted by good roads; and every dealer, and indeed every traveller, profits by them. But no men are less interested in good roads than day-labourers, or those who are commonly called *cottars;* and yet these chiefly are burdened with the reparation. Such men, at the same time having commonly many children, find it difficult to support their families, even with their utmost industry. Nothing can be more unjust, than to impose upon such men an annual tax of six days labour for repairing roads, the goodness of which contributes little or nothing to their convenience.

Our present laws are inexpedient, as well as unjust. In the first place, a tax of this nature discourages the propagation of children, in which the strength of a state consists: the poor labourer ought to be encouraged with a reward, instead of being discouraged with a tax. In the next <489> place, cottars called out to perform the statute-work, obey with reluctance, and trifle away time without doing any thing effectual. To enforce the law, and to compel such men to labour, is grievous to the gentlemen who are empowered to execute the law: they cannot punish with rigour or firmness men who have so good reason to decline the service: they are soon disgusted with being taskmasters, and the generality desist altogether.

Laws concerning private property are always kept in observance; and they execute themselves, as is commonly expressed, because there are always a multitude of individuals strongly interested to have them executed. But, in making public laws, the great difficulty has ever been, to lay down effectual measures for putting them in execution: by what means to make such laws execute themselves, is one of the most intricate problems in politics. Our laws concerning highways, are eminently defective in that respect: and accordingly, though most of them have existed near a century, they never have at any period been executed to any extent. Take the following specimen, among ma-<490>ny that may be urged, of this defect. Overseers are forced into the service under a penalty, in order to compel the peasants to perform faithfully their six days labour. To hope any good from a reluctant overseer set over a set of reluctant labourers, is a fond conceit: it is much if his resentment tempt him not to encourage their idleness. In vain would we expect, that any overseer, without a suitable reward, will exert himself in promoting the work.

To remedy the hardship of laying the burden of reparation upon those who are least able and least benefited, and at the same time to make this remedy effectual, is the purpose of the foregoing plan. And upon considering the matter in its different views, the only method that promises success, appears to be a county-tax laid upon land according to the valuation, and a capitation-tax on the inhabitants of boroughs. These taxes relieve the labouring poor, and lay the burden where it ought to be laid: and the law will execute itself, if that effect can be hoped from any public law: effectual measures are laid down for levying the tax; and, if <491> once levied, there is no danger of its being allowed to lie unemployed in the hands of the collector, for every heritor will be anxious to have some part employed for his benefit. The danger will rather be of factious disputes about the distribution. This danger also is attempted to be prevented; and, it is hoped, with success.

Some narrow-minded persons may possibly grudge a tax, that loads the present generation for the advantage of those who come after: but is it rational to grudge, that others should benefit by measures evidently calculated for advancing our own interest? Let us suppose, that the heritors of a shire were to concert measures in common, for improving their lands: to make good roads would be one effectual measure; for, supposing their reparation to cost L. 5000, their estates would be bettered double that sum.

To conclude: it is not to be expected that any regulations concerning highways, or concerning any branch of police, can be so framed as to please every individual. Wise men are practicable men, to use an expression of Lord Bacon, and will make concessions, in order to promote a general <492> good, if without such concessions it cannot be obtained. Better far to have a good law, though, in our opinion, defective in some articles, than to have no law at all; or, which is worse, a law eminently defective, unjust, and inexpedient.

FINIS.

LATIN TAGS AND PHRASES

ad valorem: according to the value

aliquando bonus dormitat Homerus: sometimes even the excellent Homer nods (a common misquotation of Horace, *Ars poetica,* l. 359)

amor patriae: love of country

cessio bonorum: surrender of the goods

credat Judeus Apella: the Jew Apella may believe that (Horace, *Satires,* bk. I, v, l. 100. The line continues *non ego:* but not I)

credo quia impossibile est: I believe it because it is impossible (a common misquotation of Tertullian's *certum est, quia impossibile est:* it is certain because it is impossible)

de hereditate viventis: concerning the inheritance of a living person

delenda est Carthago: Carthage must be destroyed

fides punica: Carthaginian fidelity (i.e., treachery)

gratis: free of charge

hic labor, hoc opus est (should be: *hoc opus, hic labour est*): this is the task, this is the toil (Virgil, *Aeneid,* bk. VI, l. 129)

in lucro captando: in the making of profit

lex talionis: the law of punishment in kind

mens sana in corpore sano: a healthy mind in a healthy body

meum et tuum: mine and thine

nudus cum nuda: a naked man with a naked woman

officina gentium: the workshop of the world

o tempora! o mores!: what times! what manners! (Cicero, *In Catilinam* I, 1)

patria potestas: the power of the father (i.e., the power bestowed by Roman law upon the father of a family over his children, grandchildren, and other descendants)

per aes et libram: by bronze and scales (a form of testament involving the fictitious sale of the inheritance to the heir)

per fas et nefas: by fair means or foul

pro aris et focis: in defense of one's altars and hearths (i.e., in defense of one's home)

quaeritur: it might be asked

quidlibet ex quolibet: everything from anything

sanctum sanctorum: holy of holies

solatium: damages awarded by way of reparation for injury to feelings

terra australis incognita: unknown southern land (i.e., a continent supposed to exist south of the Pacific Ocean)

toties quoties: as often as the thing shall happen

ultima voluntas: last will

virtute officii: by virtue of one's office

vis major: a superior force

BIBLIOGRAPHY

Aa, Pieter van der (1659–1733). *Recueil de divers voyages curieux, faite en Tartarie, en Pèrse, et ailleurs.* Leyden, 1729.

Adamnan, Saint (ca. 625–704). *Vita S. Columbae.*

Aelian (Claudius Aelianus, ca. 170–235). *Varia historia.*

Agathias (ca. 531–ca. 580). *De imperio et rebus gestis Iustiniani imperatoris.*

Aldrovandi, Ulisse (1522–ca. 1605). Author of various works of natural history.

Alexandria, Alexander of (d. 1523). *Geniales dies.*

Ammianus Marcellinus (ca. 330–95). *Rerum gestarum libri qui supersunt.* Translated by John C. Rolfe. Loeb Classical Library. Harvard University Press: Cambridge, Mass., 1935.

Anson, George, Baron (1697–1762). *A Voyage Around the World in the Years 1740, 1, 2, 3, 4.* London, 1748.

Appian (fl. ca. A.D. 160). *De bellis civilibus.*

Arnobius Afer (second half of third century A.D.). *Adversus gentes.*

Arrian (Flavius Arrianus, b. A.D. 85–90). *Anabasis,* or *De expeditione Alexandri Magni.*

Athenaeus (fl. ca. A.D. 200). *Deipnosophistai.*

Bacon, Francis (1561–1626). *The Advancement of Learning.* London, 1605.

———. *De Sapientia Veterum.* London, 1609.

———. *The Historie of the Raigne of King Henry the Seventh.* London, 1622.

———. *Novum Organum.* London, 1620.

Bancroft, Edward (1744–1821). *An Essay on the Natural History of Guiana, in South America.* London, 1769.

Barbeyrac, Jean (1674–1744). *Traité de la morale des pères de l'église.* Amsterdam, 1728.

Baretti, Giuseppe Marco Antonio (1719–89). *An Account of the Manners and Customs of Italy.* London, 1768.

Bayle, Pierre (1647–1706). *Dictionaire historique et critique.* Rotterdam, 1697.

————. *Oeuvres diverses.* La Haye, 1727–31.

Bell, John (1691–1780). *A Journey from St. Petersburg in Russia, to Diverse Parts of Asia.* Glasgow, 1763.

Bergier, Nicolas (1567–1623). *Histoire des grands chemins de l'empire Romain.* Paris, 1622.

Bernier, François (1620–88). *Histoire de la denière révolution des États du Grand Mogol.* Paris, 1670.

Björner, Erik Julius (1696–1750). *Prodromus Tractatuum de Geographica Scandinaviae Veteri, et Historicis Gothicis.* Stockholm, 1726.

Blackwell, Thomas (1701–57). *An Enquiry into the Life and Writings of Homer.* London, 1735.

Blair, Hugh (1718–1800). *A Critical Dissertation on the Poems of Ossian.* London, 1763.

Bochart, Samuel (1599–1667). *Geographia Sacra.* Cadomi, 1651.

Bosman, Willem (b. 1672). *Nauwkeurige beschryvyng van des Guinese Goud-, Tand- en Slave Kust.* Utrecht, 1704. (*A New and Accurate Description of the Coast of Guinea,* translated anonymously, London, 1705.)

Bougainville, Louis-Antoine de (1729–1811). *Voyage autour du monde.* Paris, 1771.

Boyes (or Boece), Hector (ca. 1465–1536). *Scotorum historiae.* Paris, 1526.

Brantome, Pierre de Bourdeille, seigneur de (d. 1614). *Memoires . . . contenant les vies de dames galantes.* Leiden, 1693.

Brydone, Patrick (1743–1818). *A Tour Through Sicily and Malta.* Dublin, 1773.

Buffier, Claude (1661–1737). *Traité des premières veritez: et de la source de nos jugements.* Paris, 1724.

Buffon, Georges Louis Leclerc, comte de (1707–88). *Histoire naturelle, générale et particulaire.* Paris, 1749–66, with supplements to 1789.

Bullialdus, Ismael (1605–94). *Astronomia Philolaica.* Paris, 1645.

Burgersdijck, Franco (1590–1635). *Institutionum Logicorum Libri II.* Lyons, 1634.

Busbequius, Augerius Gislenius (1522–92). *Legationis Turcice Epistole Quator.* Paris, 1595. (*Travels into Turkey,* translated anonymously, London, 1744.)

Butler, Joseph (1692–1752). *Fifteen Sermons Preached at the Rolls Chapel.* London, 1726.

Caesar, Gaius Julius (100–44 B.C.). *De bello Africo.* (Not now believed to have been written by Caesar himself.)

————. *De bello Gallico.*

Camden, William (1551–1623). *Britannia sive Florentissimorum Regnorum, Angliae, Scotiae, Hiberniae.* London, 1600.

Capitolinus, Julius. The supposed author of the (probably forged) *Vita Albini,* collected in the so-called *Historia Augusta.*

Carew, Richard (1555–1620). *The Survey of Cornwall.* London, 1602.

Cassius, Dio (ca. 150–235). *Historia Romana.*

Chardin, Sir John (1643–1713). *The Travels of Sir John Chardin into Persia and the East-Indies.* London, 1686.

Charlevoix, Pierre-François-Xavier de (1682–1761). *Histoire et description générale de la Nouvelle-France.* Paris, 1744.

Cicero, Marcus Tullius (106–43 B.C.). *De finibus bonorum et malorum.* Translated by H. Rackham. Loeb Classical Library. Cambridge, Mass.: Harvard University Press, 1914.

———. *De inventione.* Translated by H. M. Hubbell. Loeb, 1949.

———. *De natura deorum.* Translated by H. Rackham. Loeb, 1933.

———. *De officiis.* Translated by W. Miller. Loeb, 1913.

———. *De oratore.* Translated by H. Rackham. Loeb, 1942.

———. *Epistulae ad Atticam.* Translated by E. O. Winstedt. Loeb, 1912.

———. *Epistulae ad familiares.* Translated by W. G. Williams. Loeb, 1927.

———. *Epistulae ad M. Brutum.* Translated by G. L. Hendrickson. Loeb, 1939.

———. *Pro A. Licinio Archia poeta oratio.* Translated by N. H. Watts. Loeb, 1923.

———. *Tusculanae disputationes.* Translated by J. E. King. Loeb, 1927.

The Civil Law. Translated by S. P. Scott. 17 vols. Cincinnati, 1932.

Clarendon, Edward Hyde, first earl of (1609–74). *History of the Rebellion and Civil Wars in England.* Oxford, 1702.

Cocceius, Heinrich von (1644–1719). *Grotius Illustratus.* Bratislava, 1744–52.

Columella, Lucius Junius Moderatus (fl. ca. 60–65). *De re rustica.*

Commynes, Philippe de (ca. 1447–1511). *Mémoires . . . où l'on trouve l'histoire des rois de France Louis XI et Charles VIII.*

Condamine, Charles-Marie de (1701–74). *Relation abrégée d'un voyage fait dans l'intérieur de l'Amérique méridionale.* Paris. (*A Succinct Abridgment of a Voyage Made Within the Inland Parts of South America,* translated anonymously, London, 1747.)

Contarini, Gasparo (1483–1542). *Della republica et magistrati di Venetia.* Venice, 1591. (*The Common-wealth and Government of Venice,* translated by Lewes Lewkenor, London, 1599.)

Crantz, David (1723–77). *Historie von Grönland.* Barby, 1765. (*The History of Greenland,* translated anonymously, London, 1767.)

Cudworth, Ralph (1617–88). *A Treatise Concerning Eternal and Immutable Morality.* London, 1731.

Curtius Rufus, Quintus (first century A.D.). *De gestis Alexandri Magni regis Macedonum.*

Dalrymple, Sir David (1726–92). *The Annals of Scotland.* Edinburgh, 1776–79.

Damascenus, Nicholaus (b. 64 B.C.). *Mores, leges, et ritus omnium gentium.* Edited by Joannes Boemus. (*The Manners, Lawes, and Customes of All Nations,* London, 1611.)

Dampier, William (1652–1715). *A New Voyage Round the World.* London, 1697.

Dapper, Olfert (1639–89). *Naukerige beschrijvinge der Afrikaensche gewesten.* Amsterdam, 1676. (*Description de l'Afrique,* translated anonymously, Amsterdam, 1686.)

Dares Phrygius. Author of a supposed translation of a pre-Homeric poem on the destruction of Troy, at first thought to be by the character Dares Phrygius in the *Iliad,* and traditionally ascribed to Cornelius Nepos (ca. 100–ca. 25 B.C.).

Davenant, Charles (1656–1714). *The Political and Commercial Works.* Collected and revised by Sir C. Whitworth. London, 1771.

Derham, William (1657–1735). *Physico-Theology: or, A Demonstration of the Being and Attributes of God, from His Works of Creation.* London, 1713.

Diogenes Laertius (third century A.D.). *Vitae et sententiae eorum qui in philosophia probati fuerunt.*

Du Halde, Jean-Baptiste (1674–1743). *Description géographique, historique, chronologique, politique et physique de l'empire de la Chine.* Paris, 1725. (*A Description of the Empire of China and Chinese Tartary,* translated anonymously, London, 1738–41.)

Ellis, Henry (1721–1806). *A Voyage to Hudson's Bay in 1746 and 1747.* London, 1748.

Ferguson, Adam (1723–1816). *An Essay on the History of Civil Society.* 1767.

Fielding, Henry (1707–54). *A Proposal for Making an Effectual Provision for the Poor.* London, 1753.

Firmicus Maternus, Julius (fourth century A.D.). *De errore profanarum religionum.*

Fletcher, Andrew (1655–1716). *The Political Works.* London, 1732.

Fleury, Claude (1640–1723). *Histoire ecclesiastique.* Paris, 1691.

Florus, Lucius Annaeus (fl. second century A.D.). *Epitome rerum Romanarum.*

Forbin, Claude, comte de (1656–1733). *Mémoires du comte de Forbin.* Amsterdam, 1730.

Forbonnais, François Véron Duverger de (1722–1800). *Elémens du commerce.* Amsterdam, 1755.

Foster, Sir Michael (1689–1763). *A Report of Some Proceedings on the Commission of Oyer and Terminer and Gaol Delivery . . . To Which Are Added a Few Remarks of the Crown Law.* Oxford, 1762.

The Frederician Code; or, a Body of Law for the Dominions of the King of Prussia. Translated from the French anonymously. Edinburgh, 1761.

Froissart, Jean (ca. 1338–ca. 1410). *Chroniques.*

Fuller, Thomas (1608–61). *The History of the Worthies of England.* London, 1662.

Funnell, William. *A Voyage Round the World.* London, 1707.

Gellius, Aulus (ca. 130–ca. 180). *Noctes Atticae.*

Giraldus Cambrensis (ca. 1146–ca. 1223). *Itinerarium Cambriae.*

Gobien, Père Charles le. *Histoire des isles Marianes.* Paris, 1700.

Gonneville, Paulmier de, Binot. An account of his voyage to the South Seas in the sixteenth century is collected in John Callander, ed., *Terra Australis Cognita: or, Voyages to the Terra Australis, or Southern Hemisphere, During the Sixteenth, Seventeenth and Eighteenth Centuries,* Edinburgh, 1766–68.

Goudar, Ange (1720–91). *Les interêts de la France mal entendus.* Amsterdam, 1756.

Grafton, Richard (d. ca. 1572). *A Chronicle at Large and Meere History of the Affayres of Englande.* London, 1568.

Gravesande, Willem Jacob 's (1688–1742). *Physices Elementa Mathematica, experimenta confirmata.* 1725.

Grenville, George (1712–70). *The Speech of a Right Honourable Gentleman, on the Motion for Expelling Mr. Wilkes, Friday, February 3, 1769.* London, 1769.

Grotius, Hugo (1583–1645). *De Jure Belli ac Pacis.* Paris, 1625.

———. *Historia Gothorum, Vandalorum, et Langobardorum.* Amsterdam, 1655.

Guicciardini, Francesco (1483–1540). *La Historia d'Italia.* (*The Historie of Guicciardin,* translated by Geffray Fenton, London, 1599.)

Gumilla, José (d. 1750). *El Orinoco ilustrado*. Madrid, 1741. (*Histoire naturelle, civile et géographique de l'Orenoque,* translated from the Spanish by M. Eidous, Avignon, 1758.)

Hale, Sir Matthew (1609–76). *Pleas of the Crown*. London, 1678.

Hanway, Jonas (1712–86). *An Earnest Appeal for Mercy to the Children of the Poor*. London, 1766.

Harrington, James (1611–77). *The Common-wealth of Oceana*. London, 1656.

Harris, James (1709–80). *Hermes: Or a Philosophical Inquiry Concerning Universal Grammar*. London, 1751.

———. *Philosophical Arrangements*. London, 1775.

Hay, William (1695–1755). *Remarks on the Laws Relating to the Poor*. London, 1735.

Helvétius, Claude-Adrien (1715–71). *De l'esprit*. Amsterdam, 1758.

Hennepin, Louis (1626–ca. 1705). *Description de la Louisiane*. Paris, 1683.

Hentzner, Paul (1558–1623). *Itinerarium Germaniae, Galliae, Angliae, Italiae*. Norinberge, 1612. (*A Journey into England,* translated by Richard Bentley, edited by Horace Walpole, Strawberry Hill, 1757.)

Heraclides Ponticus (387–312 B.C.). *De politiis Graecorum*.

Herodian (fl. ca. A.D. 230). *Historiae de imperio post Marcum*.

Historia Augusta. A collection of biographies of Roman emperors and their heirs, apparently written in the fourth century A.D., and now recognized to be mostly forgeries of dubious historical value.

Hobbes, Thomas (1588–1679). *Leviathan: or, The Matter, Forme, and Power of a Commonwealth Ecclesiasticall and Civil*. London, 1651.

Holinshed, Raphael (d. ca. 1580). *Chronicles of England, Scotlande, and Irelande*. London, 1577.

Home, Henry (Lord Kames, 1696–1782). *Elements of Criticism*. Edinburgh, 1762. (6th ed. Edinburgh, 1785.)

———. *Essays on the Principles of Morality and Natural Religion*. Edinburgh, 1751. (2nd ed. Edinburgh, 1758; 3rd ed. Edinburgh, 1779.)

———. *The Gentleman Farmer. Being an Attempt to Improve Agriculture by Subjecting It to the Test of Rational Principles*. Edinburgh, 1776. (2nd ed. Edinburgh, 1779.)

———. *Historical Law-Tracts*. Edinburgh, 1758.

———. *Principles of Equity*. Edinburgh, 1760 (2nd ed. Edinburgh, 1767; 3rd ed., Edinburgh, 1778).

————. *Statute Law of Scotland Abridged, with Historical Notes.* Edinburgh, 1757.

Homer (probably eighth century B.C.). *The Iliad.* Translated by Alexander Pope. London, 1715–20.

————. *The Odyssey.* Translated by Alexander Pope. London, 1725–26.

Hooker, Richard (ca. 1554–1600). *Of the Lawes of Ecclesiasticall Politie.* London, 1593–1601.

Horace (Quintius Horatius Flaccus, 65–8 B.C.). *A Poetical Translation of the Works of Horace,* by Philip Francis. London, 1746.

————. *Ars poetica.* Translated by H. Rushton Fairclough. Loeb Classical Library. Cambridge, Mass.: Harvard University Press, 1926.

————. *Satires.* Translated by H. Rushton Fairclough. Loeb Classical Library. Cambridge, Mass.: Harvard University Press, 1926.

Hoyle, Edmond (1672–1769). *Mr. Hoyle's Games of Whist, Quadrille, [etc.].* London, 1748.

Huet, Pierre Daniel (1630–1721). *Huetiana, ou Pensées diverses de M. Huet.* Paris, 1722.

Hume, David (1711–76). *The History of England.* London, 1754–62.

————. "The Natural History of Religion." First published in *Four Dissertations,* London, 1757.

————. "Of the Populousness of Ancient Nations." First published in *Political Discourses,* London, 1752.

————. *A Treatise of Human Nature.* London, 1739–40.

Irenaeus, Saint (first–second centuries A.D.). *Demonstratio praedicationis apostolicae.*

Ives, Edward (d. 1786). *A Voyage from England to India, in the Year 1754.* London, 1773.

Jornandes, bishop of Ravenna (mid-sixth century A.D.). *De Getarum, sive Gothorum orgine et rebus gestis.* 1597.

Josephus, Flavius (A.D. 37–after 93). *Antiquitates Iudaicum.*

Jurieu, Pierre (1637–1713). *Apologie pour l'accomplissement des propheties.* Rotterdam, 1687.

Justin (Marcus Junianus Justinus, second or third century A.D.). *Epitoma historiae Phillippicae Pompei Trogi.*

Kaempfer, Engelbert (1651–1716). *The History of Japan: Giving an Account of the Ancient and Present State of That Empire*. Translated from the manuscript by John Scheuchter, London, 1727.

Keckermann, Bartholomeus (ca. 1571–1608). *Systema logicae*. Hanover, 1620.

Knox, John (1505–72). *The Historie of the Church of Scotland*. 1587.

Kolb, Peter (1675–1726). *Naaukerige en uitvoerige bescchryving van de Kaap Goede Hoop*. Amsterdam, 1727. (*The Present State of the Cape of Good Hope: or, A Particular Account of the Several Nations of Hottentots*, translated by Mr. Medley, London, 1731.)

Labat, Jean Baptiste (1663–1738). *Nouveau voyage aux isles de l'Amérique*. La Haye, 1724.

Lampridius, Aelius. One of the supposed contributors to the *Historia Augusta*.

Lange, Lorenz. *Journal de la résidence du sieur Lange . . . a la cour de la Chine, dans les années 1721 et 1722*. Leyden, 1726.

Lavie, Jean Charles de. *Des corps politiques et de leurs gouvernements*. Lyon, 1764.

Law, William (1686–1761). *A Practical Treatise upon Christian Perfection*. London, 1726.

Le Blanc, Jean-Bernard (1707–81). *Lettres d'un François*. La Haye, 1745.

Leland, John (ca. 1506–52). *De rebus Britannicis collectanea*. Oxford, 1715.

L'Estoile, Pierre de (1546–1611). *Journal du règne de Henri IV*. Edited by Thomas Bouges. La Haye, 1741.

Linnaeus, Carl (1707–78). *The Animal Kingdom, or Zoological System, of the Celebrated Sir Charles Linnaeus; Class I. Mammalia*. Translated by Robert Kerr, London, 1792.

———. *Flora Lapponica*. Amsterdam, 1737.

Livy (Titus Livius, 59 B.C.–A.D. 17). *Ab urbe condita libri*. Translated by B. O. Foster. Loeb Classical Library. Cambridge, Mass.: Harvard University Press, 1919–59.

Locke, John (1632–1704). *An Essay Concerning Human Understanding*. London, 1690.

———. *Of the Conduct of the Understanding*. In *Posthumous Works of Mr. John Locke*. London, 1706.

———. *Some Thoughts Concerning Education*. London, 1693.

———. *Two Treatises of Government*. London, 1690.

Longinus, Cassius (ca. 213–73). Traditionally, but erroneously, supposed to be the author of *De sublimitate*.

Lucan (Marcus Annaeus Lucanus, 39–65). *Pharsalia*. Translated by Nicholas Rowe. London, 1720.

Lucretius (Titus Lucretius Carus, ca. 99–ca. 55 B.C.). *De rerum natura.*

Machiavelli, Niccolò (1469–1527). *Historie Fiorentine*. 1532. (*The Florentine History*, translated anonymously, London, 1674.)

Macpherson, James (1736–96). *The Works of Ossian, the Son of Fingal*. London, 1765.

Macrobius, Ambrosius Theodosius (fl. ca. 400 B.C.). *Saturnalia.*

Magellan. *See* Pigafetta.

Magnus, Johannes (1488–1544). *Gothorum Sueonumque historia*. Rome, 1554.

Mallet, Paul Henri (1730–1807). *Introduction à l'histoire de Dannemarc*. Copenhagen, 1755.

Malmesbury, William of (d. ca. 1143). *Gesta regum anglorum.*

Mandeville, Bernard (1670–1733). *The Fable of the Bees*. London, 1714, 1723, 1732.

Manstein, Christoph Hermann von (1711–57). *Memoirs of Russia, Historical, Political and Military*. Translated from manuscript, London, 1770.

Marsham, John (1602–85). *Chronicus canon Aegyptiacus Ebraicus Graecus et disquisitiones*. London, 1672.

Martial (Marcus Valerius Martialis, ca. 40–103/4). *Epigrams*. Translated by D. R. Shackleton Bailey. Loeb Classical Library. Cambridge, Mass.: Harvard University Press, 1993.

Martin, Martin (d. 1719). *A Late Voyage to St. Kilda*. London, 1698.

Maupertuis, Pierre Louis Moreau de (1698–1759). *La figure de la terre*. Paris, 1738.

Meursius, Joannes (1579–1639). *Themis Attica: sive de Legibus Atticis*. Amsterdam, 1685.

Mildmay, Sir William (1705–71). *The Police of France: or, An Account of the Laws and Regulations Established in That Kingdom, for the Preservation of Peace*. London, 1763.

Minucius Felix, Marcus (fl. 200–240). *Octavius.*

Mirabeau, Victor de Riquetti, marquis de (1715–89). *Théorie de l'impôt*. Avignon, 1761.

Monlorius, Johannes. *Perfectissima in Aristotelis Analyticorum Priorum*. Frankfurt, 1593.

Monstrelet, Enguerrand (1390–1453). *Chronique.*

Montecuculi, Prince Raimondo (1609–80). *Mémorie.* (*Mémoires de Montecuculi,* translated anonymously, Paris, 1712.)

Montesquieu, Charles de Secondat, baron de (1689–1755). *Considérations sur les causes de la grandeur des Romains et de leur décadence.* Amsterdam, 1734.

———. *De l'esprit des lois.* Paris, 1748.

Morin, Jean (1591–1659). *Commentarius de Sacris Ecclesiae Ordinationibus.*

Niebuhr, Carsten (1733–1815). *Description de l'Arabie.* Amsterdam, 1774.

Olaus Magnus (1490–1555). *Historia de gentibus Septrentionalibus.*

Onosander (fourth century). *Strategicus.*

Outhier, Réginald (1694–1774). *Journal d'un voyage au Nord en 1736 et 1737.* Paris, 1744.

Ovid (Publius Ovidius Naso, 43 B.C.–A.D. 17). *Tristia.*

Parnell, Thomas (1679–1718). *An Essay on the Life, Writings, and Learning of Homer.* London, 1715. Published with Pope's translation of Homer's *Iliad* (1715–20).

Pascal, Blaise (1623–62). *Lettres provinciales.* 1656–57.

Paulus Diaconus (ca. 720–ca. 799). *De gestis Langobardorum.*

Pausanias (fl. ca. A.D. 160). *Periegesis Hellados.*

Pennant, Thomas (1726–98). *Synopsis of Quadrupeds.* Chester, 1771.

Persius Flaccus, Aulus (24–62). *Satires.* Translated by G. G. Ramsay. Loeb Classical Library. Cambridge, Mass.: Harvard University Press, 1918.

Petronius Arbiter (d. A.D. 65). *Satyricon.*

Pigafetta, Antonio (ca. 1480–ca. 1534). *Primo viaggio intorno al globo.*

Plano Carpino, Giovanni di (fl. 1240). *Relations des Mongols ou Tartares.*

Pliny (Gaius Plinius Secundus, 23/4–79). *Naturalis historiae.*

Plutarch (ca. 46–ca. 120). *Symposiacs;* or *Quaestiones conviviales.*

———. *Vitae parallelae.*

Polydore Vergil (1470–1555). *De inventoribus rerum.* Venice, 1499.

Pompadour, Jeanne Antoinette Poisson, marquise de (1721–64). *Lettres de Madame la Marquise de Pompadour.* London, 1772.

Pomponius Mela (fl. ca. A.D. 43). *De chorographia,* or *De situ orbis.*

Pope, Alexander (1688–1744). *Poetical Works.* Edited by Herbert Davis. Oxford: Oxford University Press, 1966.

Porete, Marguerite (ca. 1250–1310). *Le miroir des simples âmes.*

Porphyry (233–ca. 305). *Isagoge, sive libellus de quinque praedicabilibus.*

Porter, Sir James (1710–76). *Observations on the Religion, Law, Government, and Manners of the Turks.* London, 1771.

Price, Richard (1723–91). *Observations on Reversionary Payments.* London, 1771.

Pringle, Sir John (1707–82). *Observations on the Diseases of the Army, in Camp and in Garrison.* London, 1753.

Procopius (ca. 500–after 562). *De bellis.*

Quintilian (Marcus Fabius Quintilianus, b. ca. A.D. 35). *Institutio oratoria.*

Ramus, Petrus (1515–72). *Dialecticae libri duo.* 1556. (*The Art of Logick,* translated by S. Wotton, London, 1626.)

Ray, John (1627–1705). *The Wisdom of God Manifested in the Works of the Creation.* London, 1691.

Raynal, Guillaume-Thomas-François, Abbé (1713–96). *Histoire philosophique et politique des etablissemens des Européens dans les Deux Indes.* 6 vols. Amsterdam, 1770.

Regnard, Jean François (1655–1709). *Voyage en Laponie.* 1681.

Reid, Thomas (1710–96). *Analysis of Aristotle's Logic, with Remarks.* 2nd ed. Edinburgh, 1806.

———. *An Inquiry into the Human Mind, on the Principles of Common Sense.* London, 1764.

René, King of Naples and Jerusalem (1409–80). *Traité de la forme d'un tournoi.*

Robertson, William (1721–93). *The History of the Reign of the Emperor Charles V.* London, 1769.

Rogers, Robert (1731–95). *A Concise Account of North America.* London, 1765.

Roggeveen, Jacob (1659–1729). *Histoire de l'expédition de trois vaisseaux envoyés par la Compagnie des Indes Orientales des Provinces Unies aux terres australes.* Translated by Charles Frédéric Behrens. La Haye, 1739.

Rousseau, Jean-Jacques (1712–78). *Discours sur l'origine et les fondments de l'inégalité parmi les hommes.* Amsterdam, 1755.

———. *Émile, ou de l'éducation.* La Haye, 1762. Translated by Barbara Foxley. London: J. M. Dent, 1993.

———. *Julie, ou la nouvelle Héloïse.* Amsterdam, 1761. Translated by Philip Stewart and Jean Vaché. Hanover, N.H.: Dartmouth College: University Press of New England, 1997.

Rushworth, John (1612–90). *The London Post.* London, 1644–45.

Ruysbroeck [Rubrugius], Willem van (ca. 1210–ca. 1270). *Itenerarium.*

Saint-Réal, Abbé de (Cesar Vichard, 1639–92). *Conjuration des Espagnols de Venise en l'année 1618.* Paris, 1674.

Sallust (Gaius Sallustius Crispus, 86–35 B.C.). *Bellum Catilinae.*

Sarpi, Paolo (1552–1623). *Istoria del Concilio Tridentino.* 1619. (*The Historie of the Councel of Trent,* translated by Sir N. Brent, London, 1620.)

Saxe, Maurice, comte de (1696–1750). *Mes rêveries.* Amsterdam, 1757. (*Reveries, or Memoirs upon the Art of War,* translated by Sir W. Fawcett, London, 1757.)

Saxo Grammaticus (d. ca. 1204). *Historiae Danicae libri xvi.*

Scheffer, Johannes (1621–79). *Lappland, das ist: Neue und wahrhafftige Beschreibung von Lappland und dessen Einwohnern.* Frankfurt, 1675. (*The History of Lapland: Containing a Geographical Description, and a Natural History of That Country,* translated anonymously, London, 1704.)

Servius (Marius Servius Honoratus, early fifth century A.D.). *Commentarii in Virgilium.*

Shaftesbury, Anthony Ashley Cooper, third earl of (1671–1713). *Characteristicks of Men, Manners, Opinions, Times.* London, 1711.

Shaw, Thomas (1694–1751). *Travels, or Observations Relating to Several Parts of Barbary and the Levant.* Oxford, 1738.

Shebbeare, John (1709–88). *Letters on the English Nation, by Battista Angeloni.* London, 1755.

Siculus, Diodorus (fl. 60–30 B.C.). *Bibliotheca historica.*

Sigismundus of Herbarstain. *Rerum Moscoviticarum commentarii.* Basel, 1571.

Smith, Adam (1723–90). *The Theory of Moral Sentiments.* London, 1759

Smollett, Tobias (1721–71). *Travels Through France and Italy.* London, 1766.

Socrates Scholasticus (ca. 379–ca. 440). *Historia ecclesiastica.*

Spartianus, Aelius. One of the supposed contributors to the *Historia Augusta.*

Stobaeus, Johannes (fifth century A.D.). *Anthologion.*

Stow, John (1525–1605). *A Survay of London.* London, 1598.

Strabo (b. 64 B.C., d. after A.D. 24). *Geographica.*

Strahlenberg, Philipp Johann von (1676–1747). *Das nord- und ostliche Theil von Europa und Asia.* Stockholm, 1730. (*An Histori-Geographical Description of the North and Eastern Part of Europe and Asia,* translated anonymously, London, 1736.)

Struve, Burkhard Gotthelf (1671–1738). *Corpus Historiae Germanicae.* 1730.

Strype, John (1643–1737). *Annals of the Reformation and Establishment of Religion.* London, 1709.

Tachard, Guy le père (1651–1712). *Voyage de Siam des Pères Jésuites.* Paris, 1686.

Tacitus, Publius (b. 56 or 57, d. after 117). *Annales.*

———. *De moribus Germanorum.*

———. *Vita Agricolae.*

Tassoni, Alessandro (1565–1635). *Dieci libri di pensieri diversi.* 1627.

Temple, Sir William (1628–99). *The Works of Sir William Temple.* London, 1740.

Terence (Publius Terentius Afer, d. 159 B.C.?). *Heauton timoroumenos (The Self-Tormentor).*

Thomas, the Rhymer (ca. 1220–ca. 1297). *The Whole Prophecies of Scotland, England, France, Ireland, and Denmark.* Edinburgh and London, 1745.

Torfeus, Thormodi (1636–1719). *Historia rerum Norvegicarum.* Hafniae, 1711.

Tournefort, Joseph Pitton de (1656–1708). *Relation d'un voyage du Levant.* Lyon, 1727.

Ulloa, Antonio de (1716–95). *A Voyage to South America.* Translated anonymously, London, 1758.

Ustariz, Geronimo de (1670–1732). *Theorica y practica de commercio, y de marina.* (*The Theory and Practise of Commerce and Maritime Affairs,* translated by John Kippax, London, 1751.)

Valera, Blas (1551–97). *Las costumbres antiguas del Piru; y La historia de los Incas.*

Valerius Maximus (first century A.D.). *Facta et dictu memorabilia.*

Varro (Marcus Terentius Varro, 116–27 B.C.). *De re rustica.*

Vega, Garcilaso de la (1539–1616). *Comentarios reales de los Incas.* (*The Royal Commentaries of Peru,* London, 1688.)

Vegetius (Flavius Vegetius Renatus, 379–95). *De re militari.*

Velleius Paterculus, Gaius (ca. 19 B.C.–after A.D. 30). *Historiae Romanae.* Translated by Frederick W. Shipley. Loeb Classical Library. Cambridge, Mass.: Harvard University Press, 1924.

Venetus, Paulus. *See* Sarpi, Paolo.

Vieira, Antonio (1608–97). *Sermoens.* Lisbon, 1679.

Virgil (Publius Vergilius Maro, 70–19 B.C.). *Aeneid.* Translated by H. Rushton Fairclough, revised by G. P. Goold. Loeb Classical Library. Cambridge, Mass.: Harvard University Press, 1999.

———. *Georgics.* Translated by H. Rushton Fairclough, revised by G. P. Goold. Loeb Classical Library. Cambridge, Mass.: Harvard University Press, 1999.

Vitruvius Pollio (first century B.C.). *De architectura.*

Vives, Joannes Lodovicus (1492–1540). *Opera omnia.* Basel, 1555.

Vives, Juan Luis (1492–1540). *De civitate Dei.* 1544.

Voltaire, François Marie Arouet de (1694–1778). *Essai sur la poèsie épique.* Paris, 1726.

———. *Essai sur l'histoire générale et sur les moeurs et l'esprit des nations depuis Charlemagne jusqu'à nos jours.* Geneva, 1756.

———. "Le Mondain." Paris, 1736.

Vopiscus, Flavius. One of the supposed contributors to the *Historia Augusta.*

Winckelmann, Johann Joachim (1717–68). *Gedanken über die Nachahmung der griechischen Werke in der Malerei und Bildhauerkunst.* Dresden, 1756. (*Reflections on the Painting and Sculpture of the Greeks,* translated by Henry Fuseli, London, 1765.)

Witt, Johan de (1625–72). *Aanwissing der heilsams politike Gronden en Maximen van der Republike van Holland.* (*The True Interest and Political Maxims of the Republic of Holland and West-Friesland,* translated anonymously, 1702.)

Wollaston, William (1660–1724). *The Religion of Nature Delineated.* London, 1722.

Worster, Benjamin (fl. ca. 1722–30). *A Compendious and Methodical Account of the Principles of Natural Philosophy.* London, 1722.

Xenophon (ca. 428–ca. 354 B.C.). *Memorabilia Socratis.*

Xiphilinus, Joannes the younger (ca. 1010–75). *The History of Dion Cassius, Abridg'd by Xiphilin.* Translated by Francis Manning. London, 1704.

Young, Arthur (1741–1820). *A Six Weeks Tour, Through the Southern Counties of England and Wales.* London, 1768.

INDEX

Abderam, king of Cordova, 65

Abderites, 314

Abdoulrahman III, 480

Abino Seimei, 628

abortion, 300–301, 564n

absolute monarchies: character of sovereign and, 388; development of, 373; free press and, 382–83; Peruvian government as, 576. *See also* despotism

Abyssinians: Manicheanism of ascribing wicked acts to the devil, 813n; marriage of priests, 614; racial theories and, 23–24; restraints on women, 294

Académie des sciences, France, 104

accountability, sense of, 737–38, 747–49

Achmet (sultan), 204

Acosta, 574

active *vs.* passive courage, 33–35

Adam and Eve and Kames's racial theory, xv, 47–48, 560

Adamannus, 55

Adam of Bremen, 236

adultery, 287–89; among Romans, 204; celibacy of clergy promoting, 889; chivalry and gallantry leading to, 300–301; dress and, 166; fine as punishment for, 274; morality regarding, 717–18; moral wrongs perpetrated for sake of, 726–28n;

polygamy and, 204, 287–88; rare among savages, 166, 269; Roman women taken in adultery, prostitution of, 193; supernatural means of ascertaining, 600; of women *vs.* men, 288–89

Aelian, 873

Aeneas Silvius (Pope Paul II), 875

Aeneid. See Virgil

Aeschylus, 103, 138, 180, 769, 804, 805

Africa: adultery, 288; dress, female fondness for, 277; food and population in, 62; marital practices, 286–87; marriage, 274, 275; Portuguese exploration of, 101; strangers, aversion to, 353; sun passing over, effect of, 605; theology of, 803, 811; useful arts in, 97, 99; war and peace, effects of, 410

afterlife: Caledonian belief in, 231–32; Odin, Hall of, 237. *See also* immortality of the soul

Agatharchides of Cnidus, 45

Agathias, 845n

Agathocles, 359

Agonna, governance by women in, 290n

agreeable, the, and the disagreeable: beauty, derivation of knowledge of, 583; free will and, 745, 746; moral sense and, 738

pastoral state, development of, 56–57; paucity in America, 59n; variety in colors of, 311–12

domestic architecture, 92, 119

domestic servants: formerly forbidden to read New Testament in English, 272; hospitals for, 532; tax on, 442

Dominicans, 870

Domitius Enobarbus, 781

dowries, purchasing of women *vs.*, 271–83, 287

Drachart, Rev. Mr., 558

drama: brass pipe used to strengthen and project voice, 137–38; characters, need for variety in, 142–43; development of, 103; distress displayed in, taste for, 719, 721; Greek, 137–43; history painters valued more than players, 619; masks, use of, 138–39; morality and mystery plays, 112–13, 881–82; music and, 140, 148; naked women in portrayals of Judgment of Paris, 193; portrayal of sacred and divine persons by perhaps dissolute players, 881; women as actors in, 213–14; women, effects on drama of exclusion from society of, 142. *See also* comedy; tragedy

dramatic mode of literary composition, 123–32

drawback on exportation of commodities formerly imported, 475–78

dream interpretation, errors of, 615–16

dress, 164–66; codpieces, 193; female fondness for, 165–66, 277; luxury in, 320; morals and, 166; naturalness of, 324; pleasure afforded by, 164–66; restraints on women and, 294, 295, 296; savage fondness for, 164–65, 166, 276–77; sumptuary laws, 208, 320, 385; as useful art, 91, 94, 97

Dreux, battle of, 197

drink. *See* alcoholic drinks; food and drink

Druids, 231n, 233, 841, 900n

Dryden, John, 114, 115–16

dualism, 812, 813n

dueling, 210–11n

Du Halde, Jean-Baptiste, 398

dunking, 821

Dunstable, chronicles of, 776

Dupas, 508–9

Dutch. *See* Netherlands

Dutch East India Company: despotism practiced by, 380–81; export duties and creation of, 467–68; patriotism, degeneracy of, 425–26; Portuguese India and, 429

Dutch Guiana, 809

duties. *See* export duties; import duties; taxes

duty: active duties regarding particular persons, 716, 718–19, 721; distress, duty to relieve, 719, 721; as final cause of moral laws, 738–39; gratitude as, 719; not to harm others, 715–17, 721, 722; principles of, 723–25; prohibition on hurting others, 715–17; promises and covenants, 719–20; as right human action, 708; self, duties owed to, 720–21, 728, 741–42; truth as, 718, 741

dwarves, 113–14

dwelling places, luxury in, 318–19, 322, 325

dyers' logwood, duty on, 476–77

ear and throat, juxtaposition of, 54n

earthquakes, 792, 826

Easter Island, 28

East India Company. *See* Dutch East India Company; English East India Company

East Indies, marriage in, 262

465; writing, women's (in)decency in, 294

Francis I of France: female sex, progress of, 299n; fine arts, 114; Jewish physicians, belief in particular efficacy of, 607; morality, progress of, 773–74, 775; swearing, 194; taste, sense of, 117; Waldenses, persecution of, 896; war, mannerly conduct of, 197, 201; wrestling match with Henry VIII, 196

Franciscans, 870

Franklin, Benjamin, 898–99

Franks: cruelty of, 184; morality, progress of, 765; restraints on women, 293; women, succession and inheritance laws regarding, 289–90

fraud, negligent actions equivalent to, 734n

Frederican Code, 604, 611

Frederick the Great, 361

freedom generally. *See* liberty

free port, Kames's proposal for, 447

free press, need for, 382–83

free will and morality, 744–56; accountability, human sense of, 747–49; agreeable and disagreeable, 745, 746; arbitrary or discretionary actions, 708, 721–22; chance and contingency, 756–59; common sense as to, 752; intent or motive, 745–48, 755; laws of nature regarding moral conduct in society, 749–56; reason as to, 751–52; remorse, 754–56; voluntary actions, laws governing, 745–47

French Revolution, cruelty of Romans compared, 184

Fridlevus, king of Denmark, 247

Froissart, Jean, 184

Fro, king of Sweden, 242

frontiers of states, guarding, 402–4

Frotho, king of Denmark, 237, 245

Fuller, Thomas, 777

Fulvia (Roman empress), 183

funeral rites: dirtiness associated with mourning, 167; luxury and, 331; orations, 112; of Roman emperors, 379

Funnel, William, 190

furnishings, luxury in, 319, 322, 328

futurity: Christian prophecies not anticipating, 828; contingency of future events, human perception of, 591; human sense of, 584; prognostication of, 615–16, 825–29

Gades, siege of, 93

Gagarin, Prince, 794

Gaius, 737

Galactophagi, 241

Galen, 660, 666

Galileo, 100, 429

gallantry. *See* chivalry and gallantry

Gallway, Lord, 113

gaming, 213, 445, 534, 581

Ganghi (Chinese emperor), 205, 784

Garamantes, marriage among, 261, 262

Garcilasso de la Vega, 121, 888

gardening, 119

garments. *See* dress

Garrick, David, 629, 848

Gaston de Foix, 299

Gauls: cleanness, 167; food and drink, 313–14; food and population, 65; human sacrifice, 841; luxury used to debauch, 387; manners, 232–36, 251; marital practices, 280; racial theory and, 50; strangers, aversion to, 353

Gaures: food and internal disposition, 177n; religion and morality, 867, 876; religious worship, 842, 858

gelding cattle, 94

Geminiani, Francesco, 151

gems, importation of, 471

This book is set in Adobe Garamond, a modern adaptation by Robert Slimbach of the typeface originally cut around 1540 by the French typographer and printer Claude Garamond. The Garamond face, with its small lowercase height and restrained contrast between thick and thin strokes, is a classic "old-style" face and has long been one of the most influential and widely used typefaces.

Printed on paper that is acid-free and meets the requirements of the American National Standard for Permanence of Paper for Printed Library Materials, z39.48-1992. ∞

Book design by Louise OFarrell
Gainesville, Florida
Typography by Apex Publishing, LLC
Madison, Wisconsin
Printed and bound by Worzalla Publishing Company
Stevens Point, Wisconsin